Sustainable Management, Wertschöpfung und Effizienz

In dieser Schriftenreihe stehen insbesondere empirische und praxisnahe Studien zu nachhaltigem Wirtschaften und Effizienz im Mittelpunkt. Energie-, Umwelt-, Nachhaltigkeits-, CSR-, Innovations-, Risiko- und integrierte Managementsysteme sind nur einige Beispiele, die Sie hier wiederfinden. Ein besonderer Fokus liegt dabei auf dem Nutzen, den solche Systeme für die Anwendung in der Praxis bieten, um zu helfen die globalen Nachhaltigkeitsziele (SDGs) umzusetzen. Publiziert werden nationale und internationale wissenschaftliche Arbeiten.

This series is focusing on empirical and practical research in the fields of sustainable management and efficiency. Management systems in the context of energy, environment, sustainability, CSR, innovation, risk as well as integrated management systems are just a few examples which can be found here. A special focus is on the value such systems can offer for the application in practice supporting the implementation of the global sustainable development goals, the SDGs. National and international scientific publications are published (English and German).

More information about this series at http://www.springer.com/series/15909

Ruxandra Maria Bejinariu

Sustainable Business Performance and Risk Management

Risk Assessment Tools in the Context of Business Risk Levels Related to Threats and Opportunities

Springer Gabler

Ruxandra Maria Bejinariu
Bucharest, Romania

The Bucharest University of Economic Studies, Doctoral School in Business Administration, Bucharest, Romania, 2019

PhD Supervisor: Prof. Univ. Dr. Marieta Olaru

ISSN 2523-8620 ISSN 2523-8639 (electronic)
Sustainable Management, Wertschöpfung und Effizienz
ISBN 978-3-658-29388-8 ISBN 978-3-658-29389-5 (eBook)
https://doi.org/10.1007/978-3-658-29389-5

This Springer Gabler imprint is published by the registered company Springer Fachmedien Wiesbaden GmbH part of Springer Nature.
The registered company address is: Abraham-Lincoln-Str. 46, 65189 Wiesbaden, Germany

Dedication

I would like to dedicate the present doctoral thesis to the Romanian entrepreneurs that struggle with taking risks and balancing resources in order to ensure jobs and play a part in improving the local economy. My personal goal related to the present doctoral thesis was to propose a helpful business administration model for organizations for which risk appetite and risk attitude determine their survival in the current highly competitive business environment.

My sincere gratitude I would like to express to my PhD Professor Marieta Olaru, who besides offering me guidance during my research, has inspired me with her dedication and perseverance. I would also like to express my appreciation to Mr. Firică Popa for "opening" my appetite for risk.

I am most thankful to my family:

To my husband who has been my no. 1 supporter, an incredible father and an exquisite professional.

To my father who has always been my role model and has always had my back.

To my daughters Lara and Miruna that came in our lives during the doctoral program.

And to my godfather that has transformed me into the professional that I am today.

Dedication

Content Overview

Contents

List of abbreviations

CAGE	Cultural, Administrative, Geographic and Economic
CEO	Chief Executive Officer
EG	Edinburgh Group
EIU	Economist Intelligence Unit
ERP	Enterprise Resource Planning
et al.	et alia
etc.	et cetera
FMCG	Fast-moving commercial goods
FMEA	Failure Mode Effects analysis
GDP	Gross Domestic Product
ISO	International Organization for Standardization
KPMG	Klynveld Peat Marwick Goerdeler
MOST	Mission, Objectives, Strategy, Tactics
OECD	Organisation for Economic Co-operation and Development
PDCA	Plan, Do, Check, Act
PwC	PricewaterhouseCoopers
SMART	Specific, Measurable, Assignable, Realistic and Time-related
SME	Small and Medium Enterprise
SPC	Statistical Process Control
SWOT	Strengths, Weaknesses, Opportunities and Threats
U.S.	United States
USD	United States Dollar
5M	Machinery, Manpower, Material, Measurement, and Method
8D	Eight Disciplines

List of figures

List of tables

Summary

Purpose: Uncertainties related to the current competitive business climate have brought new challenges for organizations that had to review risk appetite statements and re-evaluate risk tolerance levels while developing cost-saving and risk-taking strategies in order to ensure sustainable performance.

Design/methodology/approach: The contribution brought by the present doctoral thesis relates to filling in gaps related to improving the risk assessment process by using unexploited methods that have been mainly used in limited areas of business and identifying both threats and opportunities that can be generated as a result of risk materialization.

Findings: Based on the results of the studies performed during the doctoral period possibilities of improving the risk assessment process were proposed with a direct impact on increasing the organizations' risk appetite and sustainable performance. The proposed methods were included in a risk assessment model that achieves the research objectives by focusing resources in order to prevent the most important possible negative effects of risks and to increase chances of tackling new business opportunities, while decreasing risk handling costs and continuously controlling risks outside the risk tolerance level intervals.

Originality: The current risk assessment methods used by organizations have limitations related to managing resources because risks are analyzed according to the probability of occurrence and consequences of risk materialization, but the conditions in which risks occur are not considered, and as a result all unacceptable or high risks are included in the risk handling plan. Another argument for resources not being harnessed is the fact that positive outcomes of risk materialization are not identified and analyzed. Organizations are losing valuable opportunities by ignoring the possible positive effects of materialized risks. Moreover, by using the proposed methods in order to perform risk assessment, organizations can save resources by focusing only on the most promising opportunities.

Limitations & Desiderata: The proposed model involves a high amount of qualitative data and has been applied in practice by a limited number of organizations. Further research including additional objective criteria is necessary in order to expand the study.

The proposed model may bring a valuable contribution to ensuring business sustainability in organizations by increasing risk appetite, lowering risk handling costs and optimizing resources.

Key words: risk assessment, sustainable performance, risk evaluation methods, business processes

1 Introduction

The unstable and uncertain economic and political environment has imposed a new set of business rules with a strong impact on the organizations' sustainable performance. In this context organizations have started focusing on cost reduction and risk assessment strategies in order to achieve competitive advantage. The scope of the present doctoral thesis is to bring a contribution to the organizations' decision-making processes related to taking risks in order to achieve new business opportunities or maintaining a defensive strategy.

Sustainable business performance can only be ensured in organizations with a solid infrastructure, a "healthy" workflow and efficient processes that are interconnected across the organization. According to the specialized literature and risk assessment experts, interactions between business processes are the main source of high risks. Therefore, risk assessment has to be performed at the interaction between organizational processes and, in case processes are contracted to a third-party provider, risks have to be assessed between the organization and the outsourced processes.

After having risks identified, evaluated and analyzed, risks that represent a threat for the organization are included in the risk handling plan and resources are allocated in order to take preventive actions. One of the most efficient risk assessment methods used so far mainly in the engineering and medical industries is the Failure Mode Effects Analysis (FMEA). This method significantly decreases risk handling costs by developing a mechanism of controlling risks and determining if risks are imminent.

Risk assessment is currently used by organizations either as a reactive method of identifying, evaluating and analyzing risks that have already materialized or in the best cases as a proactive solution that prevents risk materialization and the related possible negative outcomes. Risks are uncertainties that can also lead to positive outcomes, so that risks can be transformed in chances of tackling new business opportunities and improving business performance.

Given all these aspects, the doctoral research was oriented towards the following objectives:

R. M. Bejinariu, *Sustainable Business Performance and Risk Management*,
Sustainable Management, Wertschöpfung und Effizienz,
https://doi.org/10.1007/978-3-658-29389-5_1

1. Analyzing the conceptual framework related to business processes owned by the organization or strategically contracted to a third-party provider;
2. Determining the current approaches related to risks and risk assessment in organizations;
3. Identifying the newest trends and models related to risk assessment in the context of ensuring sustainable performance;
4. Analyzing risk assessment in small and medium-sized enterprises (SMEs) compared to large companies;
5. Determining the interrelation between risk assessment and the organizational context;
6. Identifying the critical factors that impact sustainable performance;
7. Identifying, evaluating and analysing risks related to interactions between business processes in organizations;
8. Analyzing risk assessment results related to interactions between the organization and outsourced business processes;
9. Determining the impact of using the FMEA method during risk assessment in organizations from different areas of business;
10. Analyzing the effects of using the FMEA method while harnessing risks as opportunities for the organization;
11. Developing a risk assessment model using the proposed methods in order to ensure sustainable business performance.

The results of the research performed during the doctoral period, as well as the study of national and international specialized literature and data bases developed by organizations such as the Organisation for Economic Co-operation and Development (OECD), RobecoSAM and the Maddison Project Database were used in order to achieve these objectives.

Interviews and electronic questionnaires sent to managers and risk assessment specialists were the methods of gathering data and information in order to achieve research results.

Table 1.1: Structure of the doctoral thesis, developed by the author based on the research conducted during the doctoral period

No. crt.	Objective no.	Research objective	Research methodology	Study performed related to:	Chapter
1.	1-3	Development of the theoretical framework related to business processes, risk assessment and risk assessment methods	Literature review	▪ Business processes; ▪ Outsourced and backsourced processes; ▪ Risk assessment in organizations; ▪ Risk assessment methods.	1 - 2
2.	4-5	Determining specific aspects related to risk assessment in organizations	Empirical analysis	▪ Risk assessment in SMEs; ▪ Risk assessment in large companies; ▪ Interrelation between risk assessment and the organizational context.	3
3.	6	Identifying critical factors related to business processes		▪ Business processes from sustainability point of view; ▪ Critical factors that impact sustainable performance.	4
4.	7-8	Identifying, evaluating and analyzing risks related to interactions between business processes	▪ Empirical analysis; ▪ Implementation.	Risk assessment related to business process interactions in organizations and between the organization and outsourced business processes	
5.	9	Determining the impact of the PDCA and FMEA methods during risk assessment in organizations		Risk assessment using the PDCA and FMEA methods related to business process interactions in organizations and between the organization and outsourced business processes	5
6.	10	Analyzing the effects of using the proposed methods during risk assessment in relation with identifying new business opportunities		Risk assessment using the PDCA and FMEA methods and identifying new business opportunities related to business process interactions in organizations and between the organization and outsourced business processes	
7.	11	Developing a risk assessment model using in order to ensure sustainable business performance	▪ Implemen-tation; ▪ Empirical evaluation.	▪ Description of the proposed model; ▪ Validation of the proposed model; ▪ Effects of the proposed model.	

An overview over the structure of the PhD thesis including objectives, research methodology and studies performed by the author during the doctoral period is presented in Table 1.1.

Objectives related to performing risk assessment were achieved by using various models and methods like the PDCA method, the CAGE framework, the MOST analysis, the NASA risk scorecard, the Alberta Context tool, the STEEP analysis, the FMEA method and the risk value map based on negative and positive outcomes of risk materialization.

The conceptual framework was analyzed using references from national and international literature and reports from the Economist Intelligence Unit (EIU), the international coalition of accountants Edinburgh Group (EG), the Organisation for Economic Co-operation and Development and from audit and financial counseling organizations such as KPMG, Deloitte and PwC.

In order to emphasize the current approaches and latest trends related to risk assessment different articles and books written by process specialists as well as the latest guidelines developed in 2018 by The International Organization for Standardization were used in order to identify the newest models developed in order to ensure sustainable performance.

In order to prepare the discussions related to risk assessment in SMEs and large companies, risk appetite and risk tolerance, as well as the organizations' attitude when confronted with risky situations were determined. The comparative analysis between the 2 types of organizations and the interrelation between risk assessment and the organizational context was based on information gathered during interviews with managers and specialists with risk assessment-related experience in different areas of business.

The study of the critical factors impacting sustainable performance includes results based on feedback to questionnaires and interviews related to analyzing organizational business processes from sustainability point of view and determining the impact of the main characteristics of the process or process criteria on the sustainable performance of business processes in organizations.

Objectives related to identifying risks and determining the role of performing risk assessment at the interaction between business processes in organizations and between the organization and outsourced business processes were achieved using results of interviews with managers and CEOs. Further, evaluating and analyzing the identified risks using probability of occurrence and detection as attributes were based on the study of specialized literature and research results achieved during the doctoral period.

The study related to possibilities of improving risk assessment related to interactions between business processes in organizations using the PDCA and FMEA methods and applying probability of detection as a third attribute was performed in order to identify the threats of the organizations and analyze all related risks.
The research was extended by using the proposed methods and identifying new business opportunities in the context of ensuring sustainable performance based on responses to questionnaires and interviews that have focused on researching the effects of proposed risk assessment methods related to organizational business processes and outsourced processes.

The research results achieved during the doctoral period have led to the presentation of a proposed model for the risk assessment process that aims to bring a contribution to ensuring sustainable business performance. Based on the review of national and international specialized literature, as well as the results gathered during the doctoral period and the author's professional experience with risk assessment, the proposed risk assessment model uses the FMEA method and determines risk levels for both threats and opportunities and is illustrated in bi-dimensional and tri-dimensional graphic representations. Validation and the effects of the proposed model were performed during follow-up questionnaires based on feedback from managers that have implemented or are testing the proposed risk assessment model.

Before and during the doctoral period the author has had profound insights related to risk assessment, sustainability and business performance. The author is running a medium-sized enterprise that handles road maintenance and road marking services and has created a solid base for ensuring the organization's sustainable performance - the main activities relate to medium and long-term contracts that require business sustainability and quality performance.

Based on the experience with risk assessment within small and medium-sized enterprises, as well as large companies from the FMCG, constructions and automotive areas of business, the author has also launched a start-up business in the automotive industry in the last 4 years and is managing a project related to building a traffic signs

factory. The author was involved in many other projects during the course of the doctoral research combining the study of the scientific literature with investigations related conducted during discussions with senior managers and experts.
In order to evaluate the proposed model from versatility point of view and to understand requirements and opinions related to risk assessment in organizations, the author has interacted with specialists from different areas of business: FMCG, construction, automotive, pharmaceuticals, healthcare and food industries.
The practicability of the proposed models was tested by the author in one multinational organization and 2 small and medium-sized enterprises.

The following results can be described related to the author's professional experience with risk assessment during the doctoral period:

1. Research and creating documentation related to risk assessment within a medium-sized enterprise related to operational, financial, technical, reputational and market-related risks;

2. Elaborating strategies related to all identified risks and implementing them within the organization;

3. Research, connectivity and alignment with all subsidiaries and branches owned by a multinational organization from different regions (Americas, EMEA, Asia) targeting a global approach, simplifying and strengthening existing processes and creating joint business strategies;

4. Creating risk assessment and management documentation within the multinational organization;

5. Developing and launching a pilot-project for risk assessment using the proposed model.

As a moderator and lecturer during academic seminars and university courses, as well as a concept and pilot project developer in a multinational organization, the author was able to evaluate ideas and information related to risk assessment and sustainable performance in organizations by interacting with academics and experts from different industries.

The research results were presented at several international and national conferences and were published in scientific journals and conference proceedings indexed ISI web of knowledge and recognized internationally; one of the conference papers has received "the Best PhD Paper Presentation" award at the International Conference on Management, Leadership and Governance 2016 organized in Saint Petersburg, Russia.

Research during the doctoral period was guided and supported by the author's scientific coordinator and supervisor Prof. PhD Marieta Olaru, who has pushed for innovative and value-adding results throughout the whole 3 years. The field studies were possible thanks to partners from different organizations worldwide that have shared their perspectives on the proposed topics.

2 Conceptual framework of the organizational business processes

2.1 Actual approaches and perspectives related to organizational business processes

The success of any organization is the result of a clockwork mechanism that is based on a set of business processes. Actions or reactions of any organizations are carried out through processes that aim to achieve the organizations' objectives. Research performed by the author during the doctoral thesis has shown that business processes determine the success rate of the organization's objectives and goals.

Managing business has new rules in the current competitive business environment. While the most important risks related to business sustainability are generated at operational level, managers have to monitor and control all business processes in order to successfully apply new strategies that ensure the organizations' competitive advantage or, in some cases, even business survival. As a result, in order to balance performance indicators during times of financial crisis, more and more organizations develop strategies using the process approach.

Business processes can be defined as sets of interacting or interrelated activities that transform resources or inputs into outputs. In order to add value to the organization, each process is planned as part of a workflow that is monitored and controlled. The Harvard Business School Press writes in 2010 that "processes exist in every organization and its departments and not just to make physical goods". Through business processes, people, know-how and technology are interconnected in order to achieve business objectives and to support the organization's mission and vision.
Intensive studies have been conducted in order to research methods of designing, implementing, executing process activities and monitoring processes.
While targeting business objectives, organizations apply, maintain and continuously improve their management system including all necessary business processes, process interactions and process application methods within the organization including:

- Defining the required inputs and the expected outputs of each process;
- Determining the execution order and interactions of business processes;

R. M. Bejinariu, *Sustainable Business Performance and Risk Management*,
Sustainable Management, Wertschöpfung und Effizienz,
https://doi.org/10.1007/978-3-658-29389-5_2

- Determining and applying criteria and methods including monitoring, measuring and defining performance indicators necessary in order to ensure operating efficiency and process control;
- Allocating and assigning resources for all processes and ensuring their availability;
- Assigning responsibilities and authorizations for these processes;
- Managing risks and opportunities related to all business processes and process interactions;
- Evaluating processes and implementing all necessary changes so that process achieve results according to the expected values of the performance indicators;
- Improving business processes and integrating them in the organization's management system.

According to Brocke, Mathiassen and Rosemann (2014), business process management affects the overall organization performance and "it has become an increasingly important enabling factor of organizational innovation and transforma-tion". In his research Becker et al. (2012) states that „business process management sets out to increase the effectiveness and efficiency of an organization".

Organizations have to update and keep standard operating procedures and other documentation related to applying processes according to the planned methodology in order to make sure that information is available across the organization. In many situations documentation and controlling processes are related to the clients' or other interested parties' requests or to legal requirements.
Measuring the critical performance indicators and developing strategies around the same variables are no longer enough in order to ensure business sustainability, so that organizations have started focusing on managing processes and adjusting objectives according to process results.

Business processes can include primary or support activities "depending on the (directly) extent of integration in the creation of customer value or the organization's structure" (Karavul, 2015). Every process collects and transforms inputs in order to achieve value-adding results (outputs) according to the organizational objectives. Process interactions take place across the organization crossing the barriers of structural departments.

While primary processes are involved in creating customer value, support processes are focused on internal organizational activities. According to Porter (1985), "primary business processes are directly involved in the creation of value by producing goods or services" and "are characterized by serving benefits directly for customers". Support or secondary processes provide support and service for the primary processes. Following, in a more recent study from 2013, Porter defines organizations as "a collection of activities designed by the product, manufactured, distributed, delivered and supported". Organizations with a healthy value chain strategically oriented on transforming all activities into value-adding mechanisms are organizations that are oriented on business processes (Figure 2.1).

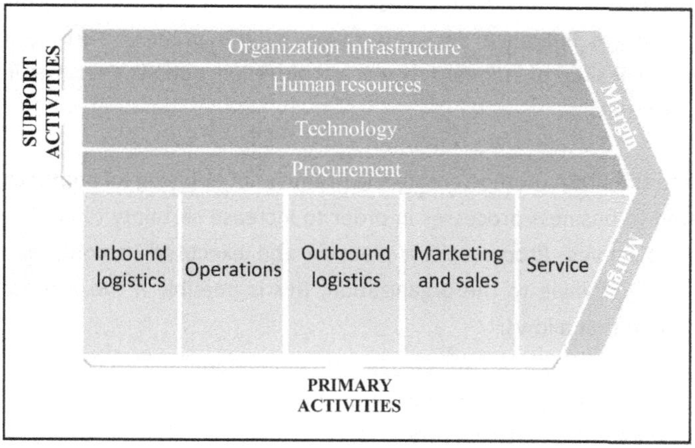

Figure 2.1: Value chain, developed by the author based on Porter, M. E., 1985. Competitive Advantage: Creating and Sustaining Superior Performance. New York: Simon and Schuster, pp. 59, http://forleadership.org/wp-content/uploads/Competitive-Advantage.pdf, accessed 30.03.2016.

2.1.1 Current aspects regarding the process approach

The process approach represents the essence of successful management by ensuring the efficiency and effectiveness of the applied management methods. One of the classic process management methods is the PDCA (Plan, Do, Act, Check) method developed by Deming in 1986. The most important conclusion of his research was that a value-adding process is a process that is permanently updated using information gathered through feedback. The steps considered by Deming were process planning (P), process execution (D = do), monitoring and measuring (C=check), analyzing and evaluating the process (A), while continuously improving the process through the feedback loop.

Feedback includes data and information related to all 4 steps of the PDCA management method:

- P – Planning: process owners receive planning data and information from all organizational levels. In this stage resources are determined, financed and assigned for all process activities;
- D – Doing: activities with the process are executed;
- C – Monitoring and measuring, analyzing and assessing: process owners monitor and evaluate business process results using the feedback loop;
- A – Actions or decisions: The analyzed process results and performance indicators related to the process influence decisions taken by the process owners; if deviations from the desired or standard results are observed, actions are taken in order to improve results.

Process approach and the PDCA method create the premises of applying an approach based on risks related to business processes in order to increase certainty related to achieving business objectives. Processes are planned and executed in controlled conditions in order to add value to the organization; this is possible if the process contains a feedback loop that allows:

- Process planning;
- Monitoring, measuring, analyzing and evaluating business processes;
- Continuous improvement of business processes.

The father of quality management and, according to many management experts, the founder of the management philosophy, Juran (1992) continued the research related to business process management and stated that "the feedback loop includes a sensor that provides data and information derived from the monitoring and measurement processes" and "the umpire compares the organization's objectives with this data". In case deviations are identified, the actuator takes corrective actions in order to realign process activities according to the business objectives. Process cannot have sustainable successful results without feedback so that most of the management tools and electronic software platforms currently include the feedback loop (Figure 2.2).

The International Organization for Standardization (2015) have defined the process approach as managing and controlling processes, interactions between processes and "the inputs and outputs that tie these processes together". In one of his researches in

2015, Popa considered that business process management involves "managing process interactions as a system".

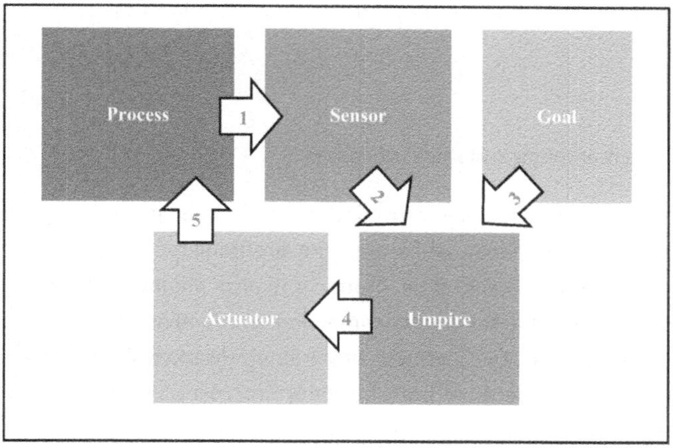

Figure 2.2: The feedback loop, developed by the author based on Juran J.M., 1992. Juran on Quality by Design: The New Steps for Planning Quality into Goods and Services, New York: The Free Press, p. 380.

Feedback prevents the negative effects of risks that occur as a result of process interactions in organizations, which is very important because the main high risks with impact on profitability and turnover can be identified at this level.

In order to design an efficient feedback loop during the planning process, the following questions need to be answered according to a study developed by the author in 2015:

- *Which are the critical performance indicators that are considered?*
- *Who compares the values of the performance indicators with the desired parameters?*
- *Who performs the analysis?*
- *Who uses the results of the diagnosis and takes actions in order to correct the deviation?*

All requirements of the process approach have to be fulfilled and applied in an efficient way in order to implement the PDCA method. By monitoring and controlling process interactions, effectiveness and compliance of inputs and outputs are ensured.

2.1.2 Specific attributes of the organizational business processes

The main business processes are presented including objectives, performance indicators, inputs and outputs, interactions with other processes, methods used and main risks.

2.1.2.1 Attributes of the marketing and sales processes

The objectives of the marketing and sales processes relate to selling products and services according to the clients' needs while ensuring profitability. The processes have to consider pricing, quantity and time frame, but also planning expenses, execution or production time, market launch time and productivity (number of produced goods and services in the defined timeframe). Marketing and sales processes are analyzed together because both business processes share the same goal: marketing promotes sales and sales activities involve preparing and delivering goods and services directly to the client. The main difference is that sales involves one-to-one interactions with clients, while marketing develops strategies related to one or more market segments.

Marketing-related business performance indicators are market share, turnover, clients' satisfaction level, number of business partnerships, number or repeat customers, number of new clients, number of clients that make only one order, marketing campaign efficiency (percentage calculated by dividing the number of inquiries by the total number of new clients x 100), marketing risk levels. When it comes to sales activities the performance indicators can be: non-conformities costs, delayed deliveries, storage costs, mounting and servicing costs and risk levels.

The main interactions are with the exterior environment: clients, creditors, competition and shareholders. Within the organization, marketing and sales processes interact with processes executed by the senior management and by the contract management and quality assurance teams. The usual methods used are market analysis, SWOT (Strengths, Weaknesses, Opportunities and Threats) analysis, Pareto analysis, benchmarking, re-engineering, risk assessment and risk handling.
Risks related to marketing and sales are usually related to not satisfying the clients' needs, not considering clients' requests , delayed production, incomplete product or service presentations or faulty external communication system that can lead to losing clients, penalties, decreased turnover, reduced sales volumes and even lawsuits.

Inputs and outputs related to marketing and sales processes are presented in Tables 2.1 and 2.2.

Table 2.1: Marketing processes inputs and outputs, developed by the author based on the research conducted during the doctoral period

Marketing processes inputs	Marketing processes outputs
▪ Market analysis reports including: targeted market, organization's position on the market, analysis of competing organizations, sales quantities, risk estimations, outsourcing or back sourcing tendencies; ▪ Studies related to the clients' needs and objectives; ▪ Laws and legal requirements; ▪ The current performance status of the products and services.	▪ Product/service specifications, such as business plans including budgets, project management and development documentation; ▪ Product or service improvement projects; ▪ Clients' knowledge concerning the organization's products and service portfolio, the performance of the organization's products and services, the performance of competing organizations.

Table 2.2: Sales processes inputs and outputs, developed by the author based on the research conducted during the doctoral period

Sales processes inputs	Sales processes outputs
▪ "Ready-for-delivery" product or project; ▪ Product specifications; ▪ Product conformity documents; ▪ Clients' information related to product or project delivery; ▪ Risk management efficiency related to the product, service or project; ▪ After-sales activities planning; ▪ Marketing offers and promotions.	▪ Product/service delivered to the client; ▪ New clients for the organization; ▪ Existing clients that want to keep collaborating with the organization; ▪ Potential clients that want details related to marketing offers and promotions.

2.1.2.2 Attributes of the contracting processes

Satisfying the clients' needs and following laws and legislation while creating performing contracts are the main objectives of the contract management team. The critical performance indicators relate to the total contracted value, performance of the offering process (percentage calculated by dividing the contracted value by the offered value x 100) and process risk levels. The contract management department usually involves a contracting team and a legal team that ensures that all contracts are legally compliant. The contracting team examines the clients' requirements in order to determine:

- The organization's capability to fulfill the clients' needs;
- Whether the clients' requests are clear or not;
- Risks related to fulfilling clients' requests (including risk assessment and risk hand-ling);
- Changes related to contract information – changes have to be registered, analyzed and implemented;
- Differences between inquiries or requests and contract information.

Business contracts are the results of processing data and information according to Table 2.3.

Table 2.3: Contracting processes inputs and outputs, developed by the author based on the research conducted during the doctoral period

Contracting processes inputs	Contracting processes outputs
▪ Information related to new clients and regular clients; ▪ Description of the clients' needs; ▪ Clients' requirements and specifications; ▪ Draft contract sent by the client; ▪ Mandatory contract clauses imposed by the organization.	▪ Clear, complete and legally compliant contract clauses; ▪ Performing contract for the organization and the client.

The methods used by the department in order to achieve business objectives are team analysis, check lists, the Pareto analysis, risk evaluation and risk handling. The main process interactions are with business processes executed by senior management and by the marketing and financial teams. Contracting risks can relate to unidentified or unquantifiable requirements that lead to increased costs, unsatisfied clients or even lost clients. Increased costs, late deliveries or clients' complaints can be consequences of non-performing contracts that can also be considered an important risk.

2.1.2.3 Attributes of the financial processes

The objective of the financial department is to manage financial resources in order to support business processes and activities while aiming to achieve organizational objectives. The main functions of the financial department relate to the following processes:

- Accounting (bookkeeping, invoicing, processing payments, etc.);
- Financial analysis and reporting (creating balance sheets and other financial reports);
- Financial planning - resources management: calculating and planning resources in order to optimize cash flow and to support production and other business processes;
- Financial risk management;
- Managing taxes and ensuring legal compliance;
- Managing payrolls.

Table 2.4: Financial processes inputs and outputs, developed by the author based on the research conducted during the doctoral period

Financial processes inputs	Financial processes outputs
▪ Financial requirements concerning resources and working capital for internal processes and ongoing contracts; ▪ Risks related to cash flow; ▪ Changes related to additional costs; ▪ Differences between initial allocated budget and ongoing costs.	▪ Financial resources allocated to departments or projects; ▪ Financial support for all ongoing projects; ▪ Budget and cash flow estimations for possible new projects.

Critical performance indicators related to financial processes are turnover, profit, working capital, cash flow, current ratio (accounts receivables against current liabilities), payroll headcount, return on equity and risk levels. Inputs and outputs are presented in Table 2.4. Excluding financial risk management, other management methods are based on the financial indicators that are calculated and analyzed. Financial processes impact and are impacted by all processes within the organization and interact directly with business processes executed by senior management and contracting, procurement and production processes.

2.1.2.4 Attributes of the procurement processes

The procurement process is a support process that ensures acquiring goods and services from the exterior environment and includes the following subprocesses: evaluating, selecting and monitoring suppliers, verifying the received products and services, controlling outsourced services. The objectives of the process are reducing sourcing costs and procurement time, ensuring stocks according to necessities and establishing partnerships with suppliers. Procurement managers monitor the following performance indicators: procurement efficiency (percentage calculated by dividing the procurement costs by 1000 units of production x 100), rate of incompliant supplied goods, procurement time for products and services, price lists changes, average payment term, risk levels. The main management methods are cause and effect analysis, Pareto analysis, check lists and team analysis.

Table 2.5 presents process inputs and outputs related to procurement processes.

Table 2.5: Procurement processes inputs and outputs, developed by the author based on the research conducted during the doctoral period

Procurement processes inputs	Procurement processes outputs
▪ Supplier information and supplier offers; ▪ Evaluation, selection and supplier monitoring criteria; ▪ Acquisition/sourcing plan including budgets; ▪ Lists of materials required by other departments (production, after-sales and others).	▪ List of accepted suppliers; ▪ Orders and contract annexes including price lists; ▪ Acquired product or service ready for production; ▪ Information resulted from supplier monitoring; ▪ Supplier partnerships.

Possible risks relate to only one supplier being evaluated and selected so that additional costs, delayed deliveries and clients' complaints may occur as consequences. Delayed procurement is also an important risk that causes reduced sales and delayed deliveries. Procurement errors can be related to incompliant products or services that leads to marketing authorizations not being obtained. Other procurement risks are not identifying acceptance criteria for products and services and unqualified suppliers that involve increased production costs, faulty products, delayed deliveries and clients' complaints.

2.1.2.5 Attributes of the production processes

Achieving sales objectives in the agreed contract terms is the goal of the production process. Also, the process aims to control production time and costs while following products specifications and decreasing associated risk levels. Production involves the following subprocesses: production and services control, products identification and traceability, control and monitoring of clients' and suppliers' property, storage, after-sales support activities and change control. The main performance indicators are production capacity, production costs, productivity (percentage calculated by dividing the manpower-related costs by the total production costs x 100), over-time productivity (percentage calculated by dividing the number of total over-time work hours by 1000 production units x 100) and production risks levels. Methods such as Failure Mode Effects Analysis (FMEA), Statistical Process Control (SPC), Pareto analysis, check lists and cause – effect diagrams are used by the production managers and specialists.

Process inputs and outputs are presented in Table 2.6.

Table 2.6: Production processes inputs and outputs, developed by the author based on the research conducted during the doctoral period

Production processes inputs	Production processes outputs
▪ "Ready-for-production" products; ▪ Sales program; ▪ Technical documentation for execution and verification; ▪ Clients' contracts and orders; ▪ Quality plan; ▪ Risk handling plan for products, services, projects and contracts; ▪ The 5M's of profitable manufacturing: Manpower, Materials, Machines, Methods and Money.	▪ "Ready-for-delivery" product or "Ready-to-be-supplied" service; ▪ Product conformity documentation; ▪ Operating manuals or other user manuals; ▪ Service logistics; ▪ Risk handling results.

The most important risks are related to defects and malfunctions signaled by clients that may lead to complaints and unsatisfied clients. Delayed deliveries are also a production-related risk which has a direct negative impact on sales. Other risks are production line malfunctions (production infrastructure) which involve repairing costs and delay deliveries and also polluting the environment and work accidents that can cause losing authorizations, decreased sales and market share. Operating with incompliant or outdated materials and equipment, using incorrect product specifications and insufficient time for verification protocols can lead to complaints from clients and decreased delivery capacity.

2.1.2.6 Attributes of the planning processes

Planning is a support process that involves preparing business processes, creating technical and technological designs and elaborating process plans. The objectives of the planning processes include reducing production times and costs, ensuring production capability, ensuring environmental protection and occupational safety and health, maintaining supplier partnerships and controlling outsourced processes. Planning managers monitor the following performance indicators:

- Planning efficiency (%) = number of contracted days / number of work days x 100;
- Delivery deadlines;
- Manpower efficiency (%) = value of salaries / 1000 production units x 100;
- Procurement efficiency (%) = inventory value / turnover x 100;
- Risk levels;
- Planning uses cause – effect diagrams, the Pareto analysis, check lists and team analysis as process methods.

Table 2.7 indicates inputs and outputs related to the planning process.

Table 2.7: Planning process inputs and outputs, developed by the author based on the research conducted during the doctoral period

Planning processes inputs	Planning processes outputs
▪ "Ready-for-production" products; ▪ Sales program; ▪ Planning production processes validation; ▪ Product and services supplier offers; ▪ Risk handling plan for products, services, projects and contracts; ▪ The 5M model of profitable manufacturing: Manpower, Materials, Machines, Methods and Money.	▪ Production program; ▪ Procurement program; ▪ List of validated products, services and suppliers; ▪ Execution technical documentation; ▪ Quality plan including acceptance and authorization criteria; ▪ Production validation reports; ▪ Risk handling plan for products, services, projects and contracts.

The identified risks can relate to generating non-compliance: transferring non-compliant products to clients and transforming non-compliant products into defects that involves additional costs, delayed deliveries and complaints. Other risks can be delayed procurement and inefficient control mechanisms that can lead to decreased sales, delayed deliveries and even losing clients. Errors in identifying compliance criteria for products and services and unqualified suppliers can cause products being delivered with defects.

2.1.2.7 Attributes of the after-sales processes

After-sales processes involve service and maintenance during the warranty period, selling after-sales products (such as components required for repairs and maintenance) and managing clients' complaints. Process objectives involve increasing product life cycles, decreasing after-sales costs during the warranty period and improving clients' satisfac-tion. Following, process indicators are warranty expenses, number of complaints and risk levels. Table 2.8 presents inputs and outputs.

Table 2.8: After-sales processes inputs and outputs, developed by the author based on the research conducted during the doctoral period

After-sales processes inputs	After-sales processes outputs
▪ Product from the client; ▪ Product operating and maintenance specifications during warranty period; ▪ Product conformity documents; ▪ Service contract or order during the warranty service; ▪ Clients' complaints; ▪ Service planning.	▪ Product ready for the client; ▪ After-sales product operating and maintenance specifications; ▪ Product conformity documents; ▪ Clients' complaints; ▪ Service planning.

Management methods used by the process are Pareto analysis, clients' visits, checklists, Eight Disciplines (8D) problem-solving model, Failure Mode Effects Analysis (FMEA) method, risk assessment and risk handling.

After-sales processes can involve the following risks:

- Incomplete documentation that can lead to inability to solve issues during the warranty period and unsatisfied clients;
- Long response times to clients' complaints with consequences related to unsatisfied clients and even losing clients;
- Inadequate service logistics that has a negative impact on the clients' trust.

2.1.2.8 Attributes of the quality assurance processes

Quality assurance is a support process that ensures that quality-related clients' requirements are met. The process aims to avoid delivering faulty or non-conforming products and services and to ensure that clients receive consistent products and services every time according to their needs. Quality assurance considers process

results and feedback from all organization departments and transmits it to the marketing department in order to improve marketing strategies and increase sales. The main indicators that are monitored are: number of clients' complaints, number of non-conforming products, service delivery time, time for dealing with clients' complaints, products and services availability and risk levels.
Inputs and outputs are indicated in Table 2.9.

Table 2.9: Quality assurance processes inputs and outputs, developed by the author based on the research conducted during the doctoral period

Quality assurance processes inputs	Quality assurance processes outputs
▪ Feedback from the organizational departments; ▪ Product defects and redundant production and after-sales issues; ▪ Product conformity documents; ▪ Product or service contract or order; ▪ Clients' complaints; ▪ Service planning.	▪ Product or service quality improvement plan; ▪ Product operating and maintenance specifications; ▪ Product conformity documents; ▪ Clients' complaints analysis; ▪ Revised service planning.

The management methods are cost of quality, cost-benefit analysis, benchmarking, statistical sampling and check lists. Related risks can be organizational image being negatively affected by faulty or non-conforming products or services and additional unforeseen costs during the warranty period caused by incomplete or incorrect product specifications and operating manuals.

2.1.3 Characteristics of the organizational business process interactions

Organizational workflows can be identified vertically from one organizational level to another, but also horizontally as processes linked together between departments (Figure 2.3). Workflows are optimized by process owners and managers by permanently identifying, analyzing and sending feedback related to all process interactions. Interactions between organizational business processes are established according to the objectives of the organization; they are controlled through the feedback mechanism, so that reports are sent from the operational level to the strategical level, where managers take decisions and develop strategies based on the received information. Following, process owners and department managers implement strategies at operational level and monitor, analyze and report performance indicators related to the process results.

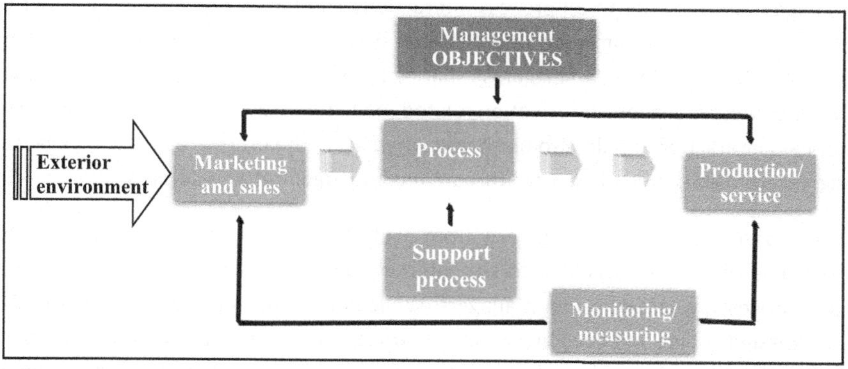

Figure 2.3: Vertical and horizontal organizational workflows, developed by the author based on the research conducted during the doctoral period

While horizontally process interactions are located between organizational business processes that are linked together in the chain of operations, vertical or hierarchical interactions are located between processes executed by the strategic management, operational management and external environment levels (Figure 2.4).

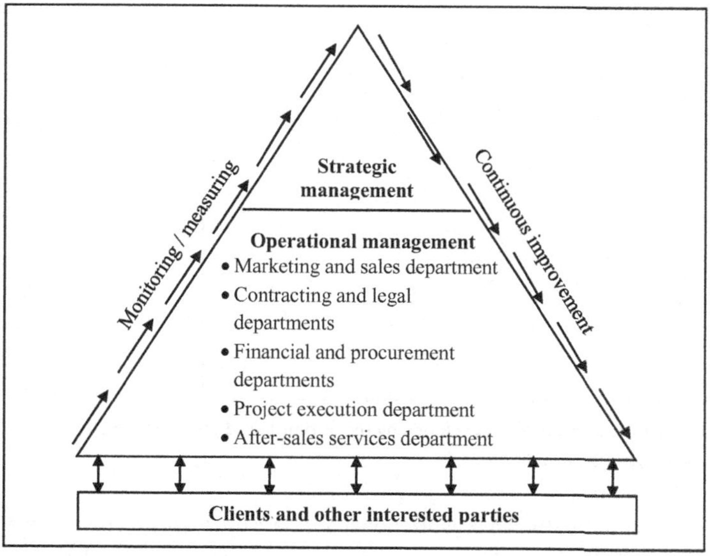

Figure 2.4: Hierarchical interactions between organizational business processes, developed by the author based on the research conducted during the doctoral period

Risk management is part of the managers' responsibilities according to the research results achieved by the author during the doctoral period, therefore the process manager is the owner of all process interactions and has to ensure their efficiency while assessing and managing risks that can occur at this level. Another important responsibility for process managers is sharing findings and providing feedback to the other process managers. Information related to identified and evaluated risks at each process interaction should also be shared when using the process approach, because significant risks can be discovered threatening the organization's success.

The transmission media can vary from websites, presentations, workshops or contracts with clients and investors to internal memos, e-mails, reports or meetings with process owners or senior managers. While data is transmitted in a "raw form", information coding and decoding is very important for successful process interactions - unclear, incorrect or incomplete information can lead to high risks and a negative impact on process results.

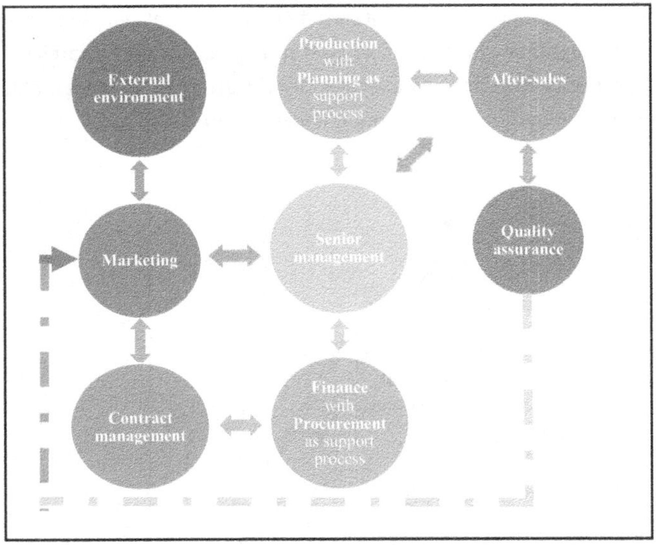

Figure 2.5: Business process interactions, developed by the author based on the research conducted during the doctoral period

An example of interactions between organizational business processes is presented in Figure 2.5. The figure shows that information and data exchange takes place between processes so that:

- each of the primary and support processes are connected horizontally with other processes that are influenced or have an influence on the processes' results;
- senior management or the strategic management team is connected to all processes across the organization.

Using the main organizational business processes presented in Figure 2.5, the following process interactions can be identified:

a) Process interactions between marketing processes and the external environment
The organization communicates with the exterior environment through marketing processes. The marketing team is permanently informed related to the "market's pulse" bringing an important contribution to decision-making related to sales and growth strategies. Given the current market conditions, developing partnerships with clients, creditors (suppliers, banks), competing organizations and shareholders is essential for ensuring business sustainability. Benchmarking with peer organizations and associating with competing organizations in projects or programs enlarges the organizations' perspectives and capabilities;

b) Process interactions between marketing processes and contracting and legal processes
Information about new business opportunities, but also threats identified in the external environment are sent from the marketing team to the contracting and legal team; this information is particularly important for verifying the viability of new clients and suppliers, editing contract clauses and setting up payment terms. The contracting and legal team sends feedback including legislative information that may involve changes in the clients' requirements;

c) Process interactions between senior management and marketing processes
It is also the marketing processes that involve sending feedback from the exterior environment to senior management that develops business strategies based on that information. Following, marketing activities are taken according to decisions taken by the strategic management;

d) Process interactions between contracting and legal processes and financial processes
Between the contracting and financial processes activities are very intense: the contracting team sends information about current and upcoming contracts, so that the financial team can optimize cash flow in order to support expenses. Also, financial

processes involve sending feedback to the contracting department related to resources and financial requirements in order to determine payment terms and other contractual clauses;

e) Process interactions between senior management and contracting and legal pro-cesses

Senior management develops strategies based on feedback from the organization and networking with other organizations; therefore, contract performance and conformity are ensured by gathering and communicating information related to the clients' needs to both the marketing and the contract management teams. Following, contracting and legal activities target elaborating contracts by using data and information received;

f) Process interactions between procurement processes and financial processes

The procurement and the financial teams work together in order to ensure profitable acquisitions. Procurement activities involves selecting suppliers based on product or service specifications, pricing and payment terms – this information has to be communicated to the financial team in order to ensure working capital and to optimize cash flow;

g) Process interactions between financial processes and production processes

Production activities involve estimating resources depending on the planned production (quantity and quality of products and services). Production costs have to be ensured by the financial department, therefore financial managers have to calculate budgets and plan financial resources according to production requirements;

h) Process interactions between senior management and financial processes

Financial business strategies are developed by senior management based on the organization's and the clients' needs. These strategies can negatively affect financial activities if they are based on erroneous or inaccurate data and information. Financial managers plan budgets and cash flow according to information from senior management and the other organization departments;

i) Process interactions between planning processes and production processes

The planning team has to consider the specifications of the products and services, budgets, timeframes, manpower and all resources that involve production planning. The production team has to share information related to quality checks including production-related issues (faulty products, delayed production times, etc.);

j) Process interactions between production processes and after-sales processes
Information related to product verifications and all related quality checks has to be sent by the production managers to the after-sales department in order to plan and prepare for issues that may be encountered during the warranty period and to update product operating manuals. Feedback from clients related to product non-conformities is received by the after-sales department and has to be sent to the production department in order to improve product specifications.

k) Process interactions between senior management and production processes
Production is highly impacted by strategical management especially by marketing and sales strategies. Senior management also takes decisions related to allocating resources and approves production budgets. Production errors that lead to faulty and non-conforming products and services affect the organization's image and business strategies have to be adjusted in order to not lose the clients' trust;

l) Process interactions between after-sales processes and quality assurance processes
Important information related to clients' complaints and non-conformities are sent by the after-sales team to the quality assurance team in order to improve product specifications. Feedback related to monitoring, measuring and verification protocols has to be sent to the after-sales team in order to prevent delivering faulty products and additional unforeseen costs during the warranty period;

m) Process interactions between senior management and after-sales processes
Business strategies developed by senior management affect after-sales processes, especially when it comes to sales of spare parts and troubleshooting during the warranty period. After-sales services are very important for the organizational image and have to be considered when elaborating business strategies and objectives;

n) Process interactions between quality assurance processes and marketing and sales processes
Information provided by the quality and assurance department is very important when developing marketing strategies – product and service specifications, operating manuals, product innovations and updates are communicated to the marketing team by the quality and assurance team.
By not analyzing the market's needs and not communicating the clients' requirements, the quality and assurance team cannot update control mechanisms and verification protocols;

o) Process interactions between procurement processes and suppliers

The relationship between the procurement and suppliers is very important for the organization. Budget delivery terms not being calculated correctly or disadvantageous negotiations can lead to non-performing contracts with the suppliers. On the other hand, suppliers' delayed production or incorrect estimations of resources can lead to delayed deliveries and even cancelled procurement contracts.

2.2 New business trends related to outsourcing and backsourcing organizational business processes

Globalization has allowed managers to seek profitability through increased revenue or profit margins and to increase corporate value by expanding their businesses across the globe. When entering overseas markets, management strategies are developed considering the business environment of the targeted countries. Elimination of the most important trade barriers, technological advancements, and decreased transportation costs have connected countries and organizations together.

There are 2 directions that have been taken by organizations when expanding business across the globe: outsourcing processes and finding new markets. Corporations have to research and understand foreign business environments and the main differences between their home country and the countries where they want to outsource processes in order to decrease production and service costs and to increase revenue by targeting new market segments worldwide.

Newly developing countries like China, India, Latin America, Southeast Asia and Africa, but also advanced regions like the United States and Europe can be major markets and can offer important outsourcing opportunities, but involve very different economies, cultures and labor conditions. Organizations have been relocating manufacturing and outsourcing services to low-wage countries; however, knowledge intensive business services have been kept inside the organization – according to Peters (2006), knowledge-intensive processes, such as very specialized production and services or research and development are not outsourced.

Managers have considered internalization as a back-up for every outsourcing strategy. Despite cost-saving estimations and forecasted profits, economic dynamics have been dominated by "the accelerating internationalization of markets and organizations" (Lange et al., 2018).

One of the most important management challenges when it comes to expanding overseas is finding control mechanisms for foreign subsidiaries and entities. Quality-related issues, flexibility, infrastructure, know-how and governance costs were the main reasons for backsourcing in the past years.

Managers have concluded that not all the outsourcing and market expansion decisions were correct, so that organizations have started repatriating business processes and activities to their home country. In a study conducted in 2007, Kinkel and Zanker state that "backsourcing is used as a short-term opportunity to correct severe strategic management errors".

2.2.1 Characteristics regarding the motivation of the outsourcing and backsourcing decisions

Since the 1980s many organizations have started relocating services by contracting work outside the organization. While outsourcing refers to moving processes and activities outside the organization without crossing country borders, offshoring is defined as outsourcing manufacturing or services in a different country.
Doh et al. (2009) and Pisani and Ricart (2016) define offshoring as "the transnational relocation or dispersion of service activities" that organizations previously performed in their home country, including captive (internal) and outsourced (external) delivery modes. According to Pressey et al. (2009), "offshoring can provide a better access to quality products, or to products or services, which required specific skills or technologies to be made".

However, many authors underline the risks related to offshoring, especially related to controlling quality and costs, so that "risks or risk criteria should be analyzed before making an offshoring decision" (Farrell, 2006) and "uncertainties and risks related to offshoring may lead to unexpected costs which offset gains from cheaper labour, or even result in losses to the outsourcer" (Song et al., 2007). A research conducted by Fel and Griette (2012) on 158 organizations investigates outsourcing decisions by organization size (Figure 2.6) and related the motivation (Figure 2.7).

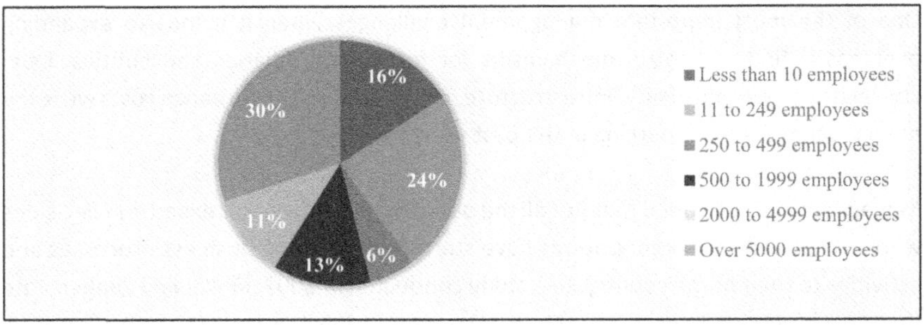

Figure 2.6: Outsourcing decisions by organization size, developed by the author based on Fel, F. and Eric, G., 2012. An analysis of the offshoring decision process: The influence of the organization's size. 8th International Strategic Management Conference, June 2012, Barcelona, 2012, pp. 599, https://www.researchgate.net/publication/257717401_An_Analysis_of_the_Offshoring_Decision_Process_The_Influence_of_the_Organization's_Size, accessed 03.03.2017.

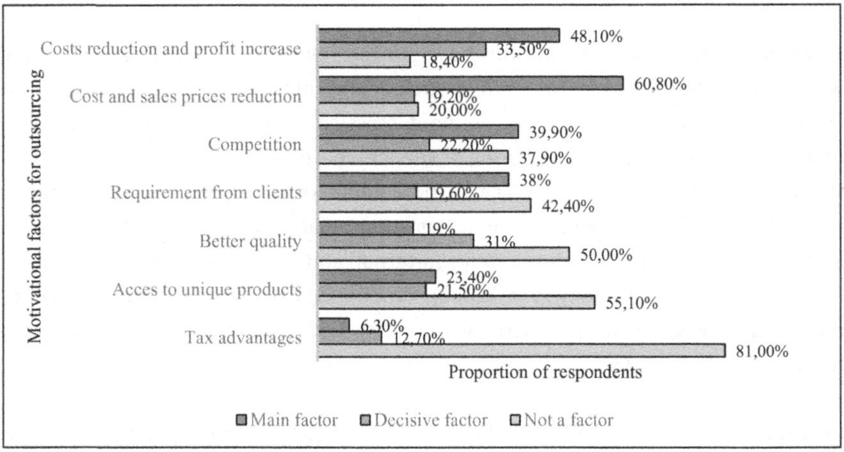

Figure 2.7: Motivation for outsourcing, developed by the author based on Fel, F. and Eric, G., 2012. An analysis of the offshoring decision process: The influence of the organization's size. 8th International Strategic Management Conference, June 2012, Barcelona, 2012, pp. 601, https://www.research gate.net/publication/257717401_An_Analysis_of_the_Offshoring_Decision_Process_The_Influence_of_the_Organization's_Size, accessed 03.03.2017.

In order to be successful, outsourcing business processes have to be prepared by gathering information related to the consumers' needs, market requirements, laws and legislation, communication and technological infrastructures, cultural differences, risks and risk management, reputation and finances related to the organization that will perform the contracted services.

Reversing decisions related to relocating work is defined as backsourcing or reshoring. More and more managers and researchers are investigating the backsourcing phenomenon in order to understand why and how organizations reshore. Recent studies by Gray et al. (2013) and Fratocchi et al. (2014) show that by revising and reversing decisions related to offshored processes and activities, managers have to consider "change of ownership, e.g. from an external overseas supplier to an in-house, domestic arrangement". Reversing decisions are mainly related to quality of products and, according to a study performed by Albrecht et al. in 2016, "this focus on improved quality, the whole area of product liability and the numerous lawsuits involved had grown out of control". A study performed by Zhai et al. in 2016 presents the main reasons for backsourcing based on 139 cases of American organizations reshoring from China (Figure 2.8).

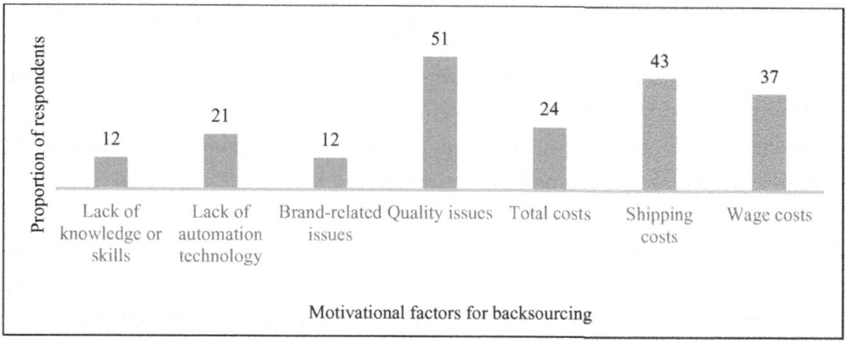

Figure 2.8: Motivation for backsourcing, developed by the author based on Zhai, W., Sun, S. and Zhang, G., 2016. Operations Management Research, pp. 62-74, https://doi.org/10.1007/s12063-016-0114-z, accessed 10.04.2018.

2.2.2 Main factors that determine decisions related to outsourcing organizational business processes

Outsourcing strategies are based on finding new countries where manufacturing or other conditions can increase business profitability. National barriers exist even in a "flattened world" (Motohashi, 2015), therefore no matter the organizations' choice, the main differences between business environments have to be understood in order to successfully expand.

Ghemawat (2007) proposes the CAGE framework as a tool for researching differences between domestic and foreign countries:

- Cultural differences: language, religion, traditions, customs, etc.;
- Administrative distance: currency, foreign investment policies, trade agreements, etc.;
- Geographic distance: transportation costs, time zones, etc.;
- Economic distance: income levels, wages, etc.

In order to ensure mid- and long-term business sustainability and development across trade borders, managers have to prepare the transition by first defining the organization's mission, objectives, strategies and tactics (the MOST analysis). The mission of the organization has to express the organization's management direction and vision; the mission has to be adapted to the foreign country's local market. Objectives have to be SMART (Specific, Measurable, Assignable, Realistic and Time-related) and when expanding overseas organizations usually choose a 3-5 years management strategy with specific objectives related to profitability and growth.

However, the changes in the global business environment have forced managers to redefine strategies and include objectives that ensure business sustainability. Tactics relate to how strategies are executed and are usually planned by department managers according to the type of strategy involved.

Developing management strategies considers both strengths and weaknesses (internal factors) and opportunities and threats (external factors). Before expanding sales in foreign markets, managers can use Porter's "Five Force" model (1980) that focuses on the external factors: threat of new entrants, threat of substitutes, bargaining power of customers, bargaining power of suppliers and industry rivalry. Relocating processes has to consider both internal and external factors and usually involves finding new manufacturers or new service and support providers.

When choosing to outsource processes in a foreign country, managers usually analyze GDP per capita (Figure 2.9), geopolitical risks, unit labor costs (specific for production), quality of the talent pool, culture, technology, laws and legislation and outsourcing reputation.

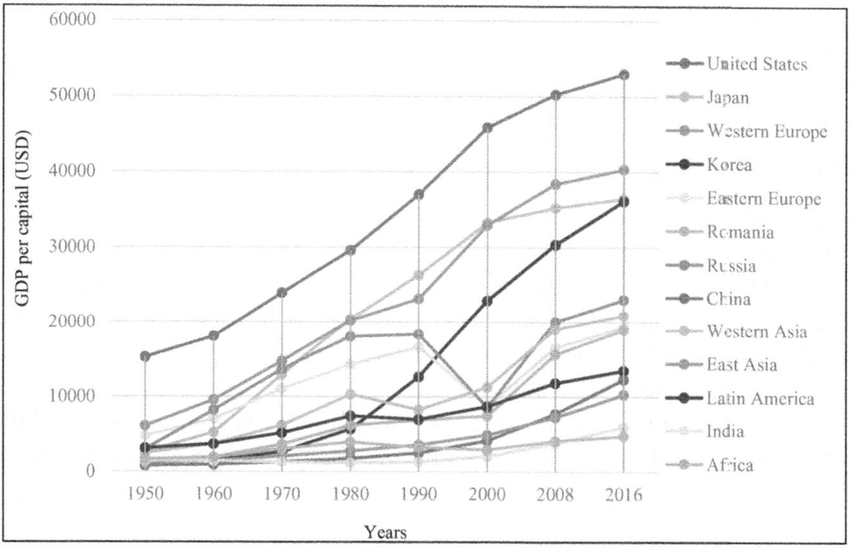

Figure 2.9: GDP per capita in U.S. Dollars, developed by the author based Jutta, B., Inklaar, R., de Jong, H. and van Zanden, J. L., 2018. Rebasing 'Maddison': new income comparisons and the shape of long-run economic development. Maddison Project Database, version 2018, Maddison Project Working paper 10, https://www.rug.nl/ggdc/historicaldevelopment/maddison/releases/ mad dison-project-database-2018, accessed 10.04.2018.

When relocating manufacturing, managers investigate unit labor costs (Figure 2.10) in order to estimate labour productivity by calculating the average cost of labour per unit of production.

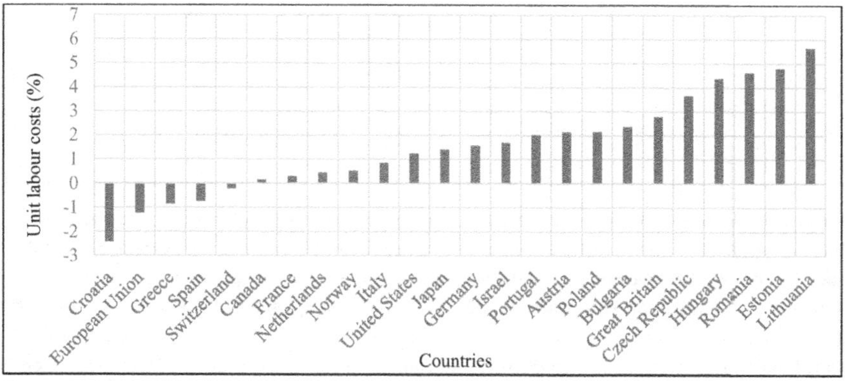

Figure 2.10: Unit labour costs in 2016, developed by the author based on data provided by Organisation for Economic Co-operation and Development (OECD), 2018. Unit labour costs (indicator), https://stats.oecd.org/Index.aspx?DataSetCode =ULC_ANN, accessed 05.05.2018.

Controlling and evaluating outsourced processed can be performed through corporate governance in order ensure business sustainability in the context of outsourcing. In a recent study by Mateiu et al. (2016) corporate governance is considered a critical factor in ensuring "long term profitability, reduction of operating costs and higher return on investment".

The success of any outsourcing model depends on communication and assigning responsibility for each of the processes that manage interactions with the new business partners while considering language, culture, common goals and objectives, trust, human rights, expectations and risks. Senior management handles the relationship with the outsourcing organization and carries out negotiations, sets standards and expectations in order to prepare the contract. Resistance to change and conflicts of interest with employees are challenges that have to be managed by communicating with the staff, explaining the transition including risks, newly assigned tasks and protocols and how this change will affect them.

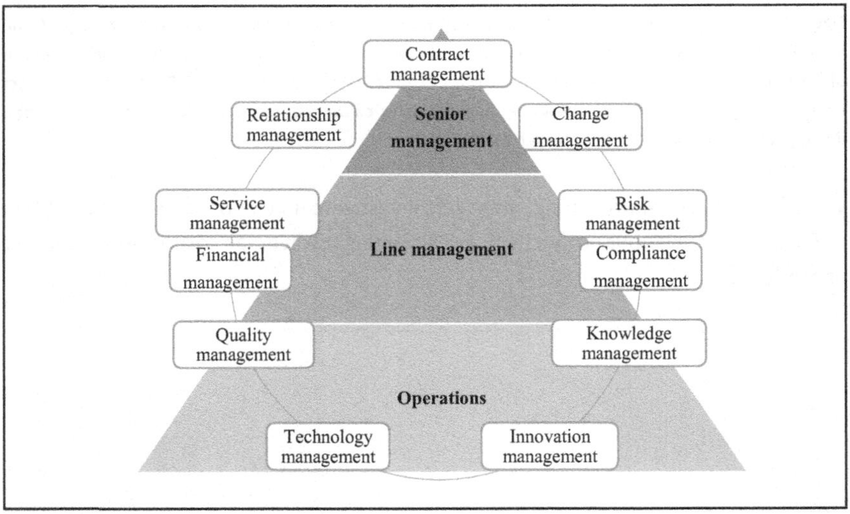

Figure 2.11: Managing outsourcing, developed by the author based on Mateiu A., Mateescu, R. M., Buchmüller, M. and Just V., 2016. Governance as a Key Factor for Ensuring the Sustainability of Outsourcing Models. Proceedings of the International Conference on Management, Leadership and Governance (4th ICMLG), St. Petersburg, Russia, 14-15.04.2016, pp. 466-474, ISBN: 978-1-910810-84-2, indexed in ISI Web of Knowledge, IDS Number: BH5MP, Accession number: WOS:000 401232800057, https://apps.webofknowledge.com/full_record.do?product=UA&search_ mode= General Search&qi d=16&SID=1E7sTR4XNLkznRxUiPJ&page=1&doc=6.

Department managers have the responsibility of ensuring quality of service and compliance, budgeting and allocating resources, managing risks and transferring knowledge. The executive teams follow the management's direction and besides are in charge of technology and innovation (Figure 2.11).

The client organization sets its own objectives, goals, strategies, structure and protocols, while the outsourcing supplier adapts its activity to the local business environment in order to achieve the required performance indicators values. Not aligning expectations and failing to analyze the differences between business environments are the main causes for third-party providers changing objectives and methods and limiting the influence of the client organizations.

While both organizations aim for profitability, when it comes to motivation each of the organizations have different incentives that fuel their activities:

- Client organizations are more concerned about quality of service and customers' satisfaction;
- Third-party providers focus on volumes being most of the times paid for each produced output (for example for one line of code (programming) or one manufactured product).

Table 2.10 shows the main issues encountered related to different strategies developed by the client organization and third-party providers.

Table 2.10: Outsourcing-related strategic challenges, developed by the author based on Bravard, L. and Morgan, R. (2009), Intelligent and successful Outsourcing, Financial Press, Munich, Dow Jones Sustainability Indices Yearbook Reports.

Client organization	Third-party provider
Develops business strategies	Defines its own strategies
Designs a new management structure	Creates a flexible structure oriented on the clients' needs
Defines new standards and protocols	Determines the level of transparency related to rewards, risks and other commercial aspects
Considers that business motivation and goals are the same for both partners	Determines the level of external influence on their organization

There is no universal outsourcing model that applies to all areas of business or countries, however industry leaders that have successfully outsourced processes have also implemented a strong governance system that permanently monitors and analyzes the outsourced process' results while considering feedback from the supplier partner. Business climate conditions have to be checked permanently and processes have to be adapted to all economic, social, political, legal and environmental changes. Any deviation from the standards that are aligned between the 2 organizations have to be com-municated so that issues are solved in a manner that is reasonable and convenient for both parties.

2.2.3 Main factors that determine decisions related to backsourcing organizational business processes

Reshoring or backsourcing have become a trend in the last years. Political and economic dynamics have brought a new set of rules that have affected outsourced solutions and proved that offshoring decisions were unsatisfactory. In 2017 Baroncelli et al. stated that "emerging political platforms oriented toward protectionism" are the main cause for reshoring but choosing a suitable business location is far more complex than that. Increased wages and production materials have forced outsourcing suppliers to choose between quality and price and have transferred these issues to their clients.

Backsourcing motivation relates mainly to quality of service, increased wages and transportation costs as well as flexibility. However, before reshoring managers have to analyze the reasons for the unsatisfying results of outsourcing. All issues encountered that have forced managers to revise outsourcing decisions have 2 root-causes: limited communication and limited control. These limitations can lead to the inability of managing risks related to interactions between business processes.

By constantly analyzing all impacting factors, risk assessment makes predictions and foresees possible changes from inside and outside the organization; this is particularly important for the success of the outsourcing process. According to the research results achieved by the author during the doctoral period, not managing risks related to critical data and information located at interaction between business processes and lack of compliance with quality standards threaten the sustainability of the chosen outsourcing model and increase governance and quality assurance costs.

Table 2.11 presents the main conclusions drawn related to outsourcing decisions according to Lange et al. (2018). Underestimating costs and overestimating the advantages of outsourcing have led to revising and reversing outsourcing decisions.

Table 2.11: Motivation for reversing outsourcing decisions, developed by the author based on Lange, S., Buchmüller, M., Heinemann, B., Mateescu, R.M., 2018. The Driver for the Backsourcing Phenome-non under the Force of Globalization, Proceedings of the 4th BASIQ International Conference on New Trends in Sustainable Business and Consumption, 11-13 June 2018, Heidelberg University, Heidelberg, Germany, pp. 116-123.

No. crt.	Factors of motivation for outsourcing decisions	Conclusion over time
1.	Flexibility and deliverability	Overestimated
2.	Quality of service and risk management	Overestimated
3.	Overhead costs which include the coordination and communication of processes	Underestimated
4.	Savings resulting from wage savings abroad	Overestimated
5.	Costs of care and coordination, which are provided by domestic locations	Underestimated
6.	Production costs - expected personnel, capital, material or manufacturing costs	Underestimated
7.	Key capabilities, governance and organization structure	Overestimated

2.2.4 New approaches related to outsourcing and backsourcing organizational business processes

Rightsourcing or “rightshoring” is a concept that involves deciding if a business process should be performed inside the organization or it should be contracted to a third-party provider. When making relocating choices related to the destination country, corporate governance and expectations, several challenges are encountered, and a series of factors can be identified that can lead to uncertainties and can delay or cancel decision-making.

The rightsourcing approach is a framework that leads to correct decision-making when it comes to locating manufacturing or business services. Recent researches performed by Tate and Bals (2017) and Vanpoucke (2016) regard rightsourcing as “as the process that leads to identify the correct location for a specific organization”.

In 2017 Baroncelli states that choices concerning offshoring and reshoring can be seen as "outcomes of a decision-making process that, when properly carried out, will lead to a "rightshoring" choice" and made a list of drivers that have to be considered in order to achieve the most from a location choice:

- Alignment between the competitive and operations strategies;
- Analyzing business environment conditions;
- Identifying and analysing organizations' and industries' specifics, so that results are not detrimental to any of the organizations' processes and activities (for example research and development or marketing and sales);
- Contingency factors that concern "endogenous conditions that must be met in order to even start considering offshoring options".

However, according to specialized literature the large number of failed outsourcing initiatives and projects shows that "the inherent decision-making process is still poorly performed" (Tate and Bals (2017), Bals et al. (2016), Joubioux and Vanpoucke (2016).

According to geographical locations, Gray (2013) defined 4 dimensions that can be considered when choosing where to execute processes: "in-house reshoring, reshoring for insourcing, reshoring for outsourcing, and outsourced reshoring".

Based on the more comprehensive model developed by Foerstl et al. in 2016, Tate and Bals (2017) have developed a model for rightshoring decision-making (Figure 2.12) that presents 8 choices related to the location where processes are carried out according to ownership, as follows:

- Full ownership of the processes can be onsite (inside the organization), offsite (processes are carried out by the organization's employees remotely for example over the internet or phone), nearshore (processes are performed by an organization subsidiary or branch in a neighbouring country) and offshore (processes are performed by an organization subsidiary or branch in a more distant location);

- Third-party providers can be located onsite (inside the organization), offsite (processes are carried out by the third part provider remotely), nearshore (the third-party provider is located in a nearby country) and offshore (the third-party provider is located in a distant country).

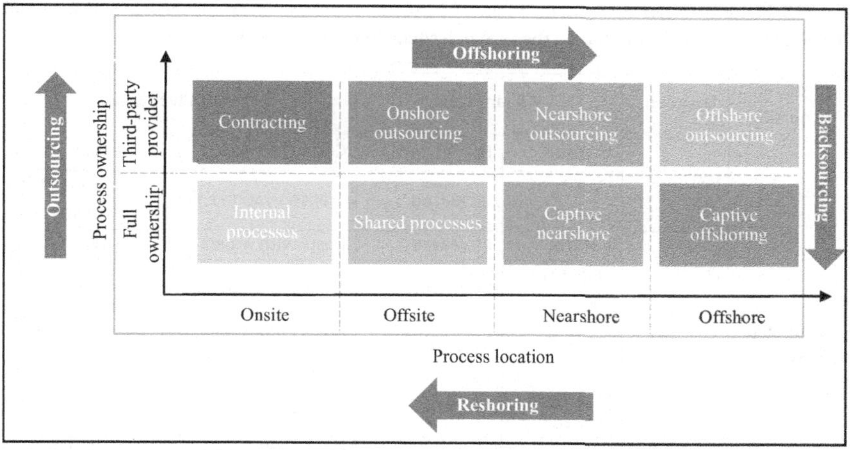

Figure 2.12: The rightshoring approach, developed by the author based on Tate W. and Bals L., 2017. Outsourcing/offshoring insights: going beyond reshoring to rightshoring. International Journal of Physical Distribution & Logistics Management, Vol. 47 Issue: 2/3, pp.106-113, https://doi.org/10.1108/IJPDLM-11-2016-0314, accessed 23.03.2018.

Managers have to balance pros and cons in order to make the right choice related to either outsourcing or backsourcing and offshoring or reshoring.

Processes performed inside the organization will always be the "safe" and a more expensive solution, while offshore solutions involve important cost savings but lower quality of service. Remote services are a good solution for IT organizations and other organizations that can offer services offsite with almost no negative effect on quality of service.

Captive models bring the advantage of lower location costs and not losing ownership of the process; nearshore or offshore solutions cannot be fully controlled and offer a moderate quality of service.

Each of the choices presented has both advantages and disadvantages related to control-ling processes, quality of service, costs with wages, relocation and transportation costs (Table 2.12).

Table 2.12: Advantages and disadvantages of executing processes by ownership and location, developed by the author based on the research conducted during the doctoral period

Process ownership	Location	**Advantages**		**Disadvantages**	
Full ownership of the processes	*Onsite*	Control	Full	Costs with wages	High
		Quality of service	Increased	Transportation costs	Replaced by facility costs
	Offsite	Control	Increased	Costs with wages	High
		Quality of service	Moderate	Transportation costs	Low
	Nearshore	Control	Moderate	Costs with wages	Medium
				Relocation costs	Medium
		Quality of service	Moderate	Transportation costs	Medium
	Offshore	Control	Decreased	Costs with wages	Medium
				Relocation costs	Increased
		Quality of service	Moderate	Transportation costs	Increased
Third-party provider	*Onsite*	Control	Increased	Costs with wages	Medium
		Quality of service	Moderate	Transportation costs	Replaced by facility costs
	Offsite	Control	Moderate	Costs with wages	Medium
		Quality of service	Moderate	Transportation costs	Low
	Nearshore	Control	Moderate	Costs with wages	Medium
		Quality of service	Decreased	Transportation costs	Medium
	Offshore	Control	Decreased	Costs with wages	Low
		Quality of service	Decreased	Transportation costs	Increased

3 Specific approaches related to risk assessment in the context of ensuring sustainable performance

3.1 Approaches related to risk assessment in specialized literature

Risk assessment has an important role in defining business objectives and strategies. Organizations have to identify, evaluate and handle the top impacting risks in order to ensure sustainable performance and increase profitability, quality assurance and clients' satisfaction. The current economic and political climate has involved changes with impact on all business process; as a consequence, organizations have to find new methods of adapting to the new challenges in order to achieve business objectives. The uncertainties related to the changes in the business environment invo ve new risks that have to be proactively assessed in order to prevent the materialization of threats and to tackle new business opportunities. In a study performed in 2010, Pfohl et al. mentions that "there has been fundamental consensus emerging that systematic risk management is required to deal with these challenges". According to the research results achieved by the author during the doctoral period, risk assessment can be considered a risk administration tool and an important process within the organization's internal control system.

The Economist Intelligence Unit (EIU) has performed a global survey in 2013 on behalf of KPMG International in order to determine the role of risk assessment and the most important threats for organizations. Feedback to the online questionnaire was gathered from 1092 respondents from 21 industries located world-wide. The results of the research show that 47% of the respondents agree that risk assessment is essential when aiming for sustainable value-adding business performance.

The global economic crisis and geopolitical instability were the greatest threats posed by risk scenarios according to almost 70% of the respondents (Figure 3.1). More than half of the respondents are worried that new risks can cause loss of major customers and 43% consider supply chain and labor disruptions important threats for business sustainability.

R. M. Bejinariu, *Sustainable Business Performance and Risk Management*,
Sustainable Management, Wertschöpfung und Effizienz,
https://doi.org/10.1007/978-3-658-29389-5_3

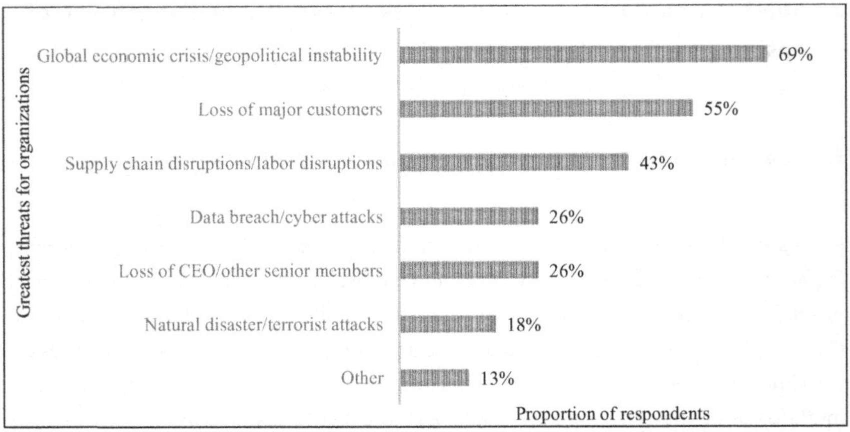

Figure 3.1: Risk scenarios that pose the greatest threats for organizations, developed by the author based on a research performed by EIU on behalf of KPMG International, 2013. Expectations of Risk assessment Outpacing Capabilities – It's Time For Action, KPMG International Cooperative, https://www.kpmg.com/LB/en/IssuesAndInsights/ArticlesPublications/Documents/expectations-risk-management-survey.pdf, accessed 08.10.2015.

High risks with a low probability of occurrence are the most common new risks that can lead to global supply chain disruptions, loss of market segments, unsatisfying results of outsourced or offshored business processes and even insolvency or bankruptcy.

Many academicians and experts agree that although many operational risk assessment tools are available, "these tools and methods have not been synthesized into a compre-hensive management system" (Kumar et al., 2013). Organizations use "firefighting me-thods" as reactive interventions to risks that have already materialized into negative events; these methods are extremely inefficient and involve important disadvantages related to costs, manpower and time.

Risk assessment has to be performed proactively as a set of coordinated activities that have the common goal of monitoring, controlling and managing risks in order to achieve business objectives and ensure sustainable performance.

3.1.1 Defining elements regarding risks in connection with sustainable performance in organizations

Risks are the measurable effects of uncertainty upon achieving business objectives. Risks are part of every process or activity, so that every day people and organizations are exposed to risks of different degrees (Damodaran, 2007). Given the ubiquity of risks related every business process it is surprising that there is very little consensus when it comes to defining risks. According to Miller (1992), "the strategic management field lacks a generally accepted definition of risk".

One of the first writings about risks date from the 1920s when Knight Frank described the difference between risk and uncertainty stating that "uncertainty must be taken in a sense radically distinct from the familiar notion of risk, from which it has never been properly separated". Knight Frank considers that risk is considered a "measurable uncertainty" and the essential fact about risk is that it means in some cases "a quantity susceptible of measurement, while at other times it is something distinctly not of this character; and there are far-reaching and crucial differences in the bearing of the phenomena depending on which of the two is really present and operating".

The effects of a risk can be a positive or negative deviation from what it is expected. Risks are characterized by referring to potential events that involve the appearance or modification of one set of the circumstances and consequences as the effect of these events. Risks are usually defined as a combination between the consequences of an event and the associated probability of appearance. Organizations have to avoid identifying risks related to events that cannot occur (fictional risks) or that will most certainly happen (certainties).

Risk profile was defined by the International Organization for Standardization in 2009 and includes the following elements:

- Risk source (usually represented by the process);
- Event generated by the source;
- Cause for the event (potential causes that did not produce, but might produce effects);
- Effect of the event;
- Impact of the effect (the negative or positive consequence of the event upon the objective);
- Probability of appearance of the event.

An example of risk profile analysis is presented in Table 3.1.

Table 3.1: Example of risk profile analysis, developed by the author based on the research conducted during the doctoral period

Risk profile analysis		Example of situation	
		Travelling by train	Market share
Risk profile elements	**Objective**	Signing a contract for 10000 EUR	Increase market share by 20%
	Source	The railway infrastructure	Internal and external markets
	Cause	Lack of resources for maintenance	Lack of market analysis based on relevant information
	Event	Interruption of power supply due to snowstorm	Appearance of unknown competitors
	Result	Loss of connection to the station X	Decreased turnover because of the two new competitors
	Risk	Delayed train	Loss of market share

When considering the impact on business objectives, the different types of organizational risks are usually split in 2 categories: financial and performance-related risks. Figure 3.2 presents operational and process-interactions risks as the main performance-related risks. Risks that occur at the interactions between business processes are operational risks between processes within the organization or between the organization and the exterior business environment.

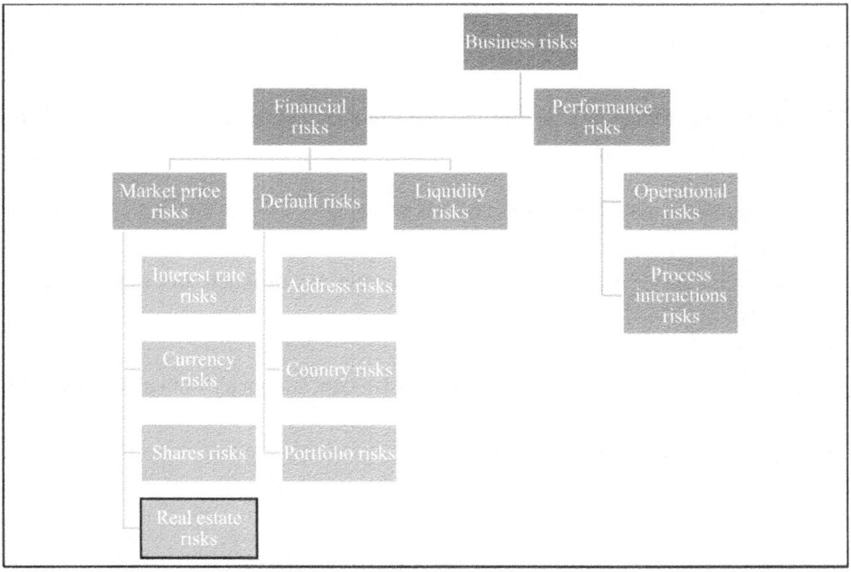

Figure 3.2 Classification of business risks, developed by the author based on Wolke T., Risk Management, De Gruyter, Oldenburg, 2017, ISBN 978-3-11-044052-2, pp.7.

According to the specific characteristics of each business risk such as source and risk level, different types of risks can be determined (Table 3.2).

Table 3.2: Types of risks depending on specific characteristics, developed by the author based on the research conducted during the doctoral period

No. crt.	Type of risk	Risk definition
1.	Inherent risk	The specific risk related to achieving objectives.
2.	Residual risk	The risk that remains after application of internal control mechanisms, such as risk handling.
3.	Secondary risk	The risk resulted after handling the inherent risk.
4.	Tolerable risk	The risk that can be tolerated by the organization.
5.	Unacceptable risk	The risk that has to be handled by the organization.
6.	Maximum risk	The risk resulted by the highest consequence and probability.
7.	Consolidated risk	The risk arising from various sources (processes).
8.	Cumulative risk	The risk whose level increases by transfer from one process to another.
9.	Individual risk	The risk identified punctually.
10.	Risks with positive or negative effects	The risk that may lead to increased or decreased process, project and product performance.
11.	Risks with major impact	Risks with very high consequences and low probability.

Sustainability is complex and multi-faceted, covering a broad spectrum of topics from habitat conservation, to energy consumption, to stakeholder satisfaction and financial results (Sebhatu, 2008). According to Schaltegger and Wagner (2006), sustainable performance can be defined as "the performance of an organization in all dimensions and for all drivers of corporate sustainability". Sustainable performance reflects corporate conformance, compliance, certifying and reporting according to predefined standards in relation to stakeholders' expectations (Epstein, 2008).

Pressure related to operating sustainably is increasing for organizations that have to consider risks related to the 3 dimensions of sustainability: social, environmental and economic (Bocken, Rana and Short, 2014). Sustainable performance can only be ensured if risks are controlled by the organizations and important threats are prevented. On the other hand, risks can also lead to positive outcomes and can be harnessed as valuable business opportunities that bring an important contribution to ensuring sustainable performance in organizations.

According to a briefing by Case (2012) for PricewaterhouseCooper, sustainability issues lead to a series of threats that affect the organization especially regarding the highly competitive business environment, scarcity of resources and regulatory changes (Figure 3.3). When it comes to business opportunities, the most important ones relate to operational efficiency, risk assessment and increasing the organizations' performance indicators. Therefore, by performing a thorough risk assessment related to organizational business processes and setting up mechanisms that control the identified risks, organizations can ensure sustainable performance.

Sustinability issues	•Economic risks (fiscal crisis, asset price collapse, energy price volatility, etc.); •Geopolitical risks (regulatory failures, political instability, geopolitical conflicts, etc.); •Environmental risks (climate change, pollution, flooding, etc.).
Threats for organizations	•Increased competition (raw materials scarcity, increased energy costs); •Increased regulation; •Reputational costs; •Penalties, fines and increased taxes; •Loss of license to operate.
Opportunities for organizations	•Improved operational efficiency; •Improved risk assessment; •Increased market share; •Increased revenue and profit; •Increased and sustained shareholder value; •Employee attraction and retention.

Figure 3.3: Threats and opportunities caused by sustainability issues, developed by the author based on Case, P., 2012. Managing Sustainability risks and opportunities in the financial services sector. Brie-fing for PricewaterhouseCooper, pp. 12, https://www.pwc.com/jg/en/publications/ ned-sustainability-presentation-may-2012.pdf, accessed 13.01.2018.

When determining whether business performance is sustainable or not, many performance indicators and sustainability evaluation methods have been discussed in the specialized literature usually referring to financial outcomes, employee satisfaction and customer satisfaction (Kantabutra, 2006).

Following, business performance is directly linked to process performance determined by operations and interactions across the organization (employees) with impact on the quality of products and services (customer satisfaction) and business results (financial outcomes). One of the most important management tool impacting sustainable performance is risk assessment related to organizational business processes; controlling risks within the organization can ensure the competitive advantage by offering a security net for organizations struggling with the high requirements of the business environment.

3.1.2 The importance of the organizational context in risk assessment related to organizational business processes

Analyzing the organizational context is one of the conditions for performing a correct risk assessment. When determining scope, risk criteria and the organizational context, involving stakeholders and taking their perspectives into account is very important. The interrelation between risk assessment and the organizational context determines the success of the process implementation and integration in the organization, as well as the sustainable performance of the process. According to a study performed by Paraxion Research Group in 2010, establishing the organizational context is defining "the external and internal parameters that organizations must consider when they manage risk".

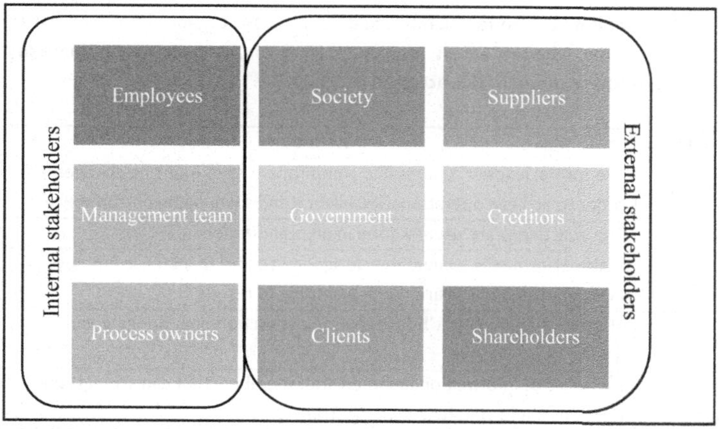

Figure 3.4 – External and internal stakeholders, developed by the author based on the research conducted during the doctoral period.

Research during the doctoral thesis has concluded that the organizational context can be described by stakeholders (Figure 3.4) and other factors with impact on business objectives, strategies and the organization's capability to achieve its targets, while

internal factors are usually related to the organization's vision, mission, strategies and culture.
The organizational context has also been defined by Kitson et al. in 1998 as "the sum of the forces at work that give the physical environment a certain character or feeling". Establishing the context means to determine internal and external factors that have to be considered by the organization when assessing risks (Pojasek, 2013).
On the other hand, risk assessment influences the organizational context and risks related to the employees' resistance to change is the main challenge encountered by managers leading to important unforeseen costs. According to a recent study developed by Maier in 2017, risk assessment is a very important process that has to be taken into account during the "development and operationalization of a model of innovation management system as part of an integrated quality-environment-safety integrated system".

Internal and external factors that define the organizational context are described below:

a) Internal factors

Table 3.3: Internal factors that determine the organizational context, developed by the author based on National Collaborating Centre for Methods and Tools, 2014. Organizational context for evidence-based practices: The Alberta Context Tool (ACT). Hamilton, ON: McMaster University, http://www.ncc mt.ca/resources/search/216, accessed 02.03.2017.

No. crt.	**Internal factor**	**Description**
1.	Leadership	The formal leaders' actions and commitment to influencing changes in order to achieve operational excellence and sustainable performance
2.	Culture	The way things are usually done in an organization
3.	Evaluation	Staff performance evaluations designed in order to increase employees' performance and reward them according to results
4.	Social capital	The active connections between employees: bonding, bridging and linking
5.	Informal interactions	Exchange of information between staff members that can strengthen relations and promote knowledge transfer
6.	Formal interactions	Exchange of information between employees through scheduled activities that promote knowledge transfer
7.	Structural and electronic resources	Structural and electronic elements that are used in order to access the organization's knowledge pool
8.	Organization slack (staff, space, time)	Organizational resources that facilitate adaptation to internal or external pressures

Table 3.3 presents the list of internal factors according to the Alberta Context Tool described as "the most compressive list of internal factors" (Estabrooks, 2009) and developed by the National Collaborating Centre for Methods and Tools in 2014 with the purpose of assessing and monitoring the organizational context.

b) External factors

The external factors are determined using the STEEP analysis (Figure 3.5) which is an extended variant of the PEST analysis for the organization's exterior environment.

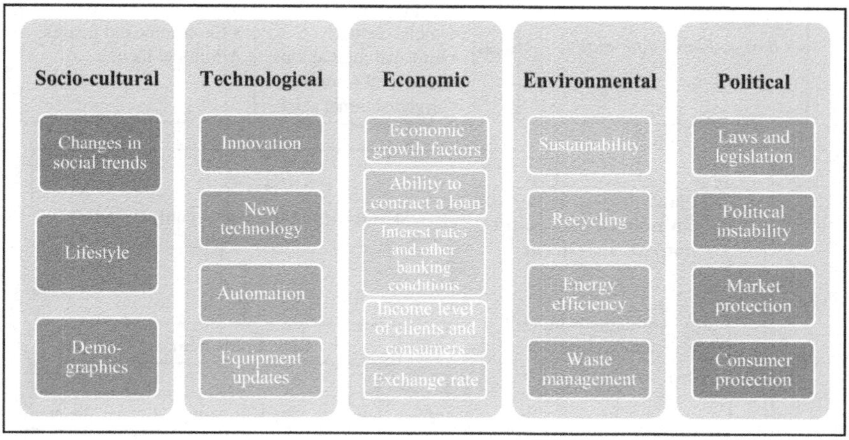

Figure 3.5: External factors that define the organizational context, developed by the author based on Szigeti, H., Messaadia, M., Majumdar, A. and Eynard, B., 2011. STEEP analysis as a tool for building technology roadmaps, Conference: eChallenges e-2011, At Florence, Italy, pp. 3, https://www.researchgate.net/publication/301295850_STEEP_analysis_as_a_tool_for_building_technology_roadmaps, accessed 08.03.2017.

According to Szigeti et al. (2011), the STEEP analysis can be defined as an "audit of an organization's environmental influences with the purpose of using this information to guide strategic decision-making"; these factors are split in 5 categories: socio-cultural, technological, economic, environmental and political factors.

3.1.3 Premises for risk assessment integration in organizations

Risk assessment has a key role in any decision-making process by detecting uncertainties and their nature related to not accomplishing something, enhancing opportunities, achieving or exceeding business targets and performance and to determine which actions have to be taken in order to handle them. In order to prepare the implementation of the process, a context analysis has to be performed and all process steps have to be planned.

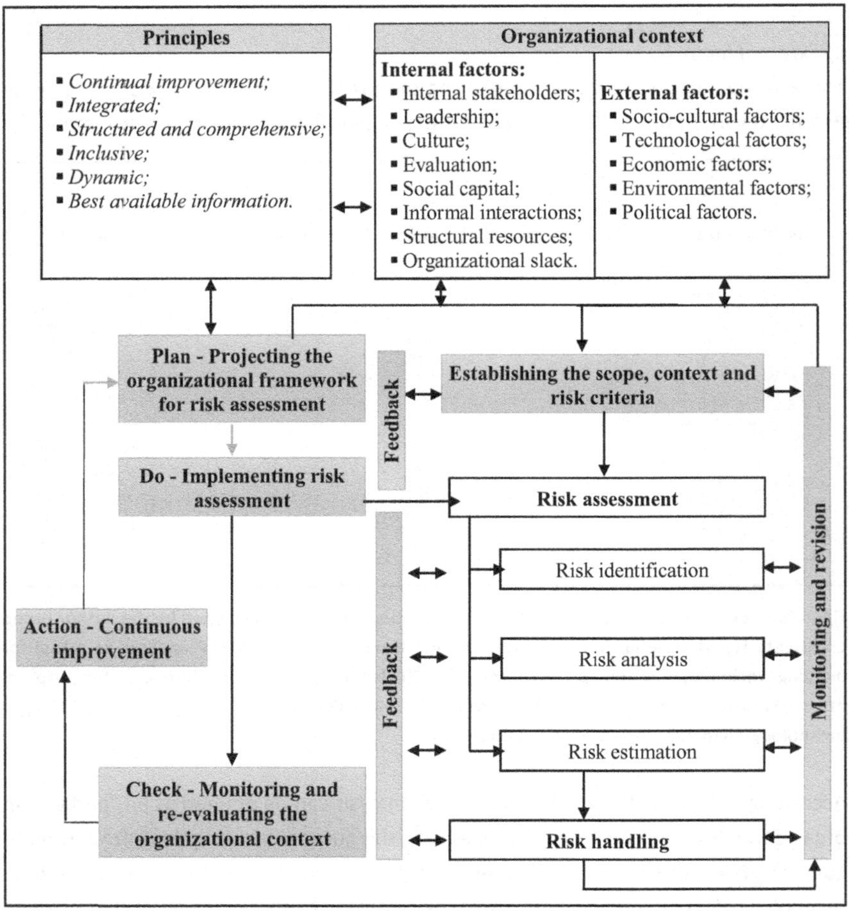

Figure 3.6: Risk assessment integration in organizations, developed by the author based on The International Organization for Standardization, ISO31000:2018, https://www.iso.org/obp/ui/#iso:std:iso:31000:ed-2:v1:en, accessed May 2018.

Figure 3.6 shows that preparing for the risk assessment process involves determining if strategic objectives, principles and organizational context were considered when planning the process and conducting a context analysis.

Risk assessment is a process that depends on interactions with all business processes and helps organizations to prioritize and to make reasoned choices by analyzing alternative directions of action. The process requires a well-structured, systematic and accurate approach that brings an important contribution to ensuring sustainable performance by achieving reliable, consistent and comparable results.

Leadership through objectives, participative management, team work and staff involvement in achieving business objectives, as well as transparency and a good communication are the critical factors that ensure the success of risk assessment.

Standardized risk assessment guidelines have been described in the specialized literature, as well as by many organizations in order to emphasize the importance of creating and protecting value within the organization, as well as committing to achieving risk assessment-related business objectives. The latest considerations concerning risk assessment relate to principles, framework and processes:

a) Principles

In order to create and conserve value, organizations have to consider the mission statement, business vision and the organizational context. Principles related to risk assessment are related to continuously improving the process, integrating it in the management system, structuring and developing it in a comprehensive way, including all aspects related to impacting and impacted factors inside and outside the organization, designing it in order to be adaptable to changes (dynamic) based on the best available information;

b) Process

According to a study performed by Verbano and Venturini in 2013, risk assessment involves identification of risks, risk evaluation and risk analysis that determine the probability and the expected magnitude associated with the occurrence of the negative effect. The results of the process are used in order to identify the most appropriate actions to reduce risks and handle unacceptable risks;

c) Framework

The framework of the process considers the defined principles and the organizational context and is structured using Deming's PDCA management method (1986), as follows:

1. Planning (P) – Designing and preparing the framework for implementing risk assessment considering both organizational principles related to risk assessment and all factors that define the organizational context;
2. Do (D) – Risk assessment implementation including risk identification, risk analysis and risk estimation that continuously send and receive feedback to the management team that committed to achieving value-adding results for the organization;
3. Check (C) – Monitoring and re-evaluating the organizational context;
4. Action (A) – Improving the process by taking corrective actions for any deviation from the expected results.

3.1.4 Risk assessment related to organizational business processes

Risk assessment is a set of coordinated activities that aim to identify, evaluate and analyze risks within an organization. These activities develop risk understanding by offering information related to risk profile including risk cause and impact on the main performance indicators. Risk assessment helps managers make reasoned choices and developing valuable business strategies. Therefore, risk assessment contributes to the achievement of business objectives and to improving long-term business performance in organizations.

The process requires a systematic and structured approach in order to achieve consistent, comparable and reliable results that are sustainable over time. Each of the steps of the risk assessment process involves the participation of individuals responsible for standardizing and ensuring process efficiency by evaluating results and developing standards, guidelines and procedures.

Business management does not involve only handling the consequences of failing to achieve objectives, but also determining the cause for the negative effects of risk materialization; this can be performed reactively by considering passed risks that have already produced effects. In order to prevent risk materialization, the management team has to have a proactive approach and evaluate potential risks.

Before taking the decision of implementing risk assessment, resources have to be allocated for risk identification, analysis and estimation. Processes related to risk assessment are presented as follows:

a) Risk identification

Identifying risks has the objective of highlighting all possible risks including risks with high or low probability of occurrence and different consequences on business results. In order to identify risks, the most important methods are brainstorming, interviews with impacting or impacted parties, "cause-effect" analysis (Ishikawa diagram or "fishbone chart"), SWOT analysis (strengths, weaknesses, opportunities and threats) and the FMEA method used mainly for technical and medical risks. Risk identification also involves determining risk profile and including risks in a risk registry adapted to the organization's needs and requirements.

b) Risk analysis

The risks analysis involves a preliminary analysis, followed by a quantitative and qualitative analysis.

The preliminary analysis is optional and has the goal of eliminating low risks for which an extensive qualitative and quantitative analysis is not necessary. The preliminary analysis considers the consequences of the risks (positive or negative) and the probability of occurrence for these risks.

Consequences are the effects of an event caused by specific sources. The planned results (objectives) and, depending on the nature of the risk, the consequences regarding objectives (outcomes) can be positive or negative. Consequences can be expressed in terms of financial results, quality, budget and costs, effort (productivity) and time (for example a delayed achievement or project).

Probability of occurrence is estimated and is a qualitative measure used to describe the organization's perspective related to the probability that a risk materializes and produces effects.

Following 4 types of risks are determined:

- *Risks with low consequences and low probability of occurrence* are risks that are removed from the analysis. This category of risks is monitored for possible changes;

- *Risks with high consequences and low probability of occurrence* have to be reviewed using historical records in order to determine if the probability was estimated correctly. These risks are monitored in order to minimize consequences;

- *Risks with low consequences and high probability of occurrence* are risks that are not important if analyzed individually, but that associated with other risks from this category can lead to high consequences with positive or negative impact on the organizational performance. For these risks a "contingency plan " has to be created in order to ensure business continuity if the organization is strongly affected by a negative event;

- *Risks with a high consequences and high probability* have a great potential of materializing. These risks are thoroughly analyzed and handled by the risk handling plan. For these risks priorities related to risk handling are established according to the estimated risk.

Figure 3.7 shows the next step of the preliminary analysis that involves risks from the risk registry being introduced in a risk diagram after establishing whether probability of occurrence and consequence are low or high for each of the risks.

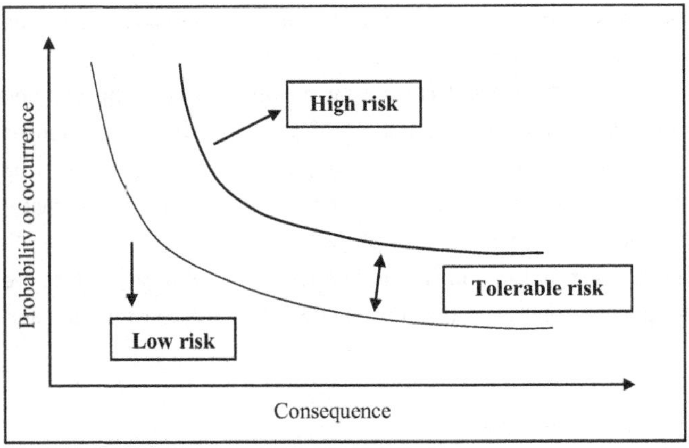

Figure 3.7: Graphic representation of the risk diagram, developed by the author based on the research conducted during the doctoral period.

The quantitative and qualitative analysis aims to provide input for risk assessment and decision-making related to risk strategies. Risk estimation includes extending the risk analysis by considering the risk criteria established after evaluating the context. One of the most common analysis methods is the risk matrix developed by NASA (Figure 3.8).

Very high	5	PROBABILITY OF OCCURENCE	5	10	15	20	25
High	4		4	8	12	16	20
Moderate (medium)	3		3	6	9	12	15
Low	2		2	4	6	8	10
Very low	1		1	2	3	4	5
			CONSEQUENCE				
		0	1	2	3	4	5
			Very low	Acceptable	Tolerable	Unacceptable	Maximum

Figure 3.8: Risk assessment using probability of occurrence and consequence as attributes, developed by the author based on Moses, K. and Malone, R., 2018. Development of Risk Assessment Matrix for NASA Engineering and Safety Center, pp. 20, https://ntrs.nasa.gov/archive/nasa/casi.ntrs.nasa.gov/ 20050123548.pdf, accessed 10.05.2018.

Table 3.4: Risk levels, risk types and risk handling actions determined using probability of occurrence and consequence as risk assessment attributes, Source: developed by the author based on Moses, K. and Malone, R., 2018. Development of Risk Assessment Matrix for NASA Engineering and Safety Center, pp. 20, https://ntrs.nasa.gov/archive/nasa/casi.ntrs.nasa.gov/ 20050123548.pdf, accessed 10.05.2018.

Tolerance intervals for risk levels	Risk type	Color coding	Risk handling actions
1	Very low risk		No action
2 – 9	Acceptable risk		Can be usually influenced indirectly through actions that are taken for tolerable or unacceptable risks
10 – 12	Tolerable risk		If it can't the influenced, control mechanisms are being established
13 – 20	Unacceptable risk		
20 – 25	Very high risk		The activity or the process has to be stopped and the risk level has to be brought to an acceptable level

Risk levels are evaluated by considering the likelihood, the impact or consequence of risk materialization and the frequency and exposure to risk. Risk levels are the mathematical product between each of the values from 1 to 5 assigned for consequence and probability of occurrence. Table 3.4 indicates the proposed color coding and risk handling actions according to risk level and risk type.

3.2 Considerations related to risk assessment in the context of ensuring sustainable performance

Risk assessment has a key role in achieving business objectives and should be considered during all decision-making business processes. While risk assessment and risk handling are essential for the organization's sustainable performance, organizations have to innovate and permanently update the process in order to adapt to the uncertainties and changes from the business environment. In order to prevent the negative effects of risk materialization, in the past years experts have researched new methods of lowering risk handling costs and improving the accuracy and efficiency of the process.

Using the FMEA method when calculating risk levels leads to important advantages related to controlling risks and significantly reducing costs with risk handling. This is very important for ensuring sustainable business performance, because resources are not wasted on managing risks for which materialization conditions may never occur and can be used in order to achieve value-adding results for the organization.

Another progress related to risk assessment is considering opportunities that can result from risk handling. An uncertain situation may lead to both negative and positive events, therefore assessing risks while aiming for new business opportunities creates additional value for the organization and in some cases, it can be "the rescue boat" that managers need when struggling with the new overwhelming challenges in the business climate.

The current specialized studies have limitations - the FMEA method is used in engineering and medicine mostly and a risk assessment approach based on opportunities is not used as a standard in organizations, so that many opportunities arise related to innovation in the risk assessment domain.

3.2.1 Methods used in the risk assessment process in relation with ensuring sustainable performance in organizations

Risk analysis can be either quantitative or qualitative or a combination of both. While qualitative risk evaluation methods use the know-how and judgement of experts in order to evaluate risk types, "quantitative tools are based on probabilistic and statistical models that calculate risk over time" (Dinmohammadi, et al, 2016).

Quantitative methods are more robust and reliable using indexed data that is not always accessible, so that most of organizations rely on subjective data in order to assess risks, so that results are determined based on qualitative data with no regard to risk materialization conditions.

One of the methods that takes risk materialization conditions into account is Failure Mode Effect Analysis (FMEA) developed by the United States Department of Defense in 1949. The method involves calculating the risk of failure that is the mathematical product of severity (consequence), occurrence (probability of occurrence) and detection (probability of detection) as an additional new attribute (Figure 3.9).

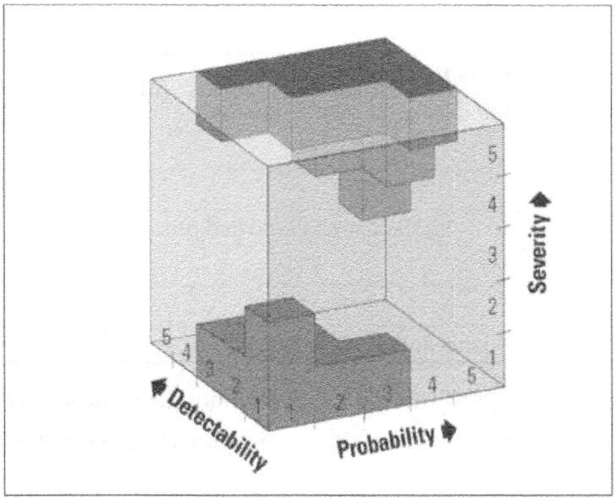

Figure 3.9: Tri-dimensional risk assessment model with high-risk zone in red and low-risk zone in blue, developed by the author based on Youssef, N. F. and Hyman W. A., 2010. Risk Analysis: Beyond Probability and Severity, Medical Device and Diagnostic Industry, http://www.mddi online.com/article/risk-analysis-beyond-probability-and-severity, accessed 10.12.2016.

Schneider (2012) defines the FMEA method as a reliability analysis by considering historical data related to failures and focusing on issues that have already occurred. The FMEA method is traditionally used in the medical and engineering industries and is "one of the first systematic techniques for failure analysis" (ArunKumar and Dillibabu, 2016). The method is also used in system reliability studies and involves identifying failure modes including causes and effects by reviewing as many assemblies, components and subsystems as possible. Considering errors, negative events and effects from the past can lead to identifying past risks that have materialized.

Preventing the negative effects of risk materialization can be managed by determining the conditions that led to the materialization of past risks; these conditions can also be indicated based on experts' judgement and experience with risk assessment. Risk materialization affects business performance indicators, so that organizations can establish the conditions that signal an important deviation from the values that are expected (Figure 3.10). Therefore, by monitoring the values of these indicators, risks can be controlled and an important part of the risks do not have to be included in the risk handling plan.

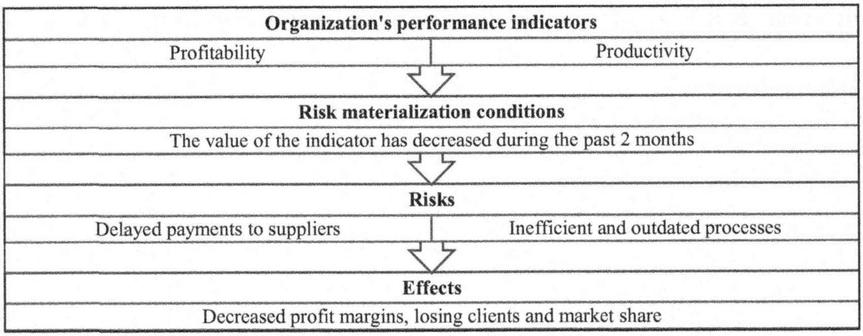

Figure 3.10: Example of the risk materialization conditions related to performance indicators that can be monitored in order to control risks and risk materialization effects, developed by the author based on the research conducted during the doctoral period.

Introducing detection as a third attribute during the risk assessment process means that risk materialization conditions are monitored, and risk handling actions are taken only if these predefined conditions are met.

Detection is used in risk assessment after performing the standard risk assessment using 2 attributes (probability of occurrence and consequence) in order to determine Risk Level 1. The next step is to determine the tolerance intervals of the risk levels for each risk type.

If considering risk values and the tolerance intervals proposed by Northey and Kinney for NASA (2014), the following limits are determined for Risk Level 1: 1, 9, 12, 20 and 25. When applying detection, a new risk level or Risk Level 2 is determined as the mathematical product between each of the values from 1 to 5 assigned for detection and Risk Level 1 (Figure 3.11).

When considering the negative effects of risk materialization, a probability of detection with the maximum value of 125 represents a low probability of detecting risk materialization conditions with a strong negative impact on performance indicators. A very high probability of detection is determined by low values and means that risk materialization conditions can be easily detected, so that risks can be controlled without involving important resources; for high values of detection it is preferable to include risks in the risks handling plan.

Very high risk	25	RISK LEVEL 1	25	50	75	100	125
Unacceptable risk	20		20	40	60	80	100
Tolerable risk	12		12	24	36	48	60
Acceptable risk	9		9	18	18	36	45
Very low risk	1		1	2	3	4	5
		0	PROBABILITY OF DETECTION				
			1	2	3	4	5
			Very high	High	Moderate (medium)	Low	Very low

Figure 3.11 – Representation of risk assessment using 3 attributes, developed by the author based on Moses K., Malone R., Development of Risk Assessment Matrix for NASA Engineering and Safety Center, pp. 20, 2018, https://ntrs.nasa.gov/archive/nasa/casi.ntrs.nasa.gov/20050123548.pdf, accessed 18.04.2018.

Table 3.5 indicates the proposed color coding and risk intervals for Risk Level 1 and Risk Level 2 for each of the risk types.

Table 3.5: Proposed risk levels and risk types using 2 and 3 attributes during risk assessment, developed by the author based on the research conducted during the doctoral period

Tolerance intervals for Risk Level 1	Tolerance intervals for Risk Level 2	Risk types
1	1	Very low risk
2 – 9	2 – 30	Acceptable risk
10 – 12	31 – 60	Tolerable risk
13 – 20	61 – 100	Unacceptable risk
21 – 25	101 – 125	Very high risk

Similar to the color coding used by the NASA developers, the proposed colors for the risk assessment scorecard are used depending on the possible impact on the organization: red for very important threats and green is assigned to very low or acceptable risks.

3.2.2 New perspectives related to ensuring sustainable business performance by harnessing risks as opportunities for organizations

In a recent study, Grigore and Drăgan (2015) consider that "in an innovation-oriented or knowledge-based economy, the function of opportunity recognition and taking the risk of realizing it becomes more prominent". In the same year Baranoff, Brockett and Kahane state that "while we typically associate "risk" with unpleasant or negative events, in reality some risky situations can result in positive outcomes". Formally and intuitively risk involves both positive and negative consequences and the number of possible outcomes is uncertain.

Sustainable business performance cannot be ensured if business risks are not controlled and risk assessment results are not used - by harnessing risks as business opportunities, the risk assessment process becomes more efficient and creates value for the organization with a strong positive impact on sustainability and business performance. Risk-taking depends on the organization's attitude when confronted with risky situations, interest in assessing and harnessing risks and risk tolerance that varies mainly by organization size.

According to Gollier, Hammitt and Treich (2013), "the economic theory of decision making under risk has seen remarkable advances over the past 50 years". The risk assessment process offers managers support when taking strategic decisions using the best available information. Organizations have to choose between a defensive risk strategy that is focused on avoiding or mitigating risks and an offensive strategy that involves taking risks while aiming for new business opportunities.

Innovating and improving risk assessment and using the process results in order to tackle new opportunities generated by risk materialization are essential for ensuring sustainable performance. Organizations also have the option of allocating resources in order to force risk materialization if the identified risks are analyzed and new business opportunities can be achieved. This method can improve risk assessment results and can transforms the process in an even more important management tool.

Risk assessment models have been described by many experts, but the method remains the same: after selecting risk criteria and identifying risks, risk analysis and evaluation determine the risk profile. In order to identify new business opportunities, the risk profile has to include both negative and positive possible effects of risk materialization. The risk handling plan includes unacceptable or very high risks that threaten the organization, but these risks can also lead to opportunities, so that they can also be considered attractive for business development.

The role of risk assessment can be understood by determining the impact on the business performance indicators in order to evaluate the effect of taking risks and using an offensive risk assessment strategy. Controlling the balance between a defensive and offensive risk strategy is essential for the stability of the organization.

Risk assessment models have not been standardized. It is easy to recommend an approach based on risks and risk assessment to an organization, but "it is very hard to indicate a good practice" according to French, Morton and Renn (2013). The most recent value map model was developed by Bugalla, Kallman and Narvaez in 2015 (Figure 3.12) that have started from the idea that "risk has an upside and a downside" and "in order to create value organizations have to take on risky projects".

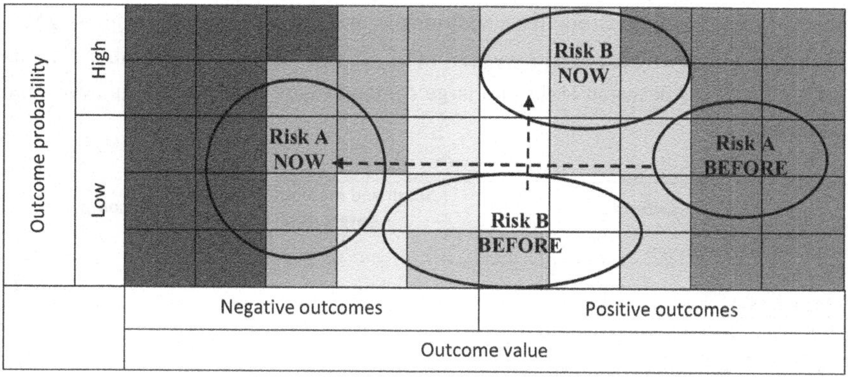

Figure 3.12: Risk value map based on negative and positive outcomes of risk materialization, developed by the author based on Bugalla, J., Kallman, J. and Narvaez, K., 2015. When you come to a fork in the road, take it. The Journal of Enterprise Risk Management, vol. 1, issue 1, pp. 51-54.

Despite of the uncertainties from the business environment more often organizations have started launching risky projects in order to add value to their business. This model differs from the traditional risk scorecard by including both negative and positive outcomes and identifying the range of outcome values as ellipses so that, according to the developers, "the wider (on the x axis) the ellipse, the greater the range of outcome values, the taller (on the y axis) the ellipse, the greater the uncertainty of the outcome".

Early studies related to the organizations' self-protection developed by Ehrlich and Becker (1972) define it as "the reduction of the probability of loss". Self-protection is meant to protect the organizations' assets and legacy and relates to the defensive strategies as risk mitigation tools. On the other hand, the current economic environment comes with a new set of requirements and challenges that affect the organizations' decisions when developing strategies. Offensive risk strategies can involve ignoring risks and "gambling" or increasing the probability of risk materialization in order to tackle new business opportunities. Given the intense competition and the uncertainties in the business climate, ensuring sustainable performance can only be achieved by correlating defensive strategies with offensive ones.

Given the fact that risk appetite and risk tolerance are highly dependent on organization size, when considering an approach based on risk, the differences between small and medium-sized enterprises (SMEs) and large companies have been determined in the specialized literature. More than 95% of the enterprises world-wide are SMEs according to a research performed in 2011 by international coalition of accountants Edinburgh Group (EG); additionally, SMEs account for approximately 52% of private sector employment (Ayyagari et al., 2011). Figure 3.13 indicates that the main differences between SMEs and large companies are number of employees and turnover.

<table>
<tr><th>Criteria</th><th>Small and medium-sized enterprises</th><th>Large companies</th></tr>
<tr><td>Number of employees</td><td rowspan="5">↓</td><td rowspan="5">↑</td></tr>
<tr><td>Turnover</td></tr>
<tr><td>Resources</td></tr>
<tr><td>Number of departments</td></tr>
<tr><td>Geographical spread</td></tr>
<tr><td>Flexibility/adaptation to change</td><td rowspan="2">↑</td><td rowspan="2">↓</td></tr>
<tr><td>Sensitivity to climate change</td></tr>
</table>

Figure 3.13: Main differences between SMEs and large companies, developed by the author based on the research conducted during the doctoral period.

Risk assessment in SMEs is required in order to "protect innovative projects, which are fundamental to gain competitive advantage and succeed in the market but involve risky decisions and activities" (Vargas-Hernández, 2011). While allocating financial resources for innovation can be easier for large companies, SMEs can struggle with budgeting new ideas. However, SMEs rely on flexibility as an advantage when developing risk strategies. As a consequence, sustainable business performance can be achieved in a different way by SMEs compared to large companies and this is mainly caused by the organization's risk appetite, tolerance and adaptability to changes related to the dynamics in the business environment, organizational resources, control mechanisms and level of risk assessment integration in the organization (Figure 3.14).

<table>
<tr><th>Criteria</th><th>Small and medium-sized enterprises</th><th>Large companies</th></tr>
<tr><td>Risk tolerance</td><td rowspan="3">↓</td><td rowspan="3">↑</td></tr>
<tr><td>Risk assessment integration in the organization</td></tr>
<tr><td>Risk assessment resources</td></tr>
<tr><td>Risk attitude</td><td rowspan="2">↑</td><td rowspan="2">↓</td></tr>
<tr><td>Risk appetite</td></tr>
</table>

Figure 3.14: Main differences between SMEs and large companies related to risk assessment, developed by the author based on the research conducted during the doctoral period.

In order to determine how SMEs and large companies take decisions when developing risk strategies, research during the doctoral period has led to developing a formula that determines which organizations use risk assessment in order to tackle opportunities and prevent threats and use these results when developing offensive and defensive strate-gies.

$$\mathbf{R_{sp} = \min (n_{OT} \cap m_{os})}$$

Risk assessment oriented on sustainable performance (%) = R_{sp} / x

Ideal state: $R_{sp} = n_{OT} = m_{os} = x$

where,

R_{sp} – no. of organizations that use risk assessment as a tool for sustainable performance;

n_{OT} – no. of organizations mapping risks as opportunities and threats;

m_{os} – no. of organizations with offensive and defensive risk strategies;

x – total no. of organizations.

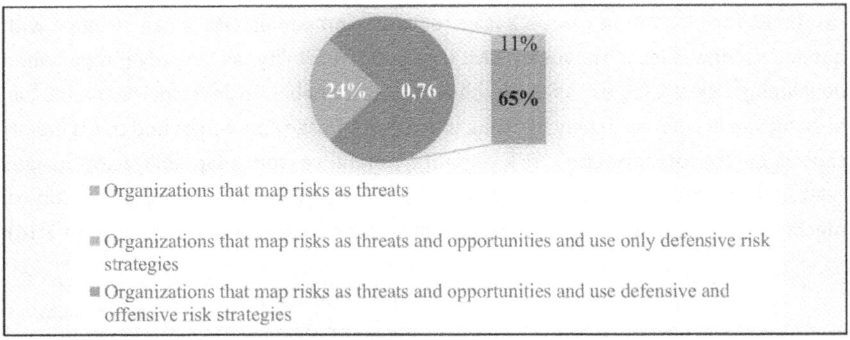

Figure 3.15: Risk assessment in SMEs, developed by the author based on the research conducted during the doctoral period.

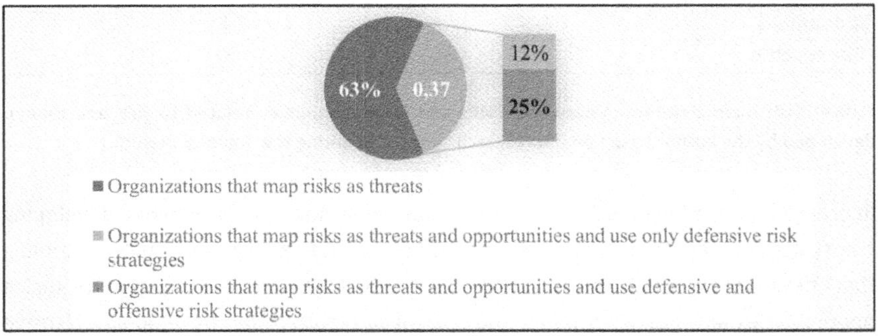

Figure 3.16: Risk assessment in large companies, developed by the author based on the research conducted during the doctoral period.

Risk assessment oriented on sustainable business performance involves mapping both positive and negative outcomes that can result from risk materialization and balancing between defensive and offensive risk strategies.

The ideal state is that organizations use the results of risk assessment in order to develop both types of strategies and to create value for the organization. The results of the doctoral studies conducted show that 76% of the SMEs and only 37% of the large companies consider both positive and negative outcomes of risk materialization and harness risks as business opportunities (Figures 3.15 and 3.16). When it comes to using risk assessment results, 65% of the SMEs and only a quarter of the large companies develop both defensive and offensive risk strategies based on the results of the process.

An approach based on taking strategic decisions considering both threats and opportunities involves using risk assessment results in an efficient way by focusing on making the most out of both positive and negative outcomes of risk materialization. Organizations like the majority of large companies that mainly develop defensive strategies in order to ensure self-protection will most likely lose many business opportunities; this can be caused by the fact that risks have a different stake or cost for large companies. When taking risks in order to achieve an opportunity and failing, organizations can destabilize, and the large companies' lack of flexibility can delay the return to the initial state so that important losses cannot be recovered.

4 Study concerning risk assessment related to organizational business processes

4.1 Study related to the risk assessment process in small and medium-sized enterprises compared to large companies

Decisions regarding risk taking have become of great strategical and tactical importance for entrepreneurs in order to ensure business survival and organization growth. When choosing between a defensive or offensive approach when facing risks, organizations have started allocating additional resources in order to predict both negative and positive outcomes that result from risk handling.

Operational performance and business finances rely on efficient and value-adding risk assessment, especially after the global economic crises. Changes in the business climate are considered "low probability, high impact changes" according to Asel, Posch and Speckbacher (2010); causes and effects of risk materialization are highly uncertain and threaten the organization's sustainable performance, so that managers are pressured to find new proactive solutions in order to predict and manage risks. Risk tolerance or risk-taking thresholds are constantly analyzed and results have always differed from one organization to another. Organization size is one of the factors that determine how risks are being perceived and handled.

The study shows the differences between the risk assessment process in small and medium-sized enterprises (SMEs) and large companies. Risk appetite and risk tolerance are relevant for determining the organization's attitude when confronted with risky situations and were analyzed in order to investigate the risk assessment process according to the size of the organization.

4.1.1 General context of the research

Many debates have been developed around the subject of risk assessment and its importance in the organizations' decision-making. Managers have started developing survival and expansion strategies only after performing a thorough risk assessment and minimizing risk exposure.

R. M. Bejinariu, *Sustainable Business Performance and Risk Management*,
Sustainable Management, Wertschöpfung und Effizienz,
https://doi.org/10.1007/978-3-658-29389-5_4

According to Weber et al. (2016), "enterprises have to react to the changing conditions simply in order to survive". The economic and political climate changes have forced organizations to redesign objectives, cut costs, find new solutions in order to preserve resources and assets, but also to reevaluate their attitude when facing risks. The new challenges have also come with a new set of risks that threaten the organizations' viability, so that managers were forced to recalibrate performance indicators and decision-making protocols.

Many organizations have passed different regimes and have always transformed in order to adapt. Democracy has quickly helped increasing the number of small and medium-sized enterprises by creating the legal framework needed for entrepreneurs in order to start developing business. Globalization has facilitated trade and commerce, so that new opportunities arrived for both small and medium-sized enterprises and large companies.

On the example of Romania, according to Văduva (2016), "the process of Europeanizing Romania is advanced" and has had positive and visible results such as the growth in GDP per capita, the presence of multinational corporations, significant progress in infrastructure, and the development of public administration. Despite progress and positive outcomes, bureaucracy, corruption and the constant changes in politics and the legal framework have always been challenges for the Romanian entrepreneurs. Additionally, the economic crises in 2008 has had a high impact on the Romanian economy, so that risk assessment has started being implemented in more and more organizations.

Both SMEs and large companies are facing the difficulties caused by the political and economic context, but the types of risks and risk levels to which organizations are exposed to are different; accordingly, the organizations' attitude in risky situations and risk thresholds should be analyzed separately in case of SMEs (for example family businesses) and large companies (for example multinational organizations). However, specialized literature agrees that SMEs "put little effort into the identification, assessment and monitoring of risks" (Brustbauer, 2014).

4.1.2 Objectives and research methodology

a) Research objectives

While risks have different effects on different organizations and choosing a defensive or offensive strategy when facing risks is highly dependent on risk tolerance, the research analyzes risk assessment separately by organization size.

Risks analysis and risk handling are performed differently by small and medium-sized enterprises compared to large companies, therefore in order to describe risk assessment in the 2 types of organizations, risk assessment integration and process execution are emphasized as results of the study.

The objectives of the research are to determine risk appetite and risk tolerance in organizations and to establish the extent in which risk assessment was integrated in the organizations. Given the important differences between SMEs and large companies related to organizational structure, resources for implementation and process execution, know-how, level of standardization and IT infrastructure, the study is performed separately depending on the organization size.

b) Research methodology

Interviews with 23 managers and specialists from different industries conducted in 2016, but also the review of specialized literature were sources for the study on the organizations' reactivity to risks and risk assessment integration.

The research focuses on qualitative information gathered from individuals with experience in 51 organizations from the following industries:

- Fast-moving commercial goods (FMCG): 8 large companies and 20 from SMEs;
- Constructions: 5 large companies and 11 from SMEs;
- Pharmaceutical and healthcare: 2 large companies and 5 from SMEs.

The interviews lasted up to one hour and included 2 parts: the first part consisted in a discussion related to risk appetite and risk tolerance for each of the researched organizations (Annex A) and the second part involves 8 questions on risk assessment integration (Annex B).

The gathered information was based on the managers' and specialists' professional experience related to assessing risks. In order to determine risk attitude, the interviewees have discussed the subjects of risk mapping and risk strategies for both types of organizations. For each question respondents have also discussed how risk assessment is handled in each of their organizations and have shared their perspective on how the process should be improved. The individuals have also discussed about how they view risk assessment integration in other peer organizations.

The last part of the research is the comparison between SMEs and large companies based on the analyzed results related to attitude when facing risks and risk assessment integration. The results of the questionnaire were analyzed as follows:

- If the answer for less than 25% of the organizations is "Yes" or "Partly" the level of integration is considered low;
- If the answer for 26% to 75% of the organizations is "Yes" or "Partly" the level of integration is considered medium;
- If the answer for more than 75% of the organizations is "Yes" or "Partly" the level of integration is considered high.

4.1.3 Research results concerning risk assessment in small and medium-sized enterprises

The first part of the survey refers to the organizations' attitude when facing risks and type of risk-related strategies (Figures 4.1 and 4.2).

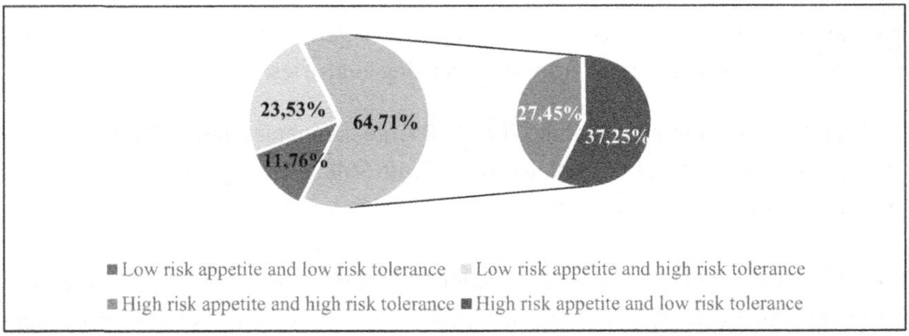

Figure 4.1: Risk appetite and tolerance in SMEs, developed by the author based on the research conducted during the doctoral period.

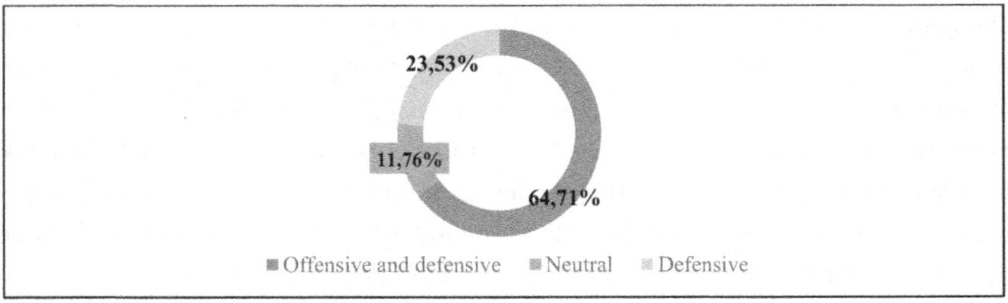

Figure 4.2: Risk attitude in SMEs developed by the author based on the research conducted during the doctoral period.

The Figures 3.1 and 3.2 show that almost 65% of the SMEs have high risk appetite and choose offensive and defensive strategies when confronted with risks.
The results of the study concerning the integration of risks assessment in SMEs show that more than half of the organizations have not implemented the risk assessment process (Figure 4.3).

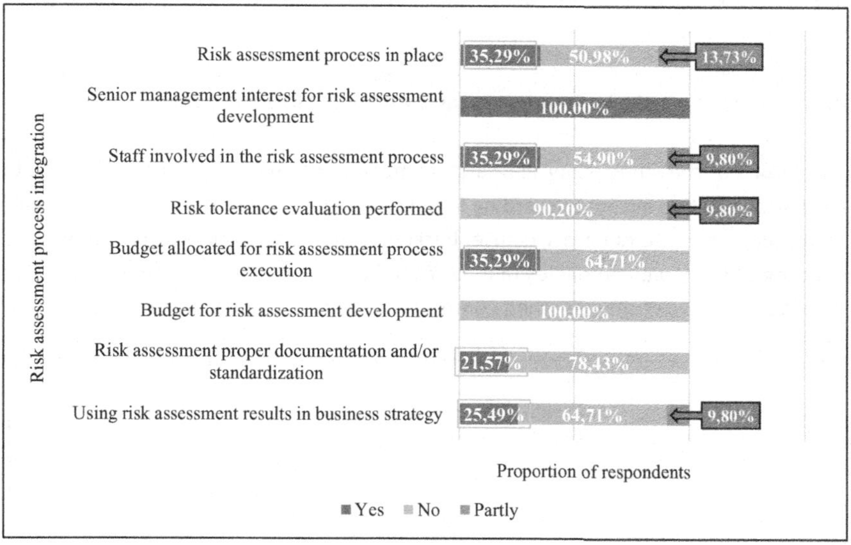

Figure 4.3: Research results related to risk assessment in small and medium-sized enterprises, developed by the author based on the research conducted during the doctoral period.

Horizontal and vertical communication between departments is an issue for this type of organizations; the members of the staff are not involved in the risk assessment process in more than half of the organizations, therefore strategies and decisions are not communicated correctly on time or at all.

While SMEs are very sensitive to climate changes, risk appetite cannot be measured because risk tolerance assessment is performed only by less than 10% of the organizations. Another worrying result is that almost 65% of the organizations have not assigned a special budget for the risk assessment process and none of the SMEs plan to allocate special resources for the development of the process. Standardization is also an issue with only 21,57% of the SMEs having proper documentation for risk assessment.

Despite the fact that flexibility and fast adaptation to change as 2 of the main advantages of SMEs, unfortunately 64,71% of these organizations do not use the results of the risk assessment process when developing their business strategy.

The interviews ended on a hopeful note because almost 14% of the SMEs have started implementing the process and all the senior managers showed interest in the topic.

4.1.4 Research results concerning risk assessment in large companies

The results of the study show that large companies usually have a high tolerance to risk materialization because according to the respondents these organizations are well organized, have a solid infrastructure, backup solutions and financial resources. The majority of the large companies (almost 75%) have a low risk appetite and prefer to develop defensive strategies when confronted with risks (Figures 4.4 and 4.5).

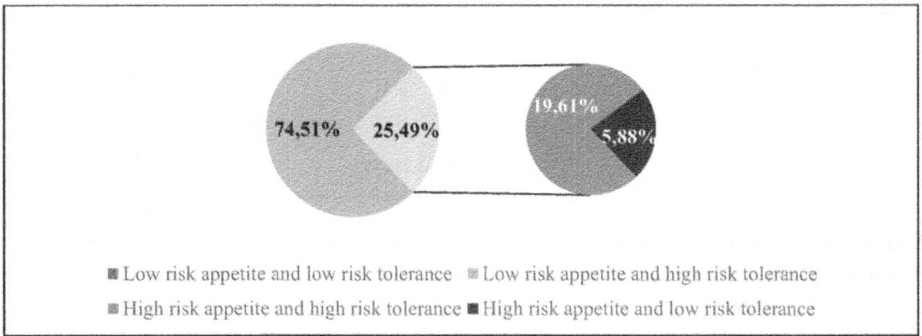

Figure 4.4: Risk appetite and risk tolerance in large companies, developed by the author based on the research conducted during the doctoral period.

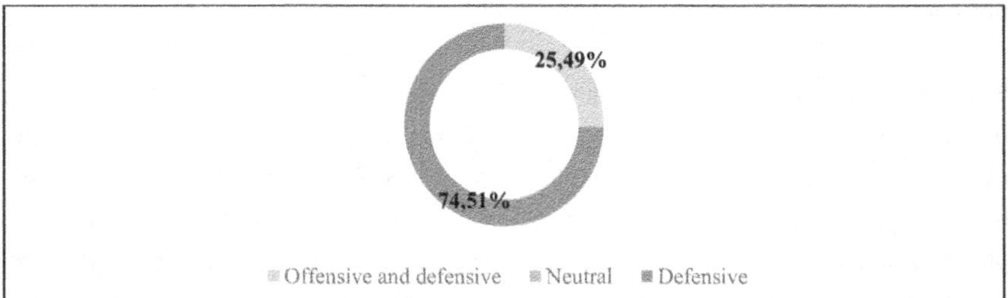

Figure 4.5: Risk attitude in large companies developed by the author based on the research conducted during the doctoral period.

The research shows that 87% of the organizations show a high interest in performing risk assessment by having already implemented the process or having started the planning phase. The majority of the senior managers consider risk assessment as a top priority and in the case of almost 14% of the organizations that have not invested in the process in the past, preparations for process development have started (Figure 4.6).

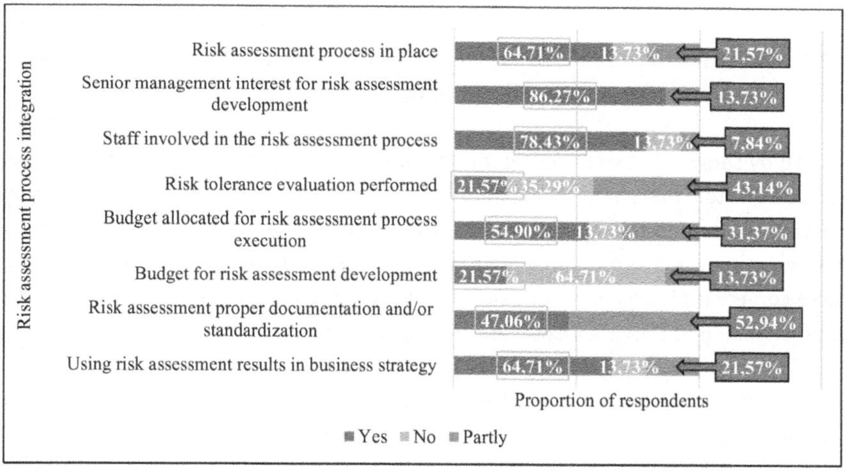

Figure 4.6: Research results related to risk assessment in large companies, developed by the author based on the research conducted during the doctoral period.

Another positive result is that staff involvement is present where risk assessment is in place and where the process has just started being implemented. Despite the fact that risk tolerance is evaluated by only 21,57% of the organizations, almost 44% of the large companies have started assessing risk tolerance because senior managers have understood that risk appetite and risk tolerance statement need to be made in order to be competitive in the current business environment.

Financial resources are not a barrier for budgeting risk assessment in large companies; unfortunately, the main barriers are bureaucracy and complex protocols that delay the process of gathering resources. In terms of implementation the process is already budgeted in more than half of the organizations and almost 32% are waiting for approvals in order to allocate resources. Despite the fact that updating the process is vital for a correct risk assessment, budget is usually assigned for process implementation and only 21,57% of the organizations have assigned special resources for further risk assessment development.

One of the large companies' advantages is standardization and documentation for the risk assessment process; most of the respondents have considered that the main issues encountered when defining a standard across the organization and between countries or continents were fighting bureaucracy, cultural differences, different market needs and points of view on risk.

4.1.5 Analysis of the research results regarding risk assessment in small and medium-sized enterprises compared to large companies

The study shows that SMEs consider offensive strategies when confronted with risks far more often than large companies. The respondents mention that in order to constantly adapt to the changes in the business environment, SMEs have to consider taking risks more often than large companies. Despite their high tolerance to risks, large companies have a different view on assessing risks and prefer to focus on self-protection and to allocate resources for risk mitigation.

The differences between the attitudes of the 2 types of organizations when confronted with risky situations is shown in Table 4.1.

Table 4.1: Risk attitude in SMEs compared to large companies, developed by the author based on the research conducted during the doctoral period

Risk attitude	When is it used?	
	Small and medium-sized enterprises	**Large companies**
Defensive	seldom	predominant
Offensive and defensive with low tolerance	sometimes	seldom
Offensive and defensive with high risk tolerance	sometimes	sometimes
Neutral	seldom	N/A
seldom <25%, 26% < sometimes used < 75%, predominant > 76%		

Defensive strategies are predominantly used by large companies, while SMEs sometimes ignore risk materialization probability and take risks in order to be competitive and improve business performance; this can also occur in case of large companies with high risk tolerance. Ignoring the identified risks or not identifying risks at all can be considered a neutral attitude – this can only rarely occur in SMEs.

Table 4.2 presents the comparison between risk assessment integration in the 2 types of organizations using the criteria established during the interviews. The results show that while both SMEs and large companies have a high interest in risk assessment, the process is far more advanced in large companies especially in terms of implementation.

Table 4.2: Risk assessment in SMEs compared to large companies, developed by the author based on the research conducted during the doctoral period

Criteria	Integration level	
	Small and medium-sized enterprises	Large companies
Risk assessment process in place	medium	high
Senior management interest	high	high
Staff involved in the risk assessment process	medium	high
Budget allocated for risk assessment	medium	medium
Budget for risk assessment development	low	low
Risk assessment documentation and standardization	low	medium
Using risk assessment results in business strategy	medium	high
low <25%, 26% < medium < 75%, high > 76%		

When it comes to resources, an average of 45% of both types of organizations have assigned budgets dedicated to process implementation, but just a few have allocated human resources and finances for process updates and development.

Risk assessment is already integrated in most of the large companies; senior managers and the staff are very involved in all the processes related to risk assessment: identifying and analyzing risks, risk monitoring and risk handling.

In case of SMEs a special attention has to be paid to documentation with 78% of the organizations not having proper documentation or any standards defined for risk assess-ment. In comparison, large companies have started writing or have finished standard ope-rating procedures and also have begun standardization across departments and regions.
Regarding risk assessment results, large companies are more focused on using them when elaborating risk strategies and developing business development plans; this is particularly important in order to harness all resources used in order to perform risk assessment and to prevent the possible negative effects of risk materialization.

4.2 Study concerning the interrelation between risk assessment related to business processes and the organizational context

No matter if manually calculated or as part of an enterprise resource planning (ERP) program, risk assessment is very sensitive to changes within the organization and in the business environment; at the same time the process has an impact on various factors within the organizational context.

The research investigates how stakeholders, social and political factors, strategy, vision and other external and internal factors related to the organizational context have an influence on risk assessment, but also how the process impacts these factors. Decision-making and business strategies should consider all risk assessment results, therefore no matter the level of operational efficiency, if not used when developing objectives, vision, mission and goals, risk assessment can become unsuccessful.

Stakeholders and senior management have a strong influence on the process – their point of view on the importance of risk assessment can determine the amount of resources assigned for the process. In order to emphasize the importance of the relation between risk assessment and the organizational context, the research was conducted by interviewing managers and specialists from different industries but also by gathering survey data from questionnaires sent by email.

Without a doubt any business process has to be supported by all stakeholders, has to be in line with the organization's strategies and vision and has to be value-adding for the organization.

4.2.1 General context of the research

Risk assessment efficiency and business performance are impacted by the symbiosis between risk assessment and the organizational context. Risk assessment has become an important tool in adapting to the constant changes in the business climate as a result of the global economic instability. The research performed by the author during the doctoral thesis has concluded that in order to choose between a defensive or offensive strategy, organizations perform extensive risk analyses and redesign organization objectives to ensure business survival and constant development.

„By changing organizational practices risk assessment can facilitate and legitimize certain ways of organizing" according to Soin and Collier (2013). Risk assessment involves a particular way of governing individuals and activities for it has the potential to change lines of accountability and responsibility within the organization.

Risk assessment is specific for every organization and can even be described as "subjective" because "relationships within the organization are mediated through the risk level perceived as acceptable by the actors involved and through the way the roles are divided among the actors" (de Reuver et al., 2009).

In the now extremely competitive environment an efficient risk assessment process can determine the success of the organization and ensure its survival and growth. Risk assessment has an essential strategic role and has a direct link to the organizations' objectives; following, all important decisions have started being linked to managing risks. In both the public and the private sectors risk assessment has become part of the organizational life.
Decisions related to risk-taking and the overall organization's attitude when facing risks are determined by the organizational context.

Pritchard (2015) states that "stakeholder risk tolerances are a vital input because different members of the customer, project, and management teams may have different perspectives on what constitutes "acceptable" risk". Also, in 2014 Hopkin suggests that "stakeholders now expect that organizations will take full account of the risks that may cause disruption within operations, late delivery of projects or failure to deliver strategy." Therefore, while stakeholders have different views on risk thresholds, they also expect that organizations take responsibility of risk materialization and its effects.

One of the main success factors of any process is communication – gathering, selecting data and sharing information for risk assessment depends on the involvement of the staff, but also all impacted or impacting parties. Unfortunately, so far "little has examined the inter-relationship between relational governance and risk assessment that affect information sharing and these relationships" (Cheng et al., 2013); therefore, another goal of the research is to determine the importance of sharing know-how and any updates that need to be considered when identifying and evaluating risks.

4.2.2 Objectives and research methodology

a) Research objectives

The objectives of the research were to determine the interrelation between risk assessment and the organizational context by establishing the influence of risk assessment on all the factors that interact with the organization, as well as the effects of the organizational context on the risk assessment process.

The study was conducted around the following research questions:

1. *How important is the interrelation between the stakeholders and risk assessment?*
2. *How does risk assessment influence organization culture, vision and communication departments and vice-versa?*
3. *What is the impact of external environment on risk assessment and which are the main effects of the risk assessment process on these factors?*
4. *How can the success of risk assessment be ensured by the organizational context within an organization?*

b) Research methodology

Feedback to the research questions was given by 52 managers and specialists that have shared their perspective on the reciprocal influence of risk assessment and the organizational context. The data was collected by interviewing 18 managers and sending electronic questionnaires to 34 managers and specialists with jobs in different industries in the period October – December 2017.

The questions related to internal and external factors from the organizational context that influence or are influenced by risk assessment. These factors were presented to all individuals and each of the respondents answered with "YES" or "NO" to each of the questions. For each question results related to the interrelation between risk assessment and each of the factors were presented as the percentage of respondents that have answered "YES". The top 3 questions and answers were presented as research results related to the questionnaire used (Annexes C and D).

Example - What is the influence of internal stakeholders on the risk assessment process?

Top answer: 94,23% of the respondents (49 out of 52 individuals) have agreed that senior management makes decisions related to budget allocation for the process and that has a strong impact on risk assessment.

4.2.3 Research results concerning the interrelation between risk assessment related to business processes and the organizational context

4.2.3.1 Risk assessment and internal factors

Leadership style, relations between employees, staff performance evaluation and infrastructure are internal factors that define the organization and have a strong impact on any business process.

a) Internal stakeholders

The success of risk assessment is mainly determined by the staff. Upper management assign resources for the process (staff, infrastructure, upgrades and automation budgets) (Figure 4.7).

The involvement of the employees, accepting and facilitating process implementation and bringing their contribution to the daily risk assessment routine are vital for successful results – staff needs to constantly update databases with information from the whole organization's knowledge pool.

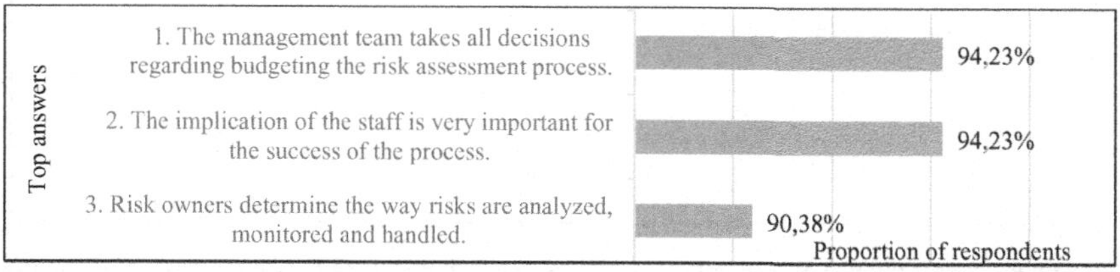

Figure 4.7: The influence of the internal stakeholders on risk assessment, developed by the author based on the research conducted during the doctoral period.

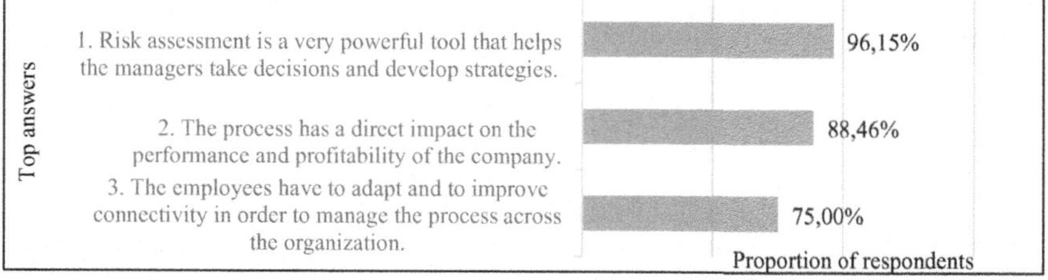

Figure 4.8: The influence of risk assessment on the internal stakeholders, developed by the author based on the research conducted during the doctoral period.

Almost all the respondents consider that risk assessment has a positive impact on business performance and profitability because it is highly important in decision-making and developing business strategies (Figure 4.8). Implementing the process across all departments and the participation of all employees are also a requirement for an efficient process according to the respondents.

b) Leadership

The senior management team determines risk assessment methods, but successfully implementing risk assessment also depends on leadership style (Figure 4.9).

Mentoring, offering guidance and motivation are essential for the involvement of the employees that has an important influence on the process.

Risk assessment involves a series of subprocesses: risk identification, assessment and risk handling. In order to monitor, control, support and help employees to find solutions and constantly being updated related to new methods and techniques, the organization needs a strong leader.

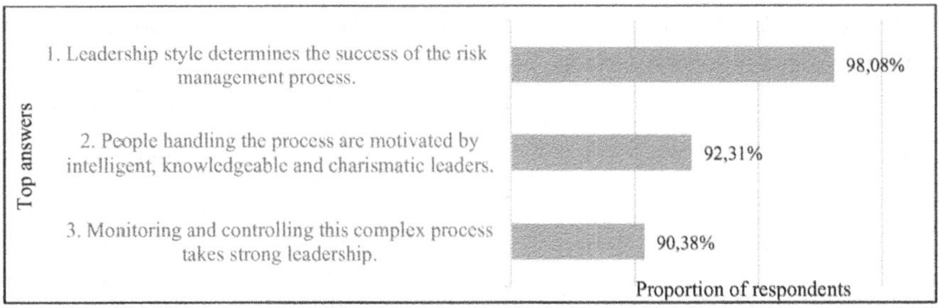

Figure 4.9: – The influence of leadership on risk assessment, developed by the author based on the research conducted during the doctoral period.

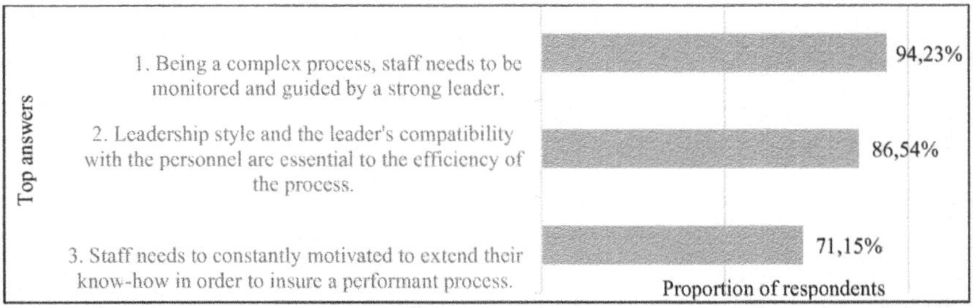

Figure 4.10: – The influence of risk assessment on leadership, developed by the author based on conducted during the doctoral period.

Figure 4.10 shows that risk assessment can influence leadership style – by being a complex process that involves intense knowledge related to business (market-related information, threats and opportunities, competition, etc.), as well as all the organizational processes, risk assessment requires a performant leadership style in order to manage staff. Senior managers have to recruit carefully and select a matching leader that can ensure a performant process by positively influencing the staff.

c) Organizational culture

The way employees behave in an organization, their principles, beliefs and values, define the organizational culture. According to O'Reilly (2014), researches on organizational culture are usually based on 2 assumptions: "senior leaders are the prime determinant of the culture, and culture is related to consequential organizational outcomes."

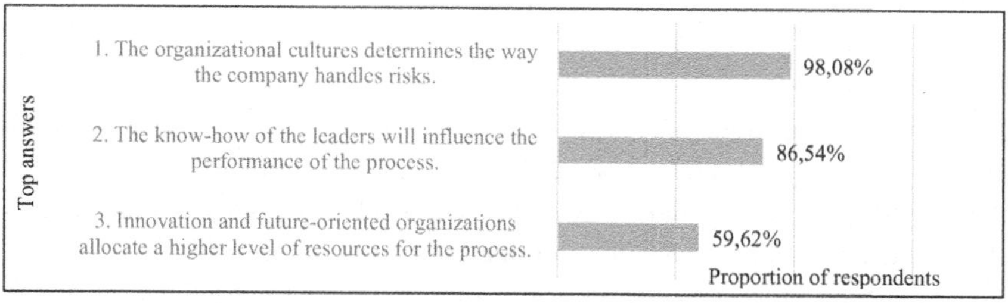

Figure 4.11: The influence of the organizational culture on risk assessment, developed by the author based on the research conducted during the doctoral period.

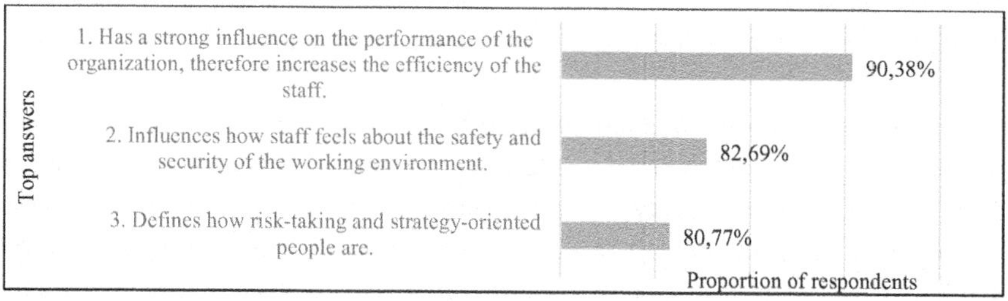

Figure 4.12: The influence of risk assessment on the organizational culture, developed by the author based on the research conducted during the doctoral period.

Figure 4.11 shows that the majority of managers and specialists state that the organizational culture can define the organization's attitude in risky situations – as example a conservative organizational culture has usually a defensive attitude by valuing self-preservation and stability. Assumptions related to possible events is subjective but can lead to risk identification, therefore the leader's judgement and knowledge is very important for the risk assessment process. Budget-related decisions are also made by senior management according to the organization's strategy and vision, therefore future-oriented organizations can assign more resources for risk assessment development such as investments in technology and human resources.

A successful business influences the organizational culture: staff is more positive, ambitious and competitive. The success of risk assessment ensures safety and stability for the organization, following a safe environment lowers the staff's stress levels – the employees have job security and do not worry about delayed salaries or the survival of the organization. Additionally, in order to achieve positive business results, managers can use the results of risk assessment as strategic opportunities – an organization that takes on new opportunities, innovates and constantly develops creates a culture of courageous, free-minded and results-oriented people (Figure 4.12).

d) Evaluation

Business knowledge, forecasting capabilities and database research are required for risk identification and analysis, as well as strategy-oriented risk handling; these requirements can only be fulfilled by performant employees - a correct and periodic staff evaluation method is vital for ensuring capable personnel for the process. The staff evaluation process has to take into consideration the requirements of risk assessment according to 95% of the respondents.

Approximately 87% of the individuals agree that risk assessment efficiency and accuracy is impacted by the staff evaluation process, so that a subjective, superficial or incorrect evaluation can led to unsuccessful risk assessment.

e) Social capital, informal and formal interactions

Any business process relies on interactions and connections between people (Figure 4.13). Team work, transparency and communication are vital for any business process – information related to process results is reported and analyzed by the organization and final decisions usually require a leader's approval. Connecting with co-workers and maintaining a healthy communication are necessary for the risk assessment process.

Figure 4.14 shows that when it comes to gathering and selecting data, connections between employees are important: in order to identify uncertainties and make estimations about the probability of appearance and consequence of possible risks, employees have to work together in order to process data correctly and determine risk levels. Risks within the risk handling plan can lead to both negative and positive outcomes - risk-taking decisions are taken by the process owner with approval from senior management. Visibility and also good relations with other members of the staff can promote ideas and facilitate access to senior managers.

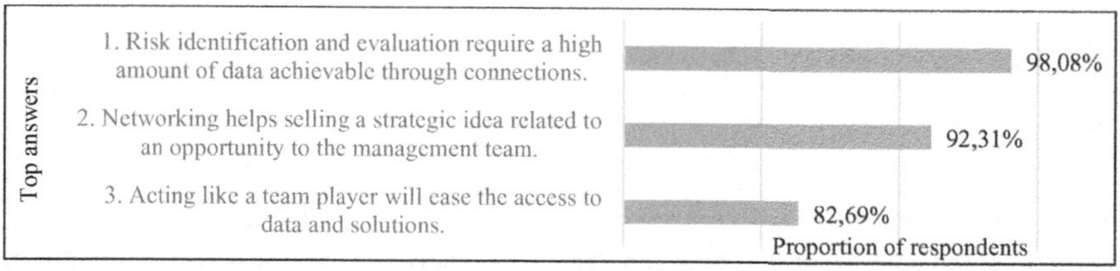

Figure 4.13: The influence of connections and interconnections on risk assessment, developed by the author based on the research conducted during the doctoral period.

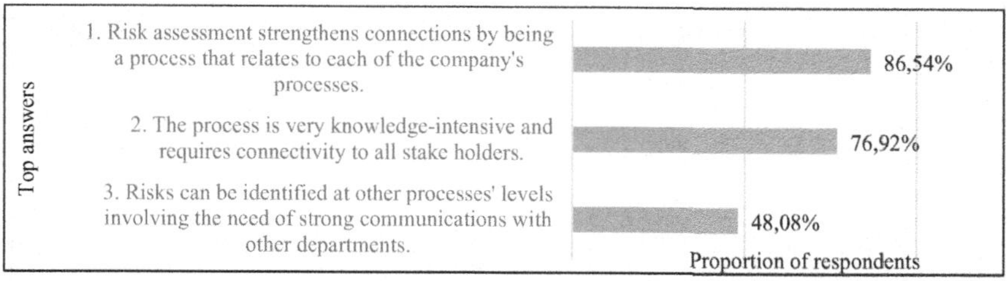

Figure 4.14: The influence of risk assessment on connections and interactions, developed by the author based on the research conducted during the doctoral period.

Each the risk assessment subprocesses has an impact on the connectivity between employees by relying its success on networking and efficient communication:

- Risk identification is performed for each business process, so that data needs to be gathered from across the organization;
- The accuracy of risk levels estimations relies on collecting data from as many sources as possible;
- Risk handling involves a strong connection between senior management and all business process owners from the organization.

f) Structural and electronic resources

Risk assessment is not handled by a special department according to the interviewed managers. Special resources have to be assigned in order to have risk assessment imple-mented correctly in the organizational structure (Figure 4.15). Human resources, hard-ware and special software are usually not dedicated for risk assessment entirely – ma-nagers assign additional risk assessment-related tasks to employees from an existing department; multitasking can lead to incorrect risk evaluation or delays in risk identifi-cation.

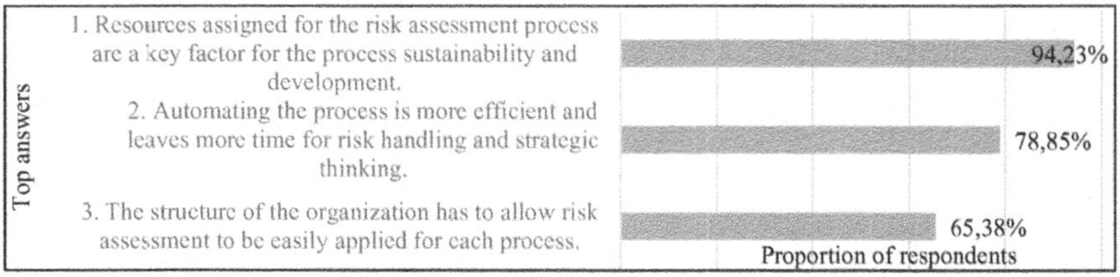

Figure 4.15: The influence of structural and electronic resources on risk assessment, developed by the author based on the research conducted during the doctoral period.

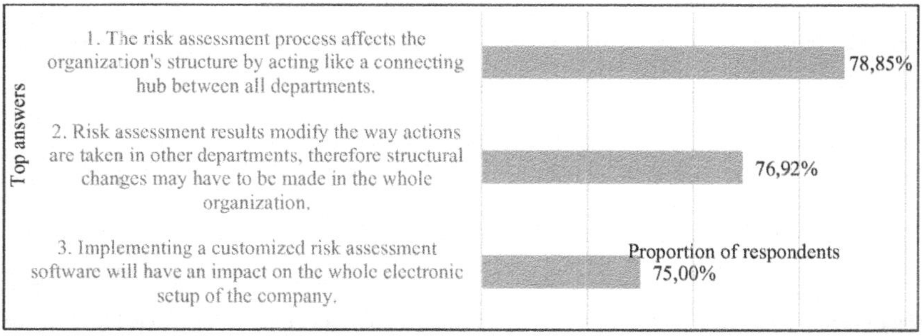

Figure 4.16: The influence of risk assessment on structural and electronic resources, developed by the author based on the research conducted during the doctoral period.

Risk assessment can also be influenced by the level of automation given the fact that a high amount of data needs to be constantly gathered, selected and transformed in order to prepare the risk analysis. Special ERP programs and setting up a dedicated team are recommended by most of the interviewees – acquiring risk assessment software is very efficient by being more efficient when it comes to historical risks analysis and cause and effect evaluation, so that managers and specialists have more time for strategic thinking.

Research results achieved by the author during the doctoral period have shown that processes interactions are the main source for high risks; in order to prevent the possible negative effects of risk materialization, risk assessment should be performed at each interaction between organizational business processes. As a consequence, the risk assessment process is directly linked and has an important impact on the structure of the organization. The influence of risk assessment on the organizational resources is presented in Figure 4.16. The process acts like a hub by collecting and selecting data across all the organization and transforming it into information that should be used as feedback for all processes and systems.

g) Organizational slack (staff, space and time)

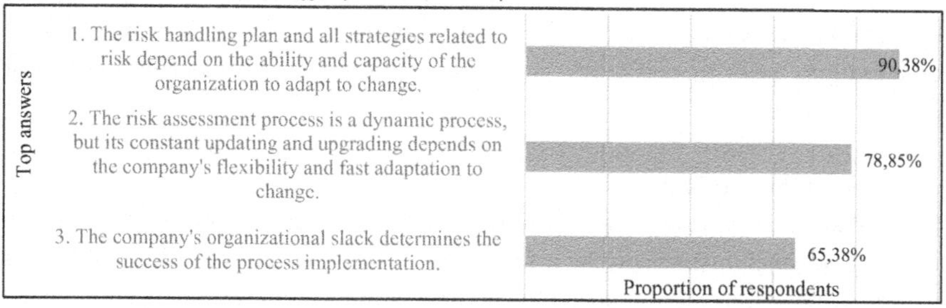

Figure 4.17: The influence of the organizationalslack resources on risk assessment, developed by the author based on the research conducted during the doctoral period.

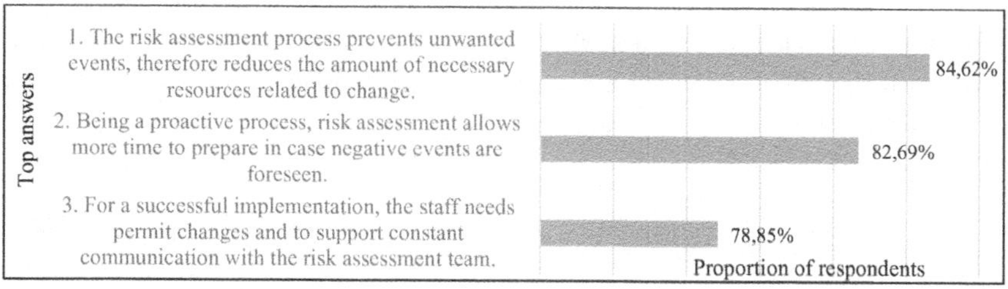

Figure 4.18: The influence of risk assessment on the organizational slack resources, developed by the author based on the research conducted during the doctoral period.

Risk assessment analyses data related to the organization in order to detect uncertainties, therefore the organizational structure has to be calibrated in order to facilitate access to data and communication, supply data for risk assessment and receive risk assessment results. Adaptation to change is vital for any business process. In order to have accurate results, risk assessment needs to be updated and upgraded on a regular basis; new changes have to be considered very often, therefore the complex and dynamic process is strongly impacted by the organizational slack. Figure 4.17 shows that the majority of the respondents consider that risk assessments reduces costs with risk handling if performed correctly – increasing predictability, mitigating and eliminating risks reduce costs with negative events. Also, by estimating risk levels, risk assessment gives more time to prepare for possible unexpected negative events. Risk assessment also influences the structure of the organization by requiring access protocols and a solid communication flow across all the organizational departments (Figure 4.18).

4.2.3.2 Risk assessment and external factors

Business strategy and organization objectives are constantly adapted to changes in the economy, but also social trends, life style, demographics and technology. Another external factor with a high impact on the business processes is competition – organizations have to constantly innovate, optimize solutions and improve their products and services.

a) External stakeholders

Shareholders, competing organizations, suppliers, creditors and customers are external stakeholders; society as a factor is discussed in the socio-cultural factors section, while government is presented in the political factors section.

Figure 4.19 shows that decisions related to investing, budgeting and assigning resources for risk assessment are influenced by the shareholders. Shareholders also influence risk handling strategies, whether the organization's attitude is a defensive one focusing on stability and self-preservation or an offensive one taking risks in order to achieve new business opportunities.

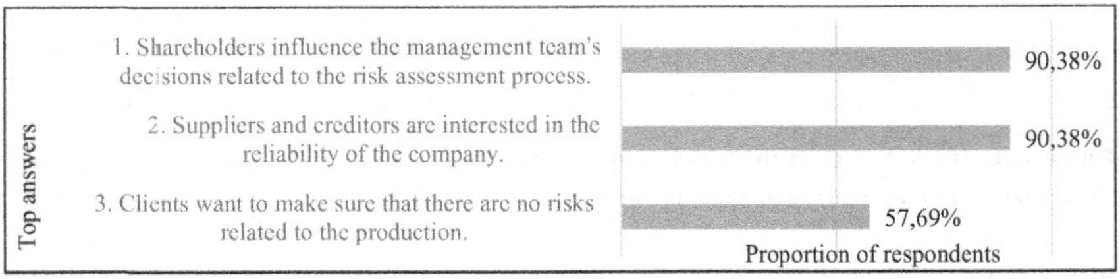

Figure 4.19: The influence of the external stakeholders on risk assessment, developed by the the author based on the research conducted during the doctoral period.

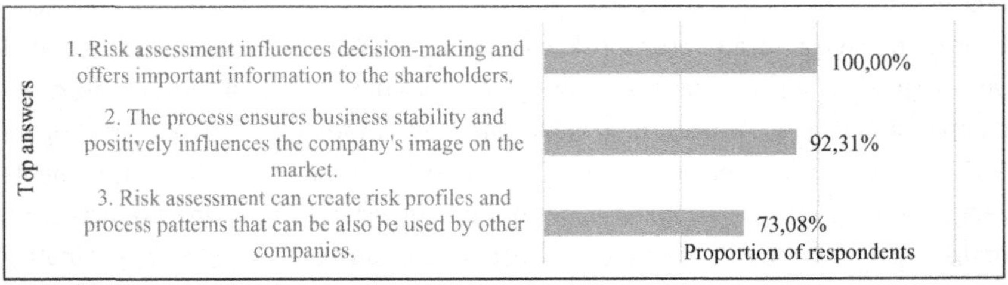

Figure 4.20: The influence of risk assessment on the external stakeholders, developed by the author based on the research conducted during the doctoral period.

When it comes to creditors, the viability of the business is essential for requesting a credit line from a bank or an extended payment term from a supplier. Clients, especially partners and supporters that sometimes base their whole activity on products or services supplied by the organization, have an important influence on risk assessment and want to make sure that production lines, outsourced services or other services are not paused or even stopped; therefore, risk monitoring and controlling is vital for clients' satisfaction and long-term partnerships.

Risk assessment influences external stakeholders by determining the shareholders' strategic actions and influencing the organization's market strategy that has an impact especially on competition (Figure 4.20). An organization with economic stability and constant growth attracts new clients, investors and knowledgeable job candidates, therefore risk assessment is also linked to the image of the organization. Benchmarking is one of the advantages of successful partnerships – risk assessment-related information can be shared with business partners in order to compare results and optimize the process.

b) Socio-cultural factors

Human resources, as well as operations and overall business profitability, are influenced by indicators related to local demographics, such as percentage of working population, education level, age and interests. Changes in local demographics influences the quality of the employees that perform risk assessment. The income levels of the organizations' customers have a direct impact on sales and revenue – economic instability can deter-mine a new set of risks for the organization so that supply and demand analyses have to be performed on a regular basis. Organizational culture also influences risk assessment especially when it comes implementation: accepting changes and acting as a team are vital for a successful process start-up (Figure 4.21).

When it comes to risk assessment, influencing socio-cultural factors (Figure 4.22), cities with good local economies and safe and reliable organizations will attract more people searching for job security. A safe working environment also relieves stress and motivates people leading to less human errors and higher performance. Being dependent on good communication between departments, risk assessment influences the organizations' socio-cultural factors by encouraging employees to work together as a team, connecting people and strengthening relationships.

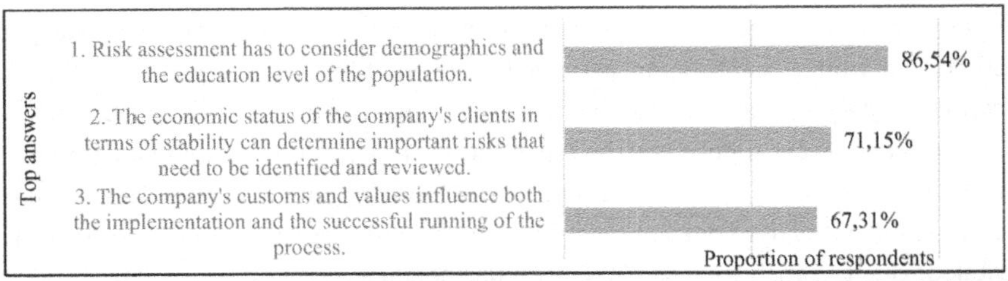

Figure 4.21: The influence of the socio-cultural factors on risk assessment, developed by the based on the research conducted during the doctoral period.

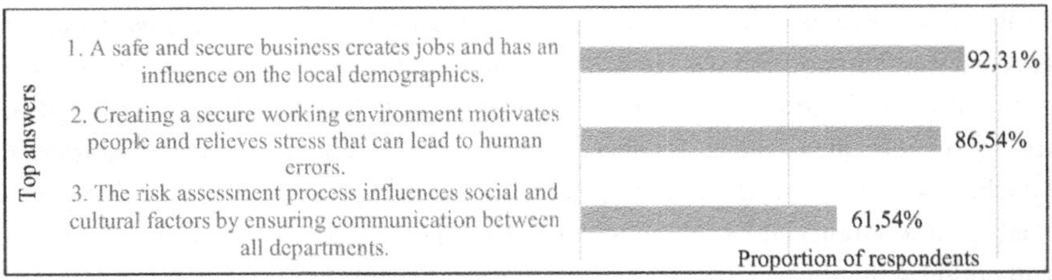

Figure 4.22: The influence of risk assessment on the socio-cultural factors, developed by the author based on the research conducted during the doctoral period.

c) Technological factors

In the past years many organizations have adopted risk assessment software programs that are able to process a high amount of data based on customized algorithms that calculate risk levels and permanently update the risk registry database. These types of programs can be very efficient especially when integrated in the organization's ERP system in order to retrieve and select data automatically related to each organizational business process. Additionally, Figure 4.23 indicates that a performant communication system facilitates data collection and reduces processing time.

Most of the respondents consider that risk assessment has created new opportunities for software development companies (Figure 4.24). By developing risk assessment software programs but also customizing their clients' existing ERP systems in order to adapt to the risk assessment process, the organizations' revenues have increased and new jobs were created for the new service and maintenance contracts. Another positive consequence of risk assessment implementation is attracting new investments for technological development.

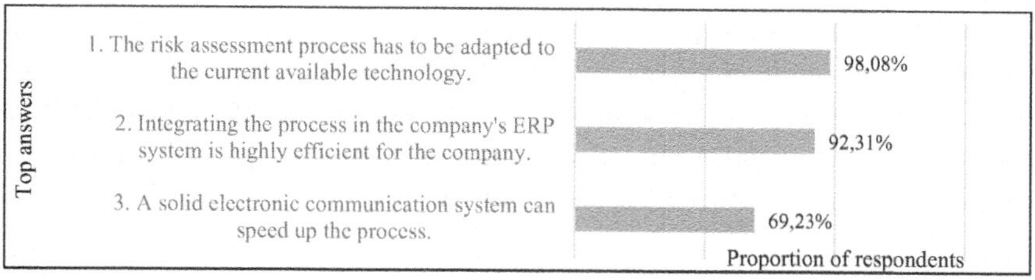

Figure 4.23: The influence of technological factors on risk assessment, developed by the author based on the research conducted during the doctoral period.

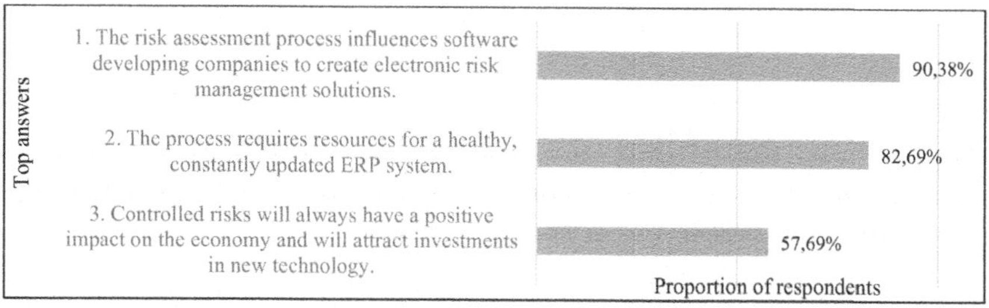

Figure 4.24: The influence of risk assessment on the technological factors, developed by the author based on the research conducted during the doctoral period.

d) Economic factors

One of the most important factors influencing risks relates to the local economy. Risk assessment-related resources are allocated depending on the status of the economic environment – a healthy environment leads to less risks, lower risk levels and a lower process complexity (Figure 4.25).

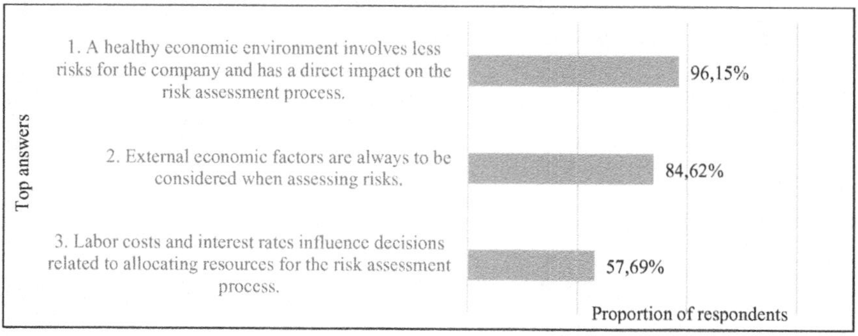

Figure 4.25: The influence of economic factors on risk assessment, developed by the author based on the research conducted during the doctoral period.

Figure 4.26 shows that by preventing negative events risk assessment has a direct influence on the results of the organization and local economy, including higher living standards for the employees: stable incomes and even higher salary levels. Finally, risk assessment has an indirect impact on attracting investors that will always prefer developing business in countries with a stable economy.

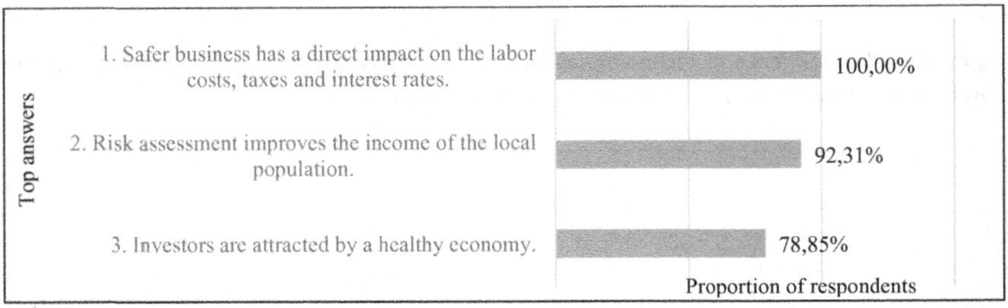

Figure 4.26: The influence of risk assessment on the economic factors, developed by the authors based on the research conducted during the doctoral period.

e) Environmental factors

When performing risk analysis and aiming for sustainable business development both abiotic and biotic factors are taken into account (Figure 4.27).

An important aspect discussed during the interviews is considering all legal requirements related to ecology and including them in the risk evaluation process. An eco-friendly environment leads to employees being more motivated according to 58% of the respondents. By improving job security risk assessment has a positive impact on the employees' morale and influences responsibility in terms of conserving the environment – satisfied employees are more often preoccupied by ecology than the ones that are constantly worried about their careers.

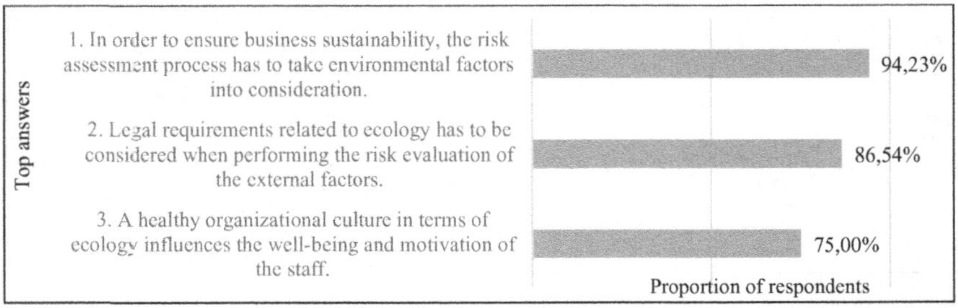

Figure 4.27: The influence of environmental factors on risk assessment, developed by the author based on the research conducted during the doctoral period.

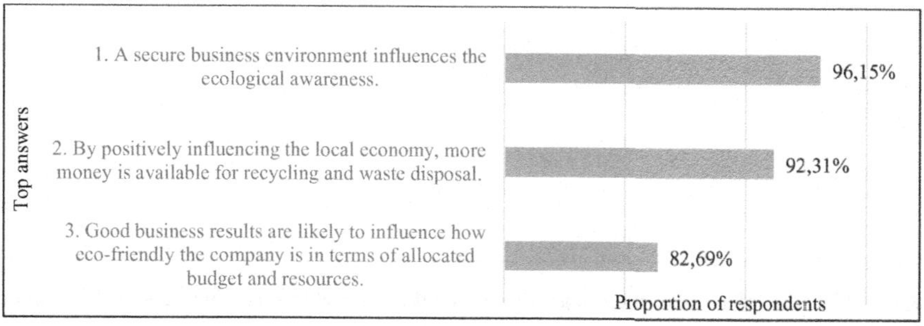

Figure 4.28: The influence of risk assessment on the environmental factors, developed by the author based on the research conducted during the doctoral period.

Figure 4.28 indicates that almost 83% of the managers and specialists say that profitable business leads to an improved local economy and more financial resources for recycling, waste disposal and other environmental activities.

f) Political factors

The political climate has to be constantly investigated in order to identify and manage risks. An unstable political environment usually involves changes in the legislative system according to more than 90% of the respondents (Figure 4.29); this also means that risk assessment becomes more complex and requires additional resources.

According to Figure 4.30 organizations that have implemented risk assessment can be an advantage for signing contracts with the public authorities: public tenders require that participants present information proving their business stability and sustainability. Risk assessment's impact on local economy has also a positive impact on the budgets administered by politicians.

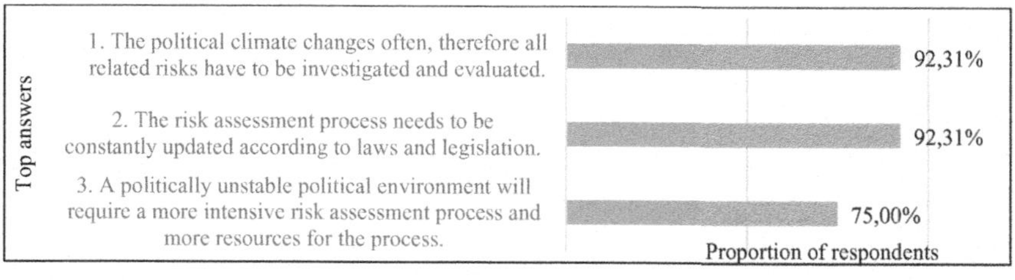

Figure 4.29: The influence of the political factors on risk assessment, developed by the author based on the research conducted during the doctoral period.

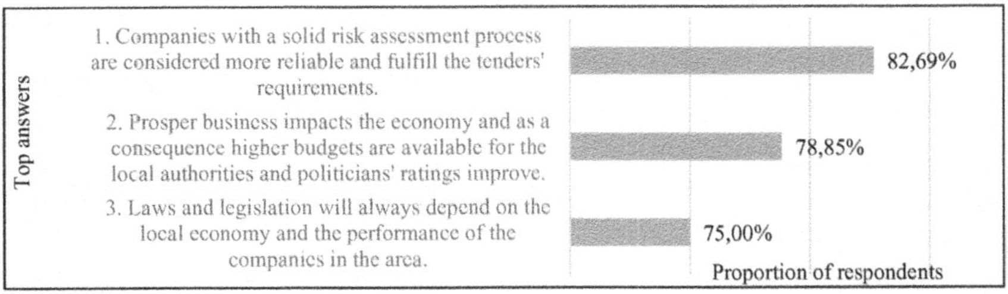

Figure 4.30: The influence of the risk assessment on the political factors, developed by the author based on the research conducted during the doctoral period.

On the other hand, respondents say that the status of the economy will always affect laws and legislation, so that the contribution of risk assessment to the economy has an indirect impact on local politics – for example taxes related to revenue or employees can be adjusted in order to support organizations, create new jobs and attract new investors.

5 Risk assessment related to the interactions between business processes in relation with the critical factors of sustainable performance

5.1 Study regarding organizational business processes and critical factors of sustainable performance

The infrastructure of any organization is based on processes that describe tasks, activities, roles and rules within the organization. Managers have understood the role of process design and business process management focused on sustainable processes that are critical factors in ensuring business sustainability. The research aims to determine the status of process sustainability in organizations and to investigate the main criteria with impact on process sustainability. Interviews with managers and process specialists from different organizations were carried out in order to gather information about business processes and analyze them from sustainability point of view.

The weakest and the strongest links in designing sustainable processes and the related risks are researched for each of the organizational departments. Additionally, interviewees discuss the critical factors that prevent process interruptions or process failures and share information related to organizational profile, core and support processes, process description, degree of formality, staff involvement, communication, risk assessment related to interactions between business processes, control mechanisms and methods of continuous improvement. In order to evaluate the level of process sustainability each of the characteristics of the process that have an impact on sustainability were analyzed.
The study intends to bring a contribution to managers and business analysts in order to design sustainable processes and successfully manage risks related to business sustain-ability.

5.1.1 General context of the research

The current competitive business environment pressures organizations to adopt new and more complex business models in order to keep up with the new market requirements. According to the research results achieved by the author during the doctoral period, international organizations but also local ones have started using new

R. M. Bejinariu, *Sustainable Business Performance and Risk Management*,
Sustainable Management, Wertschöpfung und Effizienz,
https://doi.org/10.1007/978-3-658-29389-5_5

management tools and methods with the goal of gaining a competitive advantage by focusing on the clients' needs. Sustainable business processes are a requirement for delivering high quality products and services. In his research for PricewaterhouseCoopers (PwC), Müller (2011) states that "organizations have to be in a position to create integrated business processes which are flexible and adaptable to all changes (internal or external)". In order to adapt to these new changes organizations have started acknowledging the importance of process management, but also risk assessment related to business processes and other factors that bring a contribution to business sustainability. Individual business targets as well as organizational structure, planning and control are considered when managing processes.

The research starts by gathering data on organizational profile and organizational structure, core and support processes. Following, the critical factors that are analyzed in the study are theoretical *process characteristics* that are considered the main criteria affecting process sustainability.

According to the research conducted during the doctoral period, in order to improve sustainable performance a thorough *process description* has to be made by identifying 5 characteristics for each particular process that can be considered process criteria:

1) Organizational profile and structure;
2) Process objectives and performance goals;
3) Requirements of internal or external clients;
4) Inputs and results;
5) Production and value creation;
6) Process owner and staff involvement.

Process performance is also affected by the *degree of formality*. A "formal" process is a documented process described as a set of activities and steps which should be performed under certain conditions. Harvard Business Review Press (2010) mentions that "occasionally processes might be informal procedures before the enterprise increases the degree of formality by documentation and description". In order to be sustainable and performant processes should be formalized enhancing the organization's knowledge and common understanding. Business processes can be described within a flowchart as a set of activities interleaved with decision points. Another form of representation for business process formality is the process matrix that includes a sequence of activities and rules based on process data.

Staff *level of involvement* in the process and transfer of information are also characteristics that influence sustainability. Process owners and all the employees involved in the process have to consider taking responsibility, sharing knowledge, allowing access to all the rest of the organization and ensuring a correct communication flow.

Most of the business processes range over multiple business functions and are cross-functional but are "embedded in the overall value chain and as this in the organizational structure" (Rummler et al., 1995). Therefore, *risk assessment related to interactions between business processes* is one of the most important criteria in ensuring sustainable processes.

Finally, sustainability depends on *monitoring, control and process optimization*: the responsible employees have to observe any changes in activities and identify any deviations from the process rules and procedures.

5.1.2 Objectives and research methodology

a) Research objectives

The study intends to highlight the compatibility and influence of theoretical processes regarding sustainability. The first objective is to analyze business processes in terms of sustainability in order to help managers acknowledge the need of continuously improving process design and process management. In order to achieve the objective, the research focuses on investigating the applicability of theory into business practice in order to determine the impact of the determined process criteria on the sustainable performance of business processes in organizations.

The hypothesis for the study is that sustainable processes involve a clear definition of all specific characteristics of processes, solid documentation of all steps of process mana-gement, good communication between departments concerning standard operating pro-cedures and risk assessment. The second research objective relates to identifying the critical factors of sustainable performance in organizations.

b) Research methodology

The practical research is based on a study performed between November 2015 and February 2016 that has focused on gathering data from 15 organizations and involved 2 different methodologies in order to achieve each of the research objectives:

1. For the first objective an electronic questionnaire was sent to all individuals in order to investigate business processes from sustainability point of view; each organization and each respondent shared information related to 3-5 business processes (Table 5.1);

Table 5.1: Business processes analyzed from sustainable performance point of view, developed by the author based on a study by Mateescu R., Melanie B., Vanessa J., Research on Key Factors Impacting Process Sustainability in Global Organizations, Proceedings of BASIQ 2016 - International Conference, New Trends in Sustainable Business and Consumption, Konstanz, Germany, 2-3 June 2016, ISSN: 2457-483X, pp. 22-31.

No. crt.	Business processes	No. organizations	No. processes/ organization	Total no. processes
1	Production processes	7	3	21
	Sales processes			
	Financial processes			
2	Production processes	5	4	20
	Procurement processes			
	Sales processes			
	Human resources processes			
3	Production processes	3	5	15
	Procurement processes			
	Sales processes			
	Human resources processes			
	Financial processes			
Total				**56**

2. The managers' and process specialists' perspective on the main factors that affect sustainable performance was discussed during a follow-up interview.

The questionnaire included 18 questions related to each process criteria with impact on processes in terms of sustainable performance (Table 5.2). The expected answer for each question was either "YES" or "NO".

The list of questions was designed as a checklist so that each of the investigated processes were analyzed from sustainable performance point of view:

- Organizations with the majority of the answers "YES" are considered prepared regarding the sustainable performance of business processes;

- Organizations with the majority of the answers "NO" are considered not prepared regarding the sustainable performance of business processes.

A total of 56 processes were analyzed including operational or core processes (production and sales processes) and support processes (procurement, human resources and accounting processes). For each organization all 18 questions were used for each of the investigated business processes. The results of the questionnaires were presented as the proportion between the number of managers or process specialists that have answered "YES" to a question divided by the total number of answers. Annex F presents the extended results of the questionnaire.

Table 5.2: Business processes criteria with impact on sustainable performance, developed by the author based on a study by Mateescu R., Melanie B., Vanessa J., Research on Key Factors Impacting Process Sustainability in Global Organizations, Proceedings of BASIQ 2016 - International Conference, New Trends in Sustainable Business and Consumption, Konstanz, Germany, 2-3 June 2016, ISSN: 2457-483X, pp. 22-31.

No. crt.	Process criteria	Criteria code
1.	Process description	A
2.	Degree of formality	B
3.	Level of involvement	C
4.	Transfer of information	D
5.	Risk assessment at process interactions level	E
6.	Monitoring, control and process optimization	F

In order to determine how each of the researched process criteria affects business processes in terms of sustainable performance, the background of each organization and specific process information was gathered during the follow-up interviews. Annex E presents the determined process criteria with impact on sustainable performance on the example of the procurement process in the investigated organizations. Using this methodology all process criteria were analyzed with reference to all activities within the value chain.

After having analyzed business processes from sustainable performance point of view, the second objective related to determining the critical factors that affect sustainable performance in organizations. The research objective was achieved by gathering information during interviews with managers and process specialists from the investigated organizations.

5.1.3 Research results related to organizational business process from sustainable performance point of view

The results of the first part of the questionnaire are presented in Table 5.3. The overall result is that only 71,70% of the organizations are prepared when it comes to ensuring sustainable performance for all business processes.
The best results were related to process owners being specialized for all operations required for the process (88% of the organizations) and business processes being permanently monitored (87,67% of the organizations.

The most unsatisfying results were related to the criteria "Process description" and "Level of involvement". Regarding process description, an average of only 33% of the organizations have a back-up plan in place in case the process fails and also almost 53% of the organizations have not set a clear time frame for each of the process steps and activities. With only a third of the organizations having a documented back-up plan, important risks can be identified that have to be included in the risk handling plan.

When it comes to the level of involvement, a weak result was achieved by 52,50% of the organizations that have not assigned a back-up employee in case the process owner takes a sick leave or is on vacation.

Only 66,50% of the organizations have databases in place that ensure clear information for all members of the staff. While personnel is involved in all business processes, results related to communication are worrying: 25,50% of all information is not stored in a secured database and approximately 14% of the information can be lost when an employee leaves.

Risk assessment involves identifying, evaluating and analyzing risks related to all investigated processes – the overall result is that 76,25% of the organizations manage risks related to business processes and activities with 74.50% of the organizations monitoring and controlling risks.

With an average of 80% the respondents answering "YES", organizational processes are prepared from sustainable performance point of view when it comes to monitoring, controlling and optimizing.

Table 5.3: Approaching business processes from sustainable performance point of view (general overview), developed by the author based on the research conducted during the doctoral period.

Process code	Question	Proportion of respondents with the answer YES	Overall result
A	Are processes defined completely and correctly?	80.50%	55.33%
	Is the time frame clear for each of the process steps and activities?	52.50%	
	Is there a back-up plan in place in the process fails?	33.00%	
B	Are processes fully documented in a database?	61.00%	66.50%
	Is the sequence of activities clear for all employees?	72.00%	
C	Is the process owner specialized for all operations required for the process?	88.00%	75.61%
	Is there a back-up employee in case the process owner takes a sick leave or is on vacation?	52.50%	
	Does the process owner have any experience with quality management?	86.33%	
D	Is all detailed information available for the involved employees?	86.33%	76.03%
	Do all involved personnel have the right access level for the process?	79.83%	
	Is all information available in case of personnel change?	85.67%	
	Is the process performance independent of manual input?	53.83%	
	Is there a secured database in place for all information?	74.50%	
E	Is there a risk assessment process in place for all process interactions?	78.00%	76.25%
	Are process-related risks identified being monitored and controlled?	74.50%	
F	Are all steps of the process constantly optimized?	80.33%	80.44%
	Is the process permanently monitored?	87.67%	
	Does the review of the process consider both quantitative and qualitative evaluation methods?	73.33%	
Average result for process sustainability/organization		**71,70%**	

Results related to each of the investigated business processes are presented in Figure 5.1. The average results show business processes from sustainable performance point of view by types of processes based on the answers "YES". The study shows that the results are similar, the top score being achieved by human resources processes with approximately 72% of the investigated cases being prepared regarding the sustainable performance of business processes.

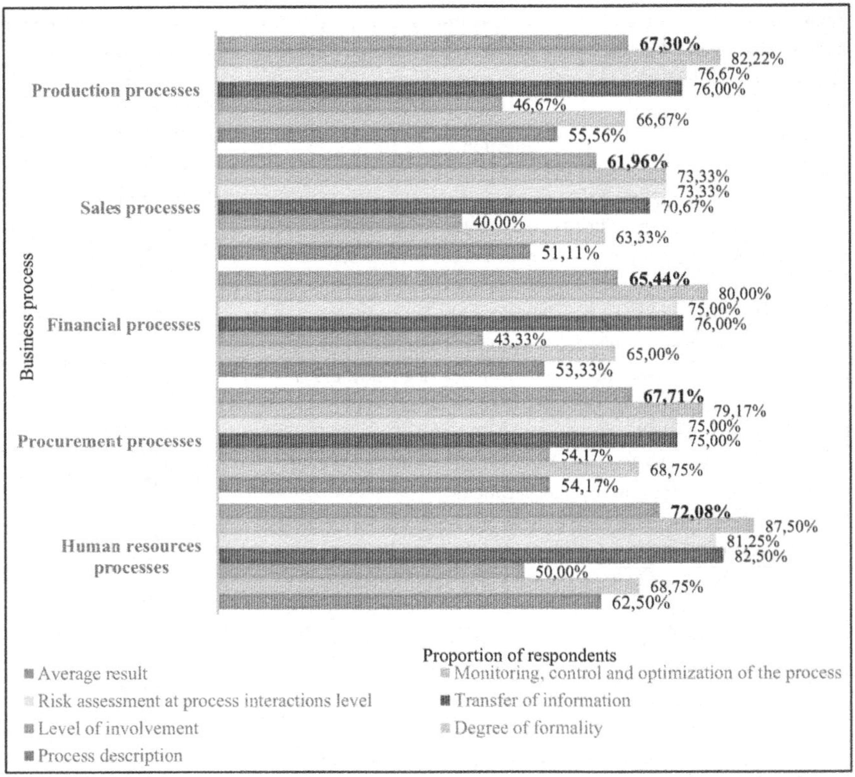

Figure 5.1: Approaching business processes from sustainable performance point of view (for each type of process), developed by the author based on the research conducted during the doctoral period.

5.1.4 Research results related to the critical factors of sustainable performance in organizations

The second part of the study relates to the respondents' perspectives on the main factors that impact sustainable performance in organizations (Figure 5.2). The discussions with the interviewees concluded that the top impacting factors are monitoring and control of processes according to almost a third of the managers and specialists, followed by solid process documentation (18%) and complete and secure database (17%).

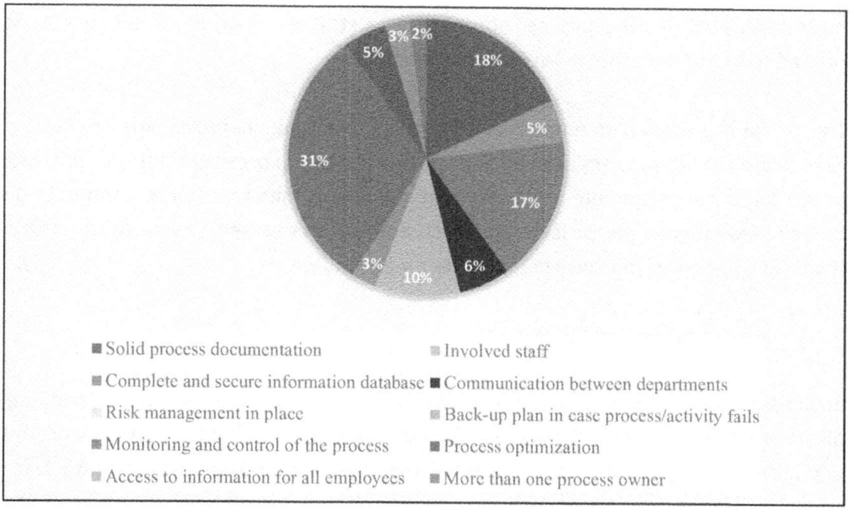

Figure 5.2: Critical factors that affect sustainable performance in organizations, developed by the author based on a study by Mateescu R., Melanie B., Vanessa J., Research on Key Factors Impacting Process Sustainability in Global Organizations, Proceedings of BASIQ 2016 - International Conference, New Trends in Sustainable Business and Consumption, Konstanz, Germany, 2-3 June 2016, ISSN: 2457-483X, pp. 22-31.

The least impacting factors mentioned by the interviewees were access to information for all employees (3%) and assigning more than one process owner for a specific process (2%). Results show that communication is also a weak factor (6%) and unfortunately just 10% of the respondents mention risk assessment as one of the critical factors.

5.2 Risk assessment related to the interactions between organizational business processes using the PDCA method

Managing business has encountered new challenges during the last years. The financial crisis has created the necessity of finding new solutions and sets of rules in order to achieve the targeted values of the performance indicators. Acting as the core of any organization, business processes have a direct impact on business performance, therefore most of the times the survival of the organizations relies on managing risks at operational management level. Controlling risks and continuous improvement of processes are essential in the current competitive business environment. More and more managers use the process approach as a strategy in order to minimize risks related to interactions between business processes.

The aim of the study is to emphasize the role of analyzing, managing and monitoring risks related to interactions between business processes in organizations with process-based quality management systems. Interviews with managers were conducted in order to investigate the process approach and risk assessment based on the PDCA (Plan-Do-Check-Act) business management method.

5.2.1 General context of the research

Business processes determine the success of any organization by being the operational pillars of any business objectives. Business process-oriented organizations are organizations with well-structured value chains that represent the framework for thinking strategically about activities involved in any business (Porter, 1985), determining the potential of their competitive advantage and fully assessing their values. Today, in order to be competitive, organizations require more than monitoring performance indicators – organizations have to develop new strategies in order to improve business results by focusing on process management.

Exchange of information between departments is essential for all subprocesses or activities that define a process: planning (P), operations (doing=D), monitoring and analysis (C=checking) and improving (decisions and actions=A). Relations between every 2 processes involve risks caused by human errors, incorrect protocols or context assessment, analysis gaps, inconsistent monitoring, communication and feedback errors, etc. The research aims to determine the main risks at the interactions between organizational business processes and to analyze the advantages of performing risk assessment at this level.

5.2.2 Objectives and research methodology

a) Research objectives

Monitoring and controlling process interactions is essential for operational management control; strategic planning and innovation can only be performed on a healthy organization framework that involves well-defined protocols and constant performance assessment. Business sustainability depends on process interactions management and its impact on organization performance and strategic direction.

The first research objective is to determine the importance of risk assessment at process interactions' level. The second objective of the study relates to performing risk assessment by identifying risks at each interaction between organizational business processes using the PDCA method, determining the cause and effect of each risk, calculating risk levels by evaluating probability of occurrence and the consequences of risks and establishing the type of risk.

b) Research methodology

For the first objective research results are based on a study conducted in October and November 2015 that involved interviewing 3 chief executive officers (CEO) and 18 department managers from the fast-moving commercial goods (FMCG) and construction industries. Each interview included series of 4 questions that invite managers and specialists to share their perspective on the role of managing risks related to interaction between organizational business processes in ensuring healthy and value-adding process results. The second objective was achieved by conducting a study related to risk identification based on interviews with managers during the period October-November 2017 (Annex G). Risk profile including risk causes and effects and risk evaluation were determined as a result of the research conducted during the doctoral period. Process interactions were considered according to Figure 5.3 and Table 5.4 and a code number was assigned for each interaction.

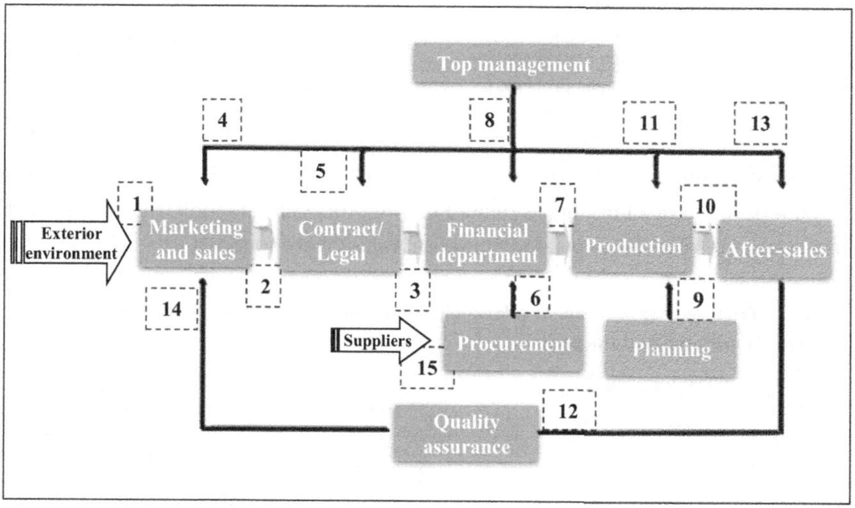

Figure 5.3 - Proposed interactions between organizational business processes, developed by the author based on the research conducted during the doctoral period.

Risks were identified using the PDCA method for each of the 5 activities related to business processes (plan, do act, check). Also, interactions were considered both ways, for example in the case of process interactions between the procurement and financial processes, risks, causes and effects were identified for each of the procuring and financial process activities. The first step of risk assessment was identifying risk levels by determining the probability of occurrence (P) and consequence (C) for each process activity.

Table 5.4: Proposed interactions between organizational business processes, developed by the author based on the research conducted during the doctoral period

Interaction code no.	Process interactions between organizational business processes:	
1	External environment	Marketing and sales processes
2	Marketing and sales processes	Contract management/legal processes
3	Senior management processes	Marketing and sales processes
4	Contract management processes	Financial processes
5	Senior management processes	Contract management processes
6	Procurement processes	Financial processes
7	Financial process processes	Production processes
8	Senior management processes	Financial processes
9	Planning processes	Production processes
10	Production processes	After-sales processes
11	Senior management processes	Production processes
12	After-sales processes	Quality assurance processes
13	Senior management processes	After-sales processes
14	Quality assurance processes	Marketing and sales processes
15	Procurement processes	Suppliers processes

The results of the research were color coded according to Table 5.5. By calculating the arithmetic mean of all risk levels related to one process interaction, the Average risk level was determined – calculated numerical values were rounded.

Table 5.5: Proposed risk assessment color coding, developed by the author based on the research conducted during the doctoral period

Color code	Tolerance intervals for risk levels	Risk type	Action
	1-9	No risk or acceptable risk	Assumed risk
	10-12	Tolerable risk	Risk monitoring
	13-20	Unacceptable risk	Risk handling plan
	21-25	Maximum risk	Risk handling plan

5.2.3 Research results concerning risk assessment related to the interactions between organizational business processes

In order to retrieve qualitative information for to risk assessment related to interactions between business processes, the second research objective is achieved based on a study conducted in 2015 and contains feedback from 21 individuals related to the topic.

Question 1 (Figure 5.4): *Which are the advantages of performing risk assessment related to interactions between business processes in organizations?*

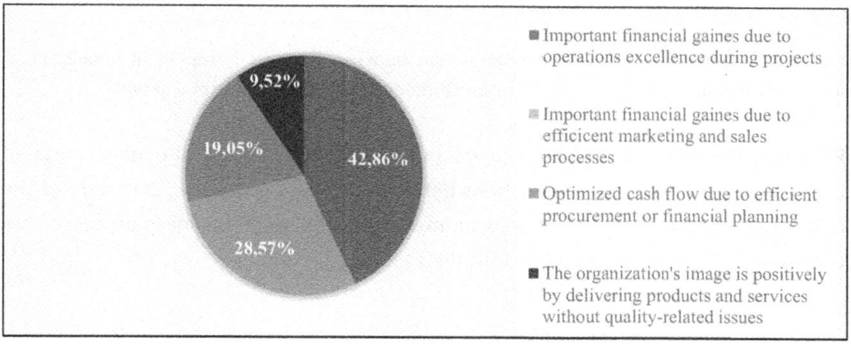

Figure 5.4: The impact of risk assessment related to business processes interactions, developed by the author based on the research conducted during the doctoral period.

Results – Financial losses are considered the most important threat according to 71,43% of the respondents from which almost 43% answer that delayed projects are the main cause for revenue loss and more than 28% refer to decreased sales. Managers believe that inefficient risk assessment related to interactions between business processes leads to decreased profit and revenue and affects overall business sustainability.

Cash flow disruptions are also an important threat according to more than 19% of the managers that state that delayed cashing in leads to delayed payments to suppliers and creditors and affects project and production planning. Less than 10% of the respondents consider that the image of the organization is negatively impacted by delivering products and services that do not satisfy the clients' needs in terms of quality.

Question 2 (Figure 5.5): *What type of risks can occur at the interactions between business processes in organizations?*

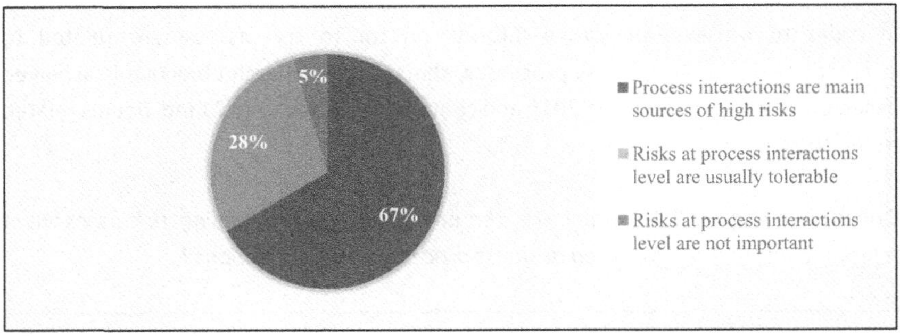

Figure 5.5: Type of risks related to interactions between business processes in organizations, developed by the author based on the research conducted during the doctoral period.

Results – The majority of the managers and specialists agree that the main source of high risks is located at the interactions between business processes. One third of the respondents state that risks related to interactions between business processes are tolerable (28%) or even not important (5%).

Question 3 (Figure 5.6): *Which business process interactions determine the highest risks?*

Results – Almost half of the interviewees answer that handling clients' data can generate the most important operational risks.

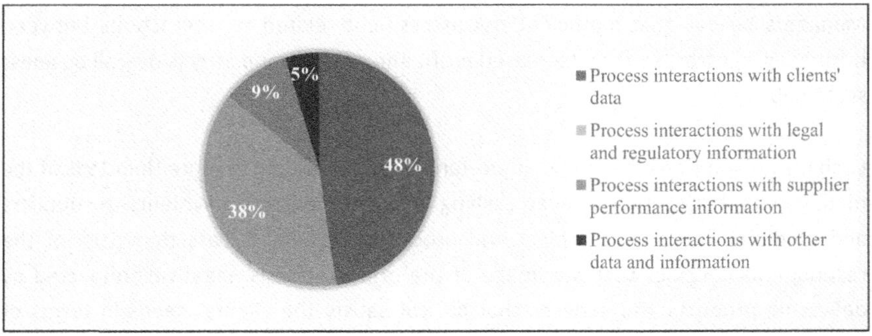

Figure 5.6: Process interactions where the most important risks can be identified, developed by the author based on the research conducted during the doctoral period.

When it comes to adapting to new rules and legislation, process interactions are critical in order to ensure legit business – all the organizational processes are impacted by changes in the business environment and have to gather and analyze all legal and regulatory information in order to adapt all processes to the new rules. Process interactions related to suppliers' performance also lead to important risks according to 9% of the managers and specialists.

Question 4 (Figure 5.7): *Do you consider risk assessment at process interactions level as value-adding?*

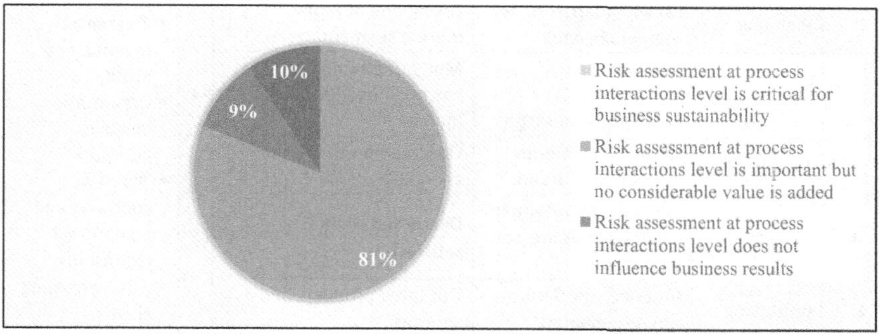

Figure 5.7: The role of risk assessment related to business process interactions, developed by the author based on the research conducted during the doctoral period.

Results – Ensuring business sustainability is one of the main roles of risk assessment related to interactions between business processes with 81% of the respondents agreeing that the process is critical for achieving organizational objectives related to sustainable performance. Less than 20% of the managers and specialists consider that risk assessment brings no considerable value or has no influence on business results.

5.2.4 Evaluating the probability of occurrence and the consequences of risks related to interactions between business processes using the PDCA method in organizations

Process interaction no. 1 – Risk assessment at process interactions between the marketing and sales processes and the exterior business environment

Process interactions between marketing and sales processes and clients determine the link between the organization and customers.

The research identifies 3 unacceptable risks that have to be handled in order to not affect this important relation (Table 5.6).

Table 5.6: Risk assessment at process interactions risks between marketing and sales processes and the exterior environment (clients and creditors) using the PDCA method, developed by the author based on the research conducted during the doctoral period

No. crt.	**Marketing activity**	Cause	Risks	P	C	Effect
Risk assessment at process interactions risks between the marketing and sales department and clients						
1.	Planning	Lack of adaptation to market changes	Losing one or more market segments	1	5	▪ Decreased revenue and profit; ▪ Organization image is altered; ▪ No new contracts and no contract extensions; ▪ Losing existing clients.
2.	Operations	Incorrect or incomplete advertising message	Marketing campaign has no impact on the market	3	4	
3a.	Monitoring	New market trends are not considered	Outdated products and services	4	5	
3b.	Analyzing	Clients' and potential clients' needs are not considered	Decreased clients' satisfaction	3	5	
4.	Improving	Products and services are not updated	Outdated products and services	4	5	
Average risk level:			Unacceptable risk	14		
Risk assessment at process interactions risks between the marketing and sales department and creditors						
1.	Planning	Resources allocated incorrectly	Cash flow disruptions	3	4	▪ Credit lines or product supply interrupted; ▪ Delayed payments to banks and suppliers; ▪ Organization is not viable for creditors; ▪ Production disruptions or stop supply.
2.	Operations	Lack of resources for the production line	Delayed deliveries, invoicing and cashing in from clients	3	5	
3a.	Monitoring	Faulty ERP system or human errors	Incorrect or incomplete financial status regarding debts and receivables	2	4	
3b.	Analyzing	Communication error or incorrect/ incomplete data input	Inefficient assignment of financial resources	3	5	
4.	Improving	Not using market feedback for process updates	Inefficient business processes	2	5	
Average risk level:			Tolerable risk	12		

When it comes to process interactions with creditors 2 risks caused by lack of resources and communication errors are unacceptable. Table 5.7 presents the main risks related to process interactions with competing organizations and shareholders - 3 unacceptable risks were identified related to delivering outdated products and services and disruptions in the production lines.

Table 5.7: Risk assessment at process interactions risks between marketing and sales processes and the exterior environment (competing organizations and shareholders) using the PDCA method, developed by the author based on the research conducted during the doctoral period

No. crt.	**Marketing activity**	Cause	Risks	P	C	Effect
Risk assessment at process interactions risks between the marketing and sales processes and competing organizations						
1.	Planning	Delayed data gathering	Outdated information about competing organizations	3	4	▪ Decreased revenue and profit; ▪ Loss of market share; ▪ Decreased revenue and profit; ▪ Loss of market share.
2. 3a.	Operations Monitoring	Incorrect or incomplete data		3	4	
3b.	Analyzing	Incorrect data processing		3	4	
4.	Improving	No benchmarking with partners	Outdated products and services	4	5	
Average risk level:			Unacceptable risk	16		
Risk assessment at process interactions between the marketing and sales processes and shareholders						
1.	Planning	Incorrect sales estimations	Disruptions in the production lines	3	5	▪ Losing support from shareholders; ▪ Decreased budgets; ▪ Decreased sales; ▪ Loss of profit and revenue.
2.	Operating	Incorrect resources assignment				
3a.	Monitoring	Faulty products and services				
3b.	Analyzing	Production costs not calculated correctly				
		Marketing data not gathered or processed	Outdated products and services	4	5	
4.	Improving					
Average risk level:			Unacceptable risk	18		

The identified risks can be caused by lack of benchmarking with partners, incorrect sales, resources and production costs estimations, delivering faulty products and services and not harnessing marketing data. The materialization of these risks can affect the organization's main performance indicators by decreasing revenue and profit, negatively affecting market share.

Process interaction no. 2 – Risk assessment at the interaction between marketing and sales processes and contracting and legal processes

Table 5.8 presents 2 unacceptable risks that can occur between marketing and sales process and contracting and legal processes. Incorrectly planned marketing campaigns can lead to no new clients and contracts, while not aligning contract clauses with organizational objectives affects the performance of the contract.

Table 5.8: Risk assessment at the interaction between marketing and sales processes and contracting and legal processes using the PDCA method, developed by the author based on the research conducted during the doctoral period

Risk assessment at the interaction between marketing and sales processes and contracting and legal processes						
No. crt.	**Marketing activity**	Cause	Risks	P	C	Effect
1.	Planning	Marketing campaigns incorrectly planned	No new contracts	3	5	▪ Decreased revenue and profit; ▪ No new contracts and no contract extensions.
2.	Operations	Communication error between departments	Contract not signed or extended	2	5	
3a.	Monitoring	Clients' needs not monitored				
3b.	Analyzing	Clients' needs not analyzed				
4.	Improving					
Average risk level:			Unacceptable risk	13		

Risk assessment at the interaction between contracting and legal processes and marketing and sales processes						
No. crt.	**Contracting activity**	Cause	Risks	P	C	Effect
1.	Planning	Contract not ready on time	Contract not signed or extended	2	5	▪ Decreased revenue and profit; ▪ No new contracts and no contract extensions; ▪ Losing existing clients.
2.	Operations					
3a.	Monitoring	New legislation not monitored				
3b.	Analyzing	Inflexible or abusive contract clauses				
4.	Improving	Contract clauses not aligned with objectives	Non-performing contracts	3	5	
Average risk level:			Unacceptable risk	13		

Process interaction no. 3 – Risk assessment at the interaction between senior management and marketing and sales processes

Inefficient marketing campaigns can be considered an unacceptable risk caused by clients' needs not monitored and analyzed. The interaction between senior management and marketing and sales processes can also lead to negatively affecting the organization's image, clients losing interest in the offered products and services and Non-performing contracts (Table 5.9).

Table 5.9: Risk assessment at the interaction between senior management and marketing and sales processes using the PDCA method, developed by the author based on the research conducted during the doctoral period

Risk assessment at the interaction between senior management and marketing and sales processes						
No. crt.	**Management activity**	Cause	Risks	P	C	Effect
1.	Planning	Marketing resources incorrectly planned	Delayed marketing campaigns	3	4	▪ Decreased revenue and profit; ▪ No new contracts and no contract extension.
2.	Operations	Limited marketing budgets	Inefficient marketing campaigns	3	5	
3a.	Monitoring	Market needs not considered				
3b.	Analyzing					
4.	Improving					
Average risk level:			Unacceptable risk	15		
Risk assessment at the interaction between marketing and sales processes and senior management						
No. crt.	**Marketing activity**	Cause	Risks	P	C	Effect
1.	Planning	Marketing campaigns incorrectly planned	Losing seasonal opportunities	2	4	▪ ▪ Decreased revenue and profit; ▪ Losing market share; ▪ No new clients; ▪ Losing existing clients.
2.	Operations	Marketing campaigns incorrectly planned	▪ Organizational image negatively affected; ▪ Clients losing interest in offered products and services.	4	5	
3a.	Monitoring	Poor quality marketing campaigns				
3b.	Analyzing	Market-related data not monitored				
4.	Improving	Market needs not analyzed	Non-performing contracts	3	5	
Average risk level:			Unacceptable risk	14		

Process interaction no. 4 – Risk assessment at the interaction between contracting and legal processes and financial processes

Table 5.10 shows that between contracting and legal processes and financial processes only one unacceptable risk can be identified related to incorrect assignment of financial resources - this can be caused by lack of know-how, insufficient budget or human resources.

Table 5.10: Risk assessment at the interaction between contracting and legal processes and financial processes using the PDCA method, developed by the author based on the research conducted during the doctoral period

Risk assessment at the interaction between contracting and legal processes and financial processes						
No. crt.	**Contracting activity**	Cause	Risks	P	C	Effect
1.	Planning	Faulty project management	Invoices not issued on time	3	2	▪ Delayed payments from clients; ▪ Delayed payments to creditors; ▪ Production disruptions or stop supply; ▪ Losing existing clients.
2.	Operations	Invoicing data not supplied on time				
3a.	Monitoring	Project status not monitored	Refused invoices	2	5	
3b.	Analyzing	Clients' needs not considered				
4.	Improving					
Average risk level:			Tolerable risk	8		
Risk assessment at the interaction between financial processes and contracting and legal processes						
No. crt.	**Financing activity**	Cause	Risks	P	C	Effect
1.	Planning	Lack of resources in the financial department	Delayed or incorrect invoicing	3	2	▪ Credit lines or product supply interrupted; ▪ Delayed payments to banks and suppliers.
2.	Operations					
3a.	Monitoring		Incorrect data related to the organization's financial processes	2	5	
3b.	Analyzing		Incorrect assignment of financial resources	3	5	
4.	Improving		Delayed or incorrect invoicing	3	2	
Average risk level:			Tolerable risk	9		

Process interaction no. 5 – Risk assessment at the interaction between senior management and contracting and legal processes

Risks related to the interaction between senior management and contracting and legal processes are described in Table 5.11 that shows that 4 out of the 6 identified risk are unacceptable.

Table 5.11: Risk assessment at the interaction between senior management and contracting and legal processes using the PDCA method, developed by the author based on the research conducted during the doctoral period

Risk assessment at the interaction between senior management and contracting and legal processes						
No. crt.	**Management activity**	Cause	Risks	P	C	Effect
1.	Planning	Unidentified or unquantifiable requirements	No new clients	3	5	▪ Decreased revenue and profit; ▪ Loss of market share; ▪ Losing existing clients; ▪ Insolvency or bankruptcy.
2.	Operations	Lack of networking				
3a.	Monitoring	Clients' needs not monitored	No new clients and loss of existing clients	4	5	
3b.	Analyzing	Clients' needs not analyzed and unforeseen additional costs	Non-performing contracts	3	5	
4.	Improving					
Average risk level:			Unacceptable risk	17		
Risk assessment at the interaction between contracting and legal processes and senior management						
No. crt.	**Contracting activity**	Cause	Risks	P	C	Effect
1.	Planning	Lack of resources in the department	Contract not signed or extended	2	5	▪ Decreased revenue and profit; ▪ Delayed payments to banks and suppliers; ▪ Production disruptions or stop supply.
2.	Operations	Insufficient or incorrect data				
3a.	Monitoring	Changes in the legislation not monitored	Delayed contracts	2	4	
3b.	Analyzing	Changes in the legislation not analyzed	Non-performing contracts	3	5	
4.	Improving					
Average risk level:			Tolerable risk	11		

No new clients, losing existing clients, non-performing contracts are the main risks that can occur as a result of activities performed by senior management in relation with contracting and legal processes. Also, contracting activities can affect the performance of the contracts if changes related to laws and legislations are not carefully monitored and analyzed.

Process interaction no. 6 – Risk assessment at the interaction between procurement processes and financial processes

Important risks such as delayed projects and deliveries, exceeded budgets, delayed payments from clients and to suppliers are the unacceptable risks that can occur between procurement and financial processes (Table 5.12).

Table 5.12: Risk assessment at the interaction between procurement processes and financial processes using the PDCA method, developed by the author based on the research conducted during the doctoral period

Risk assessment at the interaction between procurement processes and financial processes						
No. crt.	**Procurement activity**	Cause	Risks	P	C	Effect
1.	Planning	Incorrect sourcing budget planning	Cash flow disruptions	3	4	▪ Decreased revenue and profit; ▪ Production disruptions or stop supply; ▪ Losing existing clients.
2.	Operations	Sourcing errors				
3a.	Monitoring	Delivery terms not tracked	Delayed projects	3	5	
3b.	Analyzing	Budget not calculated correctly	Exceeded project budget	3	5	
4.	Improving	Disadvantageous negotiations with suppliers	Delayed projects	3	5	
Average risk level:			Unacceptable risk	14		
Risk assessment at the interaction between financial processes and procurement processes						
No. crt.	**Financing activity**	Cause	Risks	P	C	Effect
1.	Planning	Budget planning not considering payment terms in contracts	Delayed payments from clients and to suppliers	4	5	▪ Decreased revenue and profit; ▪ Delayed or disrupted projects; ▪ Losing existing clients.
2.	Operations	Payment not done on time	Delayed deliveries	3	5	
3a.	Monitoring	Payment terms not tracked	Delayed payments from clients and to suppliers	4	5	
3b.	Analyzing	Information related to payment terms not transmitted	Cash flow disruptions	3	4	
4.	Improving	Contract clauses not updated according to current fiscal policies	Invalid contract	2	5	
Average risk level:			Unacceptable risk	15		

These risks can lead to decreased revenue and profit for the organization, as well as production disruptions and decreased customers' satisfaction. The main causes for these negative effects are related to sourcing errors, delivery terms not tracked, budget not estimated correctly and disadvantageous negotiations with suppliers.

Process interaction no. 7 – Risk assessment at the interaction between financial processes and production processes

Table 5.13 presents four risks that can be identified between financial and production processes. Delays in payments, deliveries, production, quality issues and non-performing contracts are the main risks identified that can lead to decreased revenue and profit, production disruptions and losing clients.

The main causes are related to cash flow not being monitored and optimized, payment terms not being tracked, incorrect resource planning and production flow related issue not being analyzed and solved.

Table 5.13: Risk assessment at the interaction between financial processes and production processes using the PDCA method, developed by the author based on the research conducted during the doctoral period

Risk assessment at the interaction between financial processes and production processes						
No. crt.	**Financing activity**	Cause	Risks	P	C	Effect
1.	Planning	Incorrect budget planning	Cash flow disruptions	3	4	▪ Decreased revenue and profit; ▪ Production disruptions or stop supply; ▪ Losing existing clients.
2.	Operations	Incorrect / delayed payments	▪ Delayed payments; ▪ Delayed deliveries.	3	5	
3a.	Monitoring	Payment terms not tracked				
3b.	Analyzing	Cash flow not monitored				
4.	Improving	Cash flow not optimized				
Average risk level:			Unacceptable risk	14		
Risk assessment at the interaction between production processes and financial processes						
No. crt.	**Production activity**	Cause	Risks	P	C	Effect
1.	Planning	Incorrect resources planning	Delayed production	3	5	▪ Decreased revenue and profit; ▪ Delayed or disrupted projects.
2.	Operations	Incorrect execution				

2.	Operations	Incorrect execution	Products/services with quality-related issues	3	5	▪ Decreased revenue and profit; ▪ Delayed or disrupted projects; ▪ Losing existing clients.
3a.	Monitoring	Production quality checks not performed		3	5	
3b.	Analyzing	Production flow-related issues not analyzed	Delayed production	3	5	
4.	Improving	Production flow protocols not optimized	Non-performing contracts	3	5	
Average risk level:			Unacceptable risk	15		

Process interaction no. 8 – Risk assessment at the interaction between senior management and financial processes

Table 5.14 presents the risks determined at process interactions level between senior management and financial processes.

Table 5.14: Risk assessment at the interaction between senior management and financial processes using the PDCA method, developed by the author based on the research conducted during the doctoral period

Risk assessment at the interaction between senior management and financial processes						
No. crt.	**Management activity**	Cause	Risks	P	C	Effect
1.	Planning	Inefficient business strategy	▪ Delayed payments; ▪ Delayed deliveries.	3	5	▪ Decreased revenue and profit; ▪ Loss of market share; ▪ Losing existing clients; ▪ Insolvency or bankruptcy.
2.	Operations	Gathering data from irrelevant sources				
3a.	Monitoring	Clients' needs not monitored				
3b.	Analyzing	Incorrect data processing	Refused invoices or delayed payments from clients	3	5	
4.	Improving	Changes in the business climate not considered				
Average risk level:			Tolerable risk	15		

Risk assessment at the interaction between financial processes and senior management						
No. crt.	**Financing activity**	Cause	Risks	P	C	Effect
1.	Planning	Incorrect budget planning	▪ Delayed payments; ▪ Delayed deliveries to clients; ▪ Delayed deliveries from suppliers.	3	5	▪ Decreased revenue and profit; ▪ Production disruptions or stop supply; ▪ Losing existing clients.
2.	Operations	Incorrect/delayed payments				
3a.	Monitoring	Payment terms not tracked				
3b.	Analyzing	Cash flow not monitored				
4.	Improving	Cash flow not optimized				
Average risk level:			Unacceptable risk	15		

Activities performed by the management team can lead to 2 unacceptable risks caused by inefficient strategies, data not monitored, and business environment not being analyzed. Other identified risks were delayed payments and deliveries caused by financing activities. The possible effects of the identified risks are decreased revenue and profit, as well as losing existing clients, market share and even insolvency and bankruptcy.

Process interaction no. 9 – Risk assessment at the interaction between planning processes and production processes

The risks identified between planning and production processes are presented in Table 5.15. The most important risks are related to production disruption, products or services with quality issues and delayed or faulty production or service delivery.

Risks caused by planning activities can threaten business survival and can lead to insolvency and bankruptcy; risks that result from production activities are higher and have a negative impact on the relation with the clients.

Table 5.15: Risk assessment at the interaction between planning processes and production processes using the PDCA method, developed by the author based on the research conducted during the doctoral period

Risk assessment at the interactions between planning processes and production processes						
No. crt.	**Planning activity**	Cause	Risks	P	C	Effect
1.	Planning	Insufficient resources for the planning department	Production disruptions; Delayed production	3	5	▪ Decreased revenue and profit; ▪ Decreased sales; ▪ Losing existing clients; ▪ Insolvency or bankruptcy.
2.	Operations	Incorrect planning				
3a.	Monitoring	Production protocols not tracked				
			Products/services with quality-related issues	3	5	
3b.	Analyzing	Production errors not analyzed				
4.	Improving	Legislation changes not considered	Non-compliant products/services	2	5	
Average risk level:			Unacceptable risk	13		
Risk assessment at the interactions between production processes and planning processes						
No. crt.	**Production activity**	Cause	Risks	P	C	Effect
1.	Planning	Incorrect resources planning	Delayed or faulty production or service delivery	3	5	▪ Decreased revenue and profit; ▪ Production disruptions or stop supply; ▪ Losing existing clients.
2.	Operations	Production issues data not transmitted				
3a.	Monitoring	Information related to quality checks not sent to planning department				
3b.	Analyzing	Quality checks analysis not sent to planning department	Delayed or faulty production or service delivery			▪ Decreased revenue and profit; ▪ Production disruptions or stop supply; ▪ Losing existing clients.
4.	Improving	Production flow optimization data not sent to planning department				
Average risk level:			Unacceptable risk	15		

Process interaction no. 10 – Risk assessment at the interaction between production processes and after-sales processes

Table 5.16 shows that only one risk can be caused by production activities when interacting with after-sales processes – non-compliant products involve high risk during the warranty period and lead to losing the clients' trust. Risk caused by after-sales activities relate to producing troublesome or outdated products, high troubleshooting costs during warranty period. The main causes for the possible negative effects of risk materialization are incorrect planning of resources, errors related to execution and production flow, as well as quality checks not performed.

Table 5.16: Risk assessment at the interaction between production processes and after-sales processes using the PDCA method, developed by the author based on the research conducted during the doctoral period

Risk assessment at the interactions between production processes and after-sales processes						
No. crt.	**Production activity**	Cause	Risks	P	C	Effect
1.	Planning	Incorrect resources planning	▪ Non-compliant products; ▪ High costs with product replacement/repairing during the warranty period.	4	4	▪ Decreased revenue and profit; ▪ Decreased sales; ▪ Losing existing clients; ▪ Losing market share.
2.	Operations	Incorrect execution				
3a.	Monitoring	Production quality checks not performed				
3b.	Analyzing	Production flow-related issues not analyzed				
4.	Improving	Production flow not optimized				
Average risk level:			Unacceptable risk	16		
Risk assessment at the interactions between after-sales processes and production processes						
No. crt.	**After-sales activity**	Cause	Risks	P	C	Effect
1.	Planning	Incorrect warranty-related budget	Delayed troubleshooting in the warranty period	3	3	▪ Decreased revenue and profit; ▪ Decreased sales; ▪ Losing existing clients. ▪ Losing existing clients.
2.	Operations	Incorrect troubleshooting in the warranty period	High troubleshooting costs during the warranty period	2	5	
3a.	Monitoring	Faulty products not monitored	Products/services with quality-related issues	3	5	
3b.	Analyzing	Redundant errors not analyzed				
			High troubleshooting costs during the warranty period	2	5	
4.	Improving	Market needs not considered	Outdated products and services	4	5	
Average risk level:			Tolerable risk	13		

Process interaction no. 11 – Risk assessment at the interaction between senior management and production processes

Table 5.17: Risk assessment at the interaction between senior management and production processes using the PDCA method, developed by the author based on the research conducted during the doctoral period

Risk assessment at the interactions between senior management and production processes						
No. crt.	**Management activity**	**Cause**	**Risks**	**P**	**C**	**Effect**
1.	Planning	Inefficient business strategy	Producing goods and delivering services that are unappealing for potential clients	3	5	▪ Decreased revenue and profit; ▪ Loss of market share; ▪ Losing existing clients; ▪ Insolvency or bankruptcy.
2.	Operations	Gathering data from irrelevant sources				
3a.	Monitoring	Clients' needs not monitored				
3b.	Analyzing	Incorrect resources assignment	Production gaps or stopped production	3	5	
4.	Improving	Changes in the business climate not considered	Producing goods and delivering services that are unappealing for potential clients	3	5	
Average risk level:			Unacceptable risk	15		
Risk assessment at the interactions between production processes and senior management						
No. crt.	**Production activity**	**Cause**	**Risks**	**P**	**C**	**Effect**
1.	Planning	Incorrect resource planning	Decreased sales	4	5	▪ Decreased revenue and profit; ▪ Delayed or disrupted projects; ▪ Losing existing clients.
2.	Operations	Incorrect execution				
3a.	Monitoring	Production quality checks not performed	Organizational image negatively affected	3	5	
3b.	Analyzing	Production flow-related issues not analyzed	Unexpected additional production costs	3	4	
4.	Improving	Production flow protocols not optimized	Decreased sales	4	5	
Average risk level:			Unacceptable risk	17		

The majority of the risks that occur at the interactions between senior management and production processes are unacceptable (Table 5.17) – these risks have a negative effect on revenue, profitability, market share and can lead to insolvency or bankruptcy.

Process interaction no. 12 – Risk assessment at the interaction between after-sales processes and quality assurance processes

Table 5.18 presents the risk assessment performed at the interaction between after-sales and quality assurance processes. Risks identified related to limited or faulty troubleshooting affects the image of the organization and leads to additional unforeseen costs during the warranty period.

The materialization of these unacceptable risks can affect the organization's profit and revenue and can lead to decreased sales and losing clients. Therefore, these risks should be included in the risk handling plan in order to prevent possible negative outcomes.

Table 5.18: Risk assessment at the interaction between after-sales processes and quality assurance processes using the PDCA method, developed by the author based on the research conducted during the doctoral period

Risk assessment at the interactions between after-sales processes and quality assurance processes						
No. crt.	**After-sales activity**	Cause	Risks	P	C	Effect
1.	Planning	Incorrect warranty-related budget estimations	▪ Organizational image is negatively affected; ▪ Limited or faulty troubleshooting in the warranty period; ▪ Additional unforeseen costs during warranty period.	3	5	▪ Decreased revenue and profit; ▪ Decreased sales; ▪ Losing existing clients.
2.	Operations	Incorrect troubleshooting in the warranty period	▪ Organizational image is negatively affected; ▪ Limited or faulty troubleshooting in the warranty period; ▪ Additional unforeseen costs during warranty period.	3	5	▪ Decreased revenue and profit; ▪ Decreased sales; ▪ Losing existing clients.
3a.	Monitoring	Faulty products not monitored				
3b.	Analyzing	Redundant errors not analyzed				
4.	Improving	Market needs not considered				
Average risk level:			Unacceptable risk	15		

Risk assessment at the interactions between quality assurance processes and after-sales processes						
No. crt.	**Quality assurance activity**	Cause	Risks	P	C	Effect
1.	Planning	Incorrect quality assurance budget estimations	▪ Delivering faulty products; ▪ Additional unforeseen costs during warranty period.	3	5	▪ Decreased revenue and profit; ▪ Decreased sales.
2.	Operations	Incorrect measurements and verifications				
3a.	Monitoring	Incorrect or incomplete verification protocols				
3b.	Analyzing	Redundant errors not analyzed				
4.	Improving	Quality-related clients' needs not considered	Outdated products and services	3	5	
Average risk level:			Unacceptable risk	15		

Process interaction no. 13 – Risk assessment at the interaction between senior management and after-sales processes

Decreased support services and spare parts sales is the main unacceptable risk that can be caused by management activities or after-sales processes when interacting with one another.

The main causes are inefficient business strategy, incorrect assignment of resources, changes in the business climate and market needs not considered, incorrect warranty-related budget estimations, incorrect offering of spare parts or services, faulty products not monitored and redundant errors not analyzed. Table 5.19 also shows that the interaction of these processes can affect the organizational image and have a negative impact on the relation with customers leading to decreased revenue and profit and losing clients and market share.

Risks related to operations and monitoring activities performed by the management team are tolerable risks and relate to additional unforeseen costs during the warranty period; however, these risks have to be monitored and prevented being caused by gathering data from irrelevant sources and clients' needs not being monitored.

Table 5.19: Risk assessment at the interaction between senior management and after-sales processes using the PDCA method, developed by the author based on the research conducted during the doctoral period

<table>
<tr><th colspan="7">Risk assessment at the interactions between senior management and after-sales processes</th></tr>
<tr><th>No. crt.</th><th>Management activity</th><th>Cause</th><th>Risks</th><th>P</th><th>C</th><th>Effect</th></tr>
<tr><td>1.</td><td>Planning</td><td>Inefficient business strategy</td><td>Decreased support services and spare parts sales</td><td>3</td><td>5</td><td rowspan="6">▪ Decreased revenue and profit;
▪ Loss of market share;
▪ Losing existing clients.</td></tr>
<tr><td>2.</td><td>Operations</td><td>Gathering data from irrelevant sources</td><td rowspan="2">Additional unforeseen costs during warranty period</td><td rowspan="2">2</td><td rowspan="2">4</td></tr>
<tr><td>3a.</td><td>Monitoring</td><td>Clients' needs not monitored</td></tr>
<tr><td>3b.</td><td>Analyzing</td><td>Incorrect resources assignment</td><td rowspan="2">Decreased support services and spare parts sales</td><td rowspan="2">3</td><td rowspan="2">5</td></tr>
<tr><td>4.</td><td>Improving</td><td>Changes in the business climate not considered</td></tr>
<tr><td colspan="3">Average risk level:</td><td>Unacceptable risk</td><td colspan="2">13</td></tr>
<tr><th colspan="7">Risk assessment at the interactions between after-sales processes and senior management</th></tr>
<tr><th>No. crt.</th><th>After-sales activity</th><th>Cause</th><th>Risks</th><th>P</th><th>C</th><th>Effect</th></tr>
<tr><td>1.</td><td>Planning</td><td>Incorrect warranty-related budget estimations</td><td>Decreased services, support and spare parts sales</td><td>3</td><td>5</td><td>Decreased revenue and profit</td></tr>
<tr><td>2.</td><td>Operations</td><td>Incorrect offering of spare parts or services</td><td rowspan="4">▪ Organizational image is negatively affected;
▪ Decreased services, support and spare parts sales.</td><td rowspan="4">3</td><td rowspan="4">5</td><td rowspan="5">▪ Decreased revenue and profit;
▪ Decreased sales;
▪ Losing existing clients.</td></tr>
<tr><td>3a.</td><td>Monitoring</td><td>Faulty products not monitored</td></tr>
<tr><td>3b.</td><td>Analyzing</td><td>Redundant errors not analyzed</td></tr>
<tr><td>4.</td><td>Improving</td><td>Market needs not considered</td></tr>
<tr><td colspan="3">Average risk level:</td><td>Unacceptable risk</td><td colspan="2">15</td></tr>
</table>

Process interaction no. 14 – Risk assessment at the interaction between quality assurance processes and marketing and sales processes

Table 5.20 presents the main risks at the interaction between quality assurance processes and marketing and sales processes. From 5 identified risks three are identified as unacceptable affecting the organization's performance indicators (revenue and profit).

Table 5.20: Risk assessment at the interaction between quality assurance processes and marketing and sales processes using the PDCA method, developed by the author based on the research conducted during the doctoral period

Risk assessment at the interactions between quality assurance processes and marketing and sales processes						
No. crt.	**Quality assurance activity**	Cause	Risks	P	C	Effect
1.	Planning	Incorrect quality assurance budget estimations	▪ Organizational image is negatively affected; ▪ Producing goods and delivering services that are unappealing for potential clients	3	5	▪ Decreased revenue and profit; ▪ Decreased sales; ▪ Losing existing clients.
2.	Operations	Incorrect measurements and verifications				
3a.	Monitoring	Incorrect or incomplete verification protocols				
3b.	Analyzing	Redundant errors not analyzed				
4.	Improving	Quality-related clients' needs not considered	Outdated products and services	3	5	
Average risk level:			Unacceptable risk	15		
Risk assessment at the interactions between marketing and sales processes and quality assurance processes						
No. crt.	**Marketing activity**	Cause	Risks	P	C	Effect
1.	Planning	Marketing campaigns incorrectly planned	Losing seasonal opportunities	2	4	▪ Decreased revenue and profit; ▪ Losing market share; ▪ Losing existing clients.
2.	Operations	Poor quality marketing campaigns	Decreased clients' satisfaction	3	5	
3a.	Monitoring	Market-related data not monitored	Outdated marketing campaigns	2	5	
3b.	Analyzing	Market needs not analyzed				
4.	Improving	No innovations				
Average risk level:			Tolerable risk	11		

Process interaction no. 15 – Risk assessment at the interaction between procurement processes and suppliers

Delayed payments to suppliers and delayed orders can be risks generated by the procurement department when interacting with suppliers (Table 5.21). Another risks that can be generated by procurement activities relates to renegotiations that can delay projects and involve important costs for the organizations.

Table 5.21: Risk assessment at the interaction between procurement processes and suppliers using the PDCA method, developed by the author based on the research conducted during the doctoral period

Risk assessment at the interactions between procurement processes and suppliers						
No. crt.	**Procurement activity**	Cause	Risks	P	C	Effect
1.	Planning	Incorrect sourcing budget planning	Delayed payments to suppliers	4	5	▪ Decreased revenue and profit; ▪ Production disruptions or stop supply; ▪ Losing existing partnerships with suppliers.
2.	Operations	Sourcing errors				
3a.	Monitoring	Delivery terms not tracked	Delayed orders	4	4	
3b.	Analyzing	Budget not calculated correctly				
			Stop supply	2	5	
4.	Improving	Disadvantageous negotiations with suppliers	Delayed project due to renegotiations	2	5	
Average risk level:			Unacceptable risk	14		
Risk assessment at the interactions between suppliers and procurement processes						
No. crt.	**Suppliers' activity**	Cause	Risks	P	C	Effect
1.	Planning	Incorrect production and delivery planning	▪ Delayed deliveries; ▪ Sales disruptions.	4	5	▪ Decreased revenue and profit; ▪ Production disruptions or stop supply; ▪ Losing existing partnerships with clients.
2.	Operations	Incorrect order management				
3a.	Monitoring	Delivery terms not tracked				
3b.	Analyzing	Budget not calcu-lated correctly	Exceeded project budget	3	5	
4.	Improving	Disadvantageous negotiations with clients or raw materials suppliers	▪ Sales disruptions; ▪ Cancelled contracts.	3	5	Losing existing clients
Average risk level:			Unacceptable risk	17		

Summarized results related to evaluating the probability of occurrence and the consequences of risks related to interactions between business processes using the PDCA method in organizations

The average risk assessment results are presented in Table 5.22. For each interaction between two processes Average risk levels and risk types are listed. With one exception related to tolerable risks that can occur at process interactions level between contracting and financial processes all other risks are evaluated as unacceptable. Specialized literature and specialized managers consider that all unacceptable risks have to be included in the risk handling plan in order to prevent the negative effects of risk materialization.

Table 5.22: Average risk assessment results related to business process interactions using the PDCA method, developed by the author based on the research conducted during the doctoral period

Interaction no.	Process interactions between processes:		Average risk level	Average risk type
1	External environment	Marketing and sales	15	Unacceptable risk
2	Marketing and sales	Contract management and legal	13	Unacceptable risk
3	Senior management	Marketing and sales	15	Unacceptable risk
4	Contract management and legal	Financial	9	Tolerable risk
5	Senior management	Contract management and legal	14	Unacceptable risk
6	Procurement	Financial	14	Unacceptable risk
7	Financial	Production	15	Unacceptable risk
8	Senior management	Financial	15	Unacceptable risk
9	Planning	Production	14	Unacceptable risk
10	Production	After-sales	15	Unacceptable risk
11	Senior management	Production	16	Unacceptable risk
12	After-sales	Quality assurance	15	Unacceptable risk
13	Senior management	After-sales	14	Unacceptable risk
14	Quality assurance	Marketing and sales	13	Unacceptable risk
15	Procurement	Suppliers	16	Unacceptable risk

5.3 Risk assessment related to the interactions between the organization and outsourced business processes using the PDCA method

In the past years one of the most important challenges encountered by process managers was deciding which business processes to outsource in order to increase revenue and profit margin. Specialized literature, academicians and managers have concluded lately that not all the outsourcing or offshoring decisions were profitable for the organizations so that a new "business trend" was launched related to backsourcing and reshoring. While managers have rushed into revising and reversing decisions related to outsourcing and offshoring, recent studies have shown that an extensive analysis has to be performed before making a choice. It is possible that some of the business processes have to be backsourced, but at the same time organizations would benefit more from not reversing decisions related to other processes. The "rightshoring" approach refers to a model for the strategic sourcing of business processes that managers can use in order to choose whether to fully own a process or contract it and where to execute it.

The study aims to underline the importance of assessing risks related to each of the choices described by the rightshoring approach before taking decisions related to outsourcing, offshoring, backsourcing or reshoring business processes. Results are based on interviews with

5.3.1 General context of the research

Worldwide economic dynamics and globalization have set the premises for outsourcing business processes across trade borders. Managers have started contracting processes to third-party providers in order to save costs, increase sales and profit using various outsourcing models. Organizations chose newly developing countries while aiming for new outsourcing opportunities or expanding sales markets. While knowledge-intensive business services are usually kept inside the organization, managers have transferred manufacturing and support services to third-party providers or fully owned branches or subsidiaries located in low-wage countries.

In order to monitor and control process results managers have allocated resources for corporate governance in order to ensure business sustainability. Through corporate governance organizations have to acknowledge and manage all issues encountered at the interaction between the organization and each of the outsourced processes, such as decreased quality of service or manufacturing faulty products, clients' dissatisfaction, increased production costs or wages. Changes in the foreign country's economic and political climate can also be a threat for ensuring business sustainability so that organizations have to continuously identify, evaluate and analyze risks at the interaction with each of the outsourced business processes. Understanding the differences related to business and social factors with impact on sustainable performance, as well as finding efficient mechanisms to control foreign entities and third-party products and services were important challenges for the organizations.

Professional experience has shown managers in time that not all business decisions related to contracting processes to third-party providers were value-adding for the organizations. Many of the outsourced or offshored processes with quality issues lead to additional costs that significantly decreased business profitability or even resulted in losses for the organization. Increased transportation costs, taxes and wages, lack of flexibility related to adapting to clients' needs and requirements, limited know-how were the main reasons for organizations starting the internalization of business processes.

In the past years experts have developed new business models focused on taking the right decision when choosing whether to outsource, offshore, backsource or reshore business processes. While backsourcing or reshoring served the purpose of reversing outsourcing or offshoring decisions, managers and literature specialists have observed that not all decisions have to be revised - organizations with multiple business processes outsourced or offshored can internalize only part of the processes handled by third-party providers or foreign branches and subsidiaries. The "rightsourcing" model has been developed as a tool for decision-making in order to maximize value for the organizations.

5.3.2 Objectives and methodology

a) Research objectives

The main objective of the research is to evaluate the probability of occurrence and the consequences of risks at the interaction between the organization and outsourced business processes. Process interactions between processes executed in different locations that are fully owned or contracted to third-party providers were investigated in order to identify risks and determine causes for each activity according to the PDCA method. The research also determines the possible effects of risk materialization related to the main performance indicators.

b) Research methodology

In order to perform the investigation interviews with 7 managers with professional experience related to risk assessment in 11 organizations were conducted in November 2017. With the exception of internal processes, process interactions were determined between the organization and business processes executed offsite, nearshore or offshore. Depending on ownership process interactions were defined between the organization and fully owned processes or contracted to a third-party service provider or manufacturer. Risk assessment was performed in relation with each interaction between business processes defined in Table 5.23. Further causes and effects of the main identified risks were discussed; the interviewees have shared their perspective related to risk types and as a result a qualitative risk evaluation was performed (Annex H). Following, risk levels were determined with consideration to the qualitative risk evaluation.

Table 5.23: Business process categories based on ownership and location, developed by the author based on the research conducted during the doctoral period

<table>
<tr><th colspan="2" rowspan="2">Business process categories</th><th colspan="2">Business processes by ownership:</th></tr>
<tr><td>Owned by the organization</td><td>Owned by the third-party provider</td></tr>
<tr><td rowspan="4">Business processes by location:</td><td>Onsite</td><td rowspan="2">Fully owned in a domestic country</td><td rowspan="2">Third-party provider in a domestic country</td></tr>
<tr><td>Offsite</td></tr>
<tr><td>Nearshore</td><td rowspan="2">Fully owned in a foreign country</td><td rowspan="2">Third-party provider in a foreign country</td></tr>
<tr><td>Offshore</td></tr>
</table>

The risks were identified in relation with 4 categories of business processes:

a) Business processes fully owned by the organization and executed in a domestic country;
b) Business processes fully owned by the organization and executed in a foreign country;
c) Business processes owned by a third-party provider in a domestic country;
d) Business processes owned by a third-party provider in a foreign country.

The next research objective is to determine which methods are used by managers when deciding whether to internalize or externalize business processes. A qualitative analysis was performed based on answers from the interviewed managers related to evaluating options and assessing risks that can occur at the interaction between the organization and outsourced, nearshored or offshored processes.

5.3.3 Research results regarding the evaluation of the probability of occurrence and the consequences of risks related to the interactions between the organization and outsourced business processes using the PDCA method

The results of the analysis based on the information shared by the respondents indicated 6 main risks that can occur at the interaction between business processes executed inside and outside the organization:

1. Incomplete or incorrect process design as a result of planning activities;
2. Losing full control and decreased quality of service as a result of operational activities;
3. High costs with wages and transportation as a result of operational activities;
4. Outdated control mechanisms as a result of monitoring activities;
5. Inefficient processes as a result of analyzing activities;
6. Inefficient and outdated processes as a result of continuous improvement activities.

a) Results related to risk assessment at process interactions level between business processes fully owned by the organization and executed inside and outside the organization

Table 5.24 shows risk levels and risk types for each of the identified risks. The most important aspect is that full ownership decreases risk levels related to control and quality of service. Process interactions between processes executed onsite can mainly lead to tolerable risks because an improved control decreases the risks' probability of appearance.

The identified risks relate to incomplete or incorrect process design, losing full control of the process and decreased quality of service, high costs with wages and transportation and inefficient processes. These risks have to be monitored and in case the probability of occurrence increases, actions have to be taken in order to prevent possible negative outcomes. The possible effects of these risks are decreased revenue, profit and productivity, as well as losing clients.

Organizational processes performed remotely involve higher risks because distance involves less control and additional costs. The unacceptable risks identified at the interactions between the organization and shared processes executed offsite are incomplete or incorrect design, losing full control of the process and decreased quality of service, as well as inefficient and outdated processes. These risks can lead to losing market share as a result of decreased customer satisfaction.

Table 5.24: Risk assessment related to interactions between business processes owned by the organization and executed in the domestic country using the PDCA method, developed by the author based on the research conducted during the doctoral period

Risks related to interactions between business processes between processes inside the organization (full ownership, onsite)						
No. crt.	**Process activity**	Cause	Risks	P	C	Effect
1.	Planning	Lack of adaptation to organizational changes	Incomplete or incorrect process design	2	5	▪ Decreased revenue and profit; ▪ Decreased productivity; ▪ No new clients and losing existing clients.
2.	Operations	Lack of feedback between processes	Losing full control and decreased quality of service	2	5	
		Business climate changes	High costs with wages and transportation	1	5	
3a.	Monitoring	New organizational changes are not considered	Outdated control mechanisms	2	5	
3b.	Analyzing	Processes are not analyzed	Inefficient processes	2	5	
4.	Improving	Processes are not updated	Inefficient and outdated processes	4	5	
Average risk level:			Unacceptable risk	11		
Risks related to interactions between business processes between the organization and shared processes executed offsite						
No. crt.	**Process activity**	Cause	Risks	P	C	Effect
1.	Planning	Lack of adaptation to organizational changes	Incomplete or incorrect process design	3	5	▪ Decreased revenue and profit; ▪ Decreased productivity; ▪ No new clients and losing existing clients.
2.	Operations	Lack of feedback between processes	Losing full control and decreased quality of service	3	5	
		Business climate changes	High costs with wages and transportation	2	5	
3a.	Monitoring	New organizational changes are not considered	Outdated control mechanisms	2	5	
3b.	Analyzing	Processes are not analyzed	Inefficient processes	3	5	
4.	Improving	Processes are not updated	Inefficient and outdated processes	4	5	
Average risk level:			Tolerable risk	18		

Process interactions between the organization and processes executed in a foreign country are presented in Table 5.25. All risks that occur at process interactions level are unacceptable. Probability of appearance is significantly higher because of lack of control; processes executed nearshore involve high risks (risk level value = 20) related to high costs with wages and transportation and inefficient and outdated processes.

Despite the fact that processes are owned by the organization, changes in the foreign country's business climate can lead to very high or maximum risks related to increased costs that can be generated between the organization and captive processes executed offshore. Losing control of the process and decreased quality of service are also important risks that have to be considered when offshoring processes.

Table 5.25: Risk assessment related to interactions between business processes owned by the organization and executed in a foreign country using the PDCA method, developed by the author based on the research conducted during the doctoral period

Risks related to interactions between business processes between the organization and captive processes executed nearshore						
No. crt.	**Process activity**	Cause	Risks	P	C	Effect
1.	Planning	Lack of adaptation to organizational changes	Incomplete or incorrect process design	3	5	▪ Decreased revenue and profit; ▪ Decreased productivity; ▪ Closing foreign branch or subsidiary; ▪ No new clients and losing existing clients.
2.	Operations	Lack of feedback between processes	Losing full control and decreased quality of service	3	5	
		Business climate changes	High costs with wages and transportation	4	5	
3a.	Monitoring	New organizational changes are not considered	Outdated control mechanisms	3	5	
3b.	Analyzing	Processes are not analyzed	Inefficient processes	3	5	
4.	Improving	Processes are not updated	Inefficient and outdated processes	4	5	
Average risk level:			Unacceptable risk	17		
Risks related to interactions between business processes between the organization and captive processes executed offshore						
No. crt.	**Process activity**	Cause	Risks	P	C	Effect
1.	Planning	Lack of adaptation to organizational changes	Incomplete or incorrect process design	3	5	▪ Decreased revenue and profit;

2.	Operations	Lack of feedback between processes	Losing full control and decreased quality of service	4	5	▪ Decreased productivity; ▪ Closing foreign branch or subsidiary; ▪ No new clients and losing existing clients.
		Business climate changes	High costs with wages and transportation	5	5	
3a.	Monitoring	New organizational changes are not considered	Outdated control mechanisms	3	5	
3b.	Analyzing	Processes are not analyzed	Inefficient processes	3	5	
4.	Improving	Processes are not updated	Inefficient and outdated processes	4	5	
Average risk level:			Tolerable risk	18		

b) Results related to risk assessment at process interactions level between the organization and business processes fully owned by third-party providers executed inside and outside the organization

Process interactions between the organization and business processes owned by a third-party provider executed onsite involve both tolerable and unacceptable risks (Table 5.26).

Table 5.26: Risk assessment related to interactions between the organization and business processes owned by third-party providers and executed in the domestic country using the PDCA method, developed by the author based on the research conducted during the doctoral period

Risk assessment related to interactions between the organization and business processes executed by a third-party provided onsite						
No. crt.	**Process activity**	Cause	Risks	P	C	Effect
1.	Planning	Lack of adaptation to organizational changes	Incomplete or incorrect process design	2	5	▪ Decreased revenue and profit; ▪ Decreased productivity; ▪ No new clients and losing existing clients.
2.	Operations	Lack of feedback between processes	Losing full control and decreased quality of service	3	5	
		Business climate changes	High costs with wages and transportation	2	5	
3a.	Monitoring	New organizational changes are not considered	Outdated control mechanisms	2	5	
3b.	Analyzing	Processes are not analyzed	Inefficient processes	3	5	
4.	Improving	Processes are not updated	Inefficient and outdated processes	4	5	
Average risk level:			Unacceptable risk	13		

Risk assessment related to interactions between the organization and business processes executed by a third-party provided offsite						
No. crt.	**Process activity**	Cause	Risks	P	C	Effect
1.	Planning	Lack of adaptation to organizational changes	Incomplete or incorrect process design	3	5	▪ Decreased revenue and profit; ▪ Decreased productivity; ▪ No new clients and losing existing clients.
2.	Operations	Lack of feedback between processes	Losing full control and decreased quality of service	4	5	
		Business climate changes	High costs with wages and transportation	3	5	
3a.	Monitoring	New organizational changes are not considered	Outdated control mechanisms	3	5	
3b.	Analyzing	Processes are not analyzed	Inefficient processes	3	5	
4.	Improving	Processes are not updated	Inefficient and outdated processes	4	5	
Average risk level:			Tolerable risk	17		

The highest risk levels calculated were caused by process not being updated on time, so that process results provided by the third-party organization are not value-adding. Losing full control of the process and decreased quality of service, as well as inefficient and outdated processes are unacceptable risks that have to be included in the risk handling plan. Concerning interactions between the organization and processes executed by a third-party provider offsite, risk levels are higher because the risks of losing control of the process and decreased quality of service are more probable.

Table 5.27 indicates very high risks that can be caused by changes in the foreign country's economic and political climate that lead to high costs with wages and transportation.

In the case of processes executed offshore, losing control of the process and decreased quality of service have maximum risk levels. These high risks relate to high costs with wages and transportation, losing full control of the process and decreased quality of service and inefficient and outdated processes. The main possible negative outcomes of risk materialization can be decreased revenue, profit and productivity, no new clients or losing existing clients and cancelled contracts with the third-party provider.

Table 5.27: Risk assessment related to interactions between the organization and business processes owned by third-party providers and executed in a foreign country using the PDCA method, developed by the author based on the research conducted during the doctoral period

Risk assessment related to interactions between the organization and business processes executed by a third-party provided nearshore						
No. crt.	**Process activity**	Cause	Risks	P	C	Effect
1.	Planning	Lack of adaptation to organizational changes	Incomplete or incorrect process design	4	5	▪ Decreased revenue and profit; ▪ Decreased productivity; ▪ No new clients and losing existing clients; ▪ Cancelled contract with third party provider.
2.	Operations	Lack of feedback between processes	Losing full control and decreased quality of service	4	5	
		Business climate changes	High costs with wages and transportation	5	5	
3a.	Monitoring	New organizational changes are not considered	Outdated control mechanisms	4	5	
3b.	Analyzing	Processes are not analyzed	Inefficient processes	3	5	
4.	Improving	Processes are not updated	Inefficient and outdated processes	4	5	
Average risk level:			Unacceptable risk	20		
Risk assessment related to interactions between the organization and business processes executed by a third-party executed offshore						
No. crt.	**Process activity**	Cause	Risks	P	C	Effect
1.	Planning	Lack of adaptation to organizational changes	Incomplete or incorrect process design	4	5	▪ Decreased revenue and profit; ▪ Decreased productivity; ▪ No new clients and losing existing clients; ▪ Cancelled contract with third party provider.
2.	Operations	Lack of feedback between processes	Losing full control and decreased quality of service	5	5	
		Business climate changes	High costs with wages and transportation	5	5	
3a.	Monitoring	New organizational changes are not considered	Outdated control mechanisms	4	5	
3b.	Analyzing	Processes are not analyzed	Inefficient processes	4	5	
4.	Improving	Processes are not updated	Inefficient and outdated processes	5	5	
Average risk level:			Tolerable risk	23		

Summarized results related to risk assessment related to interactions between the organization and outsourced business processes using the PDCA method

Figure 5.8 indicates the average risk levels calculated for each interaction between internalized and externalized business processes. The overall result is that no matter the location of execution, risks related to business processes performed by third-party providers are higher. Also, risks levels are higher depending on the distance between the organization and the location of process execution, because business processes and all related costs are harder to control the longer the distance between the organization and the location where the process is executed.

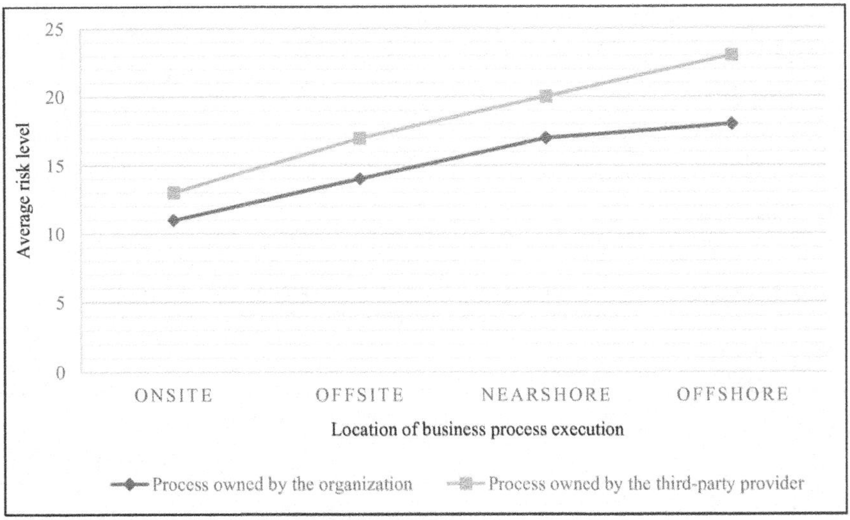

Figure 5.8: Average levels of risks related to interactions between business processes owned by the organization or third-party providers executed in the domestic country or a foreign country, developed by the author based on the research conducted during the doctoral period.

The main advantages related to outsourcing business processes are usually related to lower wages and decreased operating costs; unfortunately sometimes costs involved in solving quality-related issues can determine organizations to take backsourcing decisions. While risks related to interactions between business processes within the organization are usually tolerable or unacceptable, outsourcing and backsourcing processes involve new risks that can have immediate negative effects on the organization. Therefore, organizations have to evaluate risks related to all outsourcing or backsourcing processes and take decisions based on the complete risk analysis.

6 Possibilities of improving risk assessment related to organizational business processes in the context of ensuring sustainable performance

6.1 Applying the PDCA and FMEA methods during the risk assessment process related to organizational business processes

Today's changes in the business environment, new threats and globalization requirements have forced managers to modify their strategies and to take "certain measures in order to assure continuity of operations in any organization" (Jereb, Ivanuša and Rosi, 2013).

The research proposes extending the risk assessment process by applying the Failure Mode and Effects Analysis (FMEA) method that is traditionally used in medicine and engineering. In a study conducted in 2014, Chang, Chang and Lai state that the FMEA method has been used "to identify the critical risk events and predict a system failure to avoid or reduce the potential failure modes and their effect on operations".
Risk levels are usually calculated by determining probability of appearance and the consequence of risk materialization; however, there are no control mechanisms that analyze the conditions for risk materialization, so that managers include all unacceptable risks in the risk handling plan.

Following, resources are used and actions are taken in order to prevent these risks instead of monitoring them and acting only when certain conditions are met that can lead to risk materialization. There is no algorithm that determines when to take actions in order to control important business risks and decrease risk handling costs. Therefore, the study investigates the effect of introducing detection (also known as probability of detection), the risk assessment attribute defined by the FMEA method, as a third attribute in the risk assessment process in order to create a control mechanism that allows risks handling actions to be taken only in case of imminent risks.

Interviews with experienced managers and process specialists were carried out in order to determine if detection turns risk assessment in a more efficient process and also if it decreases risk handling costs with direct impact on the business performance indicators.

R. M. Bejinariu, *Sustainable Business Performance and Risk Management*,
Sustainable Management, Wertschöpfung und Effizienz,
https://doi.org/10.1007/978-3-658-29389-5_6

6.1.1 General context of the research

The current market conditions involve increasing quality of products or services and decreasing prices – this automatically leads to a very competitive business environment with sometimes lower profit margins. Finding the perfect balance between price and quality according to the clients' needs is a priority for any commercial organization and also involves more risks, mainly because there are no backup solutions and budgets to work with in case something goes wrong.

Organizations have started having a higher risk appetite and taking on more risks in order to stay competitive. Risk assessment results are directly linked to risk appetite and business growth; therefore, the process has become a very important tool for organizations. By ensuring the accuracy of control mechanisms, the FMEA method can improve monitoring and controlling processes and systems. Using detection as a third attribute during risk assessment ensures a more accurate and precise evaluation that directly leads to risks materializing less often and decreased risk handling costs.
While probability of appearance and consequence are usually estimated by process owners based on their experience and other subjective data, detection evaluates the conditions that determine risk materialization; by permanently monitoring the organization's performance indicators, detection can determine if certain conditions are met that can result in risk materialization.
According to a research by Carbone and Tippett (2015), "by adding the detection value to the risk quantification process, another measure beyond the typical risk score is made available to the project team".

The study is based on answers to the following questions used during a research performed in 2017:

1. *What is the role of detection in risk assessment?*
2. *Can detection be applied during the risk assessment process in organizations from all areas of business?*
3. *Which are the most important control mechanisms that should be evaluated in order to ensure risk assessment accuracy?*
4. *How can organizations reduce risk handling costs as a result of using the FMEA method?*

By verifying the accuracy of the standard risk assessment attributes (probability of appearance and consequence), detection can be considered a control mechanism itself. The extended risk assessment method involves many advantages like improved control of risks and monitoring of imminent risks, prioritizing risk contingency strategic solutions and a higher participation of the team members.

6.1.2 Objectives and research methodology

a) Research objectives

The research aims to evaluate the effects of applying detection as a third attribute in the risk assessment process and to check if this new model is applicable to any process or area of business. Activities related to any process can generate important risks when interacting with other processes and activities from different organizational departments or with the external environment (other organizations, state institutions, etc.). Process interactions are the main source for operational risks with direct impact on the organization's performance indicators and business results.

The first objective of the study is to determine the main advantages of using the FMEA method and the effects of introducing detection as a third attribute in the risk assessment process. Another objective of the research is to determine the probability of occurrence, consequences and the probability of detection during the risk assessment process related to organizational business processes.

Following, the last objective is to determine the impact of applying the FMEA method during the risk assessment related to interactions between the organization and outsourced business processes.

b) Research methodology

Determining the main advantages of the extended risk assessment process is based on data gathered during 8 interviews conducted between February and March 2017 with managers and specialists from different areas of business.

Additionally, 93 questionnaires were sent by email between November 2016 and March 2017 and 66 individuals have sent feedback, so that a total of 74 respondents from 23 organizations have answered to questions related to the proposed topic.

Given the fact that the FMEA method is usually used in medicine and engineering, the study gathers information from the following industries in order to prove the versatility of detection: fast-moving commercial goods, constructions, pharmaceuticals and agriculture.

The questionnaire was structured on 7 questions designed to test the following hypotheses:

1. *Risk assessment using the FMEA method can be used in organizations from all industries;*
2. *Organizations can reduce risks reoccurrence by eliminating the main causes for the most dangerous risks or by increasing the probability of detection;*
3. *If detected more often, a lower number risks will be introduced in the risk handling plan, therefore risk handling costs will be reduced.*

The second research objective was targeted during interviews with managers in the period October-November 2017. Based on the research conducted during the doctoral period, the results are presented in tables for each step of the methodology used. The following steps were included in the methodology:

1. Risk analysis for risks related to interactions between business processes including calculating Risk Level 1 as the mathematical product between probability of occurrence (P) and consequence (C) and determining risk type;
2. Identification of the performance indicators impacted by each of the identified risks;
3. Investigating the main risk materialization conditions associated with each organizational performance indicator;
4. Determining the probability of detection (D) for all risk materialization conditions associated with the organizational performance indicators;
5. Calculating the new risk level (Risk level 2) after applying detection to the risk analysis results by multiplying the value of Risk level 1 with the probability of detection;
6. Indicating the proposed risk type after a result of applying detection using the proposed risk tolerance intervals defined for risk assessment using 3 attributes;
7. Presenting the final results related to the number of risks introduced in the risk handling plan as a result of using the FMEA method during risk assessment related to business processes;
8. Presenting the final results related to the number of risks that impact each of the organizational performance indicators.

Risk levels and risk types were calculated using the values and color coding presented in Table 6.1.

Table 6.1: Proposed risk tolerance levels and risk types using 3 attributes during risk assessment, developed by the author based on the research conducted during the doctoral period

Proposed tolerance intervals for Risk Level 2	Proposed risk types
1	Very low risk
2 – 30	Acceptable risk
31 – 60	Tolerable risk
61 – 100	Unacceptable risk
101 – 125	Very high risk

The methodology used for determining the impact of applying the FMEA method during risk assessment related to interactions between the organization and outsourced business processes is based on a study performed in November 2017 based on interviews with 7 managers with risk assessment professional experience in 11 organizations.

For each risk identified onsite (within the organization) and between the organization and the processes executed in a different location, either owned by the organization or by a third-party provider, a qualitative risk evaluation was performed by the interviewees.

The goal of the interviews was to evaluate risks and to determine risk types after applying detection, so that the respondents have estimated Risk Level 1 (Annex H). Following, based on these results, Risk Level 2 was determined for each risk as the mathematical product between probability of detection and Risk Level 1.

6.1.3 Research results related applying the PDCA and FMEA methods during the risk assessment process related to organizational business processes

Question 1 (Figure 6.1): *Have you ever considered using the FMEA method in the risk assessment process?*

Results – The first question related to the status of integration of the FMEA method in organizations. Almost half of the organizations have never considered the FMEA method in order to improve risk assessment and only less than 18% are using it. Fortunately, almost one third are interested in testing it and 8,11% have already started pilot projects including detection.

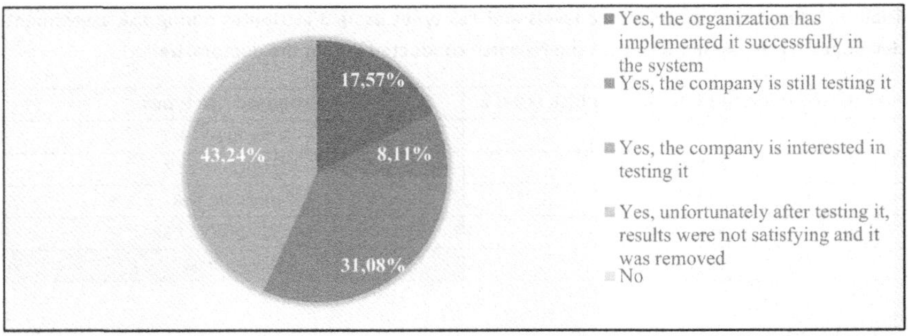

Figure 6.1: Risk assessment using the FMEA method in organizations, developed by the author based on the research conducted during the doctoral period.

Question 2 (Figure 6.2): *Which are the highest threats when performing risk assessment?*

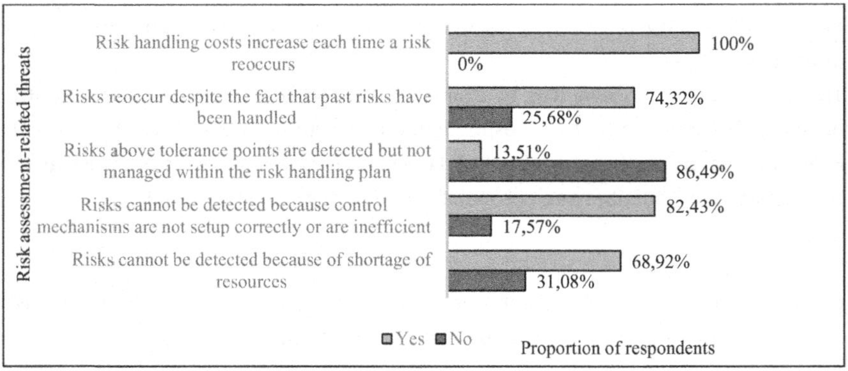

Figure 6.2 - Highest threats regarding risk assessment related to business process interactions, developed by the author based on the research conducted during the doctoral period.

Results – The highest threat and the main problem related to identifying risks is that control mechanisms are not being setup correctly or are inefficient - 82,43% of the respondents agree with this statement. According to almost 70% of the interviewees another important issue is budget. Most of the managers and specialists consider that budgets are limited and there are no special resources assigned for the process. Fortunately, 86,49% of the interviewees answer that once detected, risks are considered in the risk handling plan according to the evaluated risk levels. On the other hand, almost 75% of the respondents say that risks reoccur despite the fact that prevention actions were taken. All interviewees consider risk reoccurrence as a high threat for the organization leading to important costs with risk handling.

Question 3 (Figure 6.3): *Do you think the risk assessment process using 3 attributes should be used in your area of business?*

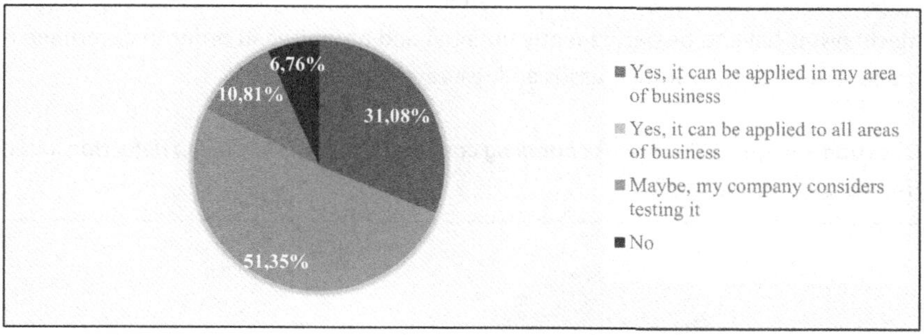

Figure 6.3: The versatility of using the FMEA method during risk assessment, developed by the author based on the research conducted during the doctoral period.

Results – Almost a third of the managers and specialists agree that detection can be used in organizations from their area of business and more than half state that the extended risk assessment process is very versatile and can be used in all areas of business. Another almost 11% of the interviewees consider testing the FMEA method in order to improve risk assessment within their organization.

Question 4 (Figure 6.4): *Which are the main advantages of using detection as a third attribute in the risk evaluation process?*

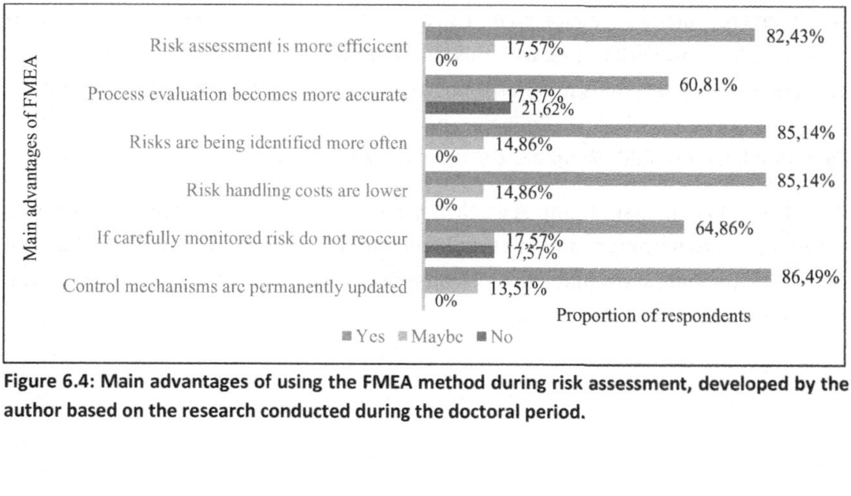

Figure 6.4: Main advantages of using the FMEA method during risk assessment, developed by the author based on the research conducted during the doctoral period.

Results – Most of the managers and specialists consider that applying detection in the risk analysis leads to a more efficient risk assessment process. Also, process evaluation becomes more accurate according to 61% of the interviewees. Risks are being identified more often and risk handling costs are considerably lower according to 85,14% of the respondents. Concerning risk reoccurrence, 65% of the interviewees agree that it can be prevented by carefully monitoring risks; additionally, control mechanisms have to be permanently updated and optimized in order to determine if probability of occurrence increases and risks are imminent.

Question 5 (Figure 6.5): *Are risk handling costs reduced by introducing detection in the risk assessment process?*

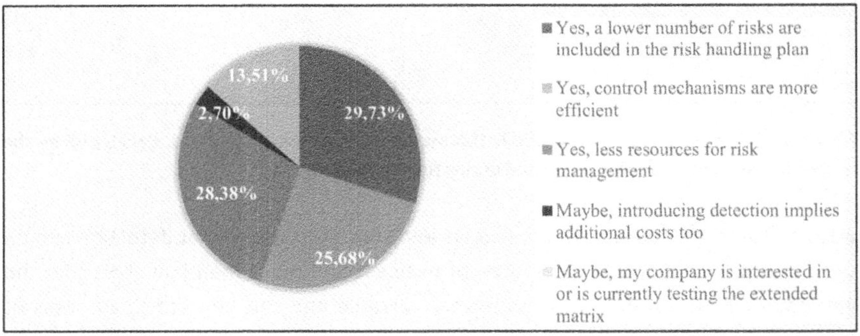

Figure 6.5: The effects of the FMEA method on risk handling costs, developed by the author based on the research conducted during the doctoral period.

Results – Risk handling costs are reduced as a result of a lower number of risks being introduced in the risk handling plan according to almost 30% of the respondents. As a result, less resources are allocated for risk assessment actions – another 28,38% of the managers and specialists agree with this statement. Also, a quarter of the interviewees consider risk assessment is more efficient as a result of applying the FMEA method.

Question 6 (Figure 6.6): *What are the main causes for detection not being used?*

Results – Finally managers and specialists were asked about their opinion related to the main causes for detection not being implemented in organizations. More than half of the respondents state that a low risk appetite is the main reason for managers not investing more in risk assessment.

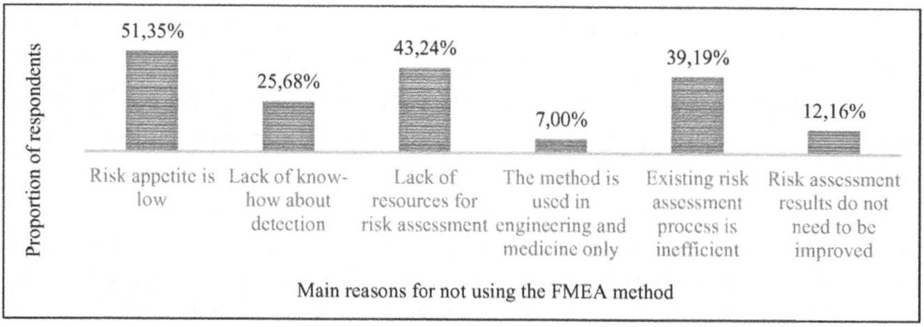

Figure 6.6: Main causes for not using the FMEA method during risk assessment, developed by the author based on the research conducted during the doctoral period.

Another 43,24% of the interviewees agree that lack of budget and other resources can lead to organizations being reluctant to applying detection; integration costs, human resources, time and effort are resources that may not be available for extending risk assessment. Interviewees (39,19%) complain about their existing risk assessment process, consider it inefficient and wouldn't invest in upgrading it.

According to a third of the managers and specialists consider that the FMEA method is only used in industries like engineering and medicine. Lack of know-how related to detection (according to 25,68% of the respondents) and risk assessment results not needing to be improved (according to 12,16% of the respondents) are also causes for organizations not extending the risk assessment process.

6.1.4 Determining the probability of occurrence, consequences and probability of detection during the risk assessment process related to organizational business processes

Process interaction no. 1 – Applying the PDCA and FMEA methods during risk assessment at the interaction between marketing and sales processes and the external business environment

Process interactions between the marketing and sales department and the external environment can lead to unacceptable risks in the relation with clients, creditors, competition and shareholders. From the 2 unacceptable risks determined by probability of occurrence and consequence identified between marketing and sales processes and clients, only one is considered a threat after applying detection (Table 6.2).

The study also shows that all the risks identified as unacceptable between the marketing and sales processes and creditors in the initial analysis turn into tolerable risks after applying detection. In the case of risks identified between marketing and sales processes and competitive organizations, these do not change after applying detection.

Table 6.2: Applying the PDCA and FMEA methods during risk assessment at the interaction between the marketing and sales processes and the external business environment (clients and creditors), developed by the author based on the research conducted during the doctoral period

No. crt.	Risks	P	C	Risk Level 1	Impacted performance indicators	Risk materialization conditions	D	Risk Level 2	Proposed risk type
Risk assessment at the interaction between the marketing and sales processes and clients									
1.	Outdated products and services	4	5	20	Number of repeat customers and new clients	Decreased during the past 2 months	2	40	Tolerable risk
					Market share	▪ New competitors ▪ New technology	4	80	Unacceptable risk
2.	Decreased clients' satisfaction	3	5	15			4	60	Tolerable risk
					Number of repeat customers and new clients	Decreased during the past 2 months	2	30	Tolerable risk
No. risks to be handled		2					1		
Risk assessment at the interaction between the marketing and sales processes and creditors									
1.	Delayed deliveries, invoicing and cashing in from clients	3	5	15	Number of repeat customers and new clients	Decreased during the past 2 months	2	30	Tolerable risk
					Liquidity	Cash flow interruptions	4	60	Tolerable risk
					Market share	▪ New competitors ▪ New technology	4	60	Tolerable risk
2.	Inefficient assignment of financial resources	3	5	15			4	60	Tolerable risk
					Profitability	Decreased during the past 2 months	2	30	Tolerable risk
No. risks to be handled		2					0		

Table 6.3 shows that only one of the risks related to organizational business processes identified between marketing and sales processes and shareholders is considered unacceptable after applying detection.

Table 6.3: Applying the PDCA and FMEA methods during risk assessment at the interaction between the marketing and sales processes and the external business environment (competing organizations and shareholders), developed by the author based on the research conducted during the doctoral period

No. crt.	Risks	P	C	Risk Level 1	Impacted performance indicators	Risk materialization conditions	D	Risk Level 2	Proposed risk type
Risk assessment at the interaction between the marketing and sales processes and competing organizations									
1.	Outdated products and services	4	5	20	Number of repeat customers and new clients	Decreased during the past 2 months	2	40	Tolerable risk
					Market share	▪ New competitors ▪ New technology	4	80	Unacceptable risk
No. risks to be handled		1					1		
Risk assessment at the interaction between the marketing and sales processes and shareholders									
1.	Disruptions in the production lines	3	5	15	Number of repeat customers and new clients	Decreased during the past 2 months	2	30	Tolerable risk
					Market share	▪ New competitors ▪ New technology	4	60	Tolerable risk
2.	Outdated products and services	4	5	20			4	80	Unacceptable risk
					Profitability	Decreased during the past 2 months	2	40	Tolerable risk
No. risks to be handled		2					1		

Process interaction no. 2 – Applying the PDCA and FMEA methods during risk assessment at the interaction between marketing and sales processes and contracting and legal processes

Table 6.4 shows that between marketing and sales processes and contract management and legal processes 2 unacceptable risks can be identified using risk assessment using the 2 classical attributes.

Table 6.4: Applying the PDCA and FMEA methods during risk assessment at the interaction between marketing and sales processes and contracting and legal processes, developed by the author based on the research conducted during the doctoral period

No. crt.	Risks	P	C	Risk Level 1	Impacted performance indicators	Risk materialization conditions	D	Risk Level 2	Proposed risk type
Risk assessment at the interaction between marketing and sales processes and contracting and legal processes									
1.	No new contracts	3	5	15	Turnover	Decreased during the past 2 months	2	30	Tolerable risk
					Market share	▪ New competitors ▪ New technology	4	60	Tolerable risk
No. risks to be handled		1					0		
Risk assessment at the interaction between contracting and legal processes and marketing and sales processes									
1.	Non-performing contracts	3	5	15	Profitability	Decreased during the past 2 months	2	30	Tolerable risk
No. risks to be handled		1					0		

These risks relate to no new contracts and non-performing contracts and have a negative impact on turnover, market share and profitability. After applying detection both risks are transformed into tolerable risks that do not require risk handling, so that important costs are saved for the organization.

Risk materialization conditions that have to be monitored by the organization relate to the impacted performance indicators. In case organizations observe that turnover or profitability have decreased in the past 2 months or market share is threatened by new competitors and technology, organizations can detect imminent risks and take preventive actions.

Process interaction no. 3 – Applying the PDCA and FMEA methods during risk assessment at the interaction between senior management and marketing and sales processes

Between senior management and marketing and sales processes interactions can lead to 4. For the risk between senior management and marketing and sales 2 risk materialization conditions were determined, but after applying the third attribute the risk becomes tolerable and no resources have to be used in order to manage this risk.

Table 6.5: Applying the PDCA and FMEA methods during risk assessment at the interaction between senior management and marketing and sales processes, developed by the author based on the research conducted during the doctoral period

No. crt.	Risks	P	C	Risk Level 1	Impacted performance indicators	Risk materialization conditions	D	Risk Level 2	Proposed risk type
Risk assessment at the interaction between senior management and marketing and sales processes									
1.	Inefficient marketing campaigns	3	5	15	Number of repeat customers and new clients	Decreased during the past 2 months	2	30	Tolerable risk
					Market share	▪ New competitors ▪ New technology	4	60	Tolerable risk
No. risks to be handled		1					0		
Risk assessment at the interaction between marketing and sales processes and senior management									
1.	Organizatio-nal image negatively affected	4	5	20	Number of repeat customers and new clients	Decreased during the past 2 months	2	30	Tolerable risk
					Market share	▪ New competitors	4	80	Unacceptable risk
2.	Clients losing interest in organization products and services	4	5	20		▪ New technology	4	80	Unacceptable risk
					Turnover	Decreased during the past 2 months	2	40	Tolerable risk
3.	Non-performing contracts	3	5	15	Profitability	Decreased during the past 2 months	2	30	Tolerable risk
No. risks to be handled		3					2		

Table 6.5 shows that between the marketing department and senior management two risks are unacceptable after applying detection.

Process interaction no. 4 – Applying the PDCA and FMEA methods during risk assessment at the interaction between contracting and legal processes and financial processes

Incorrect assignment of financial resources is the only risk that can materialize at the interaction between processes that occur between senior management and the marketing and sales department.

Table 6.6: Applying the PDCA and FMEA methods during risk assessment at the interaction between contracting and legal processes and financial processes, developed by the author based on the research conducted during the doctoral period

No. crt.	Risks	P	C	Risk Level 1	Impacted performance indicators	Risk materialization conditions	D	Risk Level 2	Proposed risk type
1.	Incorrect assignment of financial resources	3	5	15	Productivity	Decreased during the past 2 months	5	75	Unacceptable risk
					Profitability	Decreased during the past 2 months	2	30	Tolerable risk
No. risks to be handled		1					1		

Table 6.6 shows that this risk is unacceptable even after applying detection with the main cause being that risks materialization conditions for productivity can only be partially identified, controlled and monitored.

Process interaction no. 5 – Applying the PDCA and FMEA methods during risk assessment at the interaction between senior management and contracting and legal processes

Table 6.7: Applying the PDCA and FMEA methods during risk assessment at the interaction between senior management and contracting and legal processes, developed by the author based on the research conducted during the doctoral period

No. crt.	Risks	P	C	Risk Level 1	Impacted performance indicators	Risk materialization conditions	D	Risk Level 2	Proposed risk type
Risk assessment at the interaction between senior management and contracting/legal processes									
1.	No new clients	4	5	20	Number of repeat customers and new clients	Decreased during the past 2 months	2	30	Tolerable risk
1.	No new clients	4	5	20	Market share	▪ New competitors	4	80	Unacceptable risk
2.	No new clients and loss of existing clients	4	5	20		▪ New technology	4	80	Unacceptable risk
					Turnover	Decreased during the past 2 months	2	40	Tolerable risk
3.	Non-performing contracts	3	5	15	Profitability	Decreased during the past 2 months	2	30	Tolerable risk
No. risks to be handled		3					2		

Risk assessment at the interaction between contracting and legal processes and senior management									
1.	Non-performing contracts	3	5	15	Profitability	Decreased during the past 2 months	2	30	Tolerable risk
					Liquidity	Cash flow interruptions	4	60	Tolerable risk
No. risks to be handled		1					0		

Table 6.7 presents three important risks between senior management and the contract management department. Two of these risks have an impact on market share and both are still considered unacceptable after applying detection as the third risk assessment attribute. Between the contract management department and senior management only one risk was initially identified, and this risk becomes tolerable after calculating Risk Level 2.

Process interaction no. 6 – Applying the PDCA and FMEA methods during risk assessment at the interaction between procurement processes and financial processes

Four risks were identified using probability of occurrence and consequence related to interactions between procurement and the financial processes.

Table 1 from Annex I shows that none of the identified risks are unacceptable after applying detection in the case of interactions between procurement processes and finance processes; 2 of the identified risks that affect the number of supplier partners and market share are considered unacceptable even after applying detection as the third risk assessment attribute. These risks have to be included in the risk handling plan and relate to delayed payments from clients and to suppliers and delayed projects and have a negative impact on the number of supplier partners and market share.

Concerning tolerable risks organizations have to monitor risk materialization conditions determined by the impacted performance indicators: number of repeat customers and new clients, market share, liquidity and profitability.

Process interaction no. 7 – Applying the PDCA and FMEA methods during risk assessment at the interaction between financial processes and production processes

Processes between the financial department and the production department involve 5 risks from which only one is unacceptable after calculating Risk Level 2 (Table 2 from Annex I).

The unacceptable risk relates to delayed production and affects the number of supplier partners.

The tolerable risks have to be monitored by investigating risk materialization conditions related to the impacted performance indicators that have been determined: liquidity, market share, number of repeat customers and new clients and profitability.

Process interaction no. 8 – Applying the PDCA and FMEA methods during risk assessment at the interaction between senior management and financial processes

Table 3 from Annex I indicates that only 2 of the 6 risks that have been identified between senior management and financial processes are unacceptable in the second phase of the risk analysis; this means that only one third of the allocated resources have to be used in order to manage these risks.

The unacceptable risks are caused by senior management activities or errors during the financial processes and relate to delayed payments with impact on the number of supplier partners.

Process interaction no. 9 – Applying the PDCA and FMEA methods during risk assessment at the interaction between planning processes and production processes

Process interactions between the planning department and production can lead to three unacceptable risks (Table 4 from Annex I). Fortunately, these risks are transformed into tolerable risks after using detection as a third attribute in the risk analysis. These risks relate to delayed production, products or services with quality-related issues and delayed or faulty production and service delivery.

In order to monitor these risks, risks materialization conditions have to be observed related to the impacted performance indicators: number of repeat customers and new clients, liquidity and market share.

Process interaction no. 10 – Applying the PDCA and FMEA methods during risk assessment at the interaction between production processes and after-sales processes

Table 5 from Annex I presents two risks between production processes and after-sales processes and both are considered unacceptable after applying detection. All 3 unacceptable risks identified between after-sales processes and production processes are transformed into tolerable risks after applying detection during risk assessment.

Process interaction no. 11 – Applying the PDCA and FMEA methods during risk assessment at the interaction between senior management and production processes

The research shows that none of the risks identified between senior management and production processes are unacceptable after applying detection (Table 6 from Annex I). These risks relate to producing goods and delivering services that are unappealing for potential clients, production gaps or stopped production, decreased sales and the organizational image being negatively affected. These risks can have a negative impact on the following performance indicators: number of repeat customers and new clients, market share, liquidity, number of supplier partners, turnover and number of supplier partners.

Process interaction no. 12 – Applying the PDCA and FMEA methods during risk assessment at the interaction between after-sales processes and quality assurance processes

Table 7 from Annex I shows a number of 6 risks that can materialize as a result of interactions between after-sales processes and quality assurance processes. After calculating Risk Level 2 none of these risks were considered unacceptable. These risks relate to the organizational image being negatively affected, limited or faulty troubleshooting and additional unforeseen costs during warranty period, delivering faulty or outdated products and services.

The impacted organizational performance indicators are market share, number of supplier partners, number of repeat customers and new clients and profitability. These indicators have to be monitored in order to determine risk materialization conditions and prevent imminent risks.

Process interaction no. 13 – Applying the PDCA and FMEA methods during risk assessment at the interaction between senior management and after-sales processes

Process interactions between senior management and after-sales processes are another example of detection saving costs with risk handling because the both risks that were initially considered unacceptable were transformed into tolerable risks after applying detection (Table 8 from Annex I). These risks are related to decreased support services and spare parts sales, the organizational image being negatively affected and decreased services, support and spare parts sales and have an impact on turnover, market share, number of repeat customers and new clients and number of supplier partners.

Process interaction no. 14 – Applying the PDCA and FMEA methods during risk assessment at the interaction between quality assurance processes and marketing and sales processes

Table 9 from Annex I indicates that all 4 unacceptable risks were transformed into tolerable risks after using detection during the risk assessment process. These risks relate to the organizational image being negatively affected, producing goods and delivering services that are unappealing for potential clients, outdated products and services and decreased clients' satisfaction.

The performance indicators that can be affected by these tolerable risks have to be monitored in order to prevent imminent risks.

Process interaction no. 15 – Applying the PDCA and FMEA methods during risk assessment at the interaction between procurement processes and suppliers

In the case of process interactions between the procurement department and suppliers half of unacceptable risks are considered tolerable after calculating Risk Level 2 (Table 10 from Annex I).

Delayed orders, delayed deliveries and sales disruptions are the main risks that have to be handled in order to prevent negative events. Tolerable risks relate to delayed payments to suppliers, delayed orders and deliveries, sales disruptions, exceeding the project budget and cancelled contracts.

The following impacted performance indicators have to be monitored in order to prevent risks transforming into unacceptable or high risks: number of supplier partners, market share, number of repeat customers and new clients, liquidity and profitability.

Summarized results related to determining the probability of occurrence, consequences and probability of detection during the risk assessment process related to organizational business processes

Table 6.8 presents average risk types and number of risks that are included in the risk handling plan when analyzing risks using probability of occurrence and consequence (2 attributes) and when applying detection as a second phase of the risk assessment process (3 attributes).

Table 6.8: Number and type of risks determined during risk assessment using 3 attributes compared to 2 attributes, developed by the author based on the research conducted during the doctoral period

Interaction no.	Risk assessment with 2 attributes		Risk assessment with 3 attributes	
	Average risk type	No. risks to be handled	Average risk type	No. risks to be handled
1	Unacceptable risk	7	Tolerable risk	3
2	Unacceptable risk	2	Tolerable risk	0
3	Unacceptable risk	4	Tolerable risk	2
4	Tolerable risk	1	Tolerable risk	1
5	Unacceptable risk	4	Tolerable risk	2
6	Unacceptable risk	5	Tolerable risk	2
7	Unacceptable risk	5	Tolerable risk	1
8	Unacceptable risk	6	Tolerable risk	2
9	Unacceptable risk	3	Tolerable risk	0
10	Unacceptable risk	5	Tolerable risk	2
11	Unacceptable risk	4	Tolerable risk	0
12	Unacceptable risk	6	Tolerable risk	0
13	Unacceptable risk	3	Tolerable risk	0
14	Unacceptable risk	4	Tolerable risk	0
15	Unacceptable risk	6	Tolerable risk	3
Total		66		**18**

Table 6.9: Number of risks impacting the organization's performance indicators while performing risk assessment using 3 attributes compared to 2 attributes, developed by the author based on the research conducted during the doctoral period

No. crt.	Impacted performance indicators	Number of risks handled without using the FMEA method	Number of risks handled after using the FMEA method	Difference between risks handled using and not using the FMEA method during risk assessment **(B-A)**	
		A	**B**	Value	Percentage
1.	Number of repeat customers and new clients	33	0	-33	-100%
2.	Market share	45	13	-32	-71.11%
4.	Liquidity	18	1	-17	-94.44%
5.	Profitability	16	0	-16	-100%
6.	Turnover	6	0	-6	-100%
7.	Productivity	1	1	0	0%
8.	Number of supplier partners	10	4	-6	-60%
Total		129	**19**	-110	**-85.27%**

The results show that the average risk type is tolerable when using the FMEA method and only 18 out of 66 risks have to be included in the risk handling plan. The number of risks that affect the main performance indicators are indicated in Table 6.9.
The study shows that after applying detection performance indicators are affected by almost 85% less unacceptable risks.

6.1.5 Determining the probability of occurrence, consequences and probability of detection during the risk assessment process related to interactions between the organization and outsourced business processes

The following risks related to interactions between organizational business processes were identified as result of the interviews with managers during the doctoral period:

- Incomplete or incorrect process design;
- Losing full control and decreased quality of service;
- High costs with wages and transportation;
- Outdated control mechanisms;
- Inefficient processes;
- Inefficient and outdated processes.

The identified risks were analyzed in relation with the impacted performance indicators and risk materialization conditions; risk levels were calculated and as a result new risk types were proposed.

a) Results related to determining the probability of occurrence, consequences and probability of detection during the risk assessment process at process interactions level between business processes fully owned by the organization and executed in the domestic country

Table 6.10 indicates that applying the proposed methods during risk assessment related to interactions between fully owned business processes executed onsite transforms risks considered unacceptable when using only 2 risk assessment attributes into tolerable risks.

Risks related to productivity have the highest risk levels because the probability of detecting risk materialization conditions is low (Table 6.11).

Table 6.10: Applying the PDCA and FMEA methods during risk assessment related to process interactions between fully owned business processes executed onsite, developed by the author based on the research conducted during the doctoral period

No. crt.	Risks	Risk Level 1	Impacted performance indicators	Risk materialization conditions	D	Risk Level 2	Proposed risk type
1.	Inefficient and outdated processes	20	Number of repeat customers and new clients	Decreased during the past 2 months	2	30	Tolerable risk
			Productivity	Decreased during the past 2 months	4	60	Tolerable risk
No. risks to be handled		1				0	

One third of the identified risks related to process interactions between the organization and shared services executed offsite are unacceptable after applying detection.

Table 6.11: Applying the PDCA and FMEA methods during risk assessment related to process interactions between the organization and fully owned shared business processes executed offsite, developed by the author based on the research conducted during the doctoral period

No. crt.	Risks	Risk Level 1	Impacted performance indicators	Risk materialization conditions	D	Risk Level 2	Proposed risk type
1.	Incomplete or incorrect process design	15	Number of repeat customers and new clients	Decreased during the past 2 months	2	30	Tolerable risk
1.	Incomplete or incorrect process design	15	Productivity	Decreased during the past 2 months	5	75	Unacceptable risk
			Market share	▪ New competitors ▪ New technology	4	60	Tolerable risk
2.	Losing full control and decreased quality of service	15			4	60	Tolerable risk
3.	Inefficient processes	15	Profitability	Decreased during the past 2 months	2	30	Tolerable risk
4.	Inefficient and outdated processes	20			2	40	Tolerable risk
			Productivity	Decreased during the past 2 months	5	100	Unacceptable risk
No. risks to be handled		4				2	

b) Results related to determining the probability of occurrence, consequences and probability of detection during the risk assessment process at process interactions level between business processes fully owned by the organization and executed in a foreign country

Tables 6.12 and 6.13 indicate that processes owned by the organization and executed in a foreign country involve 12 risks from which only 5 have to be handled after applying detection as a third attribute during risk assessment. The most important performance indicator affected by these risks is productivity that has a negative impact on business performance and profitability.

Table 6.12: Applying the PDCA and FMEA methods during risk assessment related to process interactions between the organization and fully owned shared business processes executed nearshore, developed by the author based on the research conducted during the doctoral period

No. crt.	Risks	Risk Level 1	Impacted performance indicators	Risk materialization conditions	D	Risk Level 2	Proposed risk type
1.	Incomplete or incorrect process design	15	Number of repeat customers and new clients	Decreased during the past 2 months	2	30	Tolerable risk
			Productivity	Decreased during the past 2 months	5	75	Unacceptable risk
			Market share	▪ New competitors ▪ New technology	4	60	Tolerable risk
2.	Losing full control and decreased quality of service	15			4	60	Tolerable risk
3.	High costs with wages and transportation	20	Productivity	Decreased during the past 2 months	4	80	Unacceptable risk
4.	Outdated control mechanisms	15			4	60	Tolerable risk
5.	Inefficient processes	15	Profitability	Decreased during the past 2 months	2	30	Tolerable risk
6.	Inefficient and outdated processes	20			2	40	Tolerable risk
			Productivity	Decreased during the past 2 months	4	60	Tolerable risk
No. risks to be handled		6			2		

Table 6.12 shows when applying the PDCA and FMEA methods during risk assessment related to process interactions between the organization and fully owned shared business processes executed nearshore, risks related to incomplete or incorrect process design and high costs with wages and transportation have unacceptable levels and can have a negative impact on the organizations' productivity. Risk materialization conditions have to be monitored in relation with the tolerable risks identified that have an impact on the following organizational indicators: number of repeat customers and new clients, market share and profitability.

Table 6.13: Applying the PDCA and FMEA methods during risk assessment related to process interactions between the organization and fully owned shared business processes executed offshore, developed by the author based on the research conducted during the doctoral period

No. crt.	Risks	Risk Level 1	Impacted performance indicators	Risk materialization conditions	D	Risk Level 2	Proposed risk type
1.	Incomplete or incorrect process design	15	Number of repeat customers and new clients	Decreased during the past 2 months	2	30	Tolerable risk
			Productivity	Decreased during the past 2 months	5	75	Unacceptable risk
			Market share	▪ New competitors ▪ New technology	4	60	Tolerable risk
2.	Losing full control and decreased quality of service	15			4	60	Tolerable risk
3.	High costs with wages and transportation	25	Productivity	Decreased during the past 2 months	4	100	Unacceptable risk
4.	Outdated control mechanisms	15	Productivity	Decreased during the past 2 months	4	60	Tolerable risk
5.	Inefficient processes	15	Profitability	Decreased during the past 2 months	2	30	Tolerable risk
6.	Inefficient and outdated processes	20			2	40	Tolerable risk
			Productivity	Decreased during the past 2 months	5	100	Unacceptable risk
No. risks to be handled		6			3		

Risk materialization conditions relate to the following organizational performance indicators: number of repeat customers and new clients, market share and profitability (Table 6.13). Organizations have to analyze the trends of the performance indicators and to observe if these indicators have decreased in the last months or if new competitors and technology threaten the organization's market share. Therefore, performance indicators impacted by the tolerable risks identified between the organization and fully owned shared business processes executed offshore have to be monitored in order to prevent imminent risks.

c) Results related to determining the probability of occurrence, consequences and probability of detection during the risk assessment process at process interactions level between the organization and business processes fully owned by third-party providers executed in the domestic country

Table 6.14: Applying the PDCA and FMEA methods during risk assessment related to process interactions between the organization and processes owned by third-party providers executed onsite, developed by the author based on the research conducted during the doctoral period

No. crt.	Risks	Risk Level 1	Impacted performance indicators	Risk materialization conditions	D	Risk Level 2	Proposed risk type
1.	Incomplete or incorrect process design	15	Number of repeat customers and new clients	Decreased during the past 2 months	2	30	Tolerable risk
			Productivity	Decreased during the past 2 months	5	75	Unacceptable risk
			Market share	▪ New competitors ▪ New technology	4	60	Tolerable risk
2.	Losing full control and decreased quality of service	15			4	60	Tolerable risk
3.	High costs with wages and transportation	20	Productivity	Decreased during the past 2 months	4	80	Unacceptable risk
4.	Outdated control mechanisms	15	Productivity	Decreased during the past 2 months	4	60	Tolerable risk
5.	Inefficient processes	15	Profitability	Decreased during the past 2 months	2	30	Tolerable risk
6.	Inefficient and outdated processes	20			2	40	Tolerable risk
		20	Productivity	Decreased during the past 2 months	4	60	Tolerable risk
No. risks to be handled		6				3	

Process interactions between the organization and business processes contracted to third-party providers involve a new set of unacceptable risks. From a total of 12 unacceptable risks only half have to be included in the risk handling plan after using the FMEA method (Tables 6.14 and 6.15). Risks related to incomplete or incorrect process design, increased costs with wages and transportation and inefficient and outdated processes are still unacceptable after calculation Risk Level 2.
Table 6.15 shows by applying the PDCA and FMEA methods during risk assessment related to process interactions between the organization and processes owned by third-party providers executed offsite, risks related to incomplete or incorrect process design, high costs with wages and transportation and inefficient and outdated processes are the main unacceptable risks with impact on productivity.

Table 6.15: Applying the PDCA and FMEA methods during risk assessment related to process interactions between the organization and processes owned by third-party providers executed offsite, developed by the author based on the research conducted during the doctoral period

No. crt.	Risks	Risk Level 1	Impacted performance indicators	Risk materialization conditions	D	Risk Level 2	Proposed risk type
1.	Incomplete or incorrect process design	15	Number of repeat customers and new clients	Decreased during the past 2 months	2	30	Tolerable risk
			Productivity		5	75	Unacceptable risk
1.	Incomplete or incorrect process design	15	Market share	▪ New competitors ▪ New technology	4	60	Tolerable risk
2.	Losing full control and decreased quality of service	15			4	60	Tolerable risk
3.	High costs with wages and transportation	25	Productivity	Decreased during the past 2 months	4	100	Unacceptable risk
4.	Outdated control mechanisms	15			4	60	Tolerable risk
5.	Inefficient processes	15	Profitability	Decreased during the past 2 months	2	30	Tolerable risk
6.	Inefficient and outdated processes	20			2	40	Tolerable risk
			Productivity	Decreased during the past 2 months	5	100	Unacceptable risk
No. risks to be handled		6			3		

Tolerable risks related to interactions between the organization and processes owned by third-party providers executed offsite can have a negative impact on number of repeat customers and new clients, productivity, market share and profitability.

d) Results related to determining the probability of occurrence, consequences and probability of detection during the risk assessment process at process interactions level between the organization and business processes fully owned by third-party providers executed in a foreign country

Table 6.16 indicates risks levels after applying detection during risk assessment related to interactions between the organization and processes owned by third-party providers executed in neighboring countries.

Table 6.16: Applying the PDCA and FMEA methods during risk assessment related to process interactions between the organization and processes owned by third-party providers and executed nearshore, developed by the author based on the research conducted during the doctoral period

No. crt.	Risks	Risk Level 1	Impacted performance indicators	Risk materialization conditions	D	Risk Level 2	Proposed risk type
1.	Incomplete or incorrect process design	20	Number of repeat customers and new clients	Decreased during the past 2 months	2	40	Tolerable risk
1.	Incomplete or incorrect process design	20	Productivity	Decreased during the past 2 months	5	100	Unacceptable risk
			Market share	▪ New competitors ▪ New technology	4	80	Unacceptable risk
2.	Losing full control and decreased quality of service	20			4	80	Unacceptable risk
3.	High costs with wages and transportation	25	Productivity	Decreased during the past 2 months	4	100	Unacceptable risk
4.	Outdated control mechanisms	20			4	80	Unacceptable risk
5.	Inefficient processes	15	Profitability	Decreased during the past 2 months	2	30	Tolerable risk
6.	Inefficient and outdated processes	20			2	40	Tolerable risk
			Productivity	Decreased during the past 2 months	4	80	Unacceptable risk
No. risks to be handled		6			3		

When considering processes executed nearshore, risk levels are still unacceptable especially related to high costs with wages and transportation caused by unforeseen changes in the foreign country's business climate.

When it comes to processes owned by third-party providers and executed offshore, Table 6.17 indicates that after calculating Risk Level 2 only one out of 6 risks was evaluated as tolerable and do not have to be included in the risk handling plan. Research results indicate a maximum risk level detected related to inefficient and outdated processes that have a very strong impact on business productivity.

Table 6.17: Applying the PDCA and FMEA methods during risk assessment related to process interactions between the organization and processes owned by third-party providers and executed offshore, developed by the author based on the research conducted during the doctoral period

No. crt.	Risks	Risk Level 1	Impacted performance indicators	Risk materialization conditions	D	Risk Level 2	Proposed risk type
1.	Incomplete or incorrect process design	20	Number of repeat customers and new clients	Decreased during the past 2 months	2	40	Tolerable risk
			Productivity		5	100	Unacceptable risk
			Market share	▪ New competitors ▪ New technology	4	80	Unacceptable risk
2.	Losing full control and decreased quality of service	25			4	100	Unacceptable risk
3.	High costs with wages and transportation	25	Productivity	Decreased during the past 2 months	4	100	Unacceptable risk
4.	Outdated control mechanisms	20	Productivity	Decreased during the past 2 months	4	80	Unacceptable risk
5.	Inefficient processes	20	Profitability	Decreased during the past 2 months	2	40	Tolerable risk
6.	Inefficient and outdated processes	25			2	50	Tolerable risk
			Productivity		5	125	Very high risk
No. risks to be handled		6				5	

Summarized results related to determining the probability of occurrence, consequences and probability of detection during the risk assessment process related to interactions between the organization and outsourced business processes

Table 6.18 indicates the number of unacceptable or very high risks evaluated and analyzed using 3 attributes compared to using the classical 2 attributes.

Table 6.18: Number of risks included in the risk handling plan after applying the FMEA method during risk assessment related to interactions between the organization and outsourced business processes, developed by the author based on the research conducted during the doctoral period

Number of risks included in the risk handling plan after applying the FMEA method		Business processes by ownership:			
		Owned by the organization		Owned by the third-party provider	
		Number of risks handled without using the FMEA method	Number of risks handled after using the FMEA method	Number of risks handled without using the FMEA method	Number of risks handled after using the FMEA method
Business processes by location:	Onsite	1	0	6	3
	Offsite	5	2	6	3
	Nearshore	6	2	6	5
	Offshore	6	3	6	5
Total no. of risks		18	**7**	24	**16**

Table 6.19: Number of risks impacting the organization's performance indicators as a result of using the FMEA method during risk assessment related to interactions between the organization and outsourced business processes, developed by the author based on the research conducted during the doctoral period

No. crt.	Impacted performance indicators	Number of risks handled without using the FMEA method	Number of risks handled after using the FMEA method	Difference between risks handled using and not using the FMEA method during risk assessment **(B-A)**	
		A	**B**	Value	Percentage
1.	Number of repeat customers and new clients	8	0	-8	-100%
2.	Market share	14	4	-10	-71.43%
3.	Profitability	14	0	-14	-100%
4.	Productivity	28	23	-5	-17.85%
Total		64	**27**	-37	**-57.81%**

From a total of 42 unacceptable risks only 23 risks were still unacceptable after applying detection as the third attribute during the risk assessment process; as a result, risk handling costs are reduced by more than 45% because only 54,76% of the identified risks are included in the risk handling plan in order to prevent negative outcomes.

Almost 58% less risks are included in the risk handling plan after using the FMEA method when performing risk assessment (Table 6.19). Productivity is the performance indicator affected by the highest number of risks; also, only 5 out of 25 risks were considered tolerable after applying detection. The decreased number of risks introduced in the risk handling plan after performing risk assessment using 3 attributes leads to decreased costs and resources.

6.2 Applying the PDCA and FMEA methods during the risk assessment process related to organizational business processes in relation with the identification of business opportunities

Experts in risk assessment consider that one of the main factors that ensure business sustainability is risk appetite; introducing detection and extending the risk assessment process comes with advantages like lower risk handling costs and is a sign that organizations' risk appetite is increasing. Recently specialized literature has indicated the necessity of increasing the efficiency risk assessment even more by perceiving risks as uncertainties that can lead to both negative and positive outcomes so that risk analysis results can be used in order to identify business opportunities. A negative event is not the only possible outcome of an uncertain situation, therefore by mapping both negative and positive effects of risk materialization risk assessment efficiency can be increased.

The current competitive business environment has 2 effects on the organizations' strategic orientation related to risks: it increases risk appetite and decreases risk tolerance. Despite the fact that risk tolerance is weakened for most of the organizations, a defensive risk strategy cannot ensure business sustainability - successful results and even the survival of many organizations rely on a proactive risk assessment strategy that is oriented on identifying both threats and opportunities.

More and more publications focus on evaluating risks as uncertainties that can be transformed into added value for organizations if managers change their risk assessment strategies and even assign resources in order to take risks that can lead to positive outcomes. Organizations have started undertaking risky situations in order to achieve added value; risk assessment has become a higher responsibility by determining the managers' decisions related to risk-taking.

By using the FMEA method resources are focused on the most valuable opportunities. One of the objectives of the study relates to identifying opportunities that can be achieved as effects of the materialized risks. The extended risk assessment is performed at the interactions between business processes within the organization and also between the organization and externalized processes.
The study researches using the PDCA and FMEA methods while mapping both positive and negative possible outcomes of risk materialization. This method is intended as a useful tool for managers in order to facilitate decisions related to risk-taking in relation with ensuring business sustainability.

6.2.1 General context of the research

Organizations' risk appetite has changed according to the new challenges from the current business environment. The increasing risk attitude has influenced the organizations' attitude in front of risks and has introduced the necessity of improving risk assessment efficiency in order to have a better control of the calculated risks that are taken by managers. A study performed by Eeckhoudt (2012) concludes that "risk attitudes other than risk aversion are becoming important both in theoretical and empirical work". Risk appetite is directly influenced by risk tolerance and organizational resources.

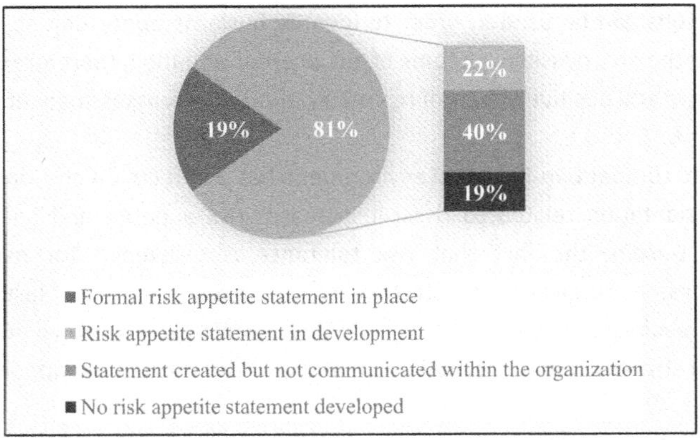

Figure 6.7: Risk appetite statement, developed by the author based on Economist Intelligence Unit on behalf of KPMG International, 2013. Expectations of Risk assessment Outpacing Capabilities – It's Time For Action, KPMG International Cooperative, https://www.kpmg.com/LB/en/Issues AndInsights/ArticlesPublications/Documents/expectations-risk-management-survey.pdf, accessed 08.10.2015.

However, not many organizations have an algorithm when it comes to decisions about risk-taking and according to a survey conducted by the Economist Intelligence Unit on behalf of KPMG in 2013, managers have difficulties developing strategies without a formal risk appetite statement (Figure 6.7).

Additionally, the survey shows that managers do not know "whether they are taking on too much risk for a given level of return or too little" – this means that managers are reluctant to assigning resources for risk assessment because they are not sure if the process is value-adding for the organization. Organizations would have an increased risk appetite if they had lower risk handling costs, if they identified opportunities more often and if tackling these opportunities led to improved business results. Introducing detection as the third attribute during risk assessment determines the conditions in which risks materialize, both risks leading to negative and positive outcomes, therefore by using the FMEA method organizations can detect which risks are worth handling in order to prevent negative effects of materialized risks or to force risk materialization in order to tackle an opportunity.

6.2.2 Objectives and research methodology

a) Research objectives

The research objectives are related to determining the advantages of using the FMEA method during the risk assessment process while aiming for new business opportunities in order to improve management efficiency and to ensure sustainable performance.

While until now the risk levels and risk types were calculated by using 3 attributes while focusing on the possible negative effects of risk materialization related to interactions between business processes, the next research objective is to determine risk levels and risk types in relation with identifying the most valuable business opportunities. Results of the studies conducted during the doctoral period were used in order to integrate detection in the risk assessment process and to determine the new risk levels that can generate both negative and positive outcomes.

Another objective of the study is to evaluate the impact of using detection as a third attribute during risk assessment related to interactions between the organization and outsourced business processes while aiming for new business opportunities.

b) Research methodology

Interviews with 7 managers in November 2017 had the goal of identifying risks that can occur between business processes in organizations, as well as between the organization and outsourced business processes (Annex J). Following, based on the information shared during the interviews and the studies conducted during the doctoral period, the research evaluated and analyzed the risks. When predicting both negative and positive outcomes of risk materialization during risk assessment risk types are different (Table 6.20) – for example a risk level of 125 corresponds to very high risks of materialization of negative outcomes when focusing on identifying threats, while when determining possible positive outcomes, a risk level of 125 relates to a very attractive opportunity.

Table 6.20: Proposed color coding, risk types and tolerance intervals for risk levels in relation with determining threats and opportunities during risk assessment, developed by the author based on the research conducted during the doctoral period

Proposed color coding	Negative outcomes	Proposed tolerance intervals for risk levels	Positive outcomes	Proposed tolerance intervals for risk levels
	-	1	Very attractive risks	101-125
	Acceptable risks	2-30	Attractive risks	61-100
	Tolerable risks	31-60	Common risks	31-60
	Unacceptable risks	61-100	Unattractive risks	2-30
	Very high risks	101-125	-	1

The research results resumed by presenting the number of risks that are handled in order to tackle opportunities compared to the number of risks that are commonly introduced in the risk handling plan. The results are presented in tables so that for each of the unacceptable risks related to interactions between business processes identified the following data is determined:

- All the possible positive outcomes that could be generated by risk materialization;
- Performance indicators that are impacted by the identified risks;
- Risk materialization conditions;
- Detection levels;
- The new risk levels (Risk Level 2);
- The new risk types (risk transformation).

Detection is calculated for each performance indicator and the new Risk Level 2 is determined. By calculating Risk Level 2 while aiming to identify the most valuable business opportunities, risk types also change according to the new risk levels. Finally, the research shows the number of risks managed in order to tackle opportunities while aiming to present:

- A comparison between the results of using 3 attributes compared to 2 attributes;
- The number of risks that have to be handled for each of the valuable opportunities that were identified at process interactions level.

6.2.3 Determining the probability of occurrence, consequences and probability of detection during the risk assessment process related to organizational business processes in relation with the identification of business opportunities

Process interaction no. 1 – Applying the FMEA method and identifying business opportunities during risk assessment at the interaction between marketing and sales processes and the external business environment while aiming for new business opportunities

The calculated Risk Level 1 shows 6 attractive risks that can materialize at process interaction level between the marketing and sales department and the external business environment. Table 6.21 indicates that only one of the two risks identified are attractive after applying detection and can lead to valuable opportunities such as attracting new investors or selling shares; this is possible if resources are used in order to force risk materialization. When it comes to creditors none of the risks are attractive while aiming for new business opportunities.

Table 6.21: Applying the FMEA method and identifying business opportunities during risk assessment at the interaction between the marketing and sales processes and the external business environment (clients and creditors), developed by the author based on the research conducted during the doctoral period

No. crt.	Risks	P	C	Risk Level 1	Possible business opportunity	Impacted performance indicators	Risk materialization conditions	D	Risk Level 2	Proposed risk type
Risk assessment at the interaction between the marketing and sales processes and clients										
1.	Offering outdated products and services	4	5	20	Investing in new technology financed by attracting new investors or selling shares	Number of repeat customers and new clients	Decreased during the past 2 months	2	40	Common risk
						Market share	▪ New competitors ▪ New technology	4	80	Attractive risk
2.	Decreased clients' satisfac-tion	3	5	15	Focusing on new marketing strategies considering the clients' needs	Market share	▪ New competitors ▪ New technology	4	60	Common risk
						Number of inquiries	Decreased during the past 2 months	2	30	Common risk
No. risks to be handled				2					1	

Risk assessment at the interaction between the marketing and sales processes and creditors										
1.	Delayed deliveries, invoicing and cashing in from clients	3	5	15	Improving delivery and invoicing protocols in order to receive payments faster and improve cash flow	Number of repeat customers and new clients	Decreased during the past 2 months	2	30	Common risk
						Liquidity	Cash flow interruptions	4	60	Common risk
						Market share	▪ New competitors ▪ New technology	4	60	Common risk
2.	Inefficient assign-ment of financial resources	3	5	15	Cash flow optimization by improving assignment of financial resources			4	60	Common risk
						Profitability	Decreased during the past 2 months	2	30	Common risk
No. risks to be handled				2					0	

Table 6.22 indicates that delivering outdated products and services is a risk that can be managed while targeting business opportunities that can be extremely valuable if the organization decides to invest in new technology.

Table 6.22: Applying the FMEA method and identifying business opportunities during risk assessment at the interaction between the marketing and sales processes and the external business environment (competing organizations and shareholders), developed by the author based on the research conducted during the doctoral period

No. crt.	Risks	P	C	Risk Level 1	Possible business opportunity	Impacted performance indicators	Risk materialization conditions	D	Risk Level 2	Proposed risk type
Risk assessment at the interaction between the marketing and sales processes and competing organizations										
1.	Outdated products and services	4	5	20	Investing in new technology financed by attracting new investors or selling shares	Number of repeat customers and new clients	Decreased during the past 2 months	2	40	Common risk
						Market share	▪ New competitors ▪ New technology	4	80	Attractive risk
No. risks to be handled				1					1	

Risk assessment at the interaction between the marketing and sales processes and shareholders										
1.	Disrup-tions in the production lines	3	5	15	Increasing turnover and profit by improving production protocols and control mechanisms	Number of repeat customers and new clients	Decreased during the past 2 months	2	30	Common risk
						Market share	▪ New competitors	4	60	Common risk
2.	Outdated products and services	4	5	20	Investing in new technology financed by attracting investors or selling shares		▪ New technology	4	80	Attractive risk
						Profitability	Decreased during the past 2 months	2	40	Common risk
No. risks to be handled		2						1		

Risks related to outdated products and services can lead to investing in new technology financed by attracting new investors or selling shares. Disruptions in the production lines are tolerable risks that have to be monitored in order to determine if risk levels increase and possible new opportunities can be tackled.

The performance indicators by the tolerable risks are number of repeat customers and new clients, profitability and market share – the first 2 indicators can signal imminent risks if their values decrease during the past 2 months, while new competitors and technology are to be monitored for the market share indicators.

Process interaction no. 2 – Applying the FMEA method and identifying business opportunities during risk assessment at the interaction between marketing and sales processes and contracting and legal processes while aiming for new business opportunities

While the initial risk analysis evaluates the 2 risks related to interactions between business processes between the marketing and sales department and contract management department as attractive, after applying detection as the third attribute in the risk evaluation process these risks become common risks and no resources should be used in order to handle them (Table 6.23).

Table 6.23: Applying the FMEA method and identifying business opportunities during risk assessment at the interaction between marketing and sales processes and contracting and legal processes, developed by the author based on the research conducted during the doctoral period

No. crt.	Risks	P	C	Risk Level 1	Possible business opportunity	Impacted performance indicators	Risk materialization conditions	D	Risk Level 2	Proposed risk type
Risk assessment at the interaction between marketing and sales processes and contracting and legal processes										
1.	No new contracts	3	5	15	Attracting new clients by improving the marketing strategy	Turnover	Decreased during the past 2 months	2	30	Common risk
						Market share	▪ New competitors ▪ New technology	4	60	Common risk
No. risks to be handled				1					0	
Risk assessment at the interaction between contracting and legal processes and marketing and sales processes										
1.	Non-performing contracts	3	5	15	Improving contract budgets and protocols in order to increase profitability	Profitability	Decreased during the past 2 months	2	30	Common risk
No. risks to be handled				1					0	

These risks are related to no new contracts and non-performing contracts that can lead to attracting new clients by improving the marketing strategy and improving contract budgets and protocols in order to increase profitability.

The performance indicators that have to be monitored are turnover, profitability and market share. If the value of the first 2 indicators decrease during the past 2 months or new competitors and technology are observed, organizations will have to reanalyze risks in order to tackle new business opportunities.

Process interaction no. 3 – Applying the FMEA method and identifying business opportunities during risk assessment at the interaction between senior management and marketing and sales processes while aiming for new business opportunities

Table 6.24 indicates 4 risks related to interactions between business processes between senior management and marketing processes. Two of these risks can lead to attracting new clients by improving the marketing strategy and investing in new technology financed by attracting new investors or selling shares. After applying detection this risk becomes unattractive for managers that are targeting new business opportunities. In the case of risks between the marketing processes and shareholders two out of three risks are attractive according to the extended risk evaluation. Performance indicators impacted by common risks should be monitored in order to detect if risk levels increase and new opportunities can be achieved. These indicators are affected by risks related to inefficient marketing campaigns, organizational image being negatively affected, clients losing interest in organization products and services and non-performing contracts.

Table 6.24: Applying the FMEA method and identifying business opportunities during risk assessment at the interaction between senior management and marketing and sales processes, developed by the author based on the research conducted during the doctoral period

No. crt.	Risks	P	C	Risk Level 1	Possible business opportunity	Impacted performance indicators	Risk materialization conditions	D	Risk Level 2	Proposed risk type
Risk assessment at the interaction between senior management and marketing and sales processes										
1.	Inefficient marketing campaigns	3	5	15	Attracting new clients by improving the marketing strategy	Number of repeat customers and new clients	Decreased during the past 2 months	2	30	Common risk
						Market share	▪ New competitors ▪ New technology	4	60	Common risk
No. risks to be handled		1						0		
Risk assessment at the interaction between marketing and sales processes and senior management										
1.	Organizatio-nal image negatively affected	4	5	20	Attracting new clients by improving the marketing strategy	Number of repeat customers and new clients	Decreased during the past 2 months	2	30	Common risk
						Market share	▪ New competitors ▪ New technology	4	80	Attractive risk
2.	Clients losing interest in organiza-tion products and services	4	5	20	Investing in new technology financed by attracting new inves-tors or selling shares			4	80	Attractive risk
						Turnover	Decreased during the past 2 months	2	40	Common risk

3.	Non-performing contracts	3	5	15	Improving contract budgets and protocols in order to increase profitability	Profitability	Decreased during the past 2 months	2	30	Common risk
No. risks to be handled		3						2		

Process interaction no. 4 – Applying the FMEA method and identifying business opportunities during risk assessment at the interaction between contracting and legal processes and financial processes while aiming for new business opportunities

Risk type does not change by extending the evaluation of the risk that is identified at process interactions level between the contract management and financial departments (Table 6.25).

Table 6.25: Applying the FMEA method and identifying business opportunities during risk assessment at the interaction between contracting and legal processes and financial processes, developed by the author based on the research conducted during the doctoral period

No. crt.	Risks	P	C	Risk Level 1	Possible business opportunity	Impacted performance indicators	Risk materialization conditions	D	Risk Level 2	Proposed risk type
1.	Incorrect assignment of financial resources	3	5	15	Assigning resources for marketing campaigns in order to increase productivity by increasing sales	Productivity	Decreased during the past 2 months	5	75	Attractive risk
2.	Incorrect assign-ment of financial resources	3	5	15	Assigning resources for marketing campaigns in order to attract new clients and increase turnover and profit	Profitability	Decreased during the past 2 months	2	30	Common risk
No. risks to be handled		1						1		

Risks related to incorrect assignment of financial resources can lead to important business opportunities such as assigning resources for marketing campaigns in order to improve productivity by increasing sales. If profitability is monitored and risk levels related to these risks increase, it is possible to tackle opportunities related to assigning resources for marketing campaigns in order to attract new clients and increase turnover and profit.

Process interaction no. 5 – Applying the FMEA method and identifying business opportunities during risk assessment at the interaction between senior management and contracting and legal processes while aiming for new business opportunities

Process between senior management and the contract management department can involve to four important risks from which only two are attractive after calculating the probability of detection for the risk materialization conditions (Tables 6.26).

Table 6.26: Applying the FMEA method and identifying business opportunities during risk assessment at the interaction between senior management and contracting and legal processes, developed by the author based on the research conducted during the doctoral period

No. crt.	Risks	P	C	Risk Level 1	Possible business opportunity	Impacted performance indicators	Risk materialization conditions	D	Risk Level 2	Proposed risk type
Risk assessment at the interaction between senior management and contracting and legal processes										
1.	No new clients	4	5	20	Improving turnover and profit by improving the marketing strategy and attracting new clients	Number of repeat customers and new clients	Decreased during the past 2 months	2	30	Common risk
						Market share	▪ New competitors	4	80	Attractive risk
2.	No new clients and loss of existing clients	4	5	20			▪ New technology	4	80	Attractive risk
						Turnover	Decreased during the past 2 months	2	40	Common risk
3.	Outdated contracts or detrimental to the organization	3	5	15	Improving contract budgets and protocols in order to increase profitability	Profitability	Decreased during the past 2 months	2	30	Common risk
No. risks to be handled		3						2		

Risk assessment at the interaction between contracting and legal processes and senior management										
1.	Outdated contracts or detrimental to the organization	3	5	15	Improving contract budgets and protocols in order to increase profitability	Profitability	Decreased during the past 2 months	2	30	Common risk
						Liquidity	Cash flow interruptions	4	60	Common risk
No. risks to be handled		1						0		

These risks affect market share performance indicators which can be controlled by monitoring competition and by keeping up with the new technologies. Finally, by improving the marketing strategy and attracting new clients these risks can lead to higher values of turnover and profit for the organization.

Process interaction no. 6 – Applying the FMEA method and identifying business opportunities during risk assessment at the interaction between procurement processes and financial processes while aiming for new business opportunities

Risks related to processes performed by the procurement department in relation with the financial department are unattractive for managers that pursue new business opportunities. Table 11 from Annex K shows that two out of the three risks identified during the initial risk analysis are attractive after applying detection. By improving payment and production procedures and protocols organizations can develop new partnerships with clients and suppliers and to increase turnover and profitability.

Performance indicators impacted by risk related to delayed projects and deliveries and exceeded project budget have to be monitored in order to determine if risk levels increase and new opportunities can be tackled (increasing turnover and profit by improving production and delivery protocols and control mechanisms, improving contract budgets and protocols in order to increase profitability and optimize cash flow and new partnerships with clients and suppliers by improving payment protocols).

Process interaction no. 7 – Applying the FMEA method and identifying business opportunities during risk assessment at the interaction between financial processes and production processes while aiming for new business opportunities

Table 12 from Annex K shows that after applying detection risks related to delayed production can lead to a value-adding opportunity that positively affects the

organizations' turnover and profit. The other risks have to be monitored and relate to delayed payments, deliveries and production, products and services with quality-related issues and non-performing contracts.
The performance indicators impacted by the common risks are liquidity, market share, number of repeat customers and new clients, number of supplier partners and profitability – these indicators have to be monitored in order to determine when risk materialization conditions are met.

Process interaction no. 8 – Applying the FMEA method and identifying business opportunities during risk assessment at the interaction between senior management and financial processes while aiming for new business opportunities

The interactions between processes between senior management and the financial department involve risks from which only 2 can lead to an increased number of supplier partners and improve the organizations' main performance indicators if payment and delivery procedures are updated (Table 13 from Annex K).
The opportunity of developing new partnerships with clients and suppliers by improving payment protocols can be achieved by including the risk related to delayed payments in the risk handling plan.

Process interaction no. 9 – Applying the FMEA method and identifying business opportunities during risk assessment at the interaction between planning processes and production processes while aiming for new business opportunities

Table 14 from Annex K shows that interactions between process from the planning and production departments do not involve any risks that can immediately lead to important business opportunities.
However, performance indicators impacted by risks related to production disruptions, products and services with quality-related issues and delayed or faulty production or service delivery should be monitored in order to determine when risk levels are higher. Such opportunities can involve increasing turnover and profit by improving production and delivery protocols and control mechanisms and keeping existing clients and attracting new clients by improving production and quality assurance protocols.

Process interaction no. 10 – Applying the FMEA method and identifying business opportunities during risk assessment at the interaction between production processes and after-sales processes while aiming for new business opportunities

Between the production and after-sales departments only production processes can generate risks that can be considered attractive after calculating Risk Level 2 (Table 15 from Annex K). Keeping the existing clients and attracting new clients while increasing turnover and profitability are the main opportunities that could derive from managing these risks.

Risks that do not immediately lead to new opportunities are related to non-compliant products, high costs with product replacement and repairing during the warranty period, producing troublesome and outdated products.
Performance indicators affected by these risks have to be monitored in order to determine if new business opportunities can be achieved.

Process interaction no. 11 – Applying the FMEA method and identifying business opportunities during risk assessment at the interaction between senior management and production processes while aiming for new business opportunities
The study shows that none of the risks that may occur at process interactions level between senior management and the production department can lead to important business opportunities (Table 16 from Annex K).

Risks related to producing goods and delivering services that are unappealing for potential clients, production gaps or stopped production, decreased sales and the organizational image being negatively affected can lead to important business opportunities if the impacted performance indicators are monitored by the organization.

Process interaction no. 12 – Applying the FMEA method and identifying business opportunities during risk assessment at the interaction between after-sales processes and quality assurance processes while aiming for new business opportunities
Table 17 from Annex K indicates that no risks are attractive for new opportunities when it comes to process interactions between the production and the planning departments.
The identified risks relate to the organizational image being negatively affected, limited or faulty troubleshooting in the warranty period, additional unforeseen costs during warranty period, delivering faulty or outdated products and services. If risk levels increase possible new business opportunities are attracting new clients by improving the marketing strategy, increasing turnover and profitability by offering high quality services, keeping existing clients and minimizing costs during warranty period.

Process interaction no. 13 – Applying the FMEA method and identifying business opportunities during risk assessment at the interaction between senior management and after-sales processes while aiming for new business opportunities

Risks at process interaction level between senior management and the after-sales department should not be managed in order to tackle new business opportunities. Table 18 from Annex K shows that none of the identified risks are attractive after performing the second phase of the analysis.

Monitoring materialization conditions of risks related to decreased support services and spare parts sales and the organizational image being negatively affected can lead to identifying new business opportunities such as increasing turnover and profitability by offering high quality services and keeping existing clients and attracting new clients by improving the marketing strategy.

Process interaction no. 14 – Applying the FMEA method and identifying business opportunities during risk assessment at the interaction between quality assurance processes and marketing and sales processes while aiming for new business opportunities

All four risks considered attractive during the preliminary analysis are transformed into common risks after applying detection (Table 19 from Annex K). Attracting new clients by improving the marketing strategy, investing in new technology financed by attracting investors or selling shares and focusing on new marketing strategies considering the clients' needs are business opportunities that can be tackled if performance indicators related to the identified risks are monitored (number of repeat customers and new clients, number of supplier partners, market share and profitability).

Process interaction no. 15 – Applying the FMEA method and identifying business opportunities during risk assessment at the interaction between procurement processes and suppliers while aiming for new business opportunities

The process interactions between the procurement department and suppliers can lead to strengthening relations with clients and increasing profitability and turnover. Table 20 from Annex K shows that by improving sourcing protocols in order to deliver goods and increasing turnover and profitability by keeping existing clients and minimizing costs during warranty period on time, as well as by updating marketing and sales strategies, organizations can tackle value-adding opportunities by managing the related risks. The attractive risks can be managed by monitoring the specific risk materialization conditions for the market share performance indicator.

Summarized results related to determining the probability of occurrence, consequences and probability of detection during the risk assessment process related to organizational business processes in relation with the identification of business opportunities

Table 6.27 shows that only 27,27% of the risks identified during the initial analysis are still attractive after calculating Risk Level 2 using the three attributes. This means that a very significant amount of resources would not be wasted and are available for managing risks that can lead to valuable business opportunities.

Table 6.27: Number of risks included in the risk handling plan as a result of using 3 attributes during risk assessment and identifying business opportunities compared risk assessment using 2 attributes at the interaction between organizational business processes, developed by the author based on the research conducted during the doctoral period

Interaction no.	Risk matrix with 2 attributes		Risk matrix with 3 attributes	
	Average proposed risk type	No. risks to be handled	Average proposed risk type	No. risks to be handled
1	Attractive risk	7	Common risk	3
2	Attractive risk	2	Common risk	0
3	Attractive risk	4	Common risk	2
4	Common risk	1	Common risk	1
5	Attractive risk	4	Common risk	2
6	Attractive risk	5	Common risk	2
7	Attractive risk	5	Common risk	1
8	Attractive risk	6	Common risk	2
9	Attractive risk	3	Common risk	0
10	Attractive risk	5	Common risk	2
11	Attractive risk	4	Common risk	0
12	Attractive risk	6	Common risk	0
13	Attractive risk	3	Common risk	0
14	Attractive risk	4	Common risk	0
15	Attractive risk	6	Common risk	3
Total		66		**18**

Table 6.28 shows that 11 out of 18 opportunities are determined by improving internal processes (61,11%) and the rest are tackled by strengthening relations with clients and suppliers.

Table 6.28: Opportunities related to risk assessment using the FMEA method and identifying new business opportunities during risk assessment related to interactions between organizational business processes, developed by the author based on the research conducted during the doctoral period

No. crt.	Possible positive effect of attractive risk materialization	Possible opportunity	No. of opportunities
1.	Investing in new technology financed by attracting new investors or selling shares	Increasing profit and turnover by improving internal processes	4
2.	Assigning resources for marketing campaigns in order to increase productivity by increasing sales		1
3.	Improving turnover and profit by improving the marketing strategy and attracting new clients		2
4.	Increasing turnover and profit by improving production protocols and control mechanisms		2
5.	Increasing turnover and profit by improving delivery protocols and control mechanisms		1
6.	Increasing turnover and profitability by keeping existing clients and minimizing costs during warranty period		1
7.	Attracting new clients by improving the marketing strategy	Increasing profit and turnover by improving relations with clients and suppliers	1
8.	Keeping existing clients and attracting new clients by improving production and quality assurance protocols		1
9.	Keeping existing clients and attracting new clients by improving the sales and marketing strategy		1
10.	New partnerships with clients and suppliers by improving payment protocols		3
11.	Improving sourcing protocols in order to deliver on time and improve relations with clients		1
Total no. of valuable opportunities to be tackled			**18**

The research shows that performance indicators are impacted by a total of 129 risks from which 110 are not managed after applying detection. In order to control the risks not included in the risk handling plan, the main performance indicators have to be monitored in order to identify if risk materialization conditions are met

Figure 6.8 shows that by monitoring the number of repeat customers and new clients, as well as market share, profitability and liquidity, organizations can control almost 90% of the attractive risks. Liquidity and profitability are each impacted by 15% of the risks that can lead to valuable business opportunities.

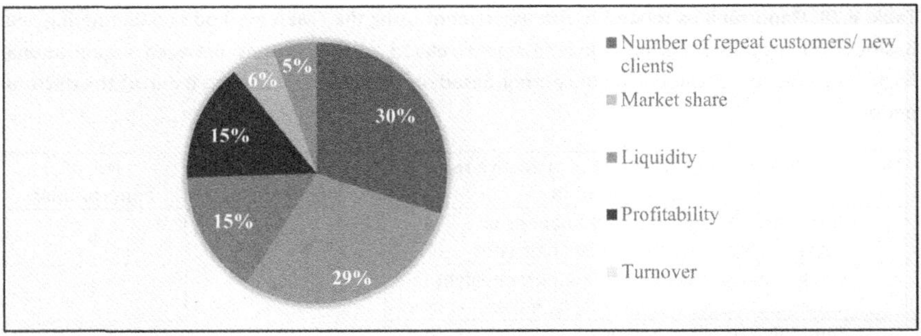

Figure 6.8: Main performance indicators that can be impacted by risks that can lead to new business opportunities, developed by the author based on the research conducted during the doctoral period.

6.2.4 Determining the probability of occurrence, consequences and probability of detection during the risk assessment process related to interactions between the organization and outsourced business processes in relation with the identification of business opportunities

a) Results related to the impact of applying the FMEA method and identifying business opportunities during risk assessment related to process interactions between business processes fully owned by the organization and executed in the domestic country

Table 6.29 indicates that by using detection during the risk assessment at process interactions level between fully owned business processes executed in the domestic country resources are focused on valuable business opportunities related to 3 risks with effect on productivity; moreover, productive processes have a direct positive impact on profitability. Only half of the risks considered unacceptable when calculating Risk Level 1 are included in the risk handling plan.

Increasing profitability and productivity by redesigning optimizing processes are the main opportunities that can be tackled by including risk related to incomplete or incorrect process design and inefficient and outdated processes in the risk handling plan.

Table 6.29: Applying the FMEA method and identifying business opportunities during risk assessment related to process interactions between processes inside the organization (full ownership, onsite), developed by the author based on the research conducted during the doctoral period

No. crt.	Risks	Risk Level 1	Possible business opportunity	Impacted performance indicators	Risk materialization conditions	D	Risk Level 2	Proposed risk type
1.	Inefficient and outdated processes	20	Increasing profitability and productivity by optimizing processes	Number of repeat customers and new clients	Decreased during the past 2 months	2	30	Common risk
				Productivity		4	60	Common risk
No. risks to be handled		1				0		

When it comes to shared processes executed remotely only 2 of the 5 unacceptable risks are to be persuaded when aiming for new business opportunities (Table 6.30).

Table 6.30: Applying the FMEA method and identifying business opportunities during risk assessment related to process interactions between the organization and shared processes executed offsite, developed by the author based on the research conducted during the doctoral period

No. crt.	Risks	Risk Level 1	Possible business opportunity	Impacted performance indicators	Risk materialization conditions	D	Risk Level 2	Proposed risk type
1.	Incomplete or incorrect process design	15	Increasing profitability and productivity by redesigning business processes	Number of repeat customers and new clients	Decreased during the past 2 months	2	30	Common risk
				Productivity		5	75	Attractive risk
				Market share	▪ New competitors ▪ New technology	4	60	Common risk
2.	Losing full control and decreased quality of service	15	Increasing clients' satisfaction by improving the quality of products and services	Market share		4	60	Common risk
3.	Inefficient processes	15	Increasing profitability and productivity by optimizing processes	Profitability	Decreased during the past 2 months	2	30	Common risk
4.	Inefficient and outdated processes	20				2	40	Common risk
				Productivity		5	100	Attractive risk
No. risks to be handled		5				2		

Common risks that have to be monitored in order to detect future business opportunities are related to incomplete or incorrect process design, losing full control and decreased quality of service and inefficient and outdated processes.
These risks affect the organization's performance indicators including number of repeat customers and new clients, productivity, market share and profitability.

b) Results related to the impact of applying the FMEA method and identifying business opportunities during risk assessment related to process interactions between business processes fully owned by the organization and executed in a foreign country

Interactions between the organization and business processes performed in neighbouring countries in subsidiaries, branches or manufacturing plants involve important risks related to productivity that can lead to profitable opportunities (Table 6.31).

Table 6.31: Applying the FMEA method and identifying business opportunities during risk assessment related to process interactions between the organization and captive processes executed nearshore, developed by the author based on the research conducted during the doctoral period

No. crt.	Risks	Risk Level 1	Possible business opportunity	Impacted performance indicators	Risk materialization conditions	D	Risk Level 2	Proposed risk type
1.	Incomplete or incorrect process design	15	Increasing profitability and productivity by redesigning business processes	Number of repeat customers and new clients	Decreased during the past 2 months	2	30	Common risk
				Productivity		5	75	Attractive risk
				Market share	▪ New competitors ▪ New technology	4	60	Common risk
2.	Losing full control and decreased quality of service	15	Increasing clients' satisfaction by improving the quality of products and services			4	60	Common risk
3.	High costs with wages and transport-tation	20	Increasing profitability and productivity by decreasing costs	Productivity	Decreased during the past 2 months	4	80	Attractive risk

4.	Outdated control mechanisms	15	Increasing productivity and business sustainability by improving control of processes	Productivity	Decreased during the past 2 months	4	60	Common risk
5.	Inefficient processes	15	Increasing profitability and productivity by optimizing processes	Profitability	Decreased during the past 2 months	2	30	Common risk
6.	Inefficient and outdated processes	20				2	40	Common risk
				Productivity		4	60	Attractive risk
No. risks to be handled		6				3		

Redesigning or optimizing business processes and finding ways of decreasing costs are efforts that need to be made by the organization in order to increase productivity and profitability. Incomplete or incorrect process design, high costs with wages and transportation and inefficient and outdated processes are the main risks that can lead to valuable business opportunities. By monitoring the number of repeat customers and new clients, market share and profitability new business opportunities can be tackled if risk materialization conditions are met.

Table 6.32: Applying the FMEA method and identifying business opportunities during risk assessment related to process interactions between the organization and captive processes executed offshore, developed by the author based on the research conducted during the doctoral period

No. crt.	Risks	Risk Level 1	Possible business opportunity	Impacted performance indicators	Risk materialization conditions	D	Risk Level 2	Proposed risk type
1.	Incomplete or incorrect process design	15	Increasing profitability and productivity by redesigning business processes	Number of repeat customers and new clients	Decreased during the past 2 months	2	30	Common risk
				Productivity		5	75	Attractive risk
				Market share	▪ New competitors ▪ New technology	4	60	Common risk
2.	Losing full control and decreased quality of service	15	Increasing clients' satisfaction by improving the quality of products and services			4	60	Common risk

3.	High costs with wages and transportation	25	Increasing profitability and productivity by decreasing costs	Productivity	Decreased during the past 2 months	4	100	Attractive risk
4.	Outdated control mechanisms	15	Increasing productivity and business sustainability by improving control of processes			4	60	Common risk
5.	Inefficient processes	15	Increasing profitability and productivity by optimizing processes	Profitability	Decreased during the past 2 months	2	30	Common risk
6.	Inefficient and outdated processes	20				2	40	Common risk
				Productivity		5	100	Attractive risk
No. risks to be handled		6					2	

While having the advantage of owning business processes, valuable opportunities can be achieved if organizations focus on cost efficiency and improving business processes executed offshore (Table 6.32). Increasing profitability and productivity by redesigning and optimizing business processes and decreasing costs are the main opportunities that can be achieved by including the identified attractive risks in the risk handling plan.

c) Results related to the impact of applying the FMEA method and identifying business opportunities during risk assessment related to process interactions between the organization and business processes owned by third-party providers executed in the domestic country

Table 6.33 shows new business opportunities can be tackled by handling risks related to incomplete or incorrect process design, high costs with wages and transportation and inefficient and outdated processes.

Increasing profitability and productivity by redesigning and optimizing processes and decreasing costs are the business opportunities that can be achieved if the identified risks are included in the risk handling plan.

Table 6.33: Applying the FMEA method and identifying business opportunities during risk assessment related to process interactions between the organization and processes executed by a third-party provider onsite, developed by the author based on the research conducted during the doctoral period

No. crt.	Risks	Risk Level 1	Possible business opportunity	Impacted performanc e indicators	Risk materializatio n conditions	D	Risk Level 2	Proposed risk type
1.	Incomplete or incorrect process design	15	Increasing profitability and productivity by redesigning business processes	Number of repeat cus-tomers and new clients	Decreased during the past 2 months	2	30	Common risk
				Productivity		5	75	Attractive risk
				Market share	▪ New competitors ▪ New technology	4	60	Common risk
2.	Losing full control and decreased quality of service	15	Increasing clients' satisfaction by improving the quality of products and services			4	60	Common risk
3.	High costs with wages and transporta-tion	20	Increasing profitability and productivity by decreasing costs	Productivity	Decreased during the past 2 months	4	80	Attractive risk
4.	Outdated control mechanisms	15	Increasing productivity and business sustainability by improving control of processes	Productivity	Decreased during the past 2 months	4	60	Common risk
5.	Inefficient processes	15	Increasing profitability and productivity by optimizing processes	Profitability	Decreased during the past 2 months	2	30	Common risk
6.	Inefficient and outdated processes	20				2	40	Common risk
				Productivity		4	60	Attractive risk
No. risks to be handled		6				3		

Common risks can lead to valuable business opportunities in the future if risk levels increase; this can only be detected by monitoring the impacted performance indicators: number of repeat customers and new clients, profitability and market share.

In case the first 2 indicators decrease in the past months or new competing organizations or innovative technology threaten the organization's position on the market risks have to be re-evaluated in order to determine if new opportunities can be tackled. Possible future opportunities can be increasing clients' satisfaction by improving the quality of products and services, increasing clients' satisfaction by improving the quality of products and services, increasing productivity and business sustainability by improving control of processes and increasing profitability and productivity by optimizing processes.

When it comes to identifying risks related to process interactions between the organization and processes executed by a third-party provider offsite 3 attractive risks can be identified (Table 6.34). The risks leading to valuable business opportunities relate to incomplete or incorrect process design, high costs with wages and transportation and inefficient and outdated processes. Increasing profitability and productivity by redesigning and optimizing business processes and decreasing costs can be achieved by including the identified risks in the risk handling plan.

Table 6.34: Applying the FMEA method and identifying business opportunities during risk assessment related to process interactions between the organization and processes executed by a third-party provider offsite, developed by the author based on the research conducted during the doctoral period

No. crt.	Risks	Risk Level 1	Possible business opportunity	Impacted performance indicators	Risk materialization conditions	D	Risk Level 2	Proposed risk type
1.	Incomplete or incorrect process design	15	Increasing profitability and productivity by redesigning business processes	Number of repeat customers and new clients	Decreased during the past 2 months	2	30	Common risk
				Productivity		5	75	Attractive risk
				Market share	▪ New competitors ▪ New technology	4	60	Common risk
2.	Losing full control and decreased quality of service	15	Increasing clients' satisfaction by improving the quality of products and services			4	60	Common risk

3.	High costs with wages and transport-tation	25	Increasing profitability and productivity by decreasing costs	Productivity	Decreased during the past 2 months	4	100	Attractive risk
4.	Outdated control mechanisms	15	Increasing productivity and business sustainability by improving control of processes			4	60	Common risk
5.	Inefficient processes	15	Increasing profitability and productivity by optimizing processes	Profitability	Decreased during the past 2 months	2	30	Common risk
6.	Inefficient and outdated processes	20				2	40	Common risk
				Productivity		5	100	Attractive risk
No. risks to be handled		6				3		

New business opportunities can be achieved by monitoring the performance indicators (number of repeat customers and new clients, market share, productivity and profitability) impacted by risks related to incomplete or incorrect process design, losing full control and decreased quality of service, outdated control mechanisms and inefficient business processes. If risk levels increase, organizations can include these risks in the risk handling plan in order to tackle value-adding opportunities.

d) *Results related to the impact of applying the FMEA method and identifying business opportunities during risk assessment related to process interactions between the organization and business processes fully owned by third-party providers executed in a foreign country*

Opportunities related to processes executed in foreign countries by third-party organi-zations can be achieved by carefully designing processes and improving control mecha-nisms in order to permanently evaluate quality of services and strategically managing all involved costs. Table 6.35 presents that the majority of the risks between the organiza-tion and third-party providers are attractive and can be introduced in the risk handling plan.

Table 6.35: Applying the FMEA method and identifying business opportunities during risk assessment related to process interactions between the organization and processes executed by a third-party provider nearshore, developed by the author based on the research conducted during the doctoral period

No. crt.	Risks	Risk Level 1	Possible business opportunity	Impacted performance indicators	Risk materialization conditions	D	Risk Level 2	Proposed risk type
1.	Incomplete or incorrect process design	20	Increasing profitability and productivity by redesigning business processes	Number of repeat customers and new clients	Decreased during the past 2 months	2	40	Common risk
				Productivity		5	100	Attractive risk
				Market share	▪ New competitors ▪ New technology	4	80	Attractive risk
2.	Losing full control and decreased quality of service	20	Increasing clients' satisfaction by improving the quality of products and services			4	80	Attractive risk
3.	High costs with wages and transporta-tion	25	Increasing profitability and productivity by decreasing costs	Productivity	Decreased during the past 2 months	4	100	Attractive risk
4.	Outdated control mechanisms	20	Increasing productivity and business sustainability by improving control of processes			4	80	Attractive risk
5.	Inefficient processes	15	Increasing profitability and productivity by optimizing processes	Profitability	Decreased during the past 2 months	2	30	Common risk
6.	Inefficient and outdated processes	20				2	40	Common risk
				Productivity	Decreased during the past 2 months	4	80	Attractive risk
No. risks to be handled		6				5		

Risk assessment at process interactions level between the organization and offshore processes executed by third-party organizations can score the highest risk levels and can be very attractive while aiming for new opportunities (Table 6.36).

Table 6.36: Applying the FMEA method and identifying business opportunities during risk assessment related to process interactions between the organization and processes executed by third-party providers offshore, developed by the author based on the research conducted during the doctoral period

No. crt.	Risks	Risk Level 1	Possible business opportunity	Impacted performance indicators	Risk materialization conditions	D	Risk Level 2	Proposed risk type
1.	Incomplete or incorrect process design	20	Increasing profitability and productivity by redesigning business processes	Number of repeat customers and new clients	Decreased during the past 2 months	2	40	Common risk
				Productivity		5	100	Attractive risk
				Market share	▪ New competitors ▪ New technology	4	80	Attractive risk
2.	Losing full control and decreased quality of service	25	Increasing clients' satisfaction by improving the quality of products and services	Market share		4	100	Attractive risk
3.	High costs with wages and transporta-tion	25	Increasing profitability and productivity by decreasing costs	Productivity	Decreased during the past 2 months	4	100	Attractive risk
4.	Outdated control mechanisms	20	Increasing productivity and business sustainability by improving control of processes	Productivity	Decreased during the past 2 months	4	80	Attractive risk
5.	Inefficient processes	20	Increasing profitability and productivity by optimizing processes	Profitability	Decreased during the past 2 months	2	40	Common risk
6.	Inefficient and outdated processes	25				2	50	Common risk
				Productivity		5	125	
No. risks to be handled		6					5	

By allocating resourcing for optimizing processes there are very high chances to increase business profitability and productivity.

Summarized results related to determining the probability of occurrence, consequences and probability of detection during risk assessment related to interactions between the organization and outsourced business processes in relation with the identification of business opportunities

Table 6.37 indicates the number of unacceptable or very high risks evaluated and analyzed using three attributes compared to using the classical two attributes. Almost 58% less risks are included in the risk handling plan after using the FMEA method when performing risk assessment.

Productivity is the key performance indicator affected by the highest number of risks with only 5 out of 25 risks were considered tolerable after applying detection. From a total of 42 attractive risks only 24 risks were still to be pursued after applying detection as the third attribute in the risk assessment process.

Table 6.37: Number of risks included in the risk handling plan as a result of using 3 attributes compared to 2 attributes during risk assessment and identifying business opportunities related to interactions between the organization and outsourced business processes, developed by the author based on the research conducted during the doctoral period

Business process categories		**Business processes by ownership:** Owned by the organization		Owned by the third-party provider	
		Number of risks handled without using the FMEA method	Number of risks handled after using the FMEA method	Number of risks handled without using the FMEA method	Number of risks handled after using the FMEA method
Business processes by location:	Onsite	1	0	6	3
	Offsite	5	2	6	3
	Nearshore	6	3	6	5
	Offshore	6	2	6	5
Total no. of risks		18	**7**	24	**16**

The organizations' performance indicators are impacted by up to 58% less risks after applying the FMEA method and identifying opportunities during risk assessment related to process interactions between the organization and outsourced business processes (Table 6.38).

Table 6.38: Number of risks impacting the organization's performance indicators as a result of applying the FMEA method and identifying business opportunities during risk assessment related to process interactions between the organization and outsourced business processes, developed by the author based on the research conducted during the doctoral period

No. crt.	Impacted performance indicators	Number of risks handled without using the FMEA method	Number of risks handled after using the FMEA method	Difference between risks handled using and not using the FMEA method during risk assessment **(B-A)**	
		A	B	Value	Percentage
1.	Number of repeat customers and new clients	8	0	-8	-100%
2.	Market share	14	4	-10	-71.43%
3.	Profitability	14	0	-14	-100%
4.	Productivity	28	23	-5	-17.85%
Total		64	**27**	-37	**-57.81%**

All risks related to the number of repeat customers and new clients and profitability are excluded from the risk handling plan and are considered tolerable by the organization after using detection during the risk assessment process. This means that the proposed method brings a significant contribution to improving sustainable performance in organizations.

6.3 Developing a model for risk assessment related to organizational business processes using the proposed methods

6.3.1 Description of the proposed risk assessment model related to organizational business processes using the proposed methods

The objective of the research related to the PDCA and FMEA methods and identifying opportunities during the risk assessment process aims to develop a model that can be used as a tool for organizations that want to ensure sustainable performance. Using the results of the studies performed during the doctoral period, the proposed model relates to improving the risk assessment process using the PDCA and FMEA methods and evaluating both negative and positive outcomes that can be generated by materialized risks.

Given the complexity of the model, different graphic representations were presented in order to facilitate integration in the organizations' risk assessment processes.

NEGATIVE OUTCOMES (RISK LEVEL 2)					RISK LEVEL 1		POSITIVE OUTCOMES (RISK LEVEL 2)				
125	-100	-75	-50	-25	-25	25	25	50	75	100	125
-100	-80	-60	-40	-20	-20	20	20	40	60	80	100
-60	-48	-36	-24	-12	-12	12	12	24	36	48	60
-45	-36	-27	-18	-9	-9	9	9	18	27	36	45
-5	-4	-3	-2	-1	-1	1	1	2	3	4	5
PROBABILITY OF DETECTION											
5	4	3	2	1			1	2	3	4	5
Very low	Low	Moderate (medium)	High	Very high			Very low	Low	Moderate (medium)	High	Very high

Figure 6.9: Proposed risk levels for the risk assessment model, developed by the author based on the research conducted during the doctoral period.

The first step in developing the risk assessment model is calculating and illustrating all risk levels and risk types. Figure 6.9 presents the proposed risk level values for Risk Level 1 calculated by multiplying probability of occurrence (P) and consequence (C) and Risk Level 2 that involves multiplying Risk Level 1 and detection (D) as a third attribute of the risk assessment process.

Additionally, Figure 6.9 includes both negative (threats) and positive outcomes (opportunities). Consequences have a positive value if the expected effects of risk materialization are positive and a negative value if the expected effects of risk materialization are negative. Therefore, risk levels have positive and negative values according to the positive or negative outcomes that are predicted as results of risk materialization.

A very low probability of detection leads to unacceptable and very high risks leading to negative outcomes and also unattractive or very low risks leading to positive outcomes. However, a very high probability of detection leads to acceptable risks that can lead to negative outcomes and attractive risks leasing to positive outcomes, therefore:

- For negative outcomes the probability of detecting risk materialization conditions starts from "very high" with the assigned value 1 to "very low" with the assigned value 5;

- For positive outcomes the probability of detecting risk materialization conditions starts from "very low" with the assigned value 1 to "very high" with the assigned value 5.

Table 6.39: Proposed risk values and risk levels for negative and positive outcomes using 2 attributes, developed by the author based on the research conducted during the doctoral period

Negative outcomes		Positive outcomes	
Tolerance intervals for Risk Level 1	Proposed risk type for Risk Level 1	Tolerance intervals for Risk Level 1	Proposed risk type for Risk Level 1
-1	Very low risk	1	Very low risk
(-2) – (-9)	Acceptable risk	2-9	Unattractive risk
(-10) – (-12)	Tolerable risk	10-12	Common risk
(-13) – (-20)	Unacceptable risk	13-20	Attractive risk
(-20) – (-25)	Very high risk	20-25	Very attractive risk

The values of Risk Level 1 using 2 attributes were negative and positive according to the consequences of the identified risks. From the 14 possible values determined by the 5x5 risk scorecard developed by NASA, the risk values +/-1, +/-9, +/-12, +/-20 and +/-25 were selected for the axe related to Risk Level 1 according to the risk levels that mark the limits between risk types (Table 6.39).

The values of the Risk Level 2 using 3 attributes were calculated by multiplying Risk level 1 with the values of detection. Further, risk level intervals and corresponding risk types were proposed in Table 6.40.

Table 6.40: Proposed risk values and risk levels for negative and positive outcomes using 3 attributes, developed by the author based on the research conducted during the doctoral period

Negative outcomes		Positive outcomes	
Tolerance intervals for Risk Level 2	Proposed risk type for Risk Level 2	Tolerance intervals for Risk Level 2	Proposed risk type for Risk Level 2
-1	Very low risk	1	Very low risk
(-2) – (-30)	Acceptable risk	2-30	Unattractive risk
(-31) – (-60)	Tolerable risk	31-60	Common risk
(-61) – (-100)	Unacceptable risk	61-100	Attractive risk
(-101) – (-125)	Very high risk	101-125	Very attractive risk

When it comes to positive outcomes, attractive and very attractive risks are to be considered when investing resources for risk handling. Risks with levels between 1 and 60 do not increase chances of tackling value-adding opportunities - risks become attractive starting with risk level 61.

In order to prepare the tri-dimensional model, Figure 6.10 presents a bi-dimensional model that involves one axis for each of the 3 attributes used during risk assessment: probability of occurrence, consequence and detection. Risk levels are presented in a standard Cartesian coordinates system using 3 axes in a two-dimensional space.

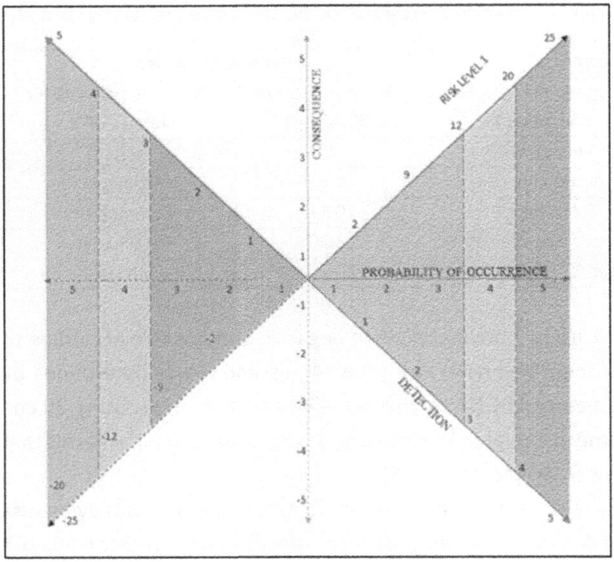

Fig. 6.10: Proposed bi-dimensional representation of the risk assessment model developed by the author based on the research conducted during the doctoral period.

The risk values indicated in Figure 6.10 (+/-2, +/-9, +/-12, +/-20 and +/-25) are represented as points at the intersection of the axes between consequence and probability of appearance and do not represent the mathematical distance between each point and the origin of the Risk Level 1 axe. In order to illustrate the tri-dimensional model the 3 axes used for the bi-dimensional model were considered in a tri-dimensional space (Figure 6.11).

The total number of risks is 250 with 125 positive values and 125 negative values that can be represented by 250 points at the intersection of the 3 axes (Figure 6.12). Each risk level has 3 coordinates: Risk level = R (p, c, d), where:

- Coordinate p = Probability axe with values from 1 to 5;
- Coordinate c = Consequence axe with values from 1 to 5;
- Coordinate d = Detection axe with values from 1 to 5.

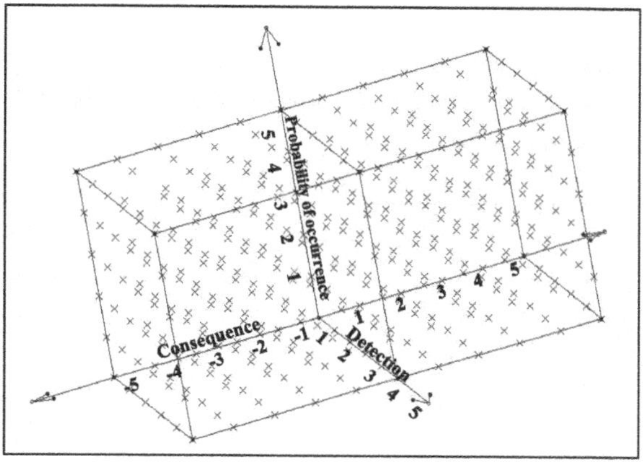

Figure 6.11: Proposed representation of risks in a tri-dimensional space, developed by the author based on the research conducted during the doctoral period.

In order to represent risk level intervals with the proposed color coding, the model includes all risk levels indicated in Figure 6.9 calculated as the mathematical product of the 3 attributes (Annex L). For example, risk level "-12" there are 2 possible combinations: (-3) x 4 x 1 and (-4) x 3 x 1. The proposed model is illustrated in Figure 6.12 presenting all the risks that can lead to negative and positive outcomes using 3 attributes.

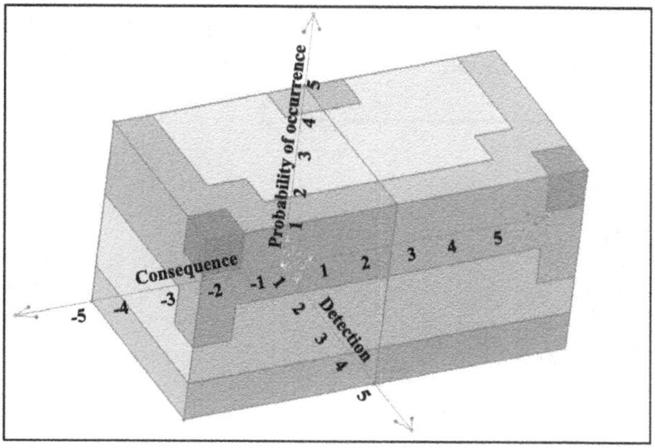

Figure 6.12: Proposed tri-dimensional risk assessment model, developed by the author based on the research conducted during the doctoral period.

In order to understand the different layers of the graphic illustrations each section of the model was separated and explained:

1. Figure 6.13 presents the risks that represent a threat for the organizations. As illustrated, consequence has negative values corresponding with the possible negative outcomes of risk materialization;

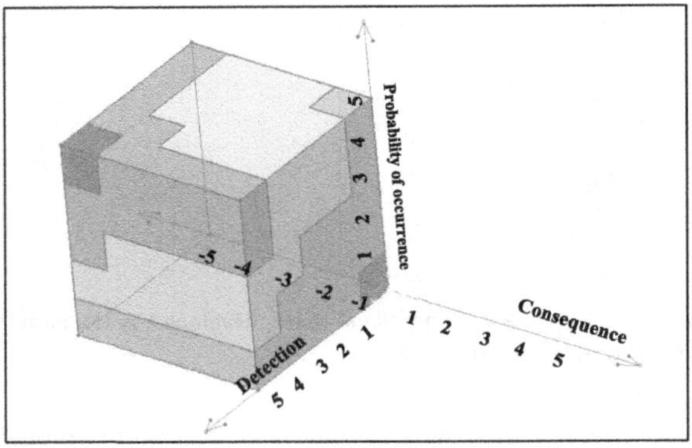

Figure 6.13 – Tri-dimensional risk assessment model for risks leading to negative outcomes as part of the proposed model, developed by the author based on the research conducted during the doctoral period.

2. Figure 6.14 presents the risks that represent an opportunity for the organizations. As illustrated, consequence has positive values corresponding with the possible positive outcomes of risk materialization;

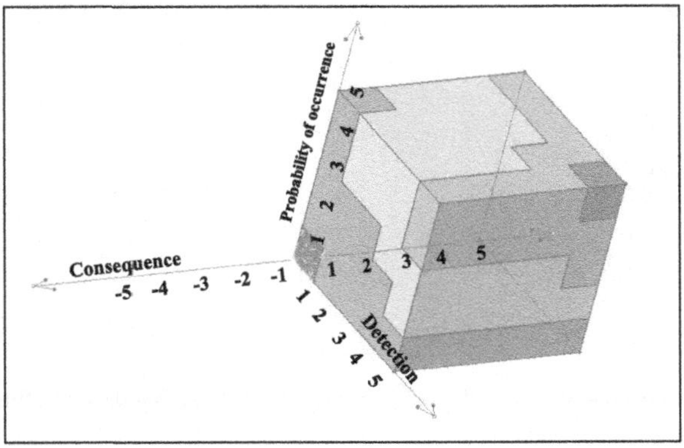

Figure 6.14 – Tri-dimensional risk assessment model for risks leading to business opportunities as part of the proposed model, developed by the author based on the research conducted during the doctoral period.

3. Figure 6.15 presents the tri-dimensional model for very high risks related to negative outcomes as part of the proposed model (risk level = -125); these risks can materialize and have a powerful negative impact on the organization;

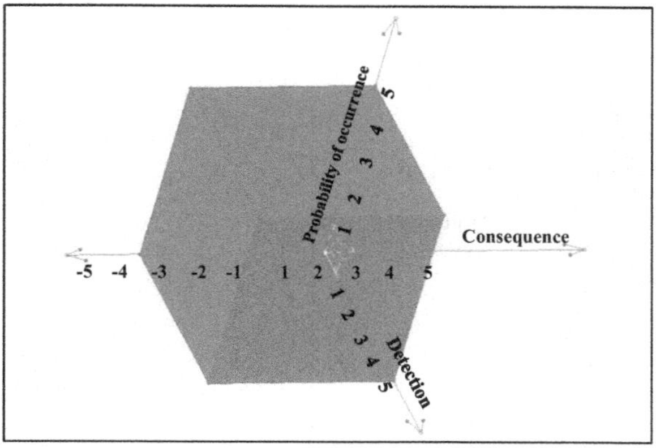

Figure 6.15 – Tri-dimensional risk assessment model for very high risks leading to negative outcomes as part of the proposed model, developed by the author based on the research conducted during the doctoral period.

4. Figure 6.16 presents the tri-dimensional model for very low risks related to positive outcomes (risk level = 1) as part of the proposed model; these risks can materialize leading to important business opportunities for the organization;

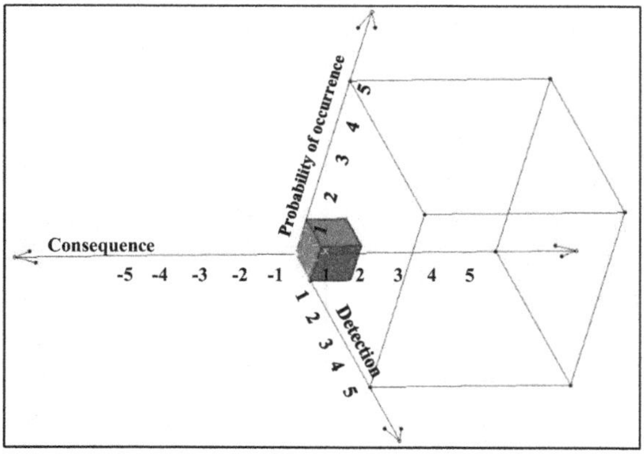

Figure 6.16 – Tri-dimensional risk assessment model for very low risks related to positive outcomes as part of the proposed model, developed by the author based on the research conducted during the doctoral period.

5. Figure 6.17 presents the tri-dimensional model for unacceptable risks related to negative outcomes as part of the proposed model (risk levels = -100, - 80 and -75);

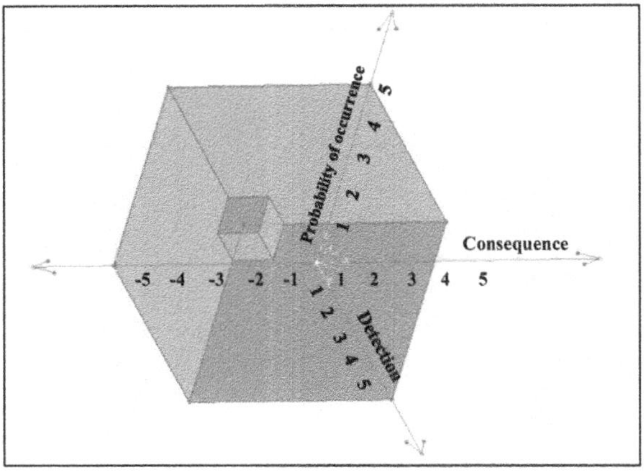

Figure 6.17 – Tri-dimensional risk assessment model for unacceptable risks leading to negative outcomes as part of the proposed model, developed by the author based on the research conducted during the doctoral period.

6. Figure 6.18 presents the tri-dimensional model for unattractive risks related to positive outcomes as part of the proposed model (risk levels = 2, 3, 4, 5, 9, 12, 18, 20, 24, 25 and 27);

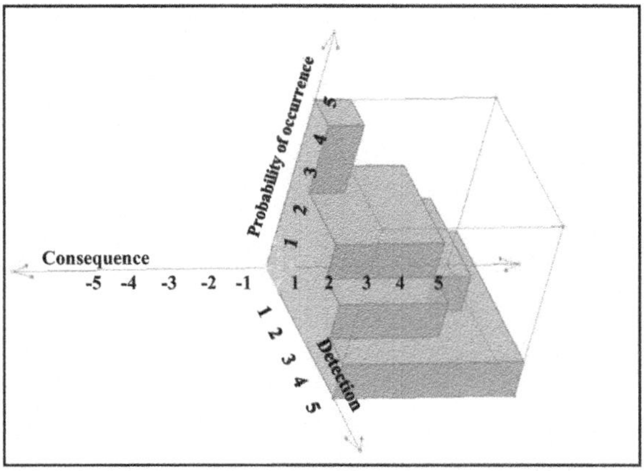

Figure 6.18 – Tri-dimensional risk assessment model for unattractive risks related to positive outcomes as part of the proposed model developed by the author based on the research conducted during the doctoral period.

7. Figure 6.19 presents the tri-dimensional model for tolerable risks related to negative outcomes as part of the proposed model (risk levels = -36, - 40, -45, - 48, -50 and -60);

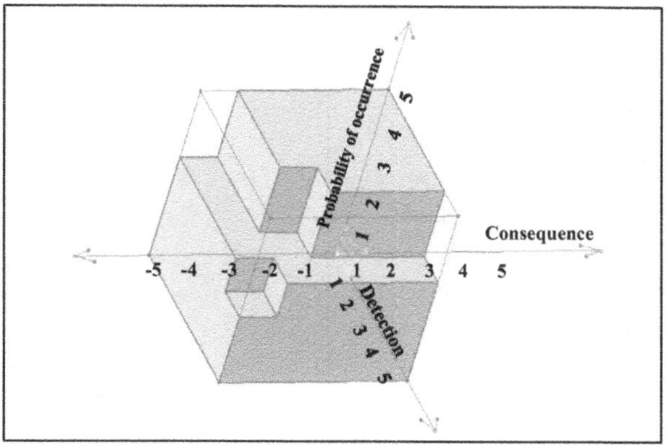

Figure 6.19 – Tri-dimensional risk assessment model for tolerable risks leading to negative outcomes as part of the proposed model, developed by the author based on the research conducted during the doctoral period.

8. Figure 6.20 presents the tri-dimensional model for common risks related to positive outcomes as part of the proposed model (risk levels = 36, 40, 45, 48, 50 and 60);

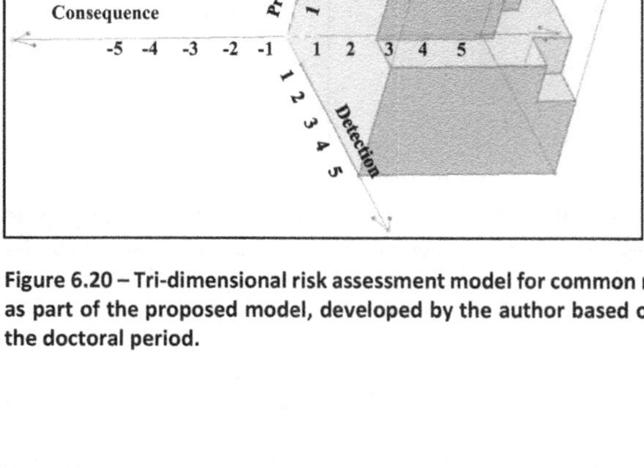

Figure 6.20 – Tri-dimensional risk assessment model for common risks related to positive outcomes as part of the proposed model, developed by the author based on the research conducted during the doctoral period.

9. Figure 6.21 presents the tri-dimensional model for acceptable risks related to negative outcomes as part of the proposed model (risk levels = -2, -3, -4, -5, -9, -12, -18, -20, -24, -25 and -27);

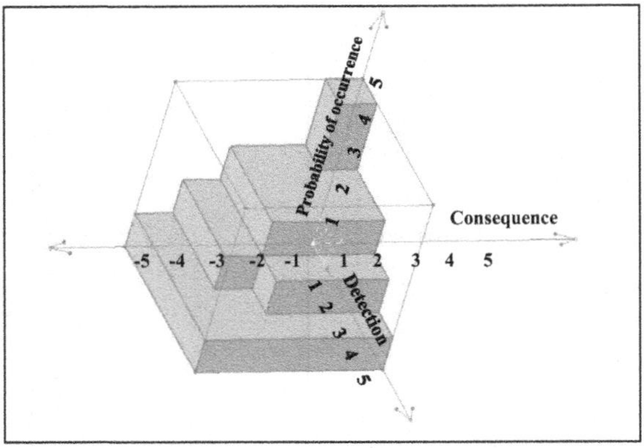

Figure 6.21 – Tri-dimensional risk assessment model for acceptable risks leading to negative outcomes as part of the proposed model, developed by the author based on the research conducted during the doctoral period.

10. Figure 6.22 presents the tri-dimensional model for attractive risks related to positive outcomes as part of the proposed model (risk levels = 75, 80 and 100);

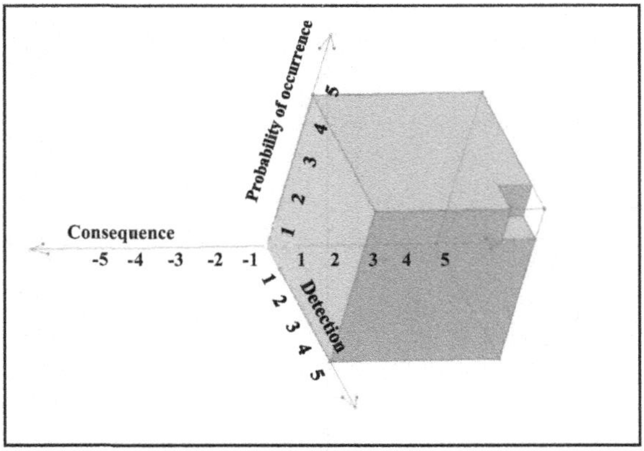

Figure 6.22 – Tri-dimensional risk assessment model for attractive risks related to positive outcomes as part of the proposed model developed by the author based on the research conducted during the doctoral period.

7. Figure 6.23 presents the tri-dimensional model for very low risks related to negative outcomes as part of the proposed model (risk level = -1);

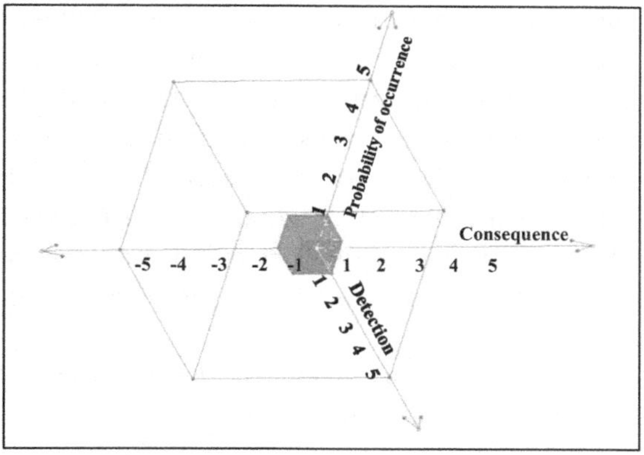

Figure 6.23 – Tri-dimensional risk assessment model for very low risks leading to negative outcomes as part of the proposed model, developed by the author based on the research conducted during the doctoral period.

8. Figure 6.24 presents the tri-dimensional model for very attractive risks related to positive outcomes as part of the proposed model (risk level = 125);

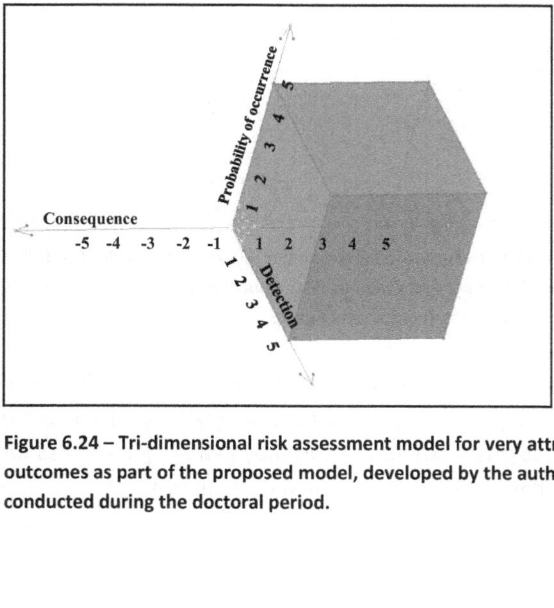

Figure 6.24 – Tri-dimensional risk assessment model for very attractive risks related to positive outcomes as part of the proposed model, developed by the author based on the research conducted during the doctoral period.

6.3.2 Research results regarding to the validation of the proposed model related to organizational business processes using the proposed methods

In order to validate the proposed risk assessment model follow-up interviews were conducted between October and December 2017 with the organizations investigated during a previous study performed between November 2016 and March 2017. The research involves questionnaires sent to 74 managers and specialists from 23 organizations that aim to determine the organizations' level of interest in implementing the proposed risk assessment model including using the PDCA and FMEA methods and analyzing both threats and opportunities and to investigate the managers' perspectives related to the advantages of the bi-dimensional or tri-dimensional models presented.
The results of the questionnaires were summarized by presenting the most relevant 4 questions related to the validation of the proposed model.

Question 1 (Figure 6.25): *Have you integrated the proposed risk assessment model that includes the FMEA method and the identification of both threats and new business opportunities?*

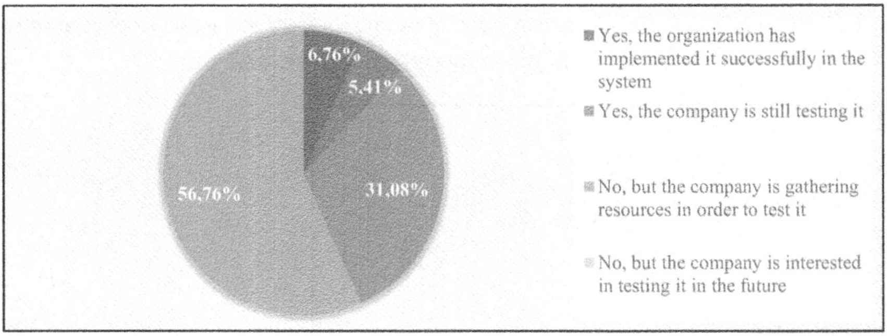

Figure 6.25 – Organizations' interest in an extended risk assessment model that includes the FMEA method and the identification of both threats and new business opportunities, developed by the author based on the research conducted during the doctoral period.

Results – Less than 7% of the organizations answer that the FMEA method has been successfully implemented in their risk evaluation process and only 4 organizations are testing it. More than 30% of the organizations are currently gathering resources for testing it and 56,76% are considering testing this method in the future.

Question 2 (Figure 6.26): *In your opinion, which are the main differences between small and medium-sized enterprises compared to large enterprises when it comes to implementing the proposed model and identifying both threats and new business opportunities?*

Results – More than 75% of the small and medium-sized enterprises perform risk assessment in order to prevent negative outcomes (threats) and to reach positive outcomes (opportunities). Unfortunately, large companies prefer a defensive strategy with only 37% investing in risk assessment while aiming or new business opportunities. This means that from risk mapping point of view, SMEs are more likely to implement the proposed model.

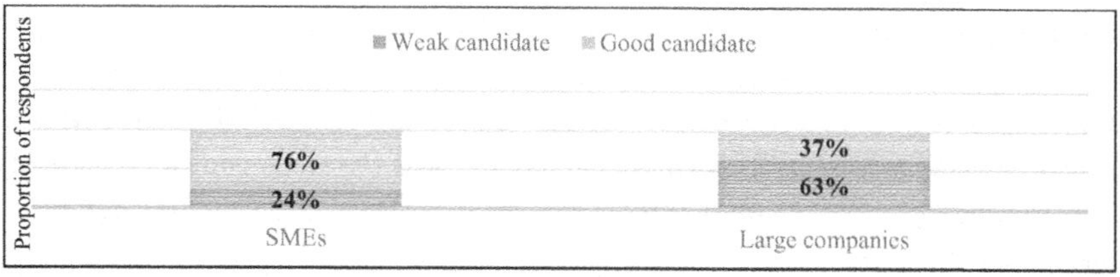

Figure 6.26 – Implementing the proposed model in SMEs compared to large companies, developed by the author based on Mateescu, R. M., Olaru, M., Sârbu, A. and Surugiu (Farcaş), I., 2016. Research on Increasing Risk assessment Efficiency as Support for Corporate Sustainable Development. International Conference on Management, Leadership and Governance (4th ICMLG), St. Petersburg, Russia, 14-15 April 2016, pp. 450, ISBN: 978-1-910810-84-2, indexed in ISI Web of Knowledge, IDS Number: BH5MP, Accession number: WOS: 000401232800055, https://apps.webofknowledge.com/full_record.do?product=UA&search_mode=GeneralSearch&qid=21&SID=1E7sTR4XNLkznRxUiPJ&page=1&doc=1.

Question 3 (Figure 6.27): *Do you think that organizations will use the proposed risk assessment model?*

Results – Almost 44% of the respondents agree that the bi-dimensional and tri-dimensional models are a useful display of applying detection in the risk evaluation process that aims to identify both threats and opportunities. The almost 7% of the managers that have already implemented the extended process agree that these models can be used in order to automate the process (new risk assessment software, less human resources). More than 30% of the respondents considered that these models involve advanced risk assessment know-how and that organizations are not ready to use them.

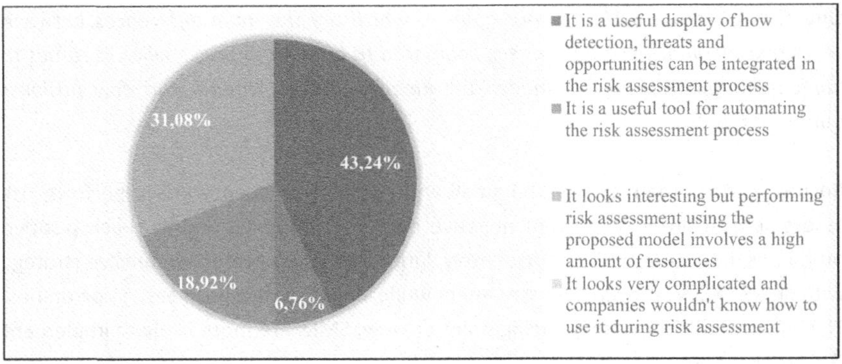

Figure 6.27: Feedback related to the potential of the proposed model, developed by the author based on the research conducted during the doctoral period.

Question 4 (Figure 6.28): *What is your opinion related to the main causes for the proposed extended risk assessment model that includes the PDCA and FMEA methods and the identification of both threats and new business opportunities not being integrated in organizations?*

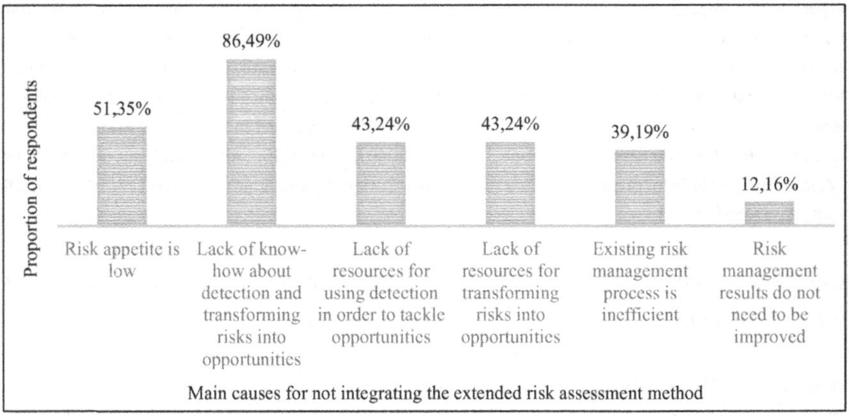

Figure 6.28: Main causes for not integrating the proposed extended risk assessment method, developed by the author based on Mateescu, R. M., Olaru, M., Sârbu, A. and Surugiu (Farcaş), I., 2016. Research on Increasing Risk assessment Efficiency as Support for Corporate Sustainable Development. International Conference on Management, Leadership and Governance (4th ICMLG), St. Petersburg, Russia, 14-15 April 2016, pp. 450, ISBN: 978-1-910810-84-2, indexed in ISI Web of Knowledge, IDS Number: BH5MP, Accession number: WOS: 000401232800055, https://apps.webofknowledge.com/full_record.do?product=UA&search_mode=GeneralSearch&qid=21&SID=1E7sTR4XNLkznRxUiPJ&page=1&doc=1.

Results – Lack of know-how is the main cause for not using detection during risk evaluation according to almost 87% of the managers. More than half of the respondents state that organizations' risk appetite is low while preferring a defensive risk strategy. Lack of resources is another cause for detection not being integrated in the risk assessment process according to 43,24% of the managers. Almost 40% do not want to invest in updating their existing risk assessment process because so far results have not been satisfying and they are not prepared to allocate more resources. According to 12,16% of the respondents their current risk assessment process delivers satisfying results so that they are not looking into improving the process.

6.3.3 Research results regarding the estimated effects of the proposed model related to organizational business processes using the proposed methods

The results were calculated based on feedback from the nine managers that have implemented (6.76% of the organizations) or are testing the proposed risk assessment model (5,41% of the organizations). The results of the questionnaires were summarized by presenting the most relevant 5 questions related to the effects of the proposed model.

Question 1 (Figure 6.29): *Which are the most valuable opportunities that can result from using the proposed risk assessment method?*

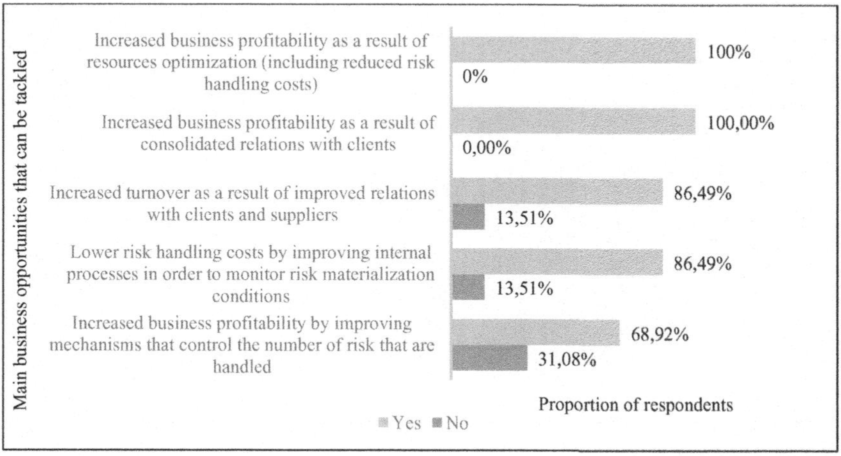

Figure 6.29: Main business opportunities related to the proposed risk assessment model, developed by the author based on the research conducted during the doctoral period.

Results – The majority of the managers agreed on all the important advantages brought by the FMEA method. All the respondents state that business profitability is increased as a result of lower risk handling costs, an improved allocation of resources and strengthened relations with clients. Improved values of organizations' turnover are also achieved by consolidating relations with both clients and suppliers according to almost 87% of the managers. Also, 86,49% of the respondents agree that lowering risk handling costs by improving internal processes is one of the most important advantages of applying detection. Almost 69% of the managers answer that profitability is increased by improving monitoring and control mechanisms in order to decrease or increase the number of risks that are managed.

Question 2 (Figure 6.30): *What is your opinion related to the contribution of the proposed risk assessment model to the organizations' sustainable performance?*

Results – Almost 44% of the respondents agree that the bi-dimensional and tri-dimensional models are a useful display of applying detection in the risk evaluation process that aims to identify both threats and opportunities. The almost 7% of the managers that have already implemented the extended process agree that these models can be used in order to automate the process (new risk assessment software, less human resources). More than 30% of the respondents considered that these models involve advanced risk assessment know-how and that organizations are not ready to use them.

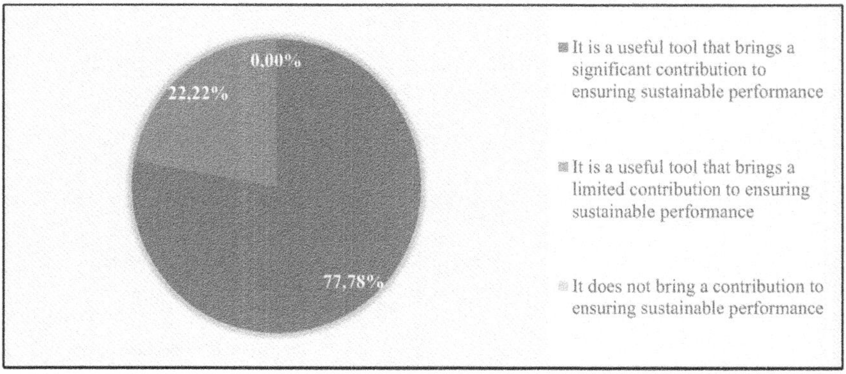

Figure 6.30: Contribution of the proposed model related to the organizations' sustainable performance, developed by the author based on the research conducted during the doctoral period.

Question 3 (Figure 6.31): *Which are the advantages of using the proposed model using the PDCA and FMEA methods and identifying both threats and opportunities?*

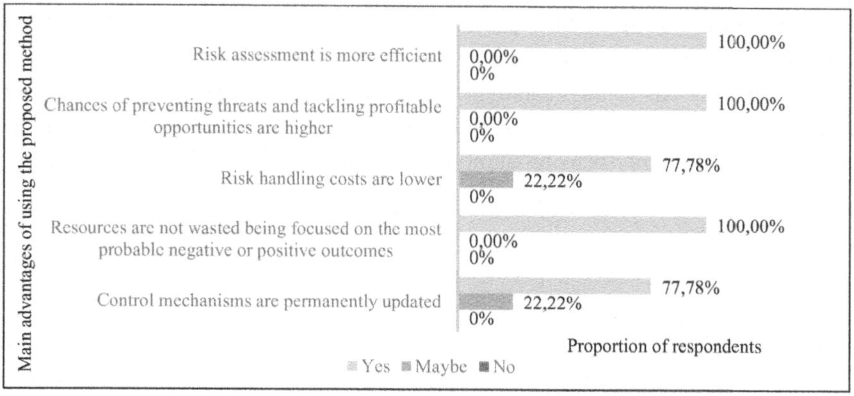

Figure 6.31 – Main advantages of using the proposed risk assessment model, developed by the author based on the research conducted during the doctoral period.

Results – All the managers agree that detection improves the chances of achieving positive outcomes by transforming risks in new business opportunities; also risk assessment becomes more efficient, resources are invested in risks leading to the most probable positive outcomes and business sustainability is ensured. More than 77% of the managers consider that risk assessment costs are lower, the rest being not sure about the resources needed in order to apply detection and monitor risk materialization conditions. By using the proposed method control mechanisms are permanently updated according to 77,78% of the respondents. All the interviewees concluded that the proposed risk assessment method ensures sustainable business performance by increasing risk assessment efficiency, lowering risk handling costs and focusing resources on achieving value-adding results.

Question 4 (Figure 6.32): *Which are the main risks related to applying the proposed risk assessment method?*

Results – The most important risk related to the implementation of the proposed model relate to the limited know-how of the employees and to specialized workforce not being available for the execution of the knowledge-intensive risk assessment model according to almost 84% of the respondents. Another important risk is related to the resourced required for monitoring risk materialization conditions; 83,78% of the respondents consider that keeping risks in a "stand-by position" by monitoring

performance indicators in order to determine risk materialization conditions can involve a high amount of resources that cannot be provided by the organization.
An important risk related to the proposed method relates to errors in the database created in order to implement the proposed model. In order to decrease the number of risks introduced in the risk handling plan, risks have to be monitored, this means that a database has to be created including the identified risks, the calculated risk levels, the analyzed risk types, the determined performance indicators impacted by risks and the analyzed risk materialization conditions.

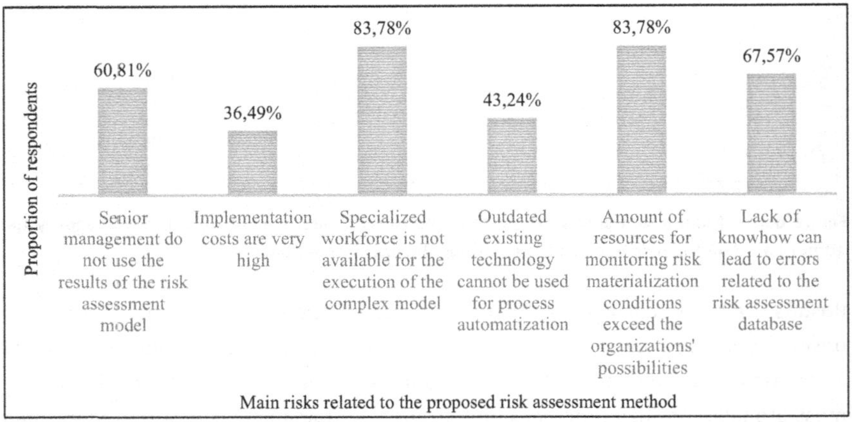

Figure 6.32: Main risks related to the proposed risk assessment model, developed by the author based on the research conducted during the doctoral period.

Almost 61% of the individuals that have sent feedback agree that it is possible that the senior management will not use the results of the proposed risk assessment model including possibilities of tackling new business opportunities. This risk is particularly important because one of the main objectives of the proposed model was to harness risks as opportunities and a large amount of resources used to perform risk assessment would be wasted. Given the fact that the complexity of the proposed model based on mathematical calculus the risk assessment process can be automatized using specialized software. Almost 44% of the respondents state that it is possible that organizations have to invest in IT infrastructure and software programs in order to implement the model. Another issue signaled by 36,49% of the individuals that have sent feedback is that implementation costs are very high. These costs mainly relate to manpower and technology used for creating the risk assessment database.

Question 5 (Figure 6.33): *Which are the possibilities of improving the proposed risk assessment method?*

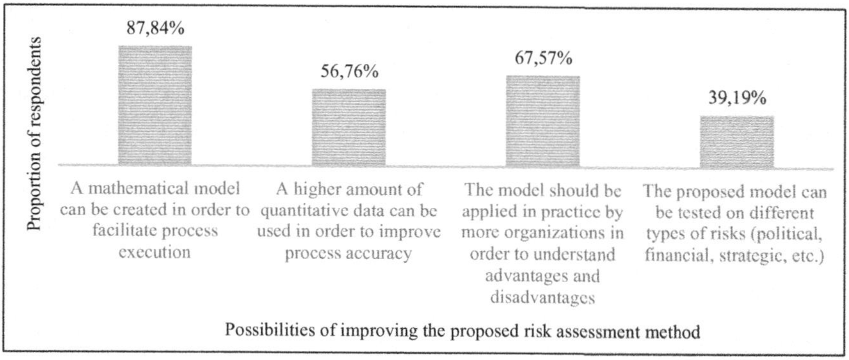

Figure 6.33: Possibilities of improving the proposed risk assessment model, developed by the author based on the research conducted during the doctoral period.

Results – According to most of the respondents the next step related to improving the proposed risk assessment model is developing a mathematical model that facilitates process execution and automatization. Almost 68% of the individuals that have sent feedback consider that the model should be applied in practice by more organizations in order to understand the related benefits and drawbacks.

Given the fact that risk assessment uses a high amount of empirical data, almost 57% of the respondents consider that the proposed model can be improved by using a higher amount of quantitative data that would improve process accuracy. Next steps related to the proposed model can involve applying the model in relation with the types of business risks that are not related to process interactions, such as political, financial, market, real estate, compliance and reputational risks.

7 Conclusions

In order to have a perspective on risk assessment related to organizational business process, the research reviews the actual trends and considerations from the specialized literature concerning assessing risks at the interactions between business processes in the context of ensuring sustainable performance. The research describes aspects related to business processes within the organization and risk assessment as premises for an approach based on processes and risk.

According to academicians and process experts, in the past years achieving business objectives has been an important challenge for organizations that had to focus on reducing costs and improving business processes. Given the unstable and highly competitive business environment organizations have adapted their business strategies in order to achieve value-adding results while aiming to ensure sustainable performance.

Successful and sustainable process results can be obtained by using the process approach as a business model according to the specialized literature. Further, studies have shown that by combining the process approach with the PDCA method managers minimize risks related to not achieving business objectives.

The first chapter is focused on establishing the conceptual framework related to business processes. Chapter 1 begins with the review of actual approaches and perspectives related to business processes. Organizations have to continuously improve by business processes by updating activities and managing risks according to the information provided by the feedback loop. Any deviation from the standard or from the expected results has to be analyzed and corrective actions have to be taken in order to not disturb the clockwork mechanism of the interlinked business processes that is the very essence of the organization. The feedback loop is present in the majority of management tools and business software programs and has a significant contribution to monitoring and controlling organizational processes and ensures successful operational results. Designing a value-adding feedback loop involves determining performance indicators and targeted values for each of them and assigning responsibility for the analysis and usage of information.

Business process interactions are the main source of high risks, therefore information provided through the feedback loop must be included in the risk assessment process in order to prevent these risks that impact the organization's main performance indicators: profit and turnover.

R. M. Bejinariu, *Sustainable Business Performance and Risk Management*,
Sustainable Management, Wertschöpfung und Effizienz,
https://doi.org/10.1007/978-3-658-29389-5_7

In order to identify risks related to interactions between business processes, the main organizational processes have been described including process objectives, performance indicators, inputs and outputs, interactions with other processes, management methods used and risks.

Within the organization business processes interact both vertically between operational processes and management processes and horizontally between departments. Each process activity from one department has an impact on each of the process activities from the connected departments, therefore risks are to be identified both ways between business processes. Relations with the external stakeholders like clients, creditors, competing organizations and shareholders are mainly managed by the marketing and sales departments, while partnerships with suppliers are the result of the procurement department's work.

New business trends related to outsourced and backsourced business processes were investigated in the second part of Chapter 1. The increasing number of announcements made by organizations that decide to backsource processes has triggered many interpretations and disputes between academicians and experts. Revising and reversing outsourcing decisions were results of unsatisfactory process results performed by third-party providers. The main causes for failed outsourcing projects were inefficient communication caused by language barriers, different time zones, technological infrastructure and cultural differences, as well as limited control mechanisms that could not find a balance between costs and quality of service that satisfies the customers' needs.
While overestimating cost advantages related to outsourcing business processes, organizations also underestimated the importance of offering quality products and services and a flexible customer experience. The increasing raw materials and wages costs and the inability to adapt to the customer's needs were the biggest disadvantages of offshore service providers. Geopolitical risks, local economy and growth possibilities of the targeted region are analyzed before investing in warehouses, production plants, service hubs or agencies. However, managers cannot take relocating decisions based on GDP, unit labor costs and other performance indicators related to productivity and costs savings; organizations have to perform qualitative investigations related to the foreign country's political and economic fluctuations, professionals' level of qualification and outsourcing reputation. Manufacturing sites in China and India were the main target of investors being able to meet the growing needs of production worldwide. Changes in the local economies led to increased wages and managers have started relocating outsourced services in other

areas like South Africa or have decided to choose backsourcing. Tax advantages like lower value-added tax, income and profit taxes, trade or property taxes and even road taxes are considered when deciding to outsource. While labor-intensive work is easier to outsource, specialized and knowledge-intensive business services are usually performed onshore. This creates a controversy between the coordination of labor-intensive and knowledge-intensive processes – for example separating production sites and research and development can involve communication barriers and temporal disadvantages.

The rightsourcing approach is a recent management model that helps managers make the "right choice" when taking decisions related to the location of business processes. Even if the initial choice offers all the advantages expected by the organizations, when outsourcing processes corporate governance is essential for the sustainability of the business model.

Chapter 2 presents specific approaches related to risk assessment in the context of ensuring sustainable performance based on the study of specialized literature. Sustainable processes and the overall sustainable performance of the organizations can only be achieved if risks are continuously assessed and handled. The current controversies are related to the costs of processing and controlling risks compared to the benefits that can be achieved by the organizations. In order to emphasize the value-adding results of risk assessment principles, framework and all related processes were investigated. Preparing for risk assessment involves defining the organizational context and determining the impact of the internal and external factors on the risk assessment process. Risk identification, analysis and evaluation were researched, the risk scorecard developed by NASA being described as the latest and most common model used by organizations when assessing risks.

In the engineering and medical industries organizations perform risk assessment by using the FMEA method in order to improve the accuracy of the process by monitoring risk materialization conditions and permanently controlling risks instead of handling them. The most important advantage of this method is that risk handling costs are decreased because a reduced number of risks are included in the risk handling plan. The FMEA method uses detection as the third attribute during risk assessment along with the standard 2 attributes: probability of occurrence and consequence. Detection indicates the probability that risk materialization conditions are met and risks are imminent. By introducing detection during the risk assessment process organizations can keep risks in a "stand-by position" and control them by monitoring risk materialization conditions.

The current limitations of the specialized publications regard the versatility of the FMEA method. There is only little research related to applying detection as the third attribute in the risk assessment process in organizations from different areas of business like fast-moving commercial goods (FMCG) and constructions, pharmaceutical and healthcare industries.
Considerations related to risk assessment in the context of ensuring sustainable performance include a new perspective related to assessing risks by considering both negative and positives outcomes that may result from risk materialization. Risks are uncertainties that can either threaten the organization or lead to new business opportunities.

The latest management model described in the specialized literature involves determining risk levels associated to negative and positive outcomes and involves a risk scorecard limited to assessing risks using only probability of occurrence and consequence as attributes. By researching possible positive effects of risk materialization and determining the opportunities that can be harnessed, organizations can develop strategies that can force risk materialization in order to tackle new business opportunities.

Personal contributions and methods of harnessing research results related to risk assessment in the context of ensuring sustainable performance

1. **Study concerning risk assessment related to organizational business processes**

Chapter 3 includes 2 studies related to the integration of risk assessment in organizations. The main factors that affect risk assessment integration are risk appetite and risk tolerance; these factors usually depend on the size of the organization. The unstable economic climate comes with new challenges for both small and medium-sized enterprises (SMEs) and large companies; new solutions and strategies are necessary in order to prevent risk materialization and to ensure sustainable competitive advantage and in more and more cases even business survival. Risk assessment protects the organizations from uncertainties that can lead to negative events and can be considered a proactive process that monitors and controls threats in order to maintain business stability and sustainability.

Worldwide both SMEs and large companies have assigned more and more resources in order to manage risks and to adapt to the unstable business climate. Performance indicators had to be recalibrated and are now closely monitored in order to identify new risks. Risks are perceived and handled differently in organizations, the main differences being caused by some characteristics of the organization such as turnover and number of employees, therefore the authors have researched risk assessment according to size of the organization. These differences can occur at operational level – risk assessment integration, allocated resources, process documentation and integration, but also at strategic management level – the organizations' attitude when confronting risks and risk tolerance.

One of the objectives of the study is to determine the extent in which risk assessment is applied and integrated in SMEs compared to large companies. The main differences relate to large companies having more resources and being better prepared for risk assessment integration – factors such as finances, technological infrastructure, human resources, documentation and know-how are the main advantages. Research objectives also relate to determining risk appetite and risk tolerance in SMEs compared to large companies and identifying the type of strategy that is developed by these organizations when facing risks. While risk assessment integration is at its early stages in SMEs, these organizations have a more offensive attitude in risky situations compared to large companies. Large companies are not flexible and prefer assigning important resources for risk mitigation while being focused on stability rather than taking risks.
The research was performed in 2016 and has gathered qualitative information from organizations with activity in the FMCG, constructions, pharmaceutical and healthcare industries.

The main results regarding risk assessment in SMEs and large companies have emphasized the following aspects:
1. The majority of SMEs have an increased risk appetite and develop offensive and defensive strategies when confronted with risks, while large companies have a decreased risk appetite and prefer defensive strategies;
2. Risk assessment is performed predominately in large companies. Senior managers from the SMEs are interested in updating and developing risk assessment, but staff is not involved and not enough resources are assigned for the process;
3. While large companies are focused on writing specific operating procedures, in most of the SMEs risk assessment is not properly documented and standardized;
4. Risk assessment results are rarely used by SMEs and large companies when developing strategies.

The following personal contributions were brought as a result of the research related to risk assessment in SMEs and large companies:

- Determining risk appetite and risk tolerance in SMEs and large companies in order to understand the organizations' decisions related to risk assessment and risk handling;
- Identifying the differences between SMEs and large companies related to risk attitude and decision-making;
- Determining the status of risk assessment integration in SMEs and large companies;
- Identifying the critical factors that influence risk assessment implementation in organizations;
- Evaluating senior management interest and staff involvement related to the process in both types of organizations;
- Determining if SMEs and large companies perform risk tolerance evaluations;
- Determining if budget is allocated for both risk assessment integration and development in organizations;
- Evaluating the risk assessment documentation and level of standardization in SMEs and large companies;
- Determining if SMEs and large companies use risk assessment results when developing business strategies.

The research evaluates the status and role of risk assessment in SMEs and large companies and determines the factors that influence risk assessment integration and risk-related decision-making in organizations of different sizes.

The second study included in Chapter 3, "study concerning the interrelation between risk assessment related to business processes and the organizational context", has the objective of determining the reciprocal influence between risk assessment and the organizational context.

Risk assessment implementation and successful process integration rely on identifying all factors within the organizational context that have an impact on the process and that are also impacted by the process. Therefore, the study analyzes the connections between risk assessment and the organizational context in order to identify how the internal and external factors that define the organizational context influence the process and how risk assessment affects these factors.

The risk assessment process depends on the organizational context when it comes to efficiently applying plans and programs. Both internal and external factors that define the organizational context have an important influence on the risk assessment process. The research shows that risk assessment has a positive impact by transforming the organization into a more stable, reliable and flexible organization. Risk assessment foresees possible changes and makes predictions by permanently analyzing impacting and impacted factors from within and outside of the organization; this also leads to organizations being more flexible to change and less vulnerable to threats.

The study was conducted in the period January-April 2017 and is based on feedback during interviews with managers and specialists from different areas of business that have shared their perspective on the reciprocal influences between risk assessment and the organizational context.

The main research results related to the interrelation between risk assessment and the organizational context are the following:

1. Stakeholders are one of the most important factors that determine the organization's integration of risk assessment, assigned resources for the ongoing process, but also attitude when confronted with risks. The effects of risk assessment on the business results are the main interest of external stakeholders; on the other hand, internal stakeholders are concerned about optimizing operations and ensuring process efficiency. Overall, stakeholders are key factors in the success of risk assessment by bringing their contribution, such as sharing information, or by setting up barriers – for example limiting budgets. Other external factors such as banks, suppliers and clients are highly interested in a risk-free and long-term collaboration with the organization; therefore, interacting with an organization with a strong risk assessment process in place can be considered an insurance for their own business;
2. Top impacting factors for any organization are politics and the local or regional economy. Risk assessment allocates a high amount of resources in constantly analyzing the business climate in order to identify new threats and opportunities. Software companies are the organizations that are most impacted by risk assessment that ensures growing their business by developing risk assessment software programs (increasing sales), creating new jobs (higher number of employees) and offering related maintenance services (ensuring long-term incomes). When it comes to ecology, job security and a safe working environment can motivate employees to become more preoccupied about the environment;
3. Identifying and analyzing risks as well as all subprocesses of risk assessment require advanced know-how and regular updates. Being a complex, resource-intensive process, risk assessment is influenced by internal factors like staff involvement, leadership style, knowledge pool of the organization and employees' skills.

4. Decisions of risk owners and senior managers are influenced by the process, so that risk assessment results are taken into consideration before setting up objectives and developing new strategies.

The research brings the following contributions related to the interrelation between risk assessment and the organization context:

- Determining both internal and external factors that determine values and parameters that should be considered when assessing and managing risks;
- Identifying the effects of risk assessment on the organization's stability, reliability and sustainable performance;
- Determining the impact of risk assessment on the business objectives, mission, values and organizational image;
- Evaluating the level of involvement and effects of internal stakeholders (such as staff, senior management) on the risk assessment process;
- Analyzing how leadership and organizational culture affect risk assessment as well as the impact of the process on these factors;
- Identifying how evaluation methods are important for the success of risk assessment;
- Determining the reciprocal relation between social, informal and formal interactions and the risk assessment process;
- Identifying how structural, electronic and organizational slack resources affect risk assessment and how the process impacts these resources;
- Determining the impact of external stakeholders (such as shareholders, competing organizations, suppliers, creditors and customers) on risk assessment;
- Evaluating the interrelation between socio-cultural factors and risk assessment;
- Identifying the impact of technological advancements and trends on the risk assessment process and how the process affects these factors;
- Determining the effect of economic and environmental factors on risk assessment;
- Analyzing the reciprocal influence between political factors and the risk assessment process.

The research brings a contribution to investigations about risk assessment efficiency by emphasizing the importance of the interrelations between risk assessment and all the impacting and impacted factors that define the organizational context.

2. Risk assessment related to the interactions between organizational business processes in relation with the critical factors of sustainable performance

The first part of Chapter 4 regards the study of critical factors impacting sustainable performance. Process performance can be determined by process efficiency and effectiveness, however, in case processes are not defined, documented, monitored and controlled, performance cannot be sustained.
Starting with process design that plays an important role in the success of the business results, organizations consider elements that bring a contribution to ensuring business sustainability. Analyzing organizational business processes from sustainability point of view can be performed by identifying and evaluating specific criteria related to each process, such as process description, degree of formality, level of staff involvement, information transfer, risk assessment at process interactions level and monitoring, control and process optimization.

The first objective of the research is to investigate business processes from sustainable performance point of view. Following, the research objectives relate to analyzing the impact of the determined process criteria on the business performance and to determine the critical factors that affect sustainable performance in organizations.

The study was conducted between November 2015 and February 2016 and involved 2 methods of collecting information: an electronic questionnaire was sent in order to determine the level of performance sustainability related to related to 56 processes and follow-up interviews with managers and specialists from different organizations were conducted in order to evaluate the impact of the process criteria on the sustainable performance of business processes and to determine the main factors that affect sustainable performance from the respondents' perspective.

The main research results regarding sustainable process performance are:

1. Most of the organizations are well prepared when it comes to process sustainability with the top results achieved by the human resources processes;
2. Results related to process criteria with impact on sustainable performance are:
- Process descriptions has an overall low score with only one third of the organizations having a back-up plan in place in case processes are interrupted or fail and time frame for each process step is clear for more than half of the investigated organizations;

- The process' degree of formality does not always support process sustainability and more than half of the interviewees consider that information databases related to processes are fully documented;
- Employees are involved in the processes with high scores retrieved related to the process owner's know-how and experience and low scores for the process owner having a backup in case of a leave of absence;
- Communication and information transfer supports process sustainability with information being available to employees according to the assigned level of access, but manual input is still important for information sharing according to almost half of the managers and specialists;

3. When it comes to the sustainable performance of business processes, risk assessment is in place at each process interaction and the identified risks are monitored and controlled. Process monitoring and controlling are top factors in ensuring sustainable process performance.

The processes related to human resources have the best results related to sustainability and this is mainly possible due to risk assessment related to interactions between business processes. Sales and financial processes have the lowest scores - this is mainly caused by the fact that the degree of formality does not support sustainability related to these business processes;

4. Risk assessment at the interactions between business processes helps organizations prevent process interruptions or even process failure;
5. Managers and specialists acknowledge that loss of information and not sharing valuable and sensitive data within the organization can lead to important risks regarding business sustainability;
6. Despite the fact that solid process documentation is the second most rated critical factor affecting sustainable performance, according to the interviewees, in practice more than half of the organizations have to make efforts in order to define and document standard operating procedures for all business processes. One of the main causes for poor documentation is that no back-up plans are in place in case processes are interrupted or fail and organizations do not acknowledge the fact that setting up a backup solution is important for sustainable performance.

The research brings the following main contributions related to sustainable performance in organizations:

- Analyzing organizational business processes from sustainable performance point of view;

- Identifying the impact of process description and degree of formality on sustainable performance;
- Evaluating the influence of staff involvement on business processes in terms of sustainable performance;
- Determining how the transfer of information affects the organization related to ensuring sustainable performance;
- Analyzing the impact of risk assessment related to interactions between business processes on the sustainable performance of organizational processes;
- Identifying the influence of monitoring, controlling and process optimization on sustainable performance;
- Determining the critical factors that affect sustainable performance in organizations.

The study emphasizes the role of process sustainability in organizations and may contribute to further research related to business process management and business sustainability.

After having emphasized the role of performing risk assessment in order to ensure sustainable performance, the research conducted in Chapter 4 continues with "risk assessment related to the interactions between organizational business processes using the PDCA method".

All departments of the organizations are interlinked and work together in order to achieve the business objectives set by senior management and shareholders. Each business process includes a series of activities that are performed by employees or software programs and that have an impact on other processes and activities. Therefore, all actions within the organization can affect the final business results and are associated with different levels of risks. By analyzing each interaction between processes and activities at chain processes level (horizontally) and hierarchically (vertically) the main risks including their causes and effects can be identified.

Further, risks related to interactions between business processes owned by the organization and executed inside and outside the organization were investigated, as well as between the organization and contracted, outsourced, nearshored or offshored processes executed by third-party providers.

The objectives of the study are to identify risks related to interactions between business processes and determining the cause and effects of each risks and evaluating risk levels and types. Risk identification was performed as result of interviews conducted between October and November 2017 and risk profile was determined based on the author's professional experience with risk assessment.

The main research results related to assessing risks related to interactions between business processes are:

1. All risks related to interactions between business processes are unacceptable with one exception: risks between the contract management and the financial department – the average result was a tolerable risk because most of the identified risks were acceptable and risks with high consequences had a low probability of appearance. For these risks no risk handling plan is necessary, but control mechanisms have to be in place in order to mitigate risks;

2. Research results related to interactions between each of the proposed business processes are:

- When it comes to process interactions between the marketing and sales department and the external environment the following conclusions can be drawn:
  - Risks caused by marketing and sales activities with impact on relations with clients are unacceptable and require risk handling;
  - Risks caused by marketing and sales activities with impact on relations with creditors are tolerable and require setting up control mechanisms in order to not affect strategic partnerships with banks or suppliers;
  - Risks caused by marketing and sales activities with impact on relations with competing organizations are unacceptable – an inefficient business strategy related to competing organizations can lead to loss of market share, decreased profit and revenue;
  - Risks caused by marketing and sales activities with impact on relations with the shareholders require a risk handling plan because not delivering the expected business results can lead to losing support from the shareholders (financing).

- Main risks generated by activities between the marketing and sales department and the contract management department relate to not signing or extending contracts and non-performing contracts; these risks are an important threat for the organization and have to be managed. Senior management activities have a strong impact on the marketing and sales department; on the other hand, marketing and sales activities affect the organizational image and the client portfolio – in both cases risks levels are unacceptable;

- Results for risks related to business process interactions between senior management and the contract management processes are different depending on which activities have caused the risk:

- Risks caused by senior management activities with impact on the marketing and sales department are unacceptable mainly because an inefficient business strategy quickly leads to bad marketing and sales results;
- Risks caused by the marketing and sales activities with impact on senior management are tolerable and mainly relate to delayed contracts;

- Procurement activities can cause risks like cash flow disruptions, delayed projects or exceeded project budget that can lead to production disruptions, stop supply and losing existing clients;

- Unacceptable risks can be generated by financing activities that can lead to delayed or disrupted projects and even losing existing clients. Process errors within the financing department can cause delayed payments and deliveries which are unacceptable risks that have to be handled in order to avoid delayed or disrupted projects and clients' dissatisfaction;

- All production activities can cause high risks that can affect the relation with clients and business objectives related to profitability and turnover;

- Financial management is one of the main challenges of any organization. Delayed payments to suppliers, delayed deliveries and payments from clients are the main risks generated at process interactions level between senior management and the financial department. These risks are unacceptable leading to decreased profit and revenue, loss of market share and even insolvency or bankruptcy;

- Planning and production processes have always depended on each other, therefore activities related to each business process have an important impact on the other organizational processes. Production disruptions delayed or faulty production or service delivery, non-compliant products and services or with quality-related issues involve risks that can be caused by activities within these 2 departments. Risks have to be handled in order to avoid negative effects on the organization, such as decreased sales, losing existing clients or even bankruptcy;

- After-sales is for some organizations the main source of revenue; risks generated by production errors can relate to non-compliant, outdated or troublesome products, as well as high costs during the warranty period. These risks have to be mitigated in order to avoid losing existing clients and market share that directly affect business profit and revenue. Risks that can be generated by after-sales processes are tolerable because planning activities and operations can lead to acceptable or tolerable risks;

- All activities with the after-sales department in relation with quality assurance lead to a series of unacceptable risks caused by incorrect budget planning and operations during the warranty period of products and services, but also not monitoring and analyzing faulty products that lead to additional unforeseen costs and negatively affect the organization's image. Processes within the quality assurance department cause important risks that are mainly related to incorrect or incomplete measurement and verification protocols that have a negative impact on customer satisfaction and sales;

- Senior management is responsible for results from all departments and the after-sales department makes no exception. Managements decisions related to after-sales can generate risks related to decreased support services and spare parts sales required for the maintenance of the products that have been sold. These risks are particularly important because many organizations (especially in the automotive industry) rely on up to half of their income from after-sales products and services;

- Very high risk levels are associated with process interactions between senior management and the production department. Senior management can have a negative impact on production by developing inefficient business strategies, not considering or not gathering data from the external environment or incorrect assignment of resources. Production activities generate even higher risks especially caused by incorrect planning of resources, not monitoring quality checks and protocols related to the production flow not being updated or optimized;

- Quality assurance and marketing and sales go hand in hand in any organization oriented on the clients' needs. Quality assurance activities can lead to decreased revenue and profit and even losing existing clients especially when not following protocols and not performing all check-ups leading to faulty products. Clients' needs have to be considered in order to avoid producing outdated products. While these risks are considered unacceptable and have to be included in the risk handling plan, risks generated by marketing and sales activities are tolerable and have to be monitored;

3. Process interactions with suppliers are carried out through the marketing and sales department. These interactions are important for the collaboration with suppliers that can lead to strategic partnerships that offer special benefits for the organization, such as low acquisition prices, extended payment terms, fast deliveries or paperless invoicing. Therefore, the research has shown that these interactions lead to very high risk levels caused by sourcing errors (incorrect or delayed orders, budget for purchasing prices not calculated correctly, disadvantageous negotiations with suppliers) that lead to delayed projects, suppliers' dissatisfaction and even losing existing partnerships. On the other hand, activities performed by suppliers can generate even higher risks: delayed deliveries and projects, sales disruptions and cancelled contracts with clients. These risks have a negative effect on relations with clients, production and of course on the organization's profitability and revenue;

4. Risks related to process interactions between the organization and business processes contracted to third-party providers are higher than risks between processes owned by the organization. No matter the ownership of the process, risk levels increase depending on the distance between the organization and the location where the process is executed.

5. Research results of the empirical study related to risk assessment related to the interactions between organizational business processes using the PDCA method are:
- Organizations acknowledge the important role of risk assessment related to organizational business processes. The majority of the respondents agree that not assessing risks related to interactions between business processes can lead to financial losses caused by delayed projects and decreased sales. Inefficient procurement or incorrect financial planning can also be the result of not managing these risks. Managers and specialists emphasize the importance of the organizational image and that delivering products and services with quality-related issues leads to clients' dissatisfaction, losing market share and decreased incomes;
- The majority of the organizations consider that process interactions are main sources of high risks. Process interactions with clients' data are an important source of risks according to almost half of the interviewees; that means that verifying clients' business viability and acknowledging or even anticipating their needs are important for a reciprocally advantageous business collaboration;

- Most of the respondents are aware of the fact that risk assessment is a value-adding process that contributes to ensuring sustainable performance.

The study related to risk assessment at process interactions level brings the following contributions:

- Identifies risks at interactions between the organization and the exterior environment;
- Identifies risks between the main organizational business processes;
- Determines the causes for each risk identified at process interactions level;
- Determines the effects of the identified risks related to interactions between business processes on the organizational results and performance indicators;
- Evaluates probability of occurrence and consequence for each identified risk at process interactions level;
- Calculates risk level and determines risk type for each identified risk at process interactions level;
- Identifies risks between the organization and outsourced, nearshored or offshored processes;
- Identifies risks between organizational processes and processes owned by the organization and executed onsite, offsite, nearshore or offshore;
- Determines causes and effects of risks related to interactions between the organization and outsourced business processes.

3. Possibilities of improving risk assessment related to organizational business processes in the context of ensuring sustainable performance

The first part of Chapter 5 relates to a study on using the PDCA and FMEA methods during risk assessment related to business processes interactions in organizations. The FMEA method has been used since the 1950s in order to detect technological malfunctions and has based its premises on historical errors. These errors are the result of risk materialization of risks that have not been identified or that haven been analyzed incorrectly. The study shows that despite the fact that detection has not been applied by organizations as a third attribute during the risk assessment process mainly because of organizations being reluctant to costs, this method increases risk assessment efficiency by considerably decreasing risk handling costs.

The research objectives are determining the effects of using the proposed methods during risk assessment in organizations and investigating if the proposed model can be used in all areas of business. The methodology used involves investigating risks related to all process activities described by the PDCA method (Plan-Do-Act-Check) and applying detection as a third attribute during the risk assessment process.

Risks were identified during interviews with managers in 2017. Risk levels and types, as well as the main performance indicators impacted by the identified risks and risk materialization conditions were determined by the author based on research conducted during the doctoral period. Determining the advantages of using the proposed methods during risk assessment was based on feedback to the electronic research questionnaires sent by email between November 2016 and March 2017.

The main results of the study related to using the PDCA and FMEA methods during risk assessment related to business process interactions are:

1. Applying detection as a third attribute during the risk assessment process can lower risk handling costs and increases risk appetite by introducing a significant lower number of risks in the risk handling plan compared to the classic risk assessment method using 2 attributes (probability of appearance and consequence). By examining the conditions for risk materialization risks can be controlled and prevented with less resources;

2. Each risk that can occur at the interaction between business processes has an effect on the organization's performance indicators, so that by using the FMEA method performance indicators are impacted by a significantly lower amount of risks;

3. Managers are still reluctant to change when it comes to risk assessment - while organizations are interested in testing the proposed methods, only a few of the investigated organizations have implemented the PDCA and FMEA methods in the risk assessment process;

4. In order to achieve value-adding results, organizations using the proposed methods have to monitor risk materialization conditions. Therefore, by simply using the advantages of applying detection in the risk analysis and selecting less risks in the risk handling plan, but not allocating resources for monitoring unacceptable risks, risks materialization can occur leading to negative effects on business results;

5. The reoccurrence of risks determines increasing risk handling costs mainly because new solutions have to be found in order to stop risk reoccurrence; this can mean that risks have been incorrectly managed the first time they were identified or that risk

materialization conditions have not been considered. A recurrent risk is not necessarily a threat for the organization and monitoring it can be a less expensive method than taking actions to prevent it from materializing. These actions involve resources and may stop risk materialization or not - according to most of the respondents risks reoccur despite risk handling;

6. The main advantages of the FMEA method relate to lower risk handling costs, risks being identified more often, and control mechanisms being permanently updated. The study once again emphasizes the fact that detection is only efficient when setting up and permanently improving control mechanisms that monitor risk materialization conditions for unacceptable risks;

7. A low interest in risk assessment is directly related to a low risk appetite. Managers are not willing to invest in extending the risk assessment process because of their defensive attitude when facing risky situations. While using a defensive strategy is considered safe, for most of the organizations managers do not allocate special resources for risk assessment; this is yet another reason for not implementing the FMEA method. Another cause for not using 3 attributes during the risk assessment process is that managers and specialists consider that their existing process is not efficient - this can be caused by allocating resources and handling risks that may never materialize;

8. Despite the fact that detection has been used during the risk assessment process mainly in the engineering and medicine industries, the FMEA method can be applied in all industries. When asked about the main reasons for detection not being applied in their risk assessment processes, approximately 7% of the respondents answer that this method is used in certain industries only;

9. Less than 45% of the risks related to interactions between the organization and outsourced business processes were included in the risk handling plan after applying detection as a third attribute during the risk assessment process. Almost 60% less risks identified between the organization and outsourced business processes with impact on the organization's performance indicators are included in the risk handling plan.

Overall, the results of the interview show that detection transforms risk assessment into a more efficient process and evaluation of business processes becomes more accurate; this ensures continuous process optimization and added value for the business results.

The study related to using the PDCA and FMEA method during risk assessment at process interactions level brings the following contributions:

- Identifying the performance indicators that are impacted by each of the identified risks;
- Determining the main risk materialization conditions associated with each business performance indicator that have to be monitored in order to control risks;
- Calculating the probability of detecting risk materialization conditions for all performance indicators;
- Evaluating risk levels after applying detection as a third attribute during the risk assessment process;
- Determining risk types after analyzing risk levels and using the predefined risk tolerance intervals;
- Analyzing the number of risks included in the risk handling plan using 3 compared to 2 risk assessment attributes;
- Determining the number of risks that impact the performance indicators included in the risk handling plan after applying detection;
- Evaluating risk levels and determining risk types for the risks related to interactions between the organization and outsourced business processes;
- Determining the number of risks identified at the interaction between the organization and outsourced business processes included in the risk handling plan after applying detection;
- Determining the status of using the FMEA method in the risk assessment process in organizations;
- Identifying the highest threats related to the risk assessment process;
- Analyzing the organizations' point of view regarding to using the FMEA method during risk assessment;
- Determining the main advantages of using the FMEA method when assessing risks;
- Identifying the main effects of the FMEA method on risk handling costs;
- Identifying the main reasons for organizations not using the FMEA method during the risk assessment process.

The next research included in Chapter 5 refers to "applying the PDCA and FMEA methods during the risk assessment process related to organizational business processes in relation with the identification of business opportunities". The research investigates the effects of correlating the proposed methods while evaluating both negative and positive outcomes of risk materialization as a follow-up study performed in order to improve the risk assessment process.

Detection increases risk appetite by decreasing costs with handling risks that can lead to both negative and positive effects. Detection can determine the probability of appear- ance for the identified risk materialization conditions and helps to identify both negative and positive possible effects of risk materialization. By identifying risks related to interactions between business processes organizations can detect both threats and opportunities but finding risks and analyzing them involves important resources; these resources are wasted if the conditions for the materialization of the unacceptable or high risks are not probable. The research also identifies the main risk materialization conditions determined by changes related to performance indicators that are affected by the identified risks.

The objectives of the research relate to identifying the main advantages of using the FMEA method in the risk assessment process while aiming for new business opportunities and to determine the impact of this method within the organization and in the context of outsourced business processes. The study was performed in 2017 and research results were based on interviews with managers and the author's research during the doctoral studies.

The main results of the study relate to using the FMEA method and the identification of new business opportunities during risk assessment are:

1. By using the FMEA method chances of tackling important opportunities are higher - this is possible because organizational resources can be used in order to aim only for the opportunities that are most likely to turn into profitable and value-adding business;

2. Organizations can use a significantly lower amount of resources in order to take risks while aiming for profitable business opportunities. Concerning risk assessment between the organization and outsourced business processes, most of the identified risks have an impact on productivity and by applying detection the number of risks included in the risk handling plan decreases significantly;

3. The 2 main categories of opportunities that have been identified relate to increasing profit and turnover and depend on improving internal processes and relations with clients and suppliers;

4. With 4 risks that can lead to new valuable business opportunities, investing in new technology financed by attracting new investors or selling shares is one of the most

probable positive outcomes of risk materialization. By improving payment protocols and managing up to 3 risks new partnerships with clients and suppliers can be ensured;

6. In order to control risks that may not lead to new opportunities according to the results achieved after applying detection, the impacted performance indicators have to be monitored in order to identify if risk materialization conditions are met. The majority of the identified risks that may lead to tackling business opportunities in the future can be controlled by monitoring market share and the performance indicators related to number of repeat customers and new clients. Liquidity and profitability are also important performance indicators that have to be checked in order to not miss any new business opportunities.

The main contributions of the study regarding using the PDCA and FMEA method during risk assessment in relation with identifying new business opportunities are:

- Determining all possible positive outcomes that can be generated by risk materialization;
- Identifying the performance indicators that are impacted by the identified risks;
- Determining risk materialization conditions that can lead to new business opportunities;
- Determining detection levels and calculating the new risk levels using 3 attributes during risk assessment;
- Evaluating risk types according to the predefined risk tolerance intervals;
- Determining risk levels and evaluating risk types for risks identified in the context of outsourced processes;
- Determining the number of risks that have to be included in the risk handling plan after applying detection in order to achieve valuable business opportunities.

The final part of Chapter 5 is focused on enhancing the results of the research performed during the doctoral period by proposing a model for risk assessment using the PDCA and FMEA methods correlated with identifying both threats and opportunities of risk materialization.

The objective related to the proposed model is to develop a risk assessment tool that can be used by organizations in order to minimize risk handling costs and to tackle important business opportunities.

By using the proposed methods and evaluating both negative and positive outcomes of risk materialization a total of 250 risk levels can be determined as the mathematical product between probability of occurrence, consequence and detection, from which 125 risk levels are identified for negative outcomes and have negative values and 125 risk levels relate to positive outcomes and have positive values. These risks can be illustrated in tri-dimensional space using the probability of occurrence, consequences of risk materialization and probability of detection as axes with values from 1 to 5.

Tolerance intervals for risk levels are the same in case of negative and positive outcomes, only risk types are different. For example, a very high risks that can lead to negative outcomes represents a threat for the organization, while a very high risk that can lead to positive outcomes can be considered an opportunity for the organization. Each risk tolerance interval was illustrated as part of the tri-dimensional risk assessment model that is created by overlaying all the proposed intervals.
In order to validate and determine the effects of the risk assessment graphic model interviews were conducted with organizations from different areas of business in 2017 with the objective of determining the organizations' level of interest related to the proposed model.

The following results were researched for the validation of the risk assessment models:
1. Almost a third of the investigated organizations are interested in introducing the proposed model in a pilot program and only a few organizations have already implemented it and are interested in investing more in the process by automating it;

2. In order to determine the potential of applying detection in organizations, the study presents results related mapping risks in small and medium-sized enterprises and large companies. While having a limited amount of resources compared to large companies, the first category of organizations is more likely to be interested in this method. Most of the large companies do not use risk assessment results in order to tackle new business opportunities; this is mainly because large companies have a lower risk appetite and take decisions based on defensive risk strategies;

3. Managers consider that the lack of knowledge and experience related to the proposed methods are the main causes for not using detection as the third attribute in the risk assessment process. Also, the defensive attitude related to risky situations is another cause for organizations being reluctant to changes when it comes to taking risks in order to achieve positive outcomes. Most of the respondents also state that

the extended process seems to involve many resources and organizations are not ready to invest in updating the risk assessment process. Also, some of the investigated organizations are very satisfied with the current risk assessment results and are not looking into making any changes;

4. Half of the managers that have sent feedback related to the proposed model consider it a useful tool for understanding how detection, threats and opportunities can be integrated in the existing risk assessment process, but also for developing software or other automation solutions.

The effects of the proposed model related to the risk assessment process using the PDCA and FMEA methods and identifying both threats and opportunities of risk materialization were investigated leading to the following results:
1. The main opportunities that can be tackled by using the extended risk assessment process involve allocating resources in order to manage risks and transform them into added value for the organizations. Increased profitability and turnover are the main improved results as a consequence of actions within the risk handling plan, such as improving resource allocation and strengthening relations with clients and suppliers. By applying detection less risks are managed so that resources are focused on improving processes and monitoring risk materialization conditions in order to observe changes related to risk levels and to detect possibilities of new opportunities;

2. The majority of the organizations agree that the proposed risk assessment model brings a significant contribution to ensuring sustainable performance. The main advantage of using the proposed method is that chances of tackling profitable opportunities are higher. Also, almost all the respondents consider that more opportunities can be achieved and risk assessment becomes more efficient by harnessing resources saved by decreasing the number of risks that are handled. By including detection in the organizations' standard operating protocols, control mechanisms have to constantly updated – resources are efficiently used because this requirement is also useful for ensuring business sustainability;

3. The most important risks related to the proposed model relate to lack of specialized workforce and know-how for the execution of the process and a high amount of resources required for monitoring risk materialization conditions. Another significant risk can be related to not using risk assessment results when developing business strategies, which would lead to a high amount of wasted resources;

4. Possibilities of improving the proposed model can be developing a mathematical model in order to facilitate process execution and automatization and testing the model on different types of risks (political, strategical, reputational, real estate, financial, etc.).

Limitations related to the model are related to using a high amount of qualitative data and being applied in practice by a limited number of organizations.

The proposed risk assessment model has brought a set of contributions described below:

- Determines both negative and positive effects of risk materialization in order to tackle the most valuable business opportunities and to prevent threats;
- Increases profitability by decreasing risk handling costs as a result of including a significantly lower amount of risks in the risk handling plan;
- Optimizes organizational resources by focusing on the most important threats and opportunities;
- Ensures efficient risk control mechanisms by monitoring risk materialization conditions and performance indicators.

Using probability of detection as a third risk assessment attribute and determining both negative and positive effects of risk materialization, the proposed model brings a significant contribution to ensuring business sustainability in organizations by lowering risk handling costs and increasing profitability and turnover.

The proposed model increases risk appetite, optimizes organizational resources and is a useful tool for entrepreneurs that are looking into finding a balance between risk-taking and defensive business strategies.

8 Bibliography

Acar, E. and Göc, Y., 2011. *Prediction of risk perception by owners' psychological traits in small building contractors*. Construction Management and Economics, Vol. 29, No. 8, pp. 841-852.

Agndal, H., 2006. *The purchasing market entry process - a study of 10 Swedish industrial SMEs*. Journal of Purchasing & Supply Management, 12, pp. 182-196.

Albrecht, A., Eidenmüller, T., Keppler, T. and Mateescu, R. M., 2016. *International Product Liability in a Global Business Environment: Ethical and Legal Perspectives for Business Managers*, Proceedings of BASIQ 2016 - International Conference, New Trends in Sustainable Business and Consumption, Konstanz, Germany, 2-3 June 2016, ISSN: 2457-483X, pp. 12-21.

Altman, E.I., Sabato, G. and Wilson, N., 2010. *The value of non-financial information in small and medium-sized enterprise risk management*. Journal of Credit Risk, Vol. 6, No. 2, pp. 95-127.

Alquier, A. M. B. and Tignol, M. H. L., 2006. *Risk Management in Small and Medium-sized Enterprises. Production Planning & Control*, 17(3), pp. 273-282.

Albrow, M. and King., E., 1990. *Globalization, Knowledge and Society*. London: Sage, pp.8.

Altman, E., Sabato, G., 2007. *Modelling Credit Risk for SMEs: Evidence from the US Market*. Abacus. 43(3), 332-357.

Altman, E., Sabato, G. and Wilson, N., 2009. The Value of Qualitative Information in SME Risk Management. CMRC, Leeds University Business School, UK. http://people.stern.nyu.edu/ealtman/SME_EA_GS_NW.pdf,accessed 30.05.2016.

Anghel, L.C., Dinu, M., 2014. *Globalizarea afacerilor*. București: Tritonic, pp.56-61.

Arnold, E., 2005. *Managing human resources to improve employee retention*. The Health Care Manager, Vol. 24 , No. 2, pp. 132-400.

Aon Risk Solutions, 2013. Global Risk Management Survey. AON plc. England, http://www.aon.com/attachments/risk-services/2013-GRMS-Executive-Summary.pdf, accessed 26.03.2016.

Arnold, M. and Holmes, S., 1999. Relative Risk Measurement in Small and Medium Enterprises. Department of Accounting and Finance, University of Newcastle, Australia. http://www.sbaer.uca.edu/research/icsb/1999/22.pdf, accessed 30.05.2016.

ArunKumar, G. and Dillibabu, R., 2016. *Design and Application of New Quality Improvement Model: Kano Lean Six Sigma for Software Maintenance Project*. Arabian Journal for Science and Engineering, Volume 41, Issue 3, pp. 997-1014.

Asakawa, K., 2011. *Global R&D management*. Tokyo: Keio University Publishing Co.

Asel, J., Posch, A. and Speckbacher, G., 2010. *Der Finanzbereich in Krisenzeiten: Vom Performance Management zum integrierten Performance-Risk assessment*. Controlling & Management, Vol 54, Issue 2 Supplement, pp. 60-67.

R. M. Bejinariu, *Sustainable Business Performance and Risk Management*,
Sustainable Management, Wertschöpfung und Effizienz,
https://doi.org/10.1007/978-3-658-29389-5

Ashenbaum, B., Maltz, A. and Rabinovich, E., 2005. Studies of Trends in Third-Party Logistics Usage: What Can We Conclude, Transportation Journal, Vol.44, No. 3, pp. 39-50.

Association of Business Schools, 2010, Academic Journal Quality Guide: Version 4, http://www.myscp.org/pdf/ABS%202010%20Combined%20Journal%20Guide.pdf, accessed 0505.2017.

Audretsch, D. B., 2002. *Entrepreneurship: A survey of the literature*. European Commission, Brussels: Enterprise Directorate General.

Audretsch, D. B. and Thurik, R., 2001. *What's new about the new economy? From the managed to the entrepreneurial economy*. Industrial and Corporate Change, 10(1), pp. 267–315.

Ayyagari, M., Beck, T., and Demirguc-Kunt, A., 2007. *Small and medium enterprises across the globe*. Small Business Economics, Vol. 29 No. 4, pp. 415-434.

Ayyagari, M., Demirgüç-Kunt, A. and Maksimovic, V., 2011. Small vs. Young Firms Across The World – Contribution to Employment, Job Creation, and Growth. Policy Research Working Paper 5631, The World Bank Development Research Group, pp. 3, http://documents.worldbank.org/curated/en/478851468161354 807/pdf/WPS56 31.pdf, accessed 26.10.2016.

Babin, R., Nicholson, B., 2012. *Sustainable Global Outsourcing*. New York: Palgrave Macmillan, pp.1.

Balkytė, A. and Tvaronavičienė, M., 2010. *Perception of competitiveness in the context of sustainable development: Facets of „sustainable competitiveness"*. Journal of Business Economics and Management, Vol. 11, No. 2.

Baldwin, R., Martin, P., 1999. *Two Waves of Globalization: Superficial Similarities, Fundamental Differences*, in: Siebert, H. (Hrsg.) Globalization and Labor, Tüb-ingen, pp. 4-52.

Bals, L., Kirchoff, J.F. and Foerstl K., 2016. *Exploring the reshoring and insourcing decision-making process: toward an agenda for future research*. Operations Management Research 9 (3–4), pp. 102–116.

Baroncelli, A., Belvedere, V. and Serio, L., 2017. Offshoring Versus Reshoring? Rather, Shouldn't It Be Rightshoring? 10.1007/ 978-3-319-58883-4_2, pp. 40-41, https://www.springer.com/cda/content/document/cda_downloaddocument/978331 9588827-2.pdf?SGWID=0-0-45-1611268-p180857128, accessed 17.02.2018.

Barratt, M., 2004. *Understanding the meaning of collaboration in the supply chain*, Supply Chain Management: An International Journal, Vol. 9, No.1, pp. 30-42.

Basel Committee, 2003. *Sound Practices for the Management and Supervision of Operational Risk*. Bank for International Settlements.

Baumgartner, R. J. and Ebner, D., 2010. *Corporate sustainability strategies. Sustainability profiles and maturity levels*. Sustainable Development, Vol.18, No. 2, pp. 23-28.

Baxter, R., Bedard, J.C., Hoitash, R., and Yezegel, A. 2013. *Enterprise risk management program quality: Determinants, value relevance, and the financial crisis*. Contemporary

Accounting Research, 30(4), pp. 1264-1295.

BCBS, 2001. *Working Paper on the Regulatory Treatment of Operational Risk*. Basel Committee on Banking Supervision.

Beachboard, J., Cole, A., Mellor, M., Hernandez, S., Aytes, K. and Massad, N., 2008. *Improving Information Security Risk Analysis Practices for Small and Medium-Sized Enterprises: A Research Agenda*. Journal of Issues in Informing Science and Information Technology Education, 5, pp. 73-85.

Beasley, M., Branson, B.C. & Pagach, D., 2014. *An Analysis of the Maturity and Strategic Impact of Investments in ERM*. Journal of Accounting & Public Policy (Forthcoming).

Beasley, M., Clune, R., and Hermanson, D., 2005. *Enterprise risk management: An empirical analysis of factors associated with the extent of implementation*. Journal of Accounting and Public Policy, 24 (6), pp. 521-531.

Beasley, M. S., Pagach, D. P., and Warr, R. S., 2008. *Information conveyed in hiring announcements of senior executives overseeing enterprise-wide risk management processes*. Journal of Accounting, Auditing & Finance, 23, 311-332.

Becker, J., Rosemann, M., Röglinger, M. and zur Muehlen, M., 2012. *Business Process Management: An introduction to the special focus issue*. Business & Information Systems Engineering, Volume 4, Issue 5, 2012, pp. 227-228.

Benedek, W., Feyter, K. and Marrella, F., 2007. *Economic globalisation and human rights*. Cambridge University Press, pp. 5.

Berra, Y., 2001. *When You Come to a Fork in the Road, Take It!* Inspiration and Wisdom From One of Baseball's Greatest Heroes, New York: Hyperion, pp. 15-29.

Best, G.A, 2011. *42 Rules for Outsourcing Your Call Center*, California: Super Star Press, pp. 6-30.

Bhagwati, J., Blinder, A., 2009. *Offshoring of American Jobs: What Response from U.S. Economic Policy?* Cambridge: MIT Press.

Bittermann, H. J., 2007. *Made in Germany – Gute Noten für den Produktionsstandort Deutschland*, in: Process, Ausgabe 5-2007, pp. 12-13.

Bocken, P., Rana, P., Short, S.W., 2014. *Value mapping for sustainable business thinking*. Journal of Industrial and Production Engineering Volume 32, 2015 - Issue 1: Decision Support for Sustainable Design and Manufacturing, https://doi.org/10.1080/21681015.2014.1000399, accessed 04.03.2017.

Bodemann, M., Verjel, A. M., Weber G., 2017. *Sustainability as foundation for practical application. Considerations from and for information technology sector*. Proceedings of BASIQ 2017 International Conference, New Trends in Sustainable Business and Consumption, Graz, Austria, 31.05 – 03.06.2017, pp. 113-121.

Bowersox, D., Closs, D. and Cooper, M.B., 2012. *Supply chain logistics management*. 4th edition., New York: McGraw-Hill/Irwin, pp. 8-12.

Brad, S., Mocan, B., Brad, E. and Fulea, M., 2014. *Leading Innovation to Improve Complex Process Performances by Systematic Problem Analysis with TRIZ*. EPFL Lausanne, TRIZ

Future Conference 14, Global Innovation Convention, Lausanne.

Brad, S., Fulea M., Mocan, B. and Brad, E., 2012. *Systematic Innovation for Improving Competitiveness of a Master Study Program*. International Conference on Engineering & Business Education, Innovation and Entrepreneurship, Sibiu.

Bravard, L and Morgan, R., 2009. *Intelligent and successful Outsourcing*. Financial Press, Munich, Robecosam Dow Jones Sustainability Indices Yearbook Reports, http://www.sustainability-indices.com, accessed 10.01.2018.

Brocke, J., Mathiassen, L. and Rosemann, M., 2014. *Business Process Management*. Business & Information Systems Engineering, Volume 6, Issue 4, pp. 189-189.

Bruns, V. and Fletcher M., 2008. *Banks' risk assessment of Swedish SMEs*. Venture Capital, Vol. 10, No. 2, pp. 171-194.

Brustbauer, J., 2014. *Enterprise risk management in SMEs: Towards a structural model*. International Small Business Journal, pp. 70-85.

Buchmüller, M., Heinemann, B., Studeny, M. and Lange, S., 2017. *Research on the modularization strategy as a key factor for the sustainability in a global organization*. Proceedings of BASIQ 2017 International Conference, New Trends in Sustainable Business and Consumption, Graz, Austria, 31.05 – 03.06.2017, pp. 122-128.

Bugalla, J., Kallman, J., Mandel, C. and Narvaez, K., 2012. *Best Practice Risk Committees*. The Corporate Board, May/June 2012 issue, pp. 6-10, http://www.erm-strategies.com/blog/wp-content/uploads/2012/06/1205Bugal laKallmanMandelNarvaez.pdf, accessed 30.03.2017.

Bugalla, J. and Kallman, J., 2014. *Before the Launch...* Credit Union Management Magazine, Vol. 37 (11), http://www.cues.org/article/view/id/Before-the-Launch, accessed 30.03.2017.

Bugalla, J. and Kallman, J., 2014. *Leverage ERM to Practice Strategic Risk Management*. In: Fraser, J.R., Simkins B.J., Narvaez K., *Implementing Enterprise Risk Management*. Hoboken, NJ: John Wiley & Sons.

Bugalla, J., Kallman, J. and Narvaez, K., 2015. *When you come to a fork in the road, take it*. The Journal of Enterprise Risk Management, vol. 1, issue 1, pp. 51-54.

Burgstaller, J. and Wagner, E., 2015. *How do family ownership and founder management affect capital structure decisions and adjustment of SMEs?* Evidence from a bank-based economy. The Journal of Risk Finance, Vol. 16, No. 1, doi: 10.1108/JRF-06-2014-0091.

Calder, A., Moir, S., 2009. *IT Governance*. Cambridgeshire Business Park.

Carbone, T. A., Tippett, D.D., 2015. *Project Risk assessment Using the Project Risk FMEA*. Engineering Management Journal, pp. 28-35, http://www.tandfon line.com/doi/abs/10.1080/10429247.2004.11415263, acces-sed 25.03.2016.

Case, P., 2012. *Managing Sustainability risks and opportunities in the financial services sector*. Briefing for PricewaterhouseCooper, pp. 12, https://www.pwc.com/jg/en /publications/ned-sustainability-presentation-may-2012.pdf, accessed 13.01.2018.

Casuality Actuarial Society, 2003. *Overview of Enterprise Risk Management*. The CAS Enterprise Risk Management Committee, Forum Summer 2003.

Chang, K., Chang, Y. and Lai P., 2014. *Applying the concept of exponential approach to enhance the assessment capability of FMEA*. Journal of Intelligent Manufacturing, Volume 25, Issue 6, pp. 1413–1427.

Changhui, Y., 2007. *Risk Management of Small and Medium Enterprise Cooperative Innovation Based on Network Environment*. 3rd International Conference on Wireless Communications, Networking, and Mobile Computing, Shanghai, China. pp. 4560 – 4563.

Chapman, C.B. and Cooper, D.F., 1983. *Risk engineering: Basic controlled interval and memory models*. Journal of the Operational Research Society, 34(1), pp. 51-60.

Chatterjee, S., Wiseman, R.M., Fiegenbaum, A. and Devers, C.E., 2003. *Integrating Behavioural and Economic Concepts of Risk into Strategic Management: The Twain Shall Meet*. Long Range Planning, 36, pp. 61-79.

Cheng, Q., 2009. *Risk Analysis and Evaluation of the Destructive Innovation in Small and Medium-Sized Enterprises*. International Conference on Management and Service Science, MASS IEEE Computer Society.

Cheng, J., Chen, S. and Chen, F., 2013. *Exploring how inter-organizational relational benefits affect information sharing in supply chains*, Information Technology and Management, 14(4), pp. 283–294.

Chesbrough, H., 2006. *Open Business Model: How to thrive in the new innovation landscape*. Boston: Harvard Business School Press.

Chesbrough, H., 2011. *The Era of Open Innovation*. MIT Sloan Management Review, Winter Issue, pp. 35-41.

Cioccio, L. and Michael, E. J., 2007. *Hazard or disaster: Tourism management for the inevitable in Northeast Victoria*. Tourism Management, Vol. 28, No. 1, pp. 1-11.

Clemens, J. and Inderfurth, K., 2015. *Supply chain coordination by contracts under binomial production yield*. Business Research, pp. 1-32.

Corbett, M.F., .2004. *The Outsourcing Revolution*, Chicago: Dearbon Trade, pp.3-4, pp.11, pp. 98, pp.177-185.

Committee of Sponsoring Organizations of the Treadway Commission (COSO), 2004. *Enterprise Risk Management - Integrated Framework. Vol. 2.* http://www.coso.org/erm-integratedframework.htm, accessed 30.05.2016.

Couto,V., Plansky, J. and Caglar, D., 2017. *Fit for Growth*. New Jersey: Wiley, pp. 103-107.

Crockford, N., 1986. *An Introduction to Risk Management (2nd Eds)*. Woodhead-Faulkner, Cambridge.

Crouhy, M., Galai, D. and Mark, R., 2014. *The Essentials of Risk Management*. USA: Mcgraw – Hill Education, pp.1.

Cruz, M., 2002. *Modeling, measuring and hedging operational risk*. West Sussex: Wiley

Cullen, S., Lacity, M. and Willcocks, L., 2014. *Outsourcing: All you need to know*. White Plume.

Cummins, J. D., Lewis, C. M., and Wei, R., 2004, *The market value impact of operational risk events for U.S. banks and insurers*.

Cummins, J. D., Wei, R. and Xie, X., 2007. *Financial sector integration and information spillovers: effects of operational risk events on U.S. banks and insurers*.

Dappar, E.M., 2013. *Personnel Outsourcing and Corporate Performance*. European Journal of Business and Management, Vol.5, No.26.

Davidson, R. and Lambert, S., 2004. *Applying the Australian and New Zealand Risk Management Standards to Information Systems in SMEs*. Australian Journal Information Systems, 12(1), pp. 4-16.

Davis, C. E. and Davis, E., 2012. *A Potential Resurgence of Outsourcing*. CPA Journal, Vol. 82, No. 10, pp. 56-61.

De Fontnouvelle, P., V. De Jesus-Rueff, J. S. Jordan, and Rosengren, E. S., 2006. *Capital and risk: new evidence on implications of large operational losses*. Journal of Money, Credit and Banking 38(7), pp. 1819-1846.

Delerue, H. and Perez, M., 2009. *Unilateral commitment in alliances: an optional behavior*. Journal of Management Development, Vol. 28, No. 2, pp. 134-149.

Delerue-Vidot, H., 2006. *Opportunism and unilateral commitment: the moderating effect of relational capital*. Management Decision, Vol. 44, No. 6, pp. 37-751.

Deming, W., 1986. *Out of the Crisis*. Massachusetts Institute of Technology Center for Advanced Engineering Study, ISBN 0911379010. OCLC 13126265, pp. 88.

Deutscher Bundestag (Hrsg.), 2002. *Schlussbericht der Enquete-Kommission „Globalisierung und Weltwirtschaft"*, Opladen, pp. 63-73.

Di Serio, L. C., de Oliveira, L. H. and Siegert Schuch, L. M., 2011. *Organizational Risk Management: A Study Case in Organizations that Have Won the Brazilian Quantity Award Prize*. Journal of Technology Management & Innovation, 6(2), pp. 230-243.

Doh, J. P., Bunyaratavej, K. and Hahn E. D., 2009. *Separable but not equal: the location determinants of discrete services offshoring activities*. Journal of International Business Studies, 40(6), pp. 926–943.

Doz, Y., Santos, J. and Williamson, P., 2001. *From global to metanational: How organization win in the knowledge economy*. Boston: Harvard Business School Press.

Dumitrescu Peculea, A., Chercia, A. E. and Sandu (Udroiu), F., 2016. Quality and Performance by Resource Control Strenghtening. Proceedings of BASIQ 2016 International Conference, Konstanz, Germany, 02-03.06.2016, pp. 91-97.

Dutta, A. and Folden, H.W., 2010. *Winning Strategies*. Singapore: John Wiley& Sons.

Duwendag, D., 2006. Globalisierung im Kreuzfeuer der Kritik, Baden Baden, pp. 34-38.

de Reuver, M., Bouwman, H. and Haaker, T., 2009. *Mobile business models: organizational and financial design issues that matter*, Electron Markets, 19(3), doi 10.1007/s12525-009-0004-4, pp.1.

Deloitte, 2016. Deloitte's 2016 Global Outsourcing Survey. https://www2.deloitte.com/content/dam/Deloitte/nl/Documents/operations/deloitte-nl-s&o-global-outsourcing-survey.pdf, accessed 25.02.2017.

Dinmohammadi, F., Alkali B., Shafiee, M., Bérenguer, C. and Labib, A., 2016. *Risk Evaluation of Railway Rolling Stock Failures Using FMECA Technique: A Case Study of Passenger Door System*, Urban Rail Transit, Volume 2, Issue 3, pp. 128–145.

Economist Intelligence Unit on behalf of KPMG International, 2013. *Expectations of Risk assessment Outpacing Capabilities – It's Time For Action*. KPMG International Cooperative, https://www.kpmg.com/LB/en/IssuesAndInsights/ArticlesPublications/Documents/expectations-risk-management-survey.pdf, accessed 08.10.2015.

Ecorys, 2012. *EU SMEs in 2012: at the crossroads: Annual report on small and medium-sized enterprises in the EU 2011/12*. European Commission, Rotterdam. http://ec.europa.eu/enterprise/policies/sme/facts-figures-analysis/performance-review/files/supporting-documents/2012/annual-report_en.pdf, accessed 30.05.2016.

Eeckhoudt, L., 2012. *Beyond risk aversion: why, how and what's next?*, The Geneva Risk and Insurance Review 37, pp. 141–155.

Ehrlich, I. and Becker, G., 1972. *Market Insurance, Self-Insurance, and Self-Protection*. Journal of Political Economy, vol. 80, issue 4, pp. 623-650, http://dx.doi.org/10.1086/259916, accessed 10.03.2018.

Ellegaard C., 2006. *Small organization purchasing: a research agenda*. Journal of Purchasing & Supply management, 12, pp. 272-283.

Ellegaard, C., 2008. *Supply Risk Management in a Small Organization Perspective*. Supply Chain Management: An International Journal, 13(6), pp. 425-434.

Epstein, M.J. and Roy, M. J., 2003. *Improving sustainability performance: specifying, implementing and measuring key principles*. Journal of General Management, Vol. 29, No. 1, pp.15–31.

Escudero, L. and Minner, S., 2013). *Robust and stochastic optimization in production systems and supply chain management*. OR Spectrum, Volume 35, Issue 4, pp. 771-772.

Estabrooks, C.A., Squires, J.E., Cummings, G.G., Birdsell, J.M. and Norton, P.G., 2009. Development and assessment of the Alberta Context Tool. BMC Health Services Research 9, pp. 234, http://bmchealthservres.biomedcentral.com/articles/10.11 86/1472-6963-9-234, accessed 05.02.2017.

European Commission, 2003. *Commission Recommendation of 6 May 2003 concerning the definition of micro, small and medium-sized enterprises*. Official Journal of the European Union, Vol. 46, May 20, 2003, pp. 36–41.

Faisal, M. N., Banwet and D.K., Shankar, R., 2006. *An Analysis of the Dynamics of Information Risk in Supply Chains of Select SME Clusters*. The Journal of Business Perspective, 10(4), pp. 49-61.

Farrell, D., 2006. *Smarter offshoring*. McKinsey Global Institute, San Francisco, USA, pp. 84-92.

Fel, F. and Eric, G., 2012. *An analysis of the offshoring decision process: The influence of the organization's size*. 8th International Strategic Management Conference, June 2012, Barcelona, 2012, pp. 596-606, https://www.researchgate.net/publication/257717401_An_Analysis_of_the_Offshoring_Decision_Process_The_Influence_of_the_Organization's_Size, accessed 03.03.2017.

Fernando A.C., 2011. *Corporate Governance: Principles, Policies and Practices*, Pearson Press, Chennai.

Fillis, I., 2001. *Small firm internalization: an investigative survey and future research direction*. Management Decision, 39, (9), pp. 767-783.

Fillis, I., 2006. *A bibliographical approach to researching entrepreneurship in the smaller firm*. Management Decision, 44, pp. 198–212.

Financial Times Deutschland, 2008. *Produktionsverlagerung – China wird Adidas zu teuer*. http://www.ftd.de/unternehmen/industrie/:Produktionsverlagerung_China_wird_Adidas_zu_teuer/390718.html, accessed 03.06.2016.

Fischer, H., Fleischmann, A. and Obermeier, S., 2006. *Geschäftsprozesse realisieren: Ein Praxisorientierter Leitfaden von der Strategie bis zur Implementierung*. Wiesbaden: Springer Verlag, pp. 8-10.

Foerstl, K., Kirchoff, J. and Bals, L., 2016. *Reshoring and Insourcing: Drivers and Future Research Directions*. International Journal of Physical Distribution and Logistics Management, Vol. 46, No. 5, pp. 492-515. Nominated for AOM Carolyn Dexter (Best International Paper) award 2015.

Fontannaz, S., Oosthuizen, H., 2007. *The development of a conceptual framework to guide sustainable organizational performance*. South African Journal of Business Management, Vol. 38, No. 4, pp. 9-19.

Forlani, D., Parthasarathy, M. and Keaveney, S.M., 2008. *Managerial risk perceptions of international entry-mode strategies: The interaction effect of control and capability*. International Marketing Review, Vol. 25 No. 3, pp. 292-311.

Fraser, I., and Henry, W., 2007. *Embedding risk management: Structures and approaches*. Managerial Auditing Journal, 22(4), pp. 392-409.

Gama, A.P.M. and Geraldes, H.S.A., 2012. *Credit risk assessment and the impact of the New Basel Capital Accord on small and medium-sized enterprises: An empirical analysis*. Management Research Review, Vol. 35, No. 8, pp. 727-749.

Gao, S.S., Sung, M.C. and Zhang, J., 2013. *Risk management capability building in SMEs: A social capital perspective*. International Small Business Journal, Vol. 31, No. 6, pp. 677-700.

Gavril, R.M., Pleșea, D. A., Hell, C. and Verjel, A.M., 2017. *Study on the business risk as a result of a performant claim management in multinational organizations*. Proceedings of BASIQ 2017 International Conference, New Trends in Sustainable Business and Consumption, Graz, Austria, 31.05 – 03.06.2017, pp. 261-268.

Georgousopoulou, M., Chipulu, M., Ojiako, U. and Johnson, J., 2014. *Investment risk preference among Greek SME proprietors: A Pilot Study*. Journal of Small Business and Enterprise Development, Vol. 21, No. 1, pp. 177-193.

Ghadge, A., Dani, S. and Kalawsky, R., 2012. *Supply chain risk management: present and future scope*. The International Journal of Logistics Management, Vol. 23 No. 3, pp. 313-339.

Ghemawat, P., 2007. *Redefining global strategy*. Boston: Harvard Business School Press, Improving Business Processes –Expert Solutions to Everyday Challenges, Pocket Mentor, Harvard Business School Publishing, Boston, Massachusetts, ISBN 978-1-4221-2973-9, pp. 13.

Gilmore, A., Carson, D. and O`Donnell, A., 2004. *Small business owner-managers and their attitude to risk*. Marketing Intelligence & Planning, Vol. 22, No. 3, pp. 349-360.

Goldin, I. and Mariathasan, M., 2014. *The butterfly defect*, Princeton University Press, pp. 36-200.

Gollier, C., Hammitt, J. K. and Treich, N., 2013. *Risk and choice: A research saga*, Journal of Risk and Uncertainty, October 2013, Vol 47, Issue 2, pp. 129-145.

Garatwa, W. and Bollin, C., 2002. *Disaster Risk Management: Working Concept*. Deutsche Gesellschaft für Technische Zusammenarbeit (GTZ), Eschborn, http://www2.gtz.de/dokumente/bib/02-5001.pdf, accessed 04.11.2016.

Gordon, L. A., Loeb, M. P. and Tseng, C.Y., 2009. *Enterprise risk management and firm performance: A contingency perspective*. Journal of Accounting & Public Policy, 28(4), pp. 301-327.

Gotesman,E., Mateiu, A. and Bercovici, A., 2017. *Evaluation of outsourcing performances: a study of outsourcing in the area/field of NGOs*. Proceedings of the Conference, New Trends in Sustainable Business and Consumption, Austria, pp.302-309.

Grahl, A., 2011. *Success Factors in Logistics Outsourcing*, Wiesbaden: Gabler.

Gray, J.V., Skowronski, K., Esenduran, G. and Rungtusanatham, J. M., 2013. *The reshoring phenomenon: what supply chain academics ought to know and should do*. Journal of Supply Chain Management, Vol. 49 No. 2, pp. 27-33.

Greaver II, M.F., 1999. *Strategic Outsourcing: A Structured Approach to Outsourcing Decisions and Initiatives*. New York: Amacom, pp.17-28.

Green, M., Cameron, E., 2015. *Making sense of change management*, London: Kogan Page, pp. 5.

Grigore, A. M. and Drăgan, I. M., 2015. *Entrepreneurship and its Economical Value in a very Dynamic Business Environment*. Amfiteatru Economic, 17(38), pp. 120-132.

Guoyu, H., Qinfen, W., Zhingjian, L., Juling, D. and Ruihua, C., 2008. *A New Quantitative Analysis Method for Financial Risk Early Warning of Unlisted Small and Medium Enterprise*. IEEE International Conference on Management of e-Commerce and e-Government, Nanchang, China. pp. 289-296.

Gurau, C. and Ranchhod, A., 2007. *Flexible Risk Management in New Product Development: The Case of Small- and Medium-Sized Biopharmaceutical Enterprises*. International Journal of Risk Assessment and Management, 7(4), pp. 474-490.

Halvey, K.J. and Melby, B.M., 2007. *Business process outsourcing*. New Jersey: John Wiley&Sons, Anexa.3.3, pp. 30-89, pp. 138-155.

Harvard Business Review Press, 2010. *Improving Business Processes –Expert Solutions to Everyday Challenges*. Pocket Mentor, Harvard Business School Publishing, Boston, Massachusetts, ISBN 978-1-4221-2973-9, pp. 6, https://books.google.ro/books?id=gJZ4_0z3XjQC&printsec=frontcover&source=gbs_ge_summary_r&cad=0#v=one page &q&f=false, accessed 20.03.2017.

Hak, T.E., Moldan, B. and Dahl, A.L., 2007. *Sustainability Indicators*. Island Press, pp. 87-112.

Haydon, R., 2016. *Value: How to Talk about What You Do So People Want to Buy It*. Australia: Durban Professionals.

Head, L.G.,2009. Risk Management – Why and How. International Risk Management Institute, Dallas, Texas.

Heinemann, B., Buchmüller, M., Lange, S., Schmid, J., 2017. *The implementation of risk management in a medium sized organization*. Proceedings of the 28th IBIMA conference on Vision 2020: Innovation Management, Development Sustainability, and Competitive Economic Growth, Seville, Spain.

Heinemann, B., Dinu., V., Vochin, O. A. and Purcărea, A., 2016, *Analysis of the Effects of the Corporate Strategy to Performance in Business*. Proceedings of BASIQ 2016 International Conference, Konstanz, Germany, 02-03.06.2016, pp. 159-166.

Henschel, T., 2009. *Implementing a Holistic Risk Management in Small and Medium Sized Enterprises (SMEs)*. Edinburgh Napier University School of Accounting, Economics & Statistics, UK. http://sbaer.uca.edu/research/icsb/2009/paper 173.pdf, accessed 15.06.2016.

Hiebl, M. R.W., 2013. *Risk aversion in family firms: what do we really know?* The Journal of Risk Finance, Vol. 14, No. 1, pp. 49-70.

Hollman, K. W. and Mohammad-Zadeh, S., 1984. *Risk Management in Small Business*. Journal of Small Business Management, Vol. 22 No. 1, pp. 7-55.

Holter, A. R., Grant, D. B., Ritchie, J., Shaw, N., 2008. *A framework for purchasing transport services in SMEs*. International Journal of Physical Distribution & Logistics Management, 38 (1), pp. 21-38.

Hopkin, P., 2014. *Fundamentals of Risk assessment: Understanding, evaluating and implementing effective risk assessment*. The Institute of Risk assessment, pp.356, https://books.google.ro/books?id=zfvTDQAAQBAJ&printsec=frontcover#v=onepage&q&f=false, accessed 22.04.2017.

Hoskisson, R. E., Eden, L., Lau, C.M. and Wright, M., 2000. *Strategy in emerging economies*. Academy of Management Journal, Vol. 43, No. 3, pp. 249-267.

Hoyt, R. E. and Liebenberg, A. P., 2011. *The value of enterprise risk management*. Journal of Risk and Insurance, 78(4), pp. 795-822.

IAOP, 2017. *World's Best Outsourcing Advisors 2016*. https://www.iaop.org/Content/ 19/165/4458, accessed 25.02.2017.

IAOP, 2017. *The 2016 Global Outsourcing 100*. https://www.iaop.org/Content/ 19/165/4454, accessed 25.02.2017.

Iskanius, P., 2009. *Risk Management in ERP Project in the Context of SMEs*. Engineering Letters, 17(4). http://web.nchu.edu.tw/pweb/users/arborfish/lesson/8613.pdf, accessed 15.06.2016.

Islam, M. A., Tedford, J. D. and Haemmerle, E., 2006. *Strategic Risk Management Approach for Small and Medium-Sized Manufacturing Enterprises (SMEs): A Theoretical Framework*. Proceedings of IEEE International Conference on Management of Innovation and Technology, Singapore, pp.694-698.

Jacques, V., 2006. *International Outsourcing Strategy and Competitiveness Study on Current Outsourcing Trends: IT, Business Processes, Contact Centers*, Paris: Éditions Publibook.

Jahns, C., Hartmann E., Bals, L., 2006. *Offshoring: dimensions and diffusion of new business concept*. Journal of Purchasing and Supply Management (12) 3, pp. 218-231.

Jansen, A., 1986. *Desinvestition – Ursachen, Probleme und Gestaltungsmöglichkeiten*. Frankfurt a. M. / Bern / New York, pp. 120-125.

Jemielniak, D., Kociatkiewicz, J., 2009. *Handbook of Research on Knowledge-intensive Organizations*. Hershey, PA: IGI Global.

Jereb, B., Ivanuša T., Rosi, B., 2013. *Systemic Thinking and Requisite Holism in Mastering Logistics Risks: the Model for Identifying Risks in Organisations and Supply Chain*. Amfiteatru economic, Vol. 15, no. 33/2013, pp. 56-73.

Jibin, M. and Yi, C., 2008. *Study on the Risk of Small and Medium-Sized Enterprises Securitization Based on Unascertained Measure Model*. Proceedings of the IEEE International Conference on Business and Information Management, Wuhan, China, pp. 285-288.

Jobst, A., 2004. *Asset Securitisation as a Risk management and Funding Tool: What Does It Hold in Store for SMEs*. Goethe-Universität Frankfurt am Main, Germany. http://www.kantakji.com/fiqh/files/markets/70081.pdf, accessed 15.06.2016.

Jobst, A. A., 2006. *Asset securitisation as a risk management and funding tool: What small firms need to know*. Managerial Finance, Vol. 32 No. 9, pp. 31-760.

Joubioux, C. and Vanpoucke, E., 2016. *Towards right-shoring: a framework for off-and re-shoring decision making*. Operations Management Research 9 (3–4), pp. 117–132.

Jovanovic, B., 2001. *New technology and the small firm. Small Business Economics*, 16, pp. 53–55.

Jutta, B., Inklaar, R., de Jong, H. and van Zanden, J. L., 2018. *Rebasing 'Maddison': new income comparisons and the shape of long-run economic development*. Maddison Project Database, version 2018, Maddison Project Working paper 10, https://www.rug.nl/ggdc/historicaldevelopment/maddison/releases/maddison - project-database-2018, accessed 10.04.2018.

Juran, J. M., 1992. *Juran on Quality by Design: The New Steps for Planning Quality Into Goods and Services*, New York: The Free Press, pp. 380.

Just,V., Buchmüller,M. and Mateiu, A., 2016. *Reasearch in sustainable business process management*. Zeitschrift für interdisziplinäre ökonomische Forschung (Journal of interdisciplinary economic research), Vol. 1, Konstanz, pp.14-27.

Kambara, H., 2013. *Production Outsourcing and Firm Performance: An Empirical Analysis of Japanese Manufacturers*, Journal of Business Studies,Vol. 5, No.1, pp. 23- 29.

Kantabutra, S., 2006. Relating Vision-based Leadership to Sustainable Business Performance: A Thai Perspective. Leadership Review, Kravis Leadership Institute, Claremont McKenna College, Vol. 6, pp. 43-44, http://citeseerx.ist.psu.edu/ viewdoc/download?doi=10.1.1.555.3901 &rep=rep1 &type=pdf, accessed 05.03.2017.

Kao, J., 2007. *Innovation Nation: How America is losing its innovation edge, why it matters, and what we can so to get it back*. New York: Free Press.

Karavul, B., 2015. Prozessmanagement. http://www.projektmanagementhand buch.de/ add-on/prozessmanagement, accessed 18.12.2015.

Karduck, A. P., Sienou, A., Lamine, E. and Pingaud, H., 2007. *Collaborative Process Driven Risk Management for Enterprise Agility*. IEEE-IES Digital EcoSystems and Technologies Conference Proceedings, Cairns, Australia, pp. 535-540.

Kefan, X., Liu, J., Peng, H., Chen, G., Chen, Y., 2009. *Earlywarning Management of Inner Logistics Risk in SMEs Based on Label-card System*. Production Planning & Control, 20(4), pp. 306-319.

Keizer, J., Halman, J. I. M. and Song, X., 2002. *From Experience: Applying the Risk Diagnosing Methodology*. Journal Product Innovation Management, 19(3), pp. 213–232.

Kim, Y. and Vonortas, N.S., 2014. *Managing risk in the formative years: Evidence from young enterprises in Europe*. Technovation, Vol. 34, No. 8, pp. 454-465.

Kinkel, S., Lay, G., 2004. *Produktionsverlagerungen unter der Lupe*. Fraunhofer Institut Systemtechnik und Innovationsforschung, No. 34, pp. 5-11, https://www.isi.fraunhofer.de/content/dam/isi/dokumente/modernisierung-roduktion/erhebung 2003/pi34.pdf, accessed 12.01.2016.

Kinkel, S., Lay, G., Maloca, S., 2004. *Produktionsverlagerungen ins Ausland und Rückverlagerungen*. No. 8, http://www.isi.fhg.de, accessed 12.11.2016.

Kinkel, S. and Zanker, C., 2007. *Globale Produktionsstrategien in der Automobilzuliefererindustrie – Erfolgsmuster und zukunftsorientierte Methoden zur Standortbewertung*, Berlin, Heidelberg, pp. 19-27.

Kirytopoulos, K., Leopoulos, V. and Malandrakis, C., 2001. *Risk Management: A Powerful Tool for Improving Efficiency of Project Oriented SMEs*. Proceedings of the 4th SME International Conference, Denmark, pp. 331-339.

Kitson, A., Harvey, G. and McCormack, B., 1998. *Enabling the implementation of evidence based practice: a conceptual framework*. Quality Health Care 1998, 7, pp. 149-158.

Klemen, M. and Biffl, S., 2002. *Economic Aspects and Needs in IT-Security Risk Management for SMEs*. Institute of Software Technology and Interactive Systems, Vienna University of Technology, Austria, http://www.soberit.hut.fi/edser-6/PDF/10_Klemen_EDSER6.pdf, accessed 14.06.2016.

Knight F.H., 1921. *Risk, Uncertainty and Profit*. Hart, Boston, MA: Hart, Schaffner & Marx; Houghton Mifflin Co., http://www.econlib.org/library/Knight/knRU P1.html# Pt.I,Ch.I, pp. 5, accessed 27.02.2018.

Knudsen, M. P., and Servais P., 2007. *Analyzing internationalization configuration of SMEs: the purchasers' perspective*. Journal of Purchasing & Supply management, 13 (2), pp. 137-151.

Kolk, A. and Puumann, K., 2008. *Co-Development of Open Innovation Strategy and Dynamic Capabilities as a Source of Corporate Growth*, University of Technology, Tallin, Economics, No. 173, pp. 73-83.

Kotter, J.P., 2012. *Leading change*. Boston: Harvard Business School Press, pp. 21.

Koulopoulos, T.M. and Roloff, T., 2006. *Smartsourcing: Driving Innovation and Growth Through Outsourcing*. Massachusetts: Platinum Press.

KPMG, 2016. Global IT-BPO Outsourcing Deals Analysis. https://assets.kpmg.com/content/dam/kpmg/pdf/2016/03/KPMG-Deal-Tracker-3Q15.pdf, accessed 30.03.2017.

Kumar, S., Boice, B. and Shepherd, M., 2013. *Risk Assessment and Operational Approaches to Manage Risk in Global Supply Chains*, Transportation Journal Vol. 52, No. 3, pp. 391-411.

Kumar S., Holden, N., Igo, L., 2009. *A decision modelling framework to analyse offshore outsourcing changes for US manufacturers*. Journal of Revenue & Pricing Management, Vol. 8, Issue 5, pp. 424-437.

Kumar, A. and Kaushik, M., 2013. *Retention of BPO Employees in India*. European Journal of Business and Management, Vol.5, No.30, pp. 111.

Lacity, M.C. and Willcocks, L.P., 2009. *Information systems and outsourcing*. New York: Palgrave Macmillan, pp. 74.

Lane, C. and Quack, S., 1999. The social dimension of risk: bank financing of SMEs in Britain and Germany. Organisation Studies, 20(6), pp. 987-1010.

Lange, S., Buchmüller, M., Heinemann, B., Kompalla, A. 2017. *Importance of a well-defined corporate Governance*. Proceedings of BASIQ 2017 International Conference, New Trends in Sustainable Business and Consumption, Graz, Austria, 31.05 – 03.06.2017, pp. 372 -379.

Lange, S., Buchmüller, M., Heinemann, B., Mateescu, R.M., 2018. *The Driver for the Backsourcing Phenomenon under the Force of Globalization*, Proceedings of the 4th BASIQ International Conference on New Trends in Sustainable Business and Consumption, 11-13 June 2018, Heidelberg University, Heidelberg, Germany.

Lange, S., Tachiciu, L., Pirnea, I. C., Maier, A. 2016. *A case study on effectiveness of organisational structures under the effect of globalization*. BASIQ 2016 Proceedings - New Trends In Sustainable Business And Consumption. 2 - 3 June 2016, Konstanz, Germany, pp. 167-174.

Lavia Lopez, O. and Hiebl, M. R.W., 2014. *Management Accounting in Small and Medium-sized Enterprises: Current Knowledge and Avenues for Further Research*. Journal of Management Accounting Research, in press, doi: 10.2308/jmar-50915.

Leggio, K.B., 2007. *Using weather derivatives to hedge precipitation exposure*. Managerial Finance, Vol. 33, No. 4, pp. 246-252.

Leopoulos, V.N., Kirytopoulos, K.A. and Malandrakis, C., 2006. *Risk Management for SMEs: Tools to Use and How*. Production Planning & Control, 17(3), pp. 322-332.

Li, J., and Matlay, H., 2006. Chinese entrepreneurship and small business development: An overview and research agenda. Journal of Small Business and Enterprise Development, 13, pp. 248–262.

Liebenberg, A. P., and Hoyt, R. E., 2003. *The determinants of enterprise risk management: Evidence from the appointment of chief risk officers*. Risk Management & Insurance Review, 6(1), pp. 37-52.

Lohrmann, M., Rau, T. and Riedel, A., 2015. *Shared Services und Business Process Outsourcing*. Weinheim: Wiley, pp. 49-57.

Louisot, J.P. and Ketcham, C., 2009. *Enterprise-Wide Risk Management: Developing and Implementing*. Malvern: American Institute for Chartered Property Casualty Underwriters/Insurance Institute of America.

Love, P. E. D., Irani, Z., Standing, C., Lin, C. and Burna, J. M., 2005. *The Enigma of Evaluation: Benefits, Costs and Risks of IT in Australian Small–Medium-Sized Enterprises*. Information &Management, 42(7), pp. 947-964.

Loveman, G. and Sengenberger, W., 1991. *The re-emergence of small-scale production: An international perspective*. Small Business Economics, 3, pp. 1–38.

Luchian, I. and Luchian, C. E., 2017. *Literature review on integrated management systems*. Proceedings of BASIQ 2017 International Conference, New Trends in Sustainable Business and Consumption, Graz, Austria, 31.05 – 03.06.2017, pp. 388-394.

Maier, D., Sven-Joachim, I., Fortmüller, A. and Maier, A., 2017. *Development and Operationalization of a Model of Innovation Management System as Part of an Integrated Quality-Environment-Safety System*, Amfiteatru Economic, 19 (44), pp. 302-314.

Mala, O., Dudnik, A. and Kostrytska, S., 2014. *The Steep Analysis As Useful Method Of Investigating The Market*. Majesty of Marketing: Materials of the conference for the students and junior research staff, http://ir.nmu.org.ua/handle/123456789/146767?show=full, accessed 05.11.2016.

Manuj, I., 2013. *Risk Management in Global Sourcing: Comparing the Business World and the Academic World*. Transportation Journal Vol. 52, No. 1, pp. 80-107.

Marcelino-Sádaba, S., Pérez-Ezcurdia, A., Echeverría Lazcano, A.M. and Villanueva, P., 2014. *Project risk management methodology for small firms*. International Journal of Project Management, Vol. 32, No. 2, pp. 327-340.

Marin, G. and Mateiu, A., 2015. *European countries and the sustainability challenge: focus on transportation*. Proceedings of IE Conference, Bucharest, IDS Number: BD6ZZ, Accession number: WOS: 000362796900078, pp. 479-484.

Marin, G. and Mateiu, A., 2015. *The evaluation and strengthening of the freight transport system, as a solution for sustainable development in Romania*. Proceedings of IE Conference, Bucharest, IDS Number: BD6ZZ, Accession number: WOS: 000362796900079, pg. 485-490.

Marin,G., Mateiu, A. and Mailinger, W., 2015. *Collaborative practices within the supply chain area, as a solution for logistic enterprises to solve the challenges in obtaining sustainability*. International Journal of Economic Practices and Theories (IJEPT), Vol. 5, No. 3, pp. 222-232.

Marshall, A.P. and Weetman, P., 2002. *Information asymmetry in disclosure of foreign exchange risk management: can regulation be effective?* Journal of Economics and Business, Vol. 54, No. 1, pp. 31-53.

Mas-Verdu´, F., 2007. *Services and innovation systems: European models of technology centres*. Service Business, 1, pp. 7–23.

Mateescu, R. M., Buchmüller, M., Just, V., 2016. *Research on Key Factors Impacting Process Sustainability in Global Organizations*. Proceedings of BASIQ 2016 - International Conference, New Trends in Sustainable Business and Consumption, Konstanz, Germany, 2-3 June 2016, ISSN: 2457-483X, pp. 22-31.

Mateescu, R. M., Dinu V. and Maftei, M.,2018. *Improving Risk Management Methods: FMEA and its Influence on Risk Handling Costs*, Springer Verlag.

Mateescu, R. M., Dinu, V. and Maftei M., 2017. *Research on Using FMEA as a Risk Assessment Method in order to Reduce Risk Handling Costs*. Proceedings of BASIQ 2017 - New Trends in Sustainable Business and Consumption, Graz, Austria, 31 May – 3 June 2017, ISSN: 2457-483X, pp. 419-427.

Mateescu, R. M., Lange S., Heinemann, B., 2015. *The Role of Process Interactions Management in Ensuring Business Sustainability*. The International Conference Global Economy Under Crisis - 4th Edition, 18-20.12.2015, Constanţa, România, published in Ovidius University Annals, Economic Sciences Series, Vol. XV, Issue 2, ISSN-L 2393-3119, ISSN 2393-3127, pp. 287-291.

Mateescu, R. M., Maftei, M., Verjel, A. and Lange, S., 2017. *The Interrelation between Risk Management and the Organizational Context: Influence, Support and Barriers*. Proceedings of the 29th IBIMA conference on Education Excellence and Innovation Management through Vision 2020: from Regional Development Sustainability to Global Economic Growth, Vienna - Austria, 3-4 May 2017, ISBN: 978-0-9860419-7-6, pp. 3292-3308.

Mateescu, R. M., Olaru, M., Sârbu, A. and Surugiu (Farcaș), I., 2016. *Research on Increasing Risk assessment Efficiency as Support for Corporate Sustainable Development.*

International Conference on Management, Leadership and Governance (4th ICMLG), St. Petersburg, Russia, 14-15 April 2016, ISBN: 978-1-910810-84-2, pp. 450.

Mateescu, R. M., Olaru, M., Lange, S., Rauch, M., 2015. *Study on Supplier Invoice Risk Management in a Global Supply Chain*. Proceedings of the International Business Information Management Conference (26th IBIMA) - Innovation Management and Sustainable Economic Competitive Advantage: From Regional Development To Global Growth, Vols I - Vi, Madrid, Spain, 11-12 November 2015, ISBN:978-0-9860419-5-2, pp. 2579-2590.

Mateiu, A., Gotesman, E., Joachim, I.S. and Maftei, M., 2016. *Research on current global market trends in the business process outsourcing industry*. Proceedings of 28th IBIMA Conference, Spain, IDS Number: BG8XT, Accession number: WOS: 000392785700116, pp. 1176-1184.

Mateiu A., Mateescu, R. M., Buchmüller, M. and Just V., 2016. *Governance as a Key Factor for Ensuring the Sustainability of Outsourcing Models*. Proceedings of the International Conference on Management, Leadership and Governance (4th ICMLG), St. Petersburg, Rusia, 14-15.04.2016, ISBN: 978-1-910810-84-2, pp. 466-474.

Mazzarol, T., and Reboud, S., 2006. *The strategic decision making of entrepreneurs within small high innovator firms*. International Entrepreneurship and Management Journal, 2, pp. 261–280.

McIvor, R., 2010. *Global Services Outsourcing*. New York: Cambridge University Press.

McMullen J. S. and Shepherd D. A., 2006. *Entrepreneurial action and the role of uncertainty in the theory of the entrepreneur*. Academy of Management Review 31(1), pp. 132–152.

McShane, M. K., Nair, A., and Rustambekov, E., 2011. *Does enterprise risk management increase firm value?* Journal of Accounting, Auditing, and Finance, 26(4), pp. 641-658.

Menardi, G., 2009. *Some Issues Emerging in Evaluating the Risk of Default for SMEs*. Department of Economic and Statistic Science, Trieste University, Italy. http://www2.mate.polimi.it/ocs/viewpaper.php?id=140&cf=7, accessed 14.06.2016.

Menzies, T., Diochon, M. and Gasse, Y., 2004. *Examining venture-related myths concerning women entrepreneurs*. Journal of Developmental Entrepreneurship, 9(2), pp. 89–97.

Meulbroek L. K., 2002. *Integrated risk management for the firm: A senior manager's guide*. Journal of Applied Corporate Finance 14(4), pp. 56–70.

Mikes A., 2009. *Risk management and calculative cultures*. Management Accounting Research 20(1), pp. 18–40.

Miller, K.D., 1992. *A framework for integrated risk management in international business*. Journal of International Business Studies, Vol. 23, No. 2, pp. 311-331.

Mocan, B., Fulea, M., Olaru, M. and Buchmueller, M., 2015. *Paradigm shift in robotic systems programming for increasing business sustainability*. Proceedings of the international Conference BASIQ– New Trends in Sustainable Business and Consumption, Bucharest, Romania, 18-19 June 2015, Bucharest: Amfiteatru Economic, pp. 338.

Mokyr, J. 1997. *Are We Living in the Middle of an Industrial Revolution?* Federal Reserve Bank of Kansas City Economic Review, 2/1997, pp. 37.

Moore, J., Culver, J. and Masterman, B., 2000. *Risk Management for Middle Market Organizations*. Journal of Applied Corporate Finance, Vol. 12, No. 4, pp. 112-119.

Morgan, R., Bravard, J., 2009. *Intelligentes und erfolgreiches Outsourcing*. München: Finanzbuch, pp. 304-310.

Morris, M. H., Myyasaki, N. N., Watters, C. E. and Coombes, S. M., 2006. *The dilemma of growth: Understanding venture size choices of women entrepreneurs*. Journal of Small Business Management, 44, pp. 221–244.

Morrissey, B. and Pittaway, L., 2006. *Buyer-supplier relationships in small firms*. International Small Business Journal, 24 (3), pp. 272-298.

Moses, K. and Malone, R., 2018. Development of Risk Assessment Matrix for NASA Engineering and Safety Center, pp. 20, https://ntrs.nasa.gov/archive/nasa/casi.ntrs.nasa.gov/20050123548.pdf, accessed 10.05.2018.

Motohashi, K., 2011. *Measuring multinational's R&D activities in China by patent database: Comparison of European. Japanese and US firms*. Proceedings of the Academy of Management conference, San Antonio.

Motohashi, K., 2015. Management Strategies for Global Businesses. In: Global Business Strategy. Springer Texts in Business and Economics. Springer, Tokyo, ISBN 978-4-431-55467-7, pp. 26, https://doi.org/10.1007/978-4-431-55468-4_2, accessed 10.04.2018.

Mutezo, A., 2013. *Credit rationing and risk management for SMEs: the way forward for South Africa*. Corporate Ownership & Control, Vol. 10, No. 2, pp. 153-163.

Müller, T., 2011. *Zukunftsthema Geschäftsprozessmanagement. Eine Studie zum Status quo des Geschäftsprozessmanagements in deutschen und österreichischen Unternehmen*. Frankfurt a, Main: PricewaterhouseCoopers AG Wirtschafts-prüfungsgesellschaft, pp. 5, https://www.pwc.de/de/prozessoptimierung/ assets/pwc-gpm-studie.pdf.

National Aeronautics and Space Administration Department of State and Regional Development, 2005. Risk management guide for small business, Global Risk Alliance Pty Ltd jointly with NSW Department of State and Regional Development, pp. 2-9, http://smallbiz.nsw.gov.au, accessed 02.10.2016.

National Aeronautics and Space Administration, 2011. *NASA Risk Management Handbook*. Washington DC, pp. 143 – 147, https://ntrs.nasa.gov/archive/nasa/ casi.ntrs.nasa.gov/20120000033.pdf, accessed 03.11.2016.

National Collaborating Centre for Methods and Tools, 2014. *Organizational context for evidence-based practices: The Alberta Context Tool (ACT)*. Hamilton, ON: McMaster University, http://www.nccmt.ca/resources/search/216, accessed 02.03.2017.

Nocco B.W. and Stulz R., 2006. *Enterprise risk management: Theory and practice*. Journal of Applied Corporate Finance 18(4), pp. 8–20.

Norman, A. and Lindroth, R., 2002. *Supply Chain Risk Management: Purchasers' vs planners' Views on Sharing Capacity Investment Risks in the Telecom Industry*. Proceedings of the

11th International Annual IPSERA Conference, Twente, The Netherlands, pp. 577–595.

Northey, J. and Kinney S., 2014. *Guidelines for Risk Management*. Independent Verification & Validation Program, Version: F, 2014, pp. 19, https://www.nasa.gov/sites/default/files/atoms/files/ivv_s3001_-_ver_f.doc, accessed 13.02.2016.

Nooteboom, B., 2007. *Service value chains and effects of scale*. Service Business, 1, pp. 119–139.

O'Regan, N. and Ghobadian A., 2005. *Innovation in SMEs: The impact of strategic orientation and environmental perceptions*. International Journal of Productivity and Performance Management 54(2), pp. 81–97.

O'Reilly, C. A., Caldwell, D. F., Chatman, J. A. and Doerr, B., 2014. The Promise and Problems of Organizational Culture. Group and Organization Management, Vol. 38(6), pp. 595-625, http://journals.sagepub.com/doi/pdf/10.1177/1059601114 550713, accessed 03.03.2017.

Ogden J. A., Rossetti C. L. and Hendrick T. E., 2007. *An exploratory cross-country comparison of strategic purchasing*. Journal of Purchasing & Supply management,13, pp. 2-16.

Olaru, M., Dinu, V., Keppler, T., Mocan, B. and Mateiu, A., 2015. *Study on the open innovation practices in Romanian SMEs*. Revista Amfiteatru Economic, Vol. 17, No. 9, pp. 769-782.

Olaru, M., Schmid,J., Maier, D. and Mateiu, A., 2016. *A study of the impact of investments in economic value of the firm in international competition.* Proceedings of the Conference New trends in sustainable business and consumption, Konstanz, IDS Number: BF6YS, Accession number: WOS: 000383845100024, pp. 210-217.

Organisation for Economic Co-operation and Development (OECD), 2018. *Unit labour costs (indicator).* https://stats.oecd.org/Index.aspx?DataSetCode=ULC_ANN, accessed 05.05.2018.

Organisation for Economic Co-operation and Development (OECD), 2018. *Outsourcing.* https://stats.oecd.org/glossary/detail.asp?ID=4950, accessed 05.02.2018.

Organisation for Economic Co-operation and Development (OECD), 2018. *Guidelines for Collecting and Interpreting Innovation Data, 3rd Edition.* http://www.oecd-ilibrary.org/science-and-technology/oslo-manual_9789264013100-en, accessed 05.02.2018.

OSF Global Services. *The real cost of outsourcing.* https://www.osf-global.com/assets/uploaded_files/en/outsourcing-costs-OSF-white-paper.pdf, accessed 25.02.2017.

Osterhammel, J. and Petersson, N., 2005. *Globalization: a short history*, Princeton University Press, pp.15-27.

Paape, L. and Speklé, R.F., 2012. *The adoption and design of enterprise risk management practices: An empirical study*. European Accounting Review 21(3), pp. 533–564.

Pagach, D. P. and Warr, R. S., 2011. *The characteristics of firms that hire chief risk officers.* Journal of Risk and Insurance, 78, pp. 185-211.

Pagach, D. and Warr R., 2011. *The characteristics of firms that hire chief risk officers*. Journal of Risk and Insurance 78(1), pp. 185–211.

Parxion Research Group, 2010. *ISO 31000:2009, Risk Management Dictionary*. http://www.praxiom.com/iso-31000-terms.htm, accessed 24.03.2017.

Peters, S., Seidel, H. and Reinhardt, K., 2006. *Wissen verlagern – Standortentscheidungen aus der Wissensperspektive*, Wissensmanagement, Ausgabe 08/06, pp. 22-24.

Petroni G., Venturini K. and Verbano C., 2012. *Open innovation and new issues in R & D organization and personnel management*. The International Journal of Human Resource Management, 23(1), pp. 147-173.

Pfohl, H., Köhler, H. and Thomas, D., 2010. *State of the art in supply chain risk management research: empirical and conceptual findings and a roadmap for the implementation in practice*. Logistics Research, Volume 2, Issue 1, pp. 33-44.

Pisani, N. and Ricart, J. E., 2016. *Offshoring of Services: A Review of the Literature and Organizing Framework*. Management International Review, ISSN 0938-8249, Volume 56, Issue 3, pp 385–424, https://doi.org/10.1007/s11575-015-0270-7, accessed 10.04.2018.

Poba-Nzaou, P., Raymond, L. and Fabi, B., 2008. *Adoption and Risk of ERP Systems in manufacturing SMEs: A Positivist Case Study*. Business Process Management Journal, 14(4), pp. 530-550.

Poba-Nzaou, P. and Raymond, L., 2011. *Managing ERP system risk in SMEs: A multiple case study*. Journal of Information Technology, Vol. 26, No. 3, pp. 170-192.

Poba-Nzaou, P., Raymond, L. and Fabi, B., 2014. *Risk of adopting mission-critical OSS applications: An interpretive case study*. International Journal of Operations & Production Management, Vol. 34, No. 4, pp. 477-512.

Pojasek, R. B., 2013. *Organization and its Context*. http://isites.harvard.edu/fs/docs/icb.topic1219851.files/Organization%20and%20its%20Context%20Week%202.pdf, accessed 09.03.2017.

Popa, F., 2015. *ISO9001:2015 Punct si de capăt! (VI)*, Calitatea, acces la succes, Vol. 16, Nr. 144, pp. 4.

Porter, M. E., 1980. *Competitive strategy: Techniques for analyzing industries and competitors*. New York: Free Press, pp. 24.

Porter, M. E., 1985. *Competitive Advantage: Creating and Sustaining Superior Performance*. New York: Simon and Schuster, pp. 59, http://forleadership.org/wp-content/uploads/Competitive-Advantage.pdf, accessed 30.03.2016.

Porter, M. E., 2013. *Wettbewerbsstrategie: Methoden zur Analyse von Branchen und Konkurrenten*. New York: Campus Verlag, Vol.7, pp. 65.

Power, M., Desouza, K. and Bonifazi, C., 2006. *The Outsourcing Handbook*. London: Kogan Page, pp. 49-161.

Pressey, A.D., Winklhofer H. M. and Tzokas N.X., 2009. *Purchasing practices in SMES: an examination of strategic purchasing adoption, supplier evaluation and supplier capabilities*. Journal of Purchasing & Supply management 15, pp. 214-226.

PricewaterhouseCoopers, 2017. *Redefining business success in a changing world.* http://www.pwc.ro/ro/Publicatii/ceo-survey-2016-web.pdf, pp.8, accessed 25.02.2018.

Pritchard, C. L., 2014. *Risk assessment: Concepts and Guidance*. CRC Press, Fifth Edition, pp. 7-10, https://books.google.ro/books?id=ONfMBQAAQBAJ&printsec=frontcover& source =gbs_ge_summary_r&cad=0#v=onepage&q&f=false, accessed 02.04.2017.

Procopie, R., Pamfilie, R., Bobe, M. and Carceag, M., 2009. *Innovation - global vision on the product in the socio-economic environment*. Textile Industry Journal, Vol. 60, No.2, pp. 90-96.

Prosci Research Organization, 2017. *What is Change Management?* https://www.pro sci.com/change-management/what-is-change-management, accessed 13.02.2017.

Raynor, E.M. and Ahmed, M., 2013. *The Three Rules: How Exceptional Organizations Think.* New York: Penguin Group, pp. 90-202.

Regan, P.J. and Patè-Cornell, M.E., 1997. *Normative engineering risk management systems.* Reliability Engineering and System Safety, 57(2), pp. 159-169.

Reichl, M., 2015. *Corporate Governance ohne Paragrafen*, Wien: Linde, pp. 15- 32.

Reichmann, T., 2001. *Controlling mit Kennzahlen und Managementberichten: Grundlagen einer systemgestützten Controlling Konzeption*. München: Vahlen Verlag, pp. 23- 39.

Richbell, S.M., Watts, H. D. and Wardle, P., 2006. *Owner-managers and business planning in the small firm*. International Small Business Journal 24(5), pp. 496–514.

Rigau, E., 2003. *Définition et Opérationalisation d'une Organisation Virtuelle à Base d'Agents Pour Contribuer à de Meilleures Pratiques de Gestion des Risques dans les PMEPMI.* Ph.D. Thesis, Ecole de Mines, Paris, pp. 7- 13.

Ritchie, B. and Brindley, C., 2000. *Disintermediation, Disintegration and Risk in the SME Global Supply Chain*. Management Decision, 38(8), pp. 575-583.

Robecosam, 2018. *Industry Group Leaders 2017*, http://www.robecosam.com/ en/sustainability-insights/about-sustainability/corporate-sustainability-assessment /industry-group-leaders.jsp, accesat 20.05.2018.

Robecosam, 2018. *The Corporate Sustainability Assessment at a glance*. http://www.robecosam.com/en/sustainability-insights/about-sustainability/cor porate-sustainability-assessment/index.jsp, accessed 26.03.2018.

Roger, M., 2013. *Don't Let Strategy Become Planning*. Harvard Business Review, February 5, 2013. https://hbr.org/2013/02/dont-let-strategy-become-plann, accessed 12.11.2016.

Romeike, F., 2005. *Modernes Risikomanagement: Die Markt-, Kredit- und operationellen Risiken zukunftsorientiert steuern*. Weinheim: Wiley-VCH.

Rummler G. and Brache A., 1995. *Improving performance: How to manage the white space in the organization Chart*. San Francisco: Jossey Bass business and management series, Jossey Bass, pp. 29-33.

Rushton, A., Walker, S., 2007. *International Logistics and Supply Chain Outsourcing*. London:

Kogan Page, pp.106.

Salavou, H., Baltas, G. and Lioukas, S., 2004. *Organizational innovation in SMEs: The importance of strategic orientation and competitive structure*. European Journal of Marketing 38(9), pp. 1091–1112.

Schaltegger, S. and Wagner, M., 2006. *Integrative management of sustainability performance, measurement and reporting*. International Journal of Accounting, Auditing and Performance Evaluation, Vol. 3, No. 1, pp. 1–19.

Schmidt, D. L., Howard, A. J., Kallman, J., Leimberg, S. R. and Riggin, D. J., 2009. *The Tools & Techniques of Risk Management & Insurance*. Erlanger, KY: National Underwriter Organization.

Schmitz, T. and Wehrheim, M., 2006. *Risikomanagement: Grundlagen, Theorie, Praxis*. Stuttgart: Kohlhammer Verlag.

Schneider, H., 2012. *Failure Mode and Effect Analysis: FMEA From Theory to Execution*. Journal Technometrics, pp. 80, http://www.tandfonline.com/doi/abs/10.1080/00401706.1996. 10484424, accessed 10.04.2016.

Schulte, A., 2002, *Das Phänomen der Rückverlagerung – Internationale Standortentscheidungen kleiner und mittlerer Unternehmen*. Springer Fachmedien Wiesbaden, ISBN 978-3-409-12375-4, pp. 15-47.

Sebhatu, S. P., 2008. *Sustainability Performance Measurement for sustainable organizations: beyond compliance and reporting*. 11th QMOD Conference. Quality Management and Organizational Development Attaining Sustainability From Organizational Excellence to Sustainable Excellence, 20-22 August; 2008 in Helsingborg, Sweden, pp. 76-77, http://www.ep.liu.se/ecp/033/005/ ecp0803305.pdf, accessed 10.11.2016.

Seth, N., Deshmukh, S. G. and Vrat, P., 2006. *A conceptual model for quality of service in the supply chain*. International Journal of Physical Distribution & Logistics Management, Vol. 36, No. 7, pp. 547-575.

Simatupang, T. M. and Sridharan R., 2005. *An integrative framework for supply chain collaboration*, The International Journal of Logistics Management, Vol. 16, No. 2, pp. 257-274.

Sinkovics, R. R. and Roath, A. S., 2004. *Strategic Orientation, Capabilities, and Performance in Manufacturer - 3PL Relationships*. Journal of Business Logistics, Vol. 25, No. 2, pp. 43-64.

Smallbone, D. and Rogut, A., 2005. *The challenge facing SMEs in the EU's new member states*. International Entrepreneurship and Management Journal, 1, pp. 219–240.

Soin, K. and Collier, P., 2013. *Risk and Risk assessment in management accounting and control*. Management Accounting Research, 24(2), pp. 82–87.

Sommer, M., Florea, I. C., Dadfar, E., 2016. *Study of the Importance of SMEs for the German Market and Their Current Challenges*. Proceedings of BASIQ 2016 International Conference, Konstanz, Germany, 02-03.06.2016, pp. 276-284.

Song, N., Platts, K. and Bance, D., 2007. *Total acquisition cost of overseas outsourcing /*

sourcing; a framework and a case study. Journal of Manufacturing Technology Management, vol. 18, no. 7, pp. 858-875.

Sourcingmag Dictionary. *Nearshore outsourcing*, http://www.sourcingmag.com/dictionary/nearshore-outsourcing/, accessed 27.01.2017.

Sparrow, J., 1999. *Using qualitative research to establish SME support needs*. Qualitative Market Research: An International Journal, Vol. 2, No. 2, pp. 21-134.

Stanislawski, R. and Lisowska, R., 2015. *The Relations between Innovation Openness (Open Innovation) and the Innovation Potential of SMEs*. Procedia Economics and Finance, No. 23, pp. 1521-1526.

Stroh, P.J., 2005. *Enterprise risk management at UnitedHealth Group*. Strategic Finance 87(1), pp. 26–35.

Sukumar, A., Edgar, D. and Grant, K., 2011. *An investigation of e-business risks in UK SMEs*. World Review of Entrepreneurship, Management and Sustainable Development, Vol. 7, No. 4, pp. 380-401.

Szigeti, H., Messaadia, M., Majumdar, A. and Eynard, B., 2011. *STEEP analysis as a tool for building technology roadmaps*. Conference: eChallenges e-2011, At Florence, Italy, pp. 3, https://www.researchgate.net/publication/301295850_STEEP _analysis_ as_a_tool_for_building_technology_roadmaps, accessed 08.03.2017.

Szymczak, M., 2013. *Managing towards supply chain maturity*. New York: Palgrave Macmillan.

Tate W. and Bals L., 2017. *Outsourcing/offshoring insights: going beyond reshoring to rightshoring*. International Journal of Physical Distribution & Logistics Management, Vol. 47 Issue: 2/3, pp.106-113, https://doi.org/10.1108/IJPDLM-11-2016-0314, accessed 23.03.2018.

The Edinburgh Group, 2011. *Growing the global economy through SMEs*. pp. 7, http://www.edinburgh-group.org/media/2776/edinburgh_group_research_-_growing_the_ global_ economy_through_smes.pdf, accessed 29.10.2015.

The International Organization for Standardization, 2010. *ISO31000:2010*. https://www.iso.org/obp/ui/#iso:std:iso:31000:ed-1:v1:en, accessed 02.05.2018.

The International Organization for Standardization, 2015. *ISO9001:2015 - ISO's Process Approach*. http://www.praxiom.com/process-approach.htm, accessed 14.11.2015.

The International Organization for Standardization, 2018. *ISO31000:2018*. https://www.iso.org/obp/ui/#iso:std:iso:31000:ed-2:v1:en, accessed 02.05.2018.

Theodorakioglou, Y., Gotzamani, K. and Tsiolvas, G., 2006. *Supplier management and its relationship to buyers' quality management*. Supply Chain Management: An International Journal, Vol. 11, No. 2, pp. 148-159.

Thevendran, V. and Mawlesley, M. J., 2004. *Perception of human risk factors in construction projects: an exploratory analysis*. International Journal of Project Management, 22, pp. 131-137.

Thun, J.H., Drüke, M. and Hoenig, D., 2011. *Managing uncertainty – an empirical analysis of supply chain risk management in small and medium-sized enterprises*. International Journal of Production Research, Vol. 49. No. 18, pp. 5511-5525.

Thurik, R., and Wennekers, S., 2004. *Entrepreneurship, small business and economic growth*. Journal of Small Business and Enterprise Development, 11(1), pp. 140–149.

Tranfield, D., Denyer, D. and Smart, P., 2003. *Towards a Methodology for Developing Evidence-Informed Management Knowledge by Means of Systematic Review*. British Journal of Management, Vol. 14 No. 3, pp. 207–222.

Troacă, V.A., Bodislav, D.A., 2012. *Externalizarea serviciilor-conceptul*, Revista de Economie teoretică și aplicată, vol.XIX, Nr.6, pp 32-39.

United States Department of Defense, 1949. *MIL-P-1629 - Procedures for performing a failure mode effect and critical analysis*. Department of Defense (US). https://src.alionscience.com/ pdf/MIL-STD-1629RevA.pdf, accessed 09.03.2017.

Urciuoli, V. and Crenca, G., 1989. *Risk Management: strategie e processi decisionali nella gestione dei rischi puri d'impresa*. ISBA, Rovereto.

Vagadia, B., 2012. *Strategic outsourcing: The Alchemy to Business Transformation in a Globally Converged World*. Heidelberg: Springer, pp. 94-99, pp.124, pp.171.

Valukas, A.R., 2014. *Report to the Board of Directors of General Motors Organization regarding Ignition Switch Recalls*. General Motors internal investigative report. Chicago: Jenner&Block. http://s3.documentcloud.org/documents/1183508/g-m-internal-investigation-report.pdf, accessed 12.11.2016.

Vanthournout, D., Olson, K., Ceisel, J., White, A., Waddington, T., Barfield,T., Desai, S., and Mindrum, C., 2006. *Training for High Performance at Accenture*. Chicago: Agate Publishing.

Vargas-Hernández, J.G., 2011. *Modelling Risk and Innovation Management*. Advances in Competitiveness Research, 19 (3-4), pp. 45-57.

Văduva S., 2016. *The Future of Public Administration Reform in Romania*. From Corruption to Modernity. SpringerBriefs in Economics, Springer, Cham, ISBN 978-3-319-26996-2, pp. 27-70.

Vătămănescu, E. M., Alexandru, V. A. and Nistoreanu, B. G., 2017. *Leveraging business relationships as SMEs internationalization drivers*. Proceedings of BASIQ 2017 International Conference, New Trends in Sustainable Business and Consumption, Graz, Austria, 31.05 – 03.06.2017, pp. 733-741.

Verbano, C. and Turra, F., 2010. *A human factors and reliability approach to clinical risk management: Evidences from Italian cases*. Safety Science, 48(59), pp. 625–39.

Verbano, C. and Venturini, K., 2011. *Development Paths of Risk Management: Approaches, Methods and Fields of Application*. Journal of Risk Research, 14(5-6), pp. 519 – 550.

Verbano, C. and Venturini, K., 2013. *Managing Risks in SMEs: A Literature Review and Research Agenda*. Journal of Technology Management & Innovation, Volume 8, Issue 3, pp. 3-15.

Vickery, J., 2008. *How and why do small firms manage interest rate risk?* Journal of Financial

Economics, Vol. 87, No. 2, pp. 446-470.

Viscelli, T.R., Beasley, M.S. and Hermanson, D. R., 2015. *Enterprise risk management: A review of the academic literature and an agenda for future research*. Working paper. Auburn University.

Vitasek, K., 2013. *Vested Outsourcing: five rules that will transform outsourcing*. 2nd edition, New York: Palgrave Macmillan, pp.18.

Wahlström, G., 2009. *Risk management versus operational action: Basel II in a Swedish context*. Management Accounting Research 20(1), pp. 53–68.

Walker, R., 2013. *Winning with Risk Management*. World Scientific Publishing Organization, pp. 37- 52.

Wallenburg, C. M, 2009. *Innovation in Logistics Outsourcing Relationships: Proactive Improvements by Logistics Service Providers as a Driver of Customer Loyalty*. Journal of Supply Chain Management, Vol.45, No. 2, pp.75-93.

Walshe, K. and Dineen, M., 1998. *Clinical Risk Management. Making a difference?* The NHS Confederation, University of Birmingham, Birmingham.

Watson, J. and Newby, R., 2005. *Biological sex, stereotypical sex-roles, and SME owner characteristics*. International Journal of Entrepreneurial Behaviour and Research, Vol. 11, No. 2, pp. 129-143.

Watt, J., 2007. *Strategic risk management in small businesses*. Reuvid J (ed.) Managing Business Risk: A Practical Guide to Protecting your Business (2nd edn). London: Kogan Page, pp.31–40.

Weber, G., Mateescu, R. M., Lange, S. and Rauch M., 2016. *Knowledge intensive Business Services (KIBS) in the context of changing energy economics in Germany*, Revista Amfiteatru Economic, "Amfiteatru Economic Journal", Vol. XVIII, No. 41, Feb. 2016, Editura ASE, Bucharest (Romania), ISSN 2247-9104, pp. 89-103.

Williams, A. and Oumlil, B., 1987. *A classification and analysis of JPMM articles*. Journal of Purchasing and Materials Management, 23(3), pp. 24–28.

Wilson, N. and Altanlar, A., 2013. *Organization failure prediction with limited information: newly incorporated organizations*. Journal of the Operational Research Society, Vol. 65, No. 2, pp. 252-264.

Wirtschaftslexikon, 2017. *Prozessmanagement*. http://www.wirtschaftslexicon24.com/d/prozessmanagement/prozessmanagement.htm, accessed 17.12.2017.

Wolke, T., 2017. *Risk Management*. De Gruyter, Oldenburg, ISBN 978-3-11-044052-2, pp.7.

World Economic Forum, 2017. *Global Risks Report 2017*. http://www3.weforum.org/docs/GRR17_Report_web.pdf, accessed 03.04.2017.

Wu, D.D. and Olson, D., 2009. *Enterprise Risk Management: Small Business Scorecard Analysis*. Production Planning & Control, 20(4), pp. 362-369.

Xiaohong, C., Ying, Z. and Jian, S., 2007. *A study of SMEs Growth Evaluation Considering Value at Risk*. IEEE International Conference on Service Systems and Service Management

Proceedings. Chengdu, China. pp. 1-5.

Yap, Q.S. and Webber, J.K., 2015. *Developing Corporate Culture in a Training Department: a Qualitative Case Study of Internal and Outsourced Staff*. Review of Business and Finance Studies, Vol.6, No.1, pp. 43-56.

Yeo, K.T. and Lai, W.C., 2004. *Risk Management Strategies for SME Investing in China: a Singaporean Perspective*. IEEE International Engineering Management Conference Proceedings. Singapore, pp. 794-798.

Youssef, N. F. and Hyman W. A., 2010. *Risk Analysis: Beyond Probability and Severity*, Medical Device and Diagnostic Industry, http://www.mddionline.com/ article/risk-analysis-beyond-probability-and-severity, accessed 10.12.2016.

Zäh, F., Rimpau, C., Wiesbeck, M., 2005. *Produktion im globalen Umfeld – Auslandsaktivitäten oder Risiken?* ZWF – Zeitschrift für wirtschaftlichen Fabrikbetrieb, Jahrgang 100 (2005) 5, pp. 248-249.

Zhai, W., Sun, S. and Zhang, G., 2016. *Operations Management Research*. pp. 62-74, https://doi.org/10.1007/s12063-016-0114-z, accessed 10.04.2018.

Zheng, J., Caldwell, N., Harland, H., Powell, P., Woerndl, M. and Xu, S., 2004. *Small firms and e-business: cautiousness, contingency and cost-benefit*. Journal of purchasing and Supply Management, 10 (1), pp. 27-39.

Zhi-Qiang, M. and Tao, H., 2008. *Risk Evaluation on Technological Innovation of Chinese Small & Medium-Sized Enterprises SMEs Based on Fuzzy Neural Network*. IEEE International Conference on Wireless Communication, Networking and Mobile Computing Proceedings, Niagara Falls, Canada, pp. 13067-13073.

Zhou, K. Z., Yim. C. K. and Tse, D. K., 2005. *The effects of strategic orientations on technology- and market-based breakthrough innovations*. Journal of Marketing 69(2), pp. 42–60.

9 Annexes

Annex A

Number and type of researched organization and interview results related to risk appetite, risk tolerance and risk attitude achieved during the study related to risk assessment integration in small and medium-sized enterprises compared to large companies

1. Number of organizations researched based on the respondents' professional experience in small and medium-sized enterprises and large companies

Interviewed individuals:	1	2	3	4	5	6	7	8	9	10	11	12	13	14	15	16	17	18	19	20	21	22	23	Total
SMEs	3	1	4	0	0	0	2	2	1	1	0	2	2	3	4	3	1	0	0	2	2	2	1	**36**
Large companies	0	1	1	1	2	2	1	0	0	1	1	0	0	1	0	0	1	1	2	0	0	0	0	**15**
Total no. of organizations	3	2	5	1	2	2	3	2	1	2	1	2	2	4	4	3	2	1	2	2	2	2	1	**51**

2. Risk appetite, risk tolerance and risk attitude in small and medium-sized enterprises and large companies

Risk appetite, tolerance and attitude	**No. of SMEs**	**No. of large companies**
Low risk appetite and low risk tolerance	6	0
Low risk appetite and high risk tolerance	12	38
High risk appetite and high risk tolerance	14	10
High risk appetite and low risk tolerance	19	3
Offensive and defensive	33	13
Neutral	6	0
Defensive	12	38

R. M. Bejinariu, *Sustainable Business Performance and Risk Management*,
Sustainable Management, Wertschöpfung und Effizienz,
https://doi.org/10.1007/978-3-658-29389-5

Annex B

Interview questions and answers during interviews conducted for the study related to risk assessment integration in small and medium-sized enterprises compared to large companies

1. Interview questions and answers related risk assessment in small and medium-sized enterprises

No. crt.	Interview questions	No. of organizations that have answered:		
		YES	NO	PARTLY
1	Is the risk assessment process implemented in your organization?	18	26	7
2	Does the senior management team show interest in investing and updating the risk assessment process?	51	0	0
3	Is the staff involved in the risk assessment process?	18	28	5
4	Has the risk tolerance evaluation been performed?	0	46	5
5	Is there a special budget allocated for risk assessment process execution?	18	33	0
6	Is there a budget for investments and updates that ensure risk assessment development?	0	51	0
7	Is there a proper documentation and standardization across the organization for the risk assessment process?	11	40	0
8	Are risk assessment results used when developing business strategies?	13	33	5

2. Interview questions and answers related to related risk assessment in large companies

No. crt.	Interview questions	No. of organizations that have answered:		
		YES	NO	PARTLY
1	Is the risk assessment process implemented in your organization?	33	7	11
2	Does the senior management team show interest in investing and updating the risk assessment process?	44	0	7
3	Is the staff involved in the risk assessment process?	40	7	4
4	Has the risk tolerance evaluation been performed?	11	18	22
5	Is there a special budget allocated for risk assessment process execution?	28	7	16
6	Is there a budget for investments and updates that ensure risk assessment development?	11	33	7
7	Is there a proper documentation and standardization across the organization for the risk assessment process?	24	0	27
8	Are risk assessment results used when developing business strategies?	33	7	11

Annex C

Questions and answers related to risk assessment and internal factors used for the study concerning the interrelation between risk assessment and the organizational context

Questions related to risk assessment and internal factors	No. of organizations that have answered:	
	YES	NO
What is the influence of internal stakeholders on the risk assessment process?		
1. Does the management team take all decisions regarding budgeting the risk assessment process?	49	3
2. The implication of the staff is very important for the success of the process.	49	3
3. Risk owners determine the way risks are analyzed, monitored and handled.	47	5
What is the influence of the risk assessment process on the internal stakeholders?		
1. Do you think that risk assessment is a very powerful tool that helps the managers take decisions and develop strategies?	50	2
2. Do you agree that the process has a direct impact on the performance and profitability of the organization?	46	6
3. Do the employees have to adapt and to improve connectivity in order to manage the process across the organization?	39	13
What is the influence of leadership on the risk assessment process?		
1. Leadership style determines the success of the risk management process. Do you agree?	51	1
2. Do people handling the process are motivated by intelligent, knowledgeable and charismatic leaders?	48	4
3. Do you think that monitoring and controlling this complex process takes strong leadership?	47	5
What is the influence of the risk assessment process on leadership?		
1. Being a complex process, do you agree that the staff needs to be monitored and guided by a strong leader?	49	3
2. Do you think that leadership style and the leader's compatibility with the personnel are essential to the efficiency of the process?	45	7
3. Staff needs to be constantly motivated to extend their know-how in order to insure a performant process. Do you agree?	37	15
What is the influence of organizational culture on the risk assessment process?		
1. Does the organizational culture determine the way the organization handles risks?	51	1

Questions related to risk assessment and internal factors	No. of organizations that have answered:	
	YES	**NO**
2. Do you agree that the know-how of the leaders will influence the performance of the process?	45	7
3. Do innovation and future-oriented organizations allocate a higher level of resources for the process?	31	21
What is the influence of the risk assessment process on the organizational culture?		
1. Does risk assessment have a strong influence on the performance of the organization, therefore increasing the efficiency of the staff?	47	5
2. Do you think that the process influences how staff feels about the safety and security of the working environment?	43	9
3. Does risk assessment define how risk-taking and strategy-oriented people are?	42	10
What is the influence of the social capital, informal and formal interactions on the risk assessment process?		
1. Do you agree that risk identification and evaluation require a high amount of data achievable through connections?	51	1
2. Does networking help selling a strategic idea related to an opportunity to the management team?	48	4
3. Does acting like a team player will ease the access to data and solutions?	43	9
What is the influence of the risk assessment process on the social capital, informal and formal interactions?		
1. Risk assessment strengthens connections by being a process that relates to each of the organization's processes. Do you agree?	45	7
2. Is the process very knowledge-intensive requiring connectivity to all stakeholders?	40	12
3. Can risks be identified at other processes' levels involving the need of strong communications with other departments?	25	27
What is the influence of the structural and electronic resources on the risk assessment process?		
1. Are resources assigned for the risk assessment process a key factor for the process sustainability and development?	49	3
2. Is automating the process more efficient and leaves more time for risk handling and strategic thinking?	41	11
3. Should the structure of the organization allow risk assessment to be easily applied for each process?	34	18
What is the influence of the risk assessment process on structural and electronic resources?		
1. Do you think that the risk assessment process affects the organization's structure by acting like a connecting hub between all departments?	41	11

Questions related to risk assessment and internal factors	No. of organizations that have answered:	
	YES	**NO**
2. Do risk assessment results modify the way actions are taken in other departments, therefore structural changes may have to be made in the whole organization?	40	12
3. Will implementing a customized risk assessment software have an impact on the whole electronic setup of the organization?	39	13
What is the influence of the organizational slack on the risk assessment process?		
1. Do you agree that risk handling plan and all strategies related to risk depend on the ability and capacity of the organization to adapt to change?	47	5
2. Do you think that while being a dynamic process, risk assessment constant updating and upgrading depends on the organization's flexibility and fast adaptation to change?	41	11
3. Does the organization's organizational slack determine the success of the process implementation?	34	18
What is the influence of the risk assessment process on the organizational slack?		
1. Do you agree that the risk assessment process prevents unwanted events, therefore reduces the amount of necessary resources related to change?	44	8
2. Being a proactive process, does risk assessment allow more time to prepare in case negative events are foreseen?	43	9
3. For a successful implementation, should the staff permit changes and to support constant communication with the risk assessment team?	41	11

Annex D

Questions and answers related to risk assessment and external factors used for the study concerning the interrelation between risk assessment and the organizational context

Questions related to risk assessment and external factors	No. of organizations that have answered:	
	YES	NO
What is the influence of external stakeholders on the risk assessment process?		
1. Do the shareholders influence the management team's decisions related to the risk assessment process?	47	5
2. Are suppliers and creditors interested in the reliability of the organization and is risk assessment implementation a factor?	47	5
3. Do clients want to make sure that there are no risks related to production?	30	22
What is the influence of the risk assessment process on the external stakeholders?		
1. Does risk assessment influence decision-making and offers important information to the shareholders?	52	0
2. Do you think that the process ensures business stability and positively influences the organization's image on the market?	48	4
3. Can risk assessment create risk profiles and process patterns that can be also be used by other organizations?	38	14
What is the influence of socio-cultural factors on the risk assessment process?		
1. Should risk assessment consider demographics and the education level of the population?	45	7
2. Can the economic status of the organization's clients in terms of stability determine important risks that need to be identified and reviewed?	37	15
3. Do the organization's customs and values influence both the implementation and the successful running of the process?	35	17
What is the influence of the risk assessment process on socio-cultural factors?		
1. Do you think that a safe and secure business creating jobs and having an influence on the local demographics is an important impact?	48	4
2. Creating a secure working environment motivates people and relieves stress that can lead to human errors. Do you agree?	45	7
3. Does the risk assessment process influence social and cultural factors by ensuring communication between all departments?	32	20
What is the influence of technological factors on the risk assessment process?		

Questions related to risk assessment and external factors	No. of organizations that have answered:	
	YES	NO
1. Do you think that the risk assessment process has to be adapted to the current available technology?	51	1
2. Is integrating the process in the organization's ERP system highly efficient for the organization?	48	4
3. Can a solid electronic communication system speed up the process?	35	17
What is the influence of the risk assessment process on technological factors?		
1. The risk assessment process influences software developing organizations to create electronic risk management solutions. Do you agree?	47	5
2. Does the process require resources for a healthy, constantly updated ERP system?	43	9
3. Will controlled risks always have a positive impact on the economy and will attract investments in new technology?	30	22
What is the influence of economic factors on the risk assessment process?		
1. Does a healthy economic environment involve less risks for the organization having a direct impact on the risk assessment process?	50	2
2. Are external economic factors always to be considered when assessing risks?	44	8
3. Do labor costs and interest rates influence decisions related to allocating resources for the risk assessment process?	30	22
What is the influence of the risk assessment process on economic factors?		
1. Safer business has a direct impact on the labor costs, taxes and interest rates. Do you agree?	52	0
2. Does risk assessment improve the income of the local population?	48	4
3. Investors are attracted by a healthy economy. Is risk assessment an important factor?	41	11
What is the influence of environmental factors on the risk assessment process?		
1. In order to ensure business sustainability, should the risk assessment process take environmental factors into consideration?	49	3
2. Legal requirements related to ecology has to be considered when performing the risk evaluation of the external factors. Do you agree?	45	7
3. Does a healthy organizational culture in terms of ecology influence the well-being and motivation of the staff?	39	13
What is the influence of the risk assessment process on environmental factors?		
1. Do you think that a secure business environment influences the ecological awareness?	50	2
2. By positively influencing the local economy, is there more money available for recycling and waste disposal?	48	4

Questions related to risk assessment and external factors	No. of organizations that have answered:	
	YES	**NO**
3. Good business results are likely to influence how eco-friendly the organization is in terms of allocated budget and resources. Do you agree?	43	9
What is the influence of political factors on the risk assessment process?		
1. The political climate changes often, therefore should all related risks be investigated and evaluated?	48	4
2. The risk assessment process needs to be constantly updated according to laws and legislation. Do you agree?	48	4
3. Do you think that a politically unstable political environment will require a more intensive risk assessment process and more resources for the process?	39	13
What is the influence of the risk assessment process on political factors?		
1. Organizations with a solid risk assessment process are considered more reliable and fulfill the tenders' requirements. Do you think risk assessment brings an important contribution?	43	9
2. Prosper business impacts the economy and as a consequence higher budgets are available for the local authorities and politicians' ratings improve. Do you agree?	41	11
3. Will laws and legislation always depend on the local economy and the performance of the organizations in the area?	39	13

Annex E

Determining process criteria with impact on sustainable performance on the example of the investigated organizations during the study related to critical factors impacting sustainable business performance

A. Process description

The procurement processes involve multiple activities: planning, budgeting, sending inquiries, supplier selection and sending orders.
In order to make a detailed description of the process the main characteristics related to sustainability have to be investigated:

a) Organization profile and structure
The investigation was carried out within a global organization with subsidiaries on three continents. The business objectives are focused on profitable growth, sustainable commercial activity based on offering high quality products and services. The corporation has a considerable market share and is perceived by clients, creditors and society as a reliable and competent organization. Senior management take strategic decisions while anticipating and adapting to the new market changes, also sustainability and business competitiveness are targeted when designing processes. Procurement, accounting, human resources and IT are supporting the organization's main processes (production, logistics and sales).

b) Process objectives and performance goals
Process owners target long-term efficiency without quality of service being compromised. Performance indicators are set up by senior management and the head of the department monitors and reviews results in order to ensure process efficiency.

c) Requirements of external or internal clients
All details related to the procurement process involving one or multiple suppliers are presented in order to adapt the process to the clients' needs and develop the sourcing strategy. All employees involved in the process must have access to information related to every step of the process – new employees have to go through the onboarding process in order to understand the process. In order to prepare the process all these requirements have to be met. Continuous monitoring and optimization ensure long-term process sustainability.

d) Inputs and outputs

The procurement process is value-adding for the commercial activity of the organization. Data gathering and data selection have to be well documented in order to ensure profitable commerce – for example the lowest price is not always the best option when selecting suppliers. Standard operating procedures related to data processing are mandatory in order to make the best deals.

e) Production and value creation

Information related to the process have to be available to all employees. The available information has to ensure that even the uninvolved staff members can purchase products from suppliers. The standard operating procedure is value-adding by sharing process-related knowledge and by facilitating process data without additional manual input. Access is ensured through the intranet so that, depending on access levels, organization employees can retrieve information from the procurement process database.

f) Process owner and staff involvement

The head of the department is the owner of the procurement process therefore ensuring an experienced and specialized perspective. The staff has also experience in the quality assurance department - this is particularly value-adding for the process. All the employees in the department are involved and one proof is that the process documentation is constantly updated.

B. Degree of formality

Solid documentation of the procurement process is available; the steps of the process are accurately defined and the sequence of activities is presented in a detailed manner.

C. Level of involvement

Despite the fact that all employees are well-trained and involved, there is no back-up in place in case one of the staff members is takes a leave of absence. The onboarding process takes up to two weeks of training for new or uninformed employees.

D. Transfer of information

All information related to the process is gathered on the intranet database as one standard operating procedures manual. Knowledge can also be shared by ensuring good communication between the procurement department and all other departments.

E. Risk management at process interactions level

Risk management offers valuable information for all the core processes such as marketing, sales and logistics. The organization manages risks across the organization but does not identify and assess risks related to communication between the procurement department and other departments; therefore, knowledge transfer and sensitive sourcing-related information can be compromised especially in case one employee leaves the organization.

F. Monitoring, control and process optimization

The process includes activities and protocols that are constantly monitored and controlled by the procurement staff. Performance indicators are reviewed by the head of the department and new optimization solutions are found in order to ensure sustainability.

The final part of the research includes the interviewees' opinion on the key factors that affect process sustainability, these are: solid process documentation, involved staff and communication between departments.

Annex F

Interview results for the study related to process criteria impacting business processes from sustainability point of view

Process criteria code	Investigated processes / Interview questions	Production processes (15 processes)		Sales processes (15 processes)		Financial processes (10 processes)		Procurement processes (8 processes)		Human resources processes (8 processes)		Average proportion of respondents with the answer YES	Overall result/ process criteria
		Respondents with the answer YES											
		No.	%	No.	%	No.	%	No.	%	No.	%		
A	Are processes defined completely and correctly?	12	80.00%	12	80.00%	8	80.00%	6	75.00%	7	87.50%	80.50%	55.33%
	Is the time frame clear for each of the process steps and activities?	8	53.33%	7	46.67%	5	50.00%	4	50.00%	5	62.50%	52.50%	
	Is there a back-up plan in place in case of the process steps fails?	5	33.33%	4	26.67%	3	30.00%	3	37.50%	3	37.50%	33.00%	
B	Are processes fully documented in a database?	9	60.00%	9	60.00%	6	60.00%	5	62.50%	5	62.50%	61.00%	66.50%
	Is the sequence of activities clear for all employees?	11	73.33%	10	66.67%	7	70.00%	6	75.00%	6	75.00%	72.00%	
C	Is the process owner specialized for all operations required for the process?	13	86.67%	11	73.33%	8	80.00%	9	112.50%	7	87.50%	88.00%	75.61%
	Is there a back-up employee in case the process owner takes a sick leave or is on vacation?	8	53.33%	7	46.67%	5	50.00%	4	50.00%	5	62.50%	52.50%	
	Does the process owner have any experience with quality management?	13	86.67%	12	80.00%	9	90.00%	7	87.50%	7	87.50%	86.33%	
D	Is all detailed information available for the involved employees?	13	86.67%	12	80.00%	9	90.00%	7	87.50%	7	87.50%	86.33%	76.03%
	Do all involved personnel have the right access level for the process?	12	80.00%	13	86.67%	7	70.00%	6	75.00%	7	87.50%	79.83%	
	Is all information available in case of personnel change?	14	93.33%	9	60.00%	10	100.00%	7	87.50%	7	87.50%	85.67%	

Process criteria code	Investigated processes	Production processes (15 processes)		Sales processes (15 processes)		Financial processes (10 processes)		Procurement processes (8 processes)		Human resources processes (8 processes)		Average propor-tion of respon-dents with the answer YES	Overall result/ process criteria
		Respondents with the answer YES											
	Interview question	No.	%	No.	%	No.	%	No.	%	No.	%		
D	Is the process performance independent of manual input?	7	46.67%	9	60.00%	5	50.00%	4	50.00%	5	62.50%	53.83 %	76.03%
	Is there a secured database in place for all information?	11	73.33%	10	66.67%	7	70.00%	6	75.00%	7	87.50%	74.50 %	
E	Is there a risk assessment process in place for all process interactions?	12	80.00%	12	80.00%	8	80.00%	6	75.00%	6	75.00%	78.00 %	76.25%
	Are process-related risks identified being monitored an controlled?	11	73.33%	10	66.67%	7	70.00%	6	75.00%	7	87.50%	74.50 %	
F	Are all steps o the process constantly optimized?	12	80.00%	10	66.67%	8	80.00%	6	75.00%	8	100.00%	80.33 %	80.44%
	Is the process permanently monitored?	14	93.33%	12	80.00%	9	90.00%	7	87.50%	7	87.50%	87.67 %	
	Does the review of the process consider both quantitative and qualitative evaluation methods?	11	73.33%	11	73.33%	7	70.00%	6	75.00%	6	75.00%	73.33 %	
Average result for sustainable performance of business processes/organization												**71.70%**	

Annex G

Risk identification during interviews for the study related to risks at the interaction between business process

Process interactions code numbers are related to the process interactions determined and listed in Table 5.5. Column with the letter „A" indicate risks that can occur at process intractions level between the first process and the second one, while the letter „B" refers to risk at process intractions level between the second process on the first one. For example, risks related to process interaction no. 2 between marketing and sales processes and contract management processes are indicated in the column „A", while risks that can occur as a result of contract management processes when interacting with marketing and sales processes are indicated in the column „B".

Process interaction / Risks code no.	1	2		3		4		5		6		7		8		9		10		11		12		13		14		15	
	A	A	B	A	B	A	B	A	B	A	B	A	B	A	B	A	B	A	B	A	B	A	B	A	B	A	B	A	B
Marketing																													
Decreased clients' satisfaction	X																										X		
No new clients								X																					
No new clients or loss of existing clients								X																					
Organizational image negatively affected					X																X	X		X		X			
Clients losing interest in offered products and services					X																								
Losing one or more market segments	X																												
Marketing campaign has no impact on the market	X																												
Delayed marketing campaigns				X																									
Inefficient marketing campaigns				X																									
Losing seasonal opportunities					X																						X		
Outdated information about competing organizations	X																												
Outdated marketing campaigns																											X		

Contracts

No new contracts		X																											
Contract not signed or extended		X	X						X																				
Non-performing contracts			X		X			X	X				X																
Delayed contracts									X																				
Invalid contract											X																		
Delayed project due to renegotiations																												X	
Cancelled contracts																													X

Production

Outdated products and services	X	X	X																X				X			X			
Products/services with quality-related issues													X			X			X										
Delivering faulty products																							X						
Producing goods and delivering services that are unappealing for potential clients																				X						X			
Non-compliant products/services																X		X											
High costs with product replacement/repairing during the warranty period																		X											
Delayed troubleshooting in the warranty period																			X										
High troubleshooting costs during the warranty period																			X										
Limited or faulty troubleshooting in the warranty period																						X							
Unexpected additional production costs																					X								
Additional unforeseen costs during warranty period																						X	X	X					
Disruptions in the production lines	X															X													
Delayed production												X				X													

Production gaps or stopped production													X							X									
Stop supply																												X	

Sales

Decreased sales																					X								
Decreased support services and spare parts sales																								X	X				
Sales disruptions																													X

Deliveries

Delayed deliveries, invoicing and cashing in from clients																													
Delayed projects										X																			
Production disruptions																													
Delayed orders																												X	
Delayed deliveries											X	X		X															X
Delayed deliveries to clients															X														
Delayed deliveries from suppliers															X														
Delayed or faulty production or service delivery																	X												

Finances

Cash flow disruptions										X	X	X																	
Incorrect or incomplete financial status regarding debts and receivables																													
Inefficient assignment of financial resources																													
Inefficient business processes																													
Exceeded project budget										X																			X
Delayed payments from clients and to suppliers											X	X		X	X														
Delayed payments to suppliers																												X	
Invoices not issued on time							X																						
Refused invoices							X																						

Refused invoices or delayed payments from clients														X															
Delayed or incorrect invoicing							X																						
Incorrect data related to the organization's financial processes							X																						
Incorrect assignment of financial resources							X																						

Annex H

Qualitative risk evaluation performed during the interviews for the study related to the impact of applying the PDCA method during risk assessment related to interactions between the organization and outsourced business processes

Process ownership	Process execution location	Identified risks					
		Incomplete or incorrect process design	Losing full control and decreased quality of service	High costs with wages and transportation	Outdated control mechanisms	Inefficient processes	Inefficient and outdated processes
Organization	Onsite	Tolerable risks	Tolerable risks	Tolerable risks	Tolerable risks	Tolerable risks	Unacceptable risks
	Offsite	Unacceptable risks	Unacceptable risks	Tolerable risks	Tolerable risks	Unacceptable risks	Unacceptable risks
	Nearshore	Unacceptable risks	Unacceptable risks	Unacceptable risks	Unacceptable risks	Unacceptable risks	Unacceptable risks
	Offshore	Unacceptable risks	Unacceptable risks	Very high risk	Unacceptable risks	Unacceptable risks	Unacceptable risks
Third-party providers	Onsite	Tolerable risks	Unacceptable risks	Tolerable risks	Unacceptable risks	Unacceptable risks	Unacceptable risks
	Offsite	Unacceptable risks	Unacceptable risks	Unacceptable risks	Unacceptable risks	Unacceptable risks	Unacceptable risks
	Nearshore	Unacceptable risks	Unacceptable risks	Very high risk	Unacceptable risks	Unacceptable risks	Unacceptable risks
	Offshore	Unacceptable risks	Very high risk	Very high risk	Unacceptable risks	Unacceptable risks	Unacceptable risks

Annex I

Applying the PDCA and FMEA methods during risk assessment related to business process interactions no. 6 – 15

Process interaction no. 6 – Applying the PDCA and FMEA methods during risk assessment at the interaction between procurement processes and financial processes

Table 1: Applying the PDCA and FMEA methods during risk assessment at the interaction between procurement processes and financial processes, developed by the author based on the research conducted during the doctoral period

No. crt.	Risks	P	C	Risk Level 1	Impacted performance indicators	Risk materialization conditions	D	Risk Level 2	Proposed risk type
Risk assessment at the interaction between procurement processes and financial processes									
1.	Delayed projects	3	5	15	Number of repeat customers and new clients	Decreased during the past 2 months	2	30	Tolerable risk
					Market share	▪ New competitors ▪ New technology	4	60	Tolerable risk
2.	Exceeded project budget	3	5	15	Liquidity	Cash flow interruptions	4	60	Tolerable risk
					Profitability	Decreased during the past 2 months	2	30	Tolerable risk
No. risks to be handled		2					0		
Risk assessment at the interaction between financial processes and procurement processes									
1.	Delayed payments from clients and to suppliers	4	5	20	Liquidity	Cash flow interruptions	4	60	Tolerable risk
					Number of supplier partners	Cash flow interruptions	4	80	Unacceptable risk
2.	Delayed deliveries	3	5	15	Liquidity	Cash flow interruptions	4	60	Tolerable risk
					Market share	▪ New competitors ▪ New technology	4	60	Tolerable risk
3.	Delayed projects	4	5	20			4	80	Unacceptable risk
					Number of repeat customers and new clients	Decreased during the past 2 months	2	40	Tolerable risk
No. risks to be handled		3					2		

Process interaction no. 7 – Applying the PDCA and FMEA methods during risk assessment at the interaction between financial processes and production processes

Table 2: Applying the PDCA and FMEA methods during risk assessment at the interaction between financial processes and production processes, developed by the author based on the research conducted during the doctoral period

No. crt.	Risks	P	C	Risk Level 1	Impacted performance indicators	Risk materialization conditions	D	Risk Level 2	Proposed risk type
Risk assessment at the interaction between financial processes and production processes									
1.	Delayed payments	3	5	15	Liquidity	Cash flow interruptions	4	60	Tolerable risk
2.	Delayed deliveries	3	5	15	Liquidity	Cash flow interruptions	4	60	Tolerable risk
					Market share	▪ New competitors ▪ New technology	4	60	Tolerable risk
					Number of repeat customers and new clients	Decreased during the past 2 months	2	30	Tolerable risk
No. risks to be handled		2					0		
Risk assessment at the interaction between production processes and financial processes									
1.	Delayed production	3	5	15	Number of repeat customers and new clients	Decreased during the past 2 months	2	30	Tolerable risk
					Number of supplier partners	Cash flow interruptions	4	80	Unacceptable risk
2.	Products/ services with quality-related issues	3	5	15	Market share	▪ New competitors ▪ New technology	4	60	Tolerable risk
					Number of repeat customers and new clients	Decreased during the past 2 months	2	30	Tolerable risk
3.	Non-performing contracts	3	5	15	Profitability	Decreased during the past 2 months	2	30	Tolerable risk
No. risks to be handled		3					1		

Process interaction no. 8 – Applying the PDCA and FMEA methods during risk assessment at the interaction between senior management and financial processes

Table 3: Applying the PDCA and FMEA methods during risk assessment at the interaction between senior management and financial processes, developed by the author based on the research conducted during the doctoral period

No. crt.	Risks	P	C	Risk Level 1	Impacted performance indicators	Risk materialization conditions	D	Risk Level 2	Risk transformation
Risk assessment at the interaction between senior management and financial processes									
1.	Delayed payments	3	5	15	Liquidity	Cash flow interruptions	4	60	Tolerable risk
					Number of supplier partners	Cash flow interruptions	4	80	Unacceptable risk
2.	Delayed deliveries	3	5	15	Market share	▪ New competitors ▪ New technology	4	60	Tolerable risk
2.	Delayed deliveries	3	5	15	Liquidity	Cash flow interruptions	4	60	Tolerable risk
3.	Refused invoices or delayed payments from clients	3	5	15			4	60	Tolerable risk
No. risks to be handled		3					1		
Risk assessment at the interaction between financial processes and senior management									
1.	Delayed payments	3	5	15	Liquidity	Cash flow interruptions	4	60	Tolerable risk
					Number of supplier partners	Cash flow interruptions	4	80	Unacceptable risk
2.	Delayed deliveries to clients	3	5	15	Market share	▪ New competitors ▪ New technology	4	60	Tolerable risk
2.	Delayed deliveries to clients	3	5	15	Liquidity	Cash flow interruptions	4	60	Tolerable risk
3.	Delayed deliveries from suppliers	3	5	15	Number of repeat customers and new clients	Decreased during the past 2 months	2	30	Tolerable risk
No. risks to be handled		3					1		

Process interaction no. 9 – Applying the PDCA and FMEA methods during risk assessment at the interaction between planning processes and production processes

Table 4: Applying the PDCA and FMEA methods during risk assessment at the interactions between planning processes and production processes, developed by the author based on the research conducted during the doctoral period

No. crt.	Risks	P	C	Risk Level 1	Impacted performance indicators	Risk materialization conditions	D	Risk Level 2	Proposed risk type
Risk assessment at the interactions between planning processes and production processes									
1.	Delayed production	3	5	15	Number of repeat customers and new clients	Decreased during the past 2 months	2	30	Tolerable risk
					Liquidity	Cash flow interruptions	4	60	Tolerable risk
					Market share	▪ New competitors	4	60	Tolerable risk
2.	Products/ services with quality-related issues	3	5	15		▪ New technology	4	60	Tolerable risk
					Number of repeat customers and new clients	Decreased during the past 2 months	2	30	Tolerable risk
No. risks to be handled		2					0		
Risk assessment at the interactions between production processes and planning processes									
1.	Delayed or faulty production or service delivery	3	5	15	Market share	▪ New competitors ▪ New technology	4	60	Tolerable risk
					Number of repeat customers and new clients	Decreased during the past 2 months	2	30	Tolerable risk
No. risks to be handled		1					0		

Process interaction no. 10 – Applying the PDCA and FMEA methods during risk assessment at the interaction between production processes and after-sales processes

Table 5: Applying the PDCA and FMEA methods during risk assessment at the interactions between production processes and after-sales processes, developed by the author based on the research conducted during the doctoral period

No. crt.	Risks	P	C	Risk Level 1	Impacted performance indicators	Risk materialization conditions	D	Risk Level 2	Proposed risk type
Risk assessment at the interactions between production processes and after-sales processes									
1.	Non-compliant products	4	4	16	Number of repeat customers and new clients	Decreased during the past 2 months	2	32	Tolerable risk
					Liquidity	Cash flow interruptions	4	64	Unacceptable risk
					Market share	▪ New competitors ▪ New technology	4	64	Unacceptable risk
2.	High costs with product replacement/repairing during the warranty period	4	4	16			4	64	Unacceptable risk
					Number of repeat customers and new clients	Decreased during the past 2 months	2	32	Tolerable risk
					Profitability		2	32	Tolerable risk
No. risks to be handled		2					2		
Risk assessment at the interactions between after-sales processes and production processes									
1.	Products/ services with quality-related issues	3	5	15	Number of repeat customers and new clients	Decreased during the past 2 months	2	30	Tolerable risk
					Market share	▪ New competitors ▪ New technology	4	40	Tolerable risk
2.	High troubleshooting costs during the warranty period	2	5	10			4	40	Tolerable risk
3.	Producing outdated goods	3	5	15	Market share		4	60	Tolerable risk
					Number of repeat customers and new clients	Decreased during the past 2 months	2	30	Tolerable risk
No. risks to be handled		3					0		

Process interaction no. 11 – Applying the PDCA and FMEA methods during risk assessment at the interaction between senior management and production processes

Table 6: Applying the PDCA and FMEA methods during risk assessment at the interactions between senior management and production processes, developed by the author based on the research conducted during the doctoral period

No. crt.	Risks	P	C	Risk Level 1	Impacted performance indicators	Risk materialization conditions	D	Risk Level 2	Proposed risk type
Risk assessment at the interactions between senior management and production processes									
1.	Producing goods and delivering services that are unappealing for potential clients	3	5	15	Number of repeat customers and new clients	Decreased during the past 2 months	2	45	Tolerable risk
					Market share	▪ New competitors ▪ New technology	4	60	Tolerable risk
2.	Production gaps or stopped production	2	5	10			4	40	Tolerable risk
					Liquidity	Cash flow interruptions	4	40	Tolerable risk
					Number of supplier partners	Cash flow interruptions	4	40	Tolerable risk
No. risks to be handled		2					0		
Risk assessment at the interactions between production processes and senior management									
1.	Decreased sales	3	5	15	Turnover	Decreased during the past 2 months	2	30	Tolerable risk
					Market share	▪ New competitors ▪ New technology	4	60	Tolerable risk
2.	Organizational image is negatively affected	3	5	15			4	60	Tolerable risk
					Number of repeat customers and new clients	Decreased during the past 2 months	2	30	Tolerable risk
					Number of supplier partners	Cash flow interruptions	4	60	Tolerable risk
No. risks to be handled		2					0		

Process interaction no. 12 – Applying the PDCA and FMEA methods during risk assessment at the interaction between after-sales processes and quality assurance processes

Table 7: Applying the PDCA and FMEA methods during risk assessment at the interactions between after-sales processes and quality assurance processes, developed by the author based on the research conducted during the doctoral period

No. crt.	Risks	P	C	Risk Level 1	Impacted performance indicators	Risk materialization conditions	D	Risk Level 2	Proposed risk type
Risk assessment at the interactions between after-sales processes and quality assurance processes									
1.	Organizational image is negatively affected	3	5	15	Market share	▪ New competitors ▪ New technology	3	45	Tolerable risk
					Number of supplier partners	Cash flow interruptions	4	60	Tolerable risk
					Number of repeat customers and new clients	Decreased during the past 2 months	2	30	Tolerable risk
2.	Limited or faulty trouble-shooting in the warranty period	2	5	10			2	20	Tolerable risk
					Market share	▪ New competitors ▪ New technology	4	40	Tolerable risk
3.	Additional unforeseen costs during warranty period	3	5	15	Profitability	Decreased during the past 2 months	2	30	Tolerable risk
No. risks to be handled			3				0		
Risk assessment at the interactions between quality assurance processes and after-sales processes									
1.	Delivering faulty products	3	5	15	Market share	▪ New competitors ▪ New technology	4	60	Tolerable risk
					Number of repeat customers and new clients	Decreased during the past 2 months	2	30	Tolerable risk
					Profitability		2	30	Tolerable risk
2.	Additional unforeseen costs during warranty period	3	5	15	Profitability	Decreased during the past 2 months	2	30	Tolerable risk

3.	Outdated products and services	3	5	15			2	30	Tolerable risk
No. risks to be handled		3					0		

Process interaction no. 13 – Applying the PDCA and FMEA methods during risk assessment at the interaction between senior management and after-sales processes

Table 8: Applying the PDCA and FMEA methods during risk assessment at the interactions between senior management and after-sales processes, developed by the author based on the research conducted during the doctoral period

No. crt.	Risks	P	C	Risk Level 1	Impacted performance indicators	Risk materialization conditions	D	Risk Level 2	Proposed risk type
Risk assessment at the interactions between senior management and after-sales processes									
1.	Decreased support services and spare parts sales	3	5	15	Turnover	Decreased during the past 2 months	2	30	Tolerable risk
					Market share	▪ New competitors ▪ New technology	4	60	Tolerable risk
No. risks to be handled		1					0		
Risk assessment at the interactions between after-sales processes and senior management									
1.	Organizatio-nal image is negatively affected	3	5	15	Number of repeat customers and new clients	Decreased during the past 2 months	2	30	Tolerable risk
					Number of supplier partners	Cash flow interruptions	4	60	Tolerable risk
					Market share	▪ New competitors ▪ New technology	4	60	Tolerable risk
2.	Decreased services, support and spare parts sales	3	5	15			4	60	Tolerable risk
					Turnover	Decreased during the past 2 months	2	30	Tolerable risk
No. risks to be handled		2					0		

Process interaction no. 14 – Applying the PDCA and FMEA methods during risk assessment at the interaction between quality assurance processes and marketing and sales processes

Table 9: Applying the PDCA and FMEA methods during risk assessment at the interactions between quality assurance processes and marketing and sales processes, developed by the author based on the research conducted during the doctoral period

No. crt.	Risks	P	C	Risk Level 1	Impacted performance indicators	Risk materialization conditions	D	Risk Level 2	Proposed risk type
Risk assessment at the interactions between quality assurance processes and marketing and sales processes									
1.	Organizational image is negatively affected	3	5	15	Number of repeat customers and new clients	Decreased during the past 2 months	2	30	Tolerable risk
					Number of supplier partners	Cash flow interruptions	4	60	Tolerable risk
					Market share	▪ New competitors ▪ New technology	4	60	Tolerable risk
2.	Producing goods and delivering services that are unappealing for potential clients	3	5	15	Market share	▪ New competitors ▪ New technology	4	60	Tolerable risk
					Number of repeat customers and new clients	Decreased during the past 2 months	2	30	Tolerable risk
3.	Outdated products and services	3	5	15	Profitability	Decreased during the past 2 months	2	30	Tolerable risk
No. risks to be handled		3					0		
Risk assessment at the interactions between marketing and sales processes and quality assurance processes									
1.	Decreased clients' satisfaction	3	5	15	Number of repeat customers and new clients	Decreased during the past 2 months	2	30	Tolerable risk
					Market share	▪ New competitors ▪ New technology	4	60	Tolerable risk
No. risks to be handled		1					0		

Process interaction no. 15 – Applying the PDCA and FMEA methods during risk assessment at the interaction between procurement processes and suppliers

Table 10: Applying the PDCA and FMEA methods during risk assessment at the interactions between procurement processes and suppliers, developed by the author based on the research conducted during the doctoral period

No. crt.	Risks	P	C	Risk Level 1	Impacted performance indicators	Risk materialization conditions	D	Risk Level 2	Proposed risk type
Risk assessment at the interactions between procurement processes and suppliers									
1.	Delayed payments to suppliers	3	5	15	Number of supplier partners	Cash flow interruptions	4	60	Tolerable risk
					Market share	▪ New competitors	4	60	Tolerable risk
2.	Delayed orders	4	4	16		▪ New technology	4	64	Unacceptable risk
					Number of repeat customers and new clients	Decreased during the past 2 months	2	32	Tolerable risk
No. risks to be handled		2					1		
Risk assessment at the interactions between suppliers and procurement processes									
1.	Delayed deliveries	4	5	20	Liquidity	Cash flow interruptions	4	60	Tolerable risk
					Market share	▪ New competitors	4	80	Unacceptable risk
2.	Sales disruptions	4	5	20		▪ New technology	4	80	Unacceptable risk
					Number of repeat customers and new clients	Decreased during the past 2 months	2	30	Tolerable risk
					Liquidity	Cash flow interruptions	4	60	Tolerable risk
3.	Exceeded project budget	3	5	15	Profitability	Decreased during the past 2 months	2	30	Tolerable risk
4.	Cancelled contracts	3	5	15	Number of repeat customers and new clients	Decreased during the past 2 months	2	30	Tolerable risk
No. risks to be handled		4					2		

Annex J

Qualitative risk evaluation performed during the interviews for the study related to the impact of applying the FMEA method and identifying new business opportunities during risk assessment related to interactions between the organization and outsourced business processes

Process ownership	Process execution location	Identified risks					
		Incomplete or incorrect process design	Losing full control and decreased quality of service	High costs with wages and transportation	Outdated control mechanisms	Inefficient processes	Inefficient and outdated processes
Organization	Onsite	Common risks	Common risks	Common risks	Common risks	Common risks	Attractive risks
	Offsite	Attractive risks	Attractive risks	Common risks	Common risks	Attractive risks	Attractive risks
	Nearshore	Attractive risks	Attractive risks	Attractive risks	Attractive risks	Attractive risks	Attractive risks
	Offshore	Attractive risks	Attractive risks	Very attractive	Attractive risks	Attractive risks	Attractive risks
Third-party providers	Onsite	Attractive risks	Attractive risks	Common risks	Attractive risks	Attractive risks	Attractive risks
	Offsite	Attractive risks	Attractive risks	Attractive risks	Attractive risks	Attractive risks	Attractive risks
	Nearshore	Attractive risks	Attractive risks	Very attractive risk	Attractive risks	Attractive risks	Attractive risks
	Offshore	Attractive risks	Very attractive	Very attractive risk	Attractive risks	Attractive risks	Attractive risks

Annex K

Applying the FMEA method and identifying business opportunities during risk assessment related to business process interactions no. 6 – 15

Process interaction no. 6 – Applying the FMEA method and identifying business opportunities during risk assessment at the interaction between procurement processes and financial processes

Table 11: Applying the FMEA method and identifying business opportunities during risk assessment at the interaction between procurement processes and financial processes, developed by the author based on the research conducted during the doctoral period

No. crt.	Risks	P	C	Risk Level 1	Possible business opportunity	Impacted performance indicators	Risk materialization conditions	D	Risk Level 2	Proposed risk type
Risk assessment at the interaction between procurement processes and financial processes										
1.	Delayed projects	3	5	15	Increasing turnover and profit by improving production protocols and control mechanisms	Number of repeat customers and new clients	Decreased during the past 2 months	2	30	Common risk
						Market share	▪ New competitors ▪ New technology	4	60	Common risk
2.	Exceeded project budget	3	5	15	Improving contract budgets and protocols in order to increase profitability and optimize cash flow	Liquidity	Cash flow interruptions	4	60	Common risk
						Profitability	Decreased during the past 2 months	2	30	Common risk
No. risks to be handled		2						0		
Risk assessment at the interaction between financial processes and procurement processes										
1.	Delayed payments from clients and to suppliers	4	5	20	New partnerships with clients and suppliers by improving payment protocols	Liquidity	Cash flow interruptions	4	60	Common risk
						Number of supplier partners	Cash flow interruptions	4	80	Attractive risk

No. crt.	Risks	P	C	Risk Level 1	Possible business opportunity	Impacted performance indicators	Risk materialization conditions	D	Risk Level 2	Proposed risk type
2.	Delayed deliveries	3	5	15	Increasing turnover and profit by improving delivery protocols and control mechanisms	Liquidity	Cash flow interruptions	4	60	Common risk
						Market share	▪ New competitors ▪ New technology	4	60	Common risk
3.	Delayed projects	4	5	20	Increasing turnover and profit by improving production protocols and control mechanisms			4	80	Attractive risk
						Number of repeat customers and new clients	Decreased during the past 2 months	2	40	Common risk
No. risks to be handled			3						2	

Process interaction no. 7 – Applying the FMEA method and identifying business opportunities during risk assessment at the interaction between financial processes and production processes while aiming for new business opportunities

Table 12: Applying the FMEA method and identifying business opportunities during risk assessment at the interaction between financial processes and production processes, developed by the author based on the research conducted during the doctoral period

No. crt.	Risks	P	C	Risk Level 1	Possible business opportunity	Impacted performance indicators	Risk materialization conditions	D	Risk Level 2	Proposed risk type
Risk assessment at the interaction between financial processes and production processes										
1.	Delayed payments	3	5	15	New partnerships with clients and suppliers by improving payment protocols	Liquidity	Cash flow interruptions	4	60	Common risk
2.	Delayed deliveries	3	5	15	Increasing turnover and profit by improving delivery protocols and control mechanisms		Cash flow interruptions	4	60	Common risk

2.	Delayed deliveries	3	5	15	Increasing turnover and profit by improving delivery protocols and control mechanisms	Market share	▪ New competitors ▪ New technology	4	60	Common risk
						Number of repeat cus-tomers and new clients	Decreased during the past 2 months	2	30	Common risk
No. risks to be handled		2						0		
Risk assessment at the interaction between production processes and financial processes										
1.	Delayed production	3	5	15	Increasing turnover and profit by improving production protocols and control mechanisms	Number of repeat customers and new clients	Decreased during the past 2 months	2	30	Common risk
						Number of supplier partners	Cash flow interruptions	4	80	Attractiv e risk
2.	Products/ services with quality-related issues	3	5	15	Keeping existing clients and attracting new clients by improving production and quality assurance protocols	Market share	▪ New competitors ▪ New technology	4	60	Common risk
						Number of repeat customers and new clients	Decreased during the past 2 months	2	30	Common risk
3.	Non-perfor-ming contracts	3	5	15	Improving contract budgets and protocols in order to increase profitability	Profitability	Decreased during the past 2 months	2	30	Common risk
No. risks to be handled		3						1		

Process interaction no. 8 – Applying the FMEA method and identifying business opportunities during risk assessment at the interaction between senior management and financial processes while aiming for new business opportunities

Table 13: Applying the FMEA method and identifying business opportunities during risk assessment at the interaction between senior management and financial processes, developed by the author based on the research conducted during the doctoral period

No. crt.	Risks	P	C	Risk Level 1	Possible business opportunity	Impacted performance indicators	Risk materialization conditions	D	Risk Level 2	Proposed risk type
Risk assessment at the interaction between senior management and financial processes										
1.	Delayed payments	3	5	15	New partnerships with clients and suppliers by improving payment protocols	Liquidity	Cash flow interruptions	4	60	Common risk
						Number of supplier partners	Cash flow interruptions	4	80	Attractive risk
2.	Delayed deliveries	3	5	15	Increasing turnover and profit by improving delivery protocols and control mechanisms	Market share	▪ New competitors ▪ New technology	4	60	Common risk
						Liquidity	Cash flow interruptions	4	60	Common risk
3.	Refused invoices or delayed payments from clients	3	5	15	New partnerships with clients and suppliers by improving payment protocols	Liquidity	Cash flow interruptions	4	60	Common risk
No. risks to be handled		3						1		
Risk assessment at the interaction between financial processes and senior management										
1.	Delayed payments	3	5	15	New partnerships with clients and suppliers by improving payment protocols	Liquidity	Cash flow interruptions	4	60	Common risk
						Number of supplier partners	Cash flow interruptions	4	80	Attractive risk

2.	Delayed deliveries to clients	3	5	15	Increasing turnover and profit by improving delivery protocols and control mechanisms	Market share	▪ New competitors ▪ New technology	4	60	Common risk
						Liquidity	Cash flow interruptions	4	60	Common risk
3.	Delayed deliveries from suppliers	3	5	15	Increasing turnover and profit by improving delivery protocols and control mechanisms	Liquidity	Cash flow interruptions	4	60	Common risk
						Number of repeat customers and new clients	Decreased during the past 2 months	2	30	Common risk
No. risks to be handled		3						1		

Process interaction no. 9 – Applying the FMEA method and identifying business opportunities during risk assessment at the interaction between planning processes and production processes while aiming for new business opportunities

Table 14: Applying the FMEA method and identifying business opportunities during risk assessment at the interactions between planning processes and production processes, developed by the author based on the research conducted during the doctoral period

No. crt.	Risks	P	C	Risk Level 1	Possible business opportunity	Impacted performance indicators	Risk materialization conditions	D	Risk Level 2	Proposed risk type
Risk assessment at the interactions between planning processes and production processes										
1.	Production disruptions	3	5	15	Increasing turnover and profit by improving production protocols and control mechanisms	Number of repeat customers and new clients	Decreased during the past 2 months	2	30	Common risk
						Liquidity	Cash flow interruptions	4	60	Common risk
						Market share	▪ New competitors ▪ New technology	4	60	Common risk

2.	Products/ services with quality-related issues	3	5	15	Keeping existing clients and attracting new clients by improving production and quality assurance protocols	Market share	▪ New competitors ▪ New technology	4	60	Common risk
						Number of repeat customers and new clients	Decreased during the past 2 months	2	30	Common risk
No. risks to be handled		2						0		
Risk assessment at the interactions between production processes and planning processes										
1.	Delayed or faulty production or service delivery	3	5	15	Increasing turnover and profit by improving production and delivery protocols	Market share	▪ New competitors ▪ New technology	4	60	Common risk
						Number of repeat customers and new clients	Decreased during the past 2 months	2	30	Common risk
No. risks to be handled		1						0		

Process interaction no. 10 – Applying the FMEA method and identifying business opportunities during risk assessment at the interaction between production processes and after-sales processes while aiming for new business opportunities

Table 15: Applying the FMEA method and identifying business opportunities during risk assessment at the interactions between production processes and after-sales processes, developed by the author based on the research conducted during the doctoral period

No. crt.	Risks	P	C	Risk Level 1	Possible business opportunity	Impacted performance indicators	Risk materialization conditions	D	Risk Level 2	Proposed risk type
Risk assessment at the interactions between production processes and after-sales processes										
1.	Non-compliant products	4	4	16	Keeping existing clients and attracting new clients by improving production and quality assurance protocols	Number of repeat customers and new clients	Decreased during the past 2 months	2	32	Common risk
						Liquidity	Cash flow interruptions	4	64	Attractive risk
						Market share	▪ New competitors ▪ New technology	4	64	Attractive risk

2.	High costs with product replace-ment and repairing during the warranty period	4	4	16	Increasing turnover and profitability by keeping existing clients and minimizing costs during warranty period	Market share	▪ New competitors ▪ New technology	4	64	Attractive risk
						Number of repeat customers and new clients	Decreased during the past 2 months	2	32	Common risk
						Profitability		2	32	Common risk
No. risks to be handled		2						2		
Risk assessment at the interactions between after-sales processes and production processes										
1.	Producing trouble-some products	3	5	15	Keeping existing clients and attracting new clients by improving production and quality assurance protocols	Number of repeat customers and new clients	Decreased during the past 2 months	2	30	Common risk
						Market share	▪ New competitors ▪ New technology	4	60	Common risk
2.	High trouble-shooting costs during the warranty period	2	5	10	Increasing turnover and profitability by keeping existing clients and minimizing costs during warranty period			4	40	Common risk
3.	Producing outdated goods	3	5	15	Investing in new technology financed by attracting investors or selling shares			4	60	Common risk
						Number of repeat customers and new clients	Decreased during the past 2 months	2	30	Common risk
No. risks to be handled		3						0		

Process interaction no. 11 – Applying the FMEA method and identifying business opportunities during risk assessment at the interaction between senior management and production processes while aiming for new business opportunities

Table 16: Applying the FMEA method and identifying business opportunities during risk assessment at the interactions between senior management and production processes, developed by the author based on the research conducted during the doctoral period

No. crt.	Risks	P	C	Risk Level 1	Possible business opportunity	Impacted performance indicators	Risk materialization conditions	D	Risk Level 2	Proposed risk type
Risk assessment at the interactions between senior management and production processes										
1.	Producing goods and delivering services that are unappealing for potential clients	3	5	15	Investing in new technology financed by attracting investors or selling shares	Number of repeat customers and new clients	Decreased during the past 2 months	2	45	Common risk
						Market share	▪ New competitors ▪ New technology	4	60	Common risk
2.	Production gaps or stopped production	2	5	10	Increasing turnover and profit by improving production protocols and control mechanisms			4	40	Common risk
						Liquidity	Cash flow interruptions	4	40	Common risk
						Number of supplier partners	Cash flow interruptions	4	40	Common risk
No. risks to be handled		2						0		
Risk assessment at the interactions between production processes and senior management										
1.	Decreased sales	3	5	15	Attracting new clients by improving the sales and marketing strategy	Turnover	Decreased during the past 2 months	2	30	Common risk
						Market share	▪ New competitors ▪ New technology	4	60	Common risk
2.	Organiza-tional image is negatively affected	3	5	15	Attracting new clients by improving the marketing strategy			4	60	Common risk
2.	Organiza-tional image is negatively affected	3	5	15	Attracting new clients by improving the marke-ting strategy	Number of repeat cus-tomers and new clients	Decreased during the past 2 months	2	30	Common risk
						Number of supplier partners	Cash flow interruptions	4	60	Common risk
No. risks to be handled		2						0		

Process interaction no. 12 – Applying the FMEA method and identifying business opportunities during risk assessment at the interaction between after-sales processes and quality assurance processes while aiming for new business opportunities

Table 17: Applying the FMEA method and identifying business opportunities during risk assessment at the interactions between after-sales processes and quality assurance processes, developed by the author based on the research conducted during the doctoral period

No. crt.	Risks	P	C	Risk Level 1	Possible business opportunity	Impacted performance indicators	Risk materialization conditions	D	Risk Level 2	Proposed risk type
Risk assessment at the interactions between after-sales processes and quality assurance processes										
1.	Organiza-tional image is negatively affected	3	5	15	Attracting new clients by improving the marketing strategy	Market share	▪ New competitors ▪ New technology	3	45	Common risk
					Attracting new clients by improving the marketing strategy	Number of supplier partners	Cash flow interruptions	4	60	Common risk
						Number of repeat customers and new clients	Decreased during the past 2 months	2	30	Common risk
2.	Limited or faulty trouble-shooting in the warranty period	2	5	10	Increasing turnover and profitability by offering high quality services and keeping existing clients			2	20	Common risk
						Market share	▪ New competitors ▪ New technology	4	40	Common risk
3.	Additional unforeseen costs during warranty period	3	5	15	Increasing turnover and profitability by keeping existing clients and minimizing costs during warranty period	Profitability	Decreased during the past 2 months	2	30	Common risk
No. risks to be handled				3					0	

Risk assessment at the interactions between quality assurance processes and after-sales processes										
1.	Delivering faulty products	3	5	15	Keeping existing clients and attracting new clients by improving production and quality assurance protocols	Market share	▪ New competitors ▪ New technology	4	60	Common risk
						Number of repeat customers and new clients	Decreased during the past 2 months	2	30	Common risk
						Profitability	Decreased during the past 2 months	2	30	Common risk
2.	Additional unfore-seen costs during warranty period	3	5	15	Increasing turnover and profitability by keeping existing clients and minimizing costs during warranty period		Decreased during the past 2 months	2	30	Common risk
3.	Outdated products and services	3	5	15	Investing in new technology financed by attracting investors or selling shares		Decreased during the past 2 months	2	30	Common risk
No. risks to be handled		3						0		

Process interaction no. 13 – Applying the FMEA method and identifying business opportunities during risk assessment at the interaction between senior management and after-sales processes while aiming for new business opportunities

Table 18: Applying the FMEA method and identifying business opportunities during risk assessment at the interactions between senior management and after-sales processes

No. crt.	Risks	P	C	Risk Level 1	Possible business opportunity	Impacted performance indicators	Risk materialization conditions	D	Risk Level 2	Proposed risk type
Risk assessment at the interactions between senior management and after-sales processes										
1.	Decreased support services and spare parts sales	3	5	15	Increasing turnover and profitability by offering high quality services and keeping existing clients	Turnover	Decreased during the past 2 months	2	30	Common risk
						Market share	▪ New competitors ▪ New technology	4	60	Common risk
No. risks to be handled		1						0		
Risk assessment at the interactions between after-sales processes and senior management										
1.	Organiza-tional image is negatively affected	3	5	15	Attracting new clients by improving the marketing strategy	Number of repeat customers and new clients	Decreased during the past 2 months	2	30	Common risk
						Number of supplier partners	Cash flow interruption s	4	60	Common risk
						Market share	▪ New competitor s ▪ New technology	4	60	Common risk
2.	Decreased services, support and spare parts sales	3	5	15	Increasing turnover and profitability by offering high quality services and keeping existing clients			4	60	Common risk
						Turnover	Decreased during the past 2 months	2	30	Common risk
No. risks to be handled		2						0		

Process interaction no. 14 – Applying the FMEA method and identifying business opportunities during risk assessment at the interaction between quality assurance processes and marketing and sales processes while aiming for new business opportunities

Table 19: Applying the FMEA method and identifying business opportunities during risk assessment at the interactions between quality assurance processes and marketing and sales processes, developed by the author based on the research conducted during the doctoral period

No. crt.	Risks	P	C	Risk Level 1	Possible business opportunity	Impacted performance indicators	Risk materialization conditions	D	Risk Level 2	Proposed risk type
Risk assessment at the interactions between quality assurance processes and marketing and sales processes										
1.	Organiza-tional image is negatively affected	3	5	15	Attracting new clients by improving the marketing strategy	Number of repeat customers and new clients	Decreased during the past 2 months	2	30	Common risk
						Number of supplier partners	Cash flow interruptions	4	60	Common risk
						Market share	▪ New competitors	4	60	Common risk
2.	Producing goods and delivering services that are unappea-ling for potential clients	3	5	15	Investing in new technology financed by attracting investors or selling shares		▪ New technology	4	60	Common risk
						Number of repeat customers and new clients	Decreased during the past 2 months	2	30	Common risk
3.	Outdated products and services	3	5	15	Investing in new technology financed by attracting investors or selling shares	Profitability	Decreased during the past 2 months	2	30	Common risk
No. risks to be handled		3						0		

Risk assessment at the interactions between marketing and sales processes and quality assurance processes										
1.	Decreased clients' satisfaction	3	5	15	Focusing on new marketing strategies considering the clients' needs	Number of repeat customers and new clients	Decreased during the past 2 months	2	30	Common risk
						Market share	▪ New competitors ▪ New technology	4	60	Common risk
No. risks to be handled		1						0		

Process interaction no. 15 – Applying the FMEA method and identifying business opportunities during risk assessment at the interaction between procurement processes and suppliers while aiming for new business opportunities

Table 20: Applying the FMEA method and identifying business opportunities during risk assessment at the interactions between procurement processes and suppliers, developed by the author based on the research conducted during the doctoral period

No. crt.	Risks	P	C	Risk Level 1	Possible business opportunity	Impacted performance indicators	Risk materialization conditions	D	Risk Level 2	Proposed risk type
Risk assessment at the interactions between procurement processes and suppliers										
1.	Delayed payments to suppliers	3	5	15	New partnerships with suppliers by improving payment protocols	Number of supplier partners	Cash flow interruptions	4	60	Common risk
						Market share	▪ New competitors ▪ New technology	4	60	Common risk
2.	Delayed orders	4	4	16	Improving sourcing protocols in order to deliver on time and improve relations with clients	Market share	▪ New competitors ▪ New technology	4	64	Attractiv e risk
						Number of repeat customers and new clients	Decreased during the past 2 months	2	32	Common risk
No. risks to be handled		2						1		

Risk assessment at the interactions between suppliers and procurement processes										
1.	Delayed deliveries	4	5	20	Increasing turnover and profit by improving delivery protocols and control mechanisms	Liquidity	Cash flow interruptions	4	60	Common risk
						Market share	▪ New competitors ▪ New technology	4	80	Attractive risk
2.	Sales disruptions	4	5	20	Keeping existing clients and attracting new clients by improving the sales and marketing strategy	Market share	▪ New competitors ▪ New technology	4	80	Attractive risk
						Number of repeat customers and new clients	Decreased during the past 2 months	2	30	Common risk
						Liquidity	Cash flow interruptions	4	60	Common risk
3.	Exceeded project budget	3	5	15	Improving contract budgets and protocols in order to increase profitability and optimize cash flow	Profitability	Decreased during the past 2 months	2	30	Common risk
4.	Cancelled contracts	3	5	15	Keeping existing clients by improving the sales and marketing strategy	Number of repeat customers and new clients	Decreased during the past 2 months	2	30	Common risk
No. risks to be handled		4						2		

Annex L

Calculated values for the proposed tri-dimensional risk assessment model

Negative outcomes (Risk Level 2)	Conse-quence	Probability of occurrence	Detection	Positive outcomes (Risk Level 2)	Consequence	Probability of occurrence	Detection
-1	-1	1	1	1	1	1	1
-2	-1	1	2	2	1	1	2
-3	-1	1	3	3	1	1	3
-4	-1	1	4	4	1	1	4
-5	-1	1	5	5	1	1	5
-9	-3	3	1	9	3	3	1
-12	-3	4	1	12	3	4	1
	-4	3	1		4	3	1
-18	-3	3	2	18	3	3	2
-20	-4	5	1	20	4	5	1
	-5	4	1		5	4	1
-24	-3	4	2	24	3	4	2
	-4	3	2		4	3	2
-25	-5	5	1	25	5	5	1
-27	-3	3	3	27	3	3	3
-36	-3	4	3	36	3	4	3
	-4	3	3		4	3	3
-40	-4	5	2	40	4	5	2
	-5	4	2		5	4	2
-45	-3	3	5	45	3	3	5
-48	-3	4	4	48	3	4	4
	-4	3	4		4	3	4
-50	-5	5	2	50	5	5	2
-60	-3	4	5	60	3	4	5
	-4	3	5		5	4	3
	-5	3	4		4	5	3
	-5	4	3		4	3	5
-75	-5	5	3	75	5	5	3
-80	-4	5	4	80	4	5	4
	-5	4	4		5	4	4
-100	-5	5	4	100	5	5	4
	-5	4	5		5	4	5
	-4	5	5		4	5	5
-125	-5	5	5	125	5	5	5

Annex M

List of publications

1. **Published scientific articles**

a) Literature published in ISI proceedings

[1] **Mateescu Ruxandra Maria doctorand**, Dinu V., Maftei M., 3 - *Research on Using FMEA as a Risk Assessment Method in order to Reduce Risk Handling Costs*, Proceedings of BASIQ 2017 - New Trends in Sustainable Business and Consumption, Graz, Austria, **31 May – 3 June 2017**, ISSN: 2457-483X, pp. 419-427, indexed in **ISI Web of Knowledge**, IDS Number: BJ6MF, Accession number: WOS:000426833400048, http://apps.webofknowledge.com/full_record.do?product=WOS&search_mode=GeneralSearch&qid=5&SID=C3lG5LGFwucAMLbEPDa&page=1&doc=1.

[2] **Mateescu Ruxandra Maria doctorand**, Maftei M., Verjel A., Lange S., 4 - *The Interrelation between Risk Management and the Organizational Context: Influence, Support and Barriers,* The 29th IBIMA conference on Education Excellence and Innovation Management through Vision 2020: from Regional Development Sustainability to Global Economic Growth, Vienna - Austria, **3-4 May 2017**, ISBN: 978-0-9860419-7-6, pp. 3292-3308, indexed in **ISI Web of Knowledge**, IDS Number: BI2TP, Accession number: WOS:000410252702078, http://apps.webofknowledge.com/full_record.do?product=WOS&search_mode=GeneralSearch&qid=9&SID=C3lG5LGFwucAMLbEPDa&page=1&doc=1.

[3] **Mateescu Ruxandra Maria doctorand**, Melanie Buchmüller, Vanessa Just, 3- *Research on Key Factors Impacting Process Sustainability in Global Organizations*, Proceedings of BASIQ 2016 - International Conference, New Trends in Sustainable Business and Consumption, Konstanz, Germany, **2-3 June 2016**, ISSN: 2457-483X, pp. 22-31, indexed in **ISI Web of Knowledge**, IDS Number: BF6YS, Accession number: WOS:000383845100002, http://apps.webofknowledge.com/full_record.do?product=WOS&search_mode=GeneralSearch&qid=12&SID=C3lG5LGFwucAMLbEPDa&page=1&doc=2.

[4] Achim Albrecht, Thorsten Eidenmüller, Timo Keppler, **Mateescu Ruxandra Maria doctorand**, 4 - *International Product Liability in a Global Business Environment: Ethical and Legal Perspectives for Business Managers*, Proceedings of BASIQ 2016 - International Conference, New Trends in Sustainable Business and Consumption, Konstanz, Germany, **2-3 June 2016**, ISSN: 2457-483X, pp. 12-21, indexed in **ISI Web of Knowledge**, indexed in ISI Web of Knowledge, IDS Number: BF6YS, Accession number: WOS:000383845100001, http://apps.webofknowledge.com/full_record.do?product =WOS&search_mode=GeneralSearch&qid=15&SID=C3lG5LGFwucAMLbEPDa&page= 1&doc=1.

[5] **Mateescu Ruxandra Maria doctorand**, Professor Olaru Marieta, Sârbu Alexandra, Surugiu (Farcaş) Ioana, 4 - *Research on Increasing Risk Management Efficiency as Support for Corporate Sustainable Development,* Proceedings of the 4th International Conference on Management, Leadership and Governance (ICMLG 2016), organized at Sankt Petersburg, Russia, **14-15 April 2016**, pp. 450, ISBN: 978-1-910810-84-2, indexed in **ISI Web of Knowledge**, IDS Number: BH5MP, Accession number: WOS: 000401232800055, https://apps.webofknowledge.com/full_record.do?product=UA &search_mode=GeneralSearch&qid=21&SID=1E7sTR4XNLkznRxUiPJ&page=1&doc=1 .

[6] Mateiu Alexandra, **Mateescu Ruxandra Maria doctorand**, Buchmüller Melanie, Just Vanessa, 4 – *Governance as a key factor for ensuring the sustainability of outsourcing models,* Proceedings of the International Conference on Management, Leadership and Governance (ICMLG 2016), organized at Sankt Petersburg, Russia, **14-15 April 2016**, pp. 466-474, ISBN: 978-1-910810-84-2, indexed in **ISI Web of Knowledge**, IDS Number: BH5MP, Accession number:WOS:000401232800057, https://apps.webofknowledge.com/full_record.do?product=UA&search_mode=Gen eralSearch&qid=16&SID=1E7sTRXNLkz nRxUiPJ&page=1&doc=6.
Best Phd. Paper Presentation, http://www.academic-conferences.org/conferences/ icmlg/icmlg-future-and-past/.

[7] **Mateescu Ruxandra Maria doctorand**, Professor Marieta Olaru, Lange Steffen, Rauch Manfred, 4- *Study on Supplier Invoice Risk Management in a Global Supply Chain*, Proceedings of the International Business Information Management Conference (26th IBIMA) - Innovation Management and Sustainable Economic Competitive Advantage: From Regional Development To Global Growth, Vols I - Vi, Madrid, Spain, **11-12 November 2015**, ISBN:978-0-9860419-5-2, pp. 2579-2590, indexed in **ISI Web of Knowledge**, IDS Number: BE0SX, Accession number:

WOS:000366872700265, http://apps.webofknowledge.com/full_record.do?product =WOS&search_mode=GeneralSearch&qid=18&SID=C3lG5LGFwucAMLbEPDa&page= 1&doc=1.

[8] Steffen Lange, Melanie Buchmüller, Bastian Heinemann, **Mateescu Ruxandra Maria doctorand**, 4 - The *Driver for the Backsourcing Phenomenon under the Force of Globalization*, 4th BASIQ International Conference on New Trends in Sustainable Business and Consumption, **11-13 June 2018**, Heidelberg University, Heidelberg, Germany, pp. 116-123, **ISI Web of Knowledge** indexing in progress.

b) Literature published in scientific ISI magazines

[1] Gregor Weber, **Mateescu Ruxandra Maria doctorand**, Lange Steffen, Rauch Manfred, 4 – *Knowledge intensive Business Services (KIBS) in the context of changing energy economics in Germany*, Revista Amfiteatru Economic, "Amfiteatru Economic Journal", Vol. XVIII, No. 41, pp. 89-103, **February 2016,** Editura ASE, Bucharest (Romania), ISSN 2247-9104, the journal is indexed CNCSIS in category A, included in **ISI Thomson Reuters Services**: Social Sciences Citation Index®, Social Scisearch®, Journal Citation Reports/Social Sciences Edition. Impact factor for the year 2012: 0,953. The article is available on the website http://www.amfiteatru economic.ase.ro. IDS Number: 710QA, Accession number: WOS:0002865251000 13, http://apps.webofknowledge.com/full_record.do?product=WOS&search_mo de=GeneralSearch&qid=3&SID=R1OH4eicMMf5M8i6pPp&page=1&doc=1, http://www.amfiteatrueconomic.ase.ro

c) Literature published in national non ISI-magazines (B+)

[1] **Mateescu Ruxandra Maria doctorand**, Lange Steffen, Bastian Heinemann, 3 - *The Role of Process Interactions Management in Ensuring Business Sustainability*, The International Conference Global Economy Under Crisis - 4th Edition, **18 – 20 December 2015**, Constanţa, România, published in Ovidius University Annals, Economic Sciences Series, Vol. XV, Issue 2, pp. 287-291, 2015, ISSN-L 2393-3119, ISSN 2393-3127, recognized by the National Council of Scientific Research in Higher Education (CNCSIS) in B+ category, code 444, indexed in RePEc, DOAJ, EBSCO host, Cabell's Directories, Ulrichs Web, J-Gate, Erih Plus, Index Copernicus, Scientific Indexing Services, INFOBASE INDEX, ResearchBib, https://ideas.re

pec.org/a/ovi/oviste/vxvy2015i2p287-291.html, http://stec.univ-ovidius.ro/html /anale/ENG/wp-content/uploads/2015/03/ANALE-vol-15-issue_2_2015_site_v2.pdf.

d) Publishing in non ISI scientific literature

[1] **Mateescu Ruxandra Maria doctorand**, Vasile Dinu, Mihaela Maftei, 3 - *Improving Risk Management Methods: FMEA and its Influence on Risk Handling Costs*, **2018**, Springer Verlag.

2. Citations published in scientific literature

[1] **Mateescu Ruxandra Maria doctorand**, Maftei M., Verjel A., Lange S., 4 - *The Interrelation between Risk Management and the Organizational Context: Influence, Support and Barriers,* The 29th IBIMA conference on Education Excellence and Innovation Management through Vision 2020: from Regional Development Sustainability to Global Economic Growth, Vienna - Austria, **3-4 May 2017**, ISBN: 978-0-9860419-7-6, pp. 3292-3308, indexed in **ISI Web of Knowledge**, IDS Number: BI2TP, Accession number: WOS:000410252702078, http://apps.webofknowledge.com/full _record.do?product=WOS&search_mode=GeneralSearch&qid=9&SID=C3lG5LGFwuc AMLbEPDa&page=1&doc=1, cited by:

- Steffen Lange, Melanie Buchmüller, Bastian Heinemann, **Mateescu Ruxandra Maria doctorand**, 4 - The *Driver for the Backsourcing Phenomenon under the Force of Globalization*, 4th BASIQ International Conference on New Trends in Sustainable Business and Consumption, **11-13 June 2018**, Heidelberg University, Heidelberg, Germany, pp. 116-123, **ISI Web of Knowledge** indexing in progress.

[2] **Mateescu Ruxandra Maria doctorand**, Professor Olaru Marieta, Sârbu Alexandra, Surugiu (Farcaş) Ioana, 4 - *Research on Increasing Risk Management Efficiency as Support for Corporate Sustainable Development*, International Conference on Management, Leadership and Governance (4th ICMLG), St. Petersburg, Rusia, **14-15 April 2016**, pp. 450, ISBN: 978-1-910810-84-2, indexed in **ISI Web of Knowledge**, IDS Number: BH5MP, Accession number: WOS: 000401232800055, https://apps.webof knowledge.com/full_record.do?product=UA&search_mode=GeneralSearch&qid=21 &SID=1E7sTR4XNLkznRxUiPJ&page=1&doc=1, cited by:

- Elisa Gotesman Bercovici, Alexandra Mateiu (Sârbu) and Adrian Bercovici, *Evaluation of Outsourcing Performances a Study of Outsourcing in the Area/Field of NGOs*, Proceedings of BASIQ 2017 - New Trends in Sustainable Business and Consumption, Graz, Austria, **31 May – 3 June 2017**, pp. 302, **ISI Web of Knowledge**, IDS Number: BJ6MF, Accession number: WOS:000426833400034, http://apps.webofknow ledge.com/full_record.do?product=WOS&search_mode=GeneralSearch&qid=21&SID =C3lG5LGFwucAMLbEPDa&page=1&doc=1.

[3] **Mateescu Ruxandra Maria doctorand**, Professor Olaru Marieta, Sârbu Alexandra, Surugiu (Farcaş) Ioana, 4 - *Research on Increasing Risk Management Efficiency as Support for Corporate Sustainable Development,* International Conference on Management, Leadership and Governance (4th ICMLG), St. Petersburg, Rusia, **14-15 April 2016**, pp. 450, ISBN: 978-1-910810-84-2, indexed in ISI Web of Knowledge, IDS Number: BH5MP, Accession number: WOS: 000401232800055, https://apps.webof knowledge.com/full_record.do?product=UA&search_mode=GeneralSearch&qid=21 &SID=1E7sTR4XNLkznRxUiPJ&page=1&doc=1, cited by:

- **Mateescu Ruxandra Maria doctorand**, Maftei M., Verjel A., Lange S., 4 - *The Interrelation between Risk Management and the Organizational Context: Influence, Support and Barriers,* The 29th IBIMA conference on Education Excellence and Innovation Management through Vision 2020: from Regional Development Sustainability to Global Economic Growth, Vienna - Austria, **3-4 May 2017**, ISBN: 978-0-9860419-7-6, pp. 3292-3308, indexed in **ISI Web of Knowledge**, IDS Number: BI2TP, Accession number: WOS:000410252702078, http://apps.webofknowledge.com/ full_record.do?product= WOS&search_mode=GeneralSearch&qid=9&SID=C3lG5LGF wucAMLbEPDa&page=1&doc=1.

[4] **Mateescu Ruxandra Maria doctorand**, Melanie Buchmüller, Vanessa Just, 3- *Research on Key Factors Impacting Process Sustainability in Global Organizations*, Proceedings of BASIQ 2016 - International Conference, New Trends in Sustainable Business and Consumption, Konstanz, Germany, **2-3 June 2016**, ISSN: 2457-483X, pp. 22-31, indexed in **ISI Web of Knowledge**, IDS Number: BF6YS, Accession number: WOS:000383845100002, http://apps.webofknowledge.com/full_record.do?product =WOS&search_mode=GeneralSearch&qid=12&SID=C3lG5LGFwucAMLbEPDa&page= 1&doc=2, cited by:

- **Mateescu Ruxandra Maria doctorand**, Dinu V., Maftei M., 3 - *Research on Using FMEA as a Risk Assessment Method in order to Reduce Risk Handling Costs*, Proceedings of BASIQ 2017 - New Trends in Sustainable Business and Consumption, Graz, Austria, **31 May – 3 June 2017**, ISSN: 2457-483X, pp. 419-427, indexed in ISI Web of Knowledge, IDS Number: BJ6MF, Accession number: WOS:000426833400048, http://apps.webofknowledge.com/full_record.do?product=WOS&search_mode= GeneralSearch&qid=5&SID=C3lG5LGFwucAMLbEPDa&page=1&doc=1.

[5] **Mateescu Ruxandra Maria doctorand**, Melanie Buchmüller, Vanessa Just, 3- *Research on Key Factors Impacting Process Sustainability in Global Organizations*, Proceedings of BASIQ 2016 - International Conference, New Trends in Sustainable Business and Consumption, Konstanz, Germany, **2-3 June 2016**, ISSN: 2457-483X, pp. 22-31, indexed in **ISI Web of Knowledge**, IDS Number: BF6YS, Accession number: WOS:000383845100002, http://apps.webofknowledge.com/full_record.do?product =WOS&search_mode=GeneralSearch&qid=12&SID=C3lG5LGFwucAMLbEPDa&page= 1&doc=2, cited by:

- **Mateescu Ruxandra Maria doctorand**, Vasile Dinu, Mihaela Maftei, 3 - *Improving Risk Management Methods: FMEA and its Influence on Risk Handling Costs*, **2018**, Springer Verlag.

[6] **Mateescu Ruxandra Maria doctorand**, Lange Steffen, Bastian Heinemann, 3 - *The Role of Process Interactions Management in Ensuring Business Sustainability*, The International Conference Global Economy Under Crisis - 4th Edition, **18-20 December 2015**, Constanţa, România, published in Ovidius University Annals, Economic Sciences Series, Vol. XV, Issue 2, pp. 287-291, 2015, ISSN-L 2393-3119, ISSN 2393-3127. The journal "Ovidius University Annals, Series: Economics" is recognized by the National Council of Scientific Research in Higher Education (CNCSIS) in B+ category, code 444. The journal is indexed in RePEc, DOAJ, EBSCO host, Cabell's Directories, Ulrichs Web, J-Gate, Erih Plus, Index Copernicus, Scientific Indexing Services, INFOBASE INDEX, ResearchBib, http://stec.univ-ovidius.ro/html/anale/ENG/wp-content/uploads/2015/ 03/ANALE-vol-15-issue_2_2015_site_v2.pdf, cited by:

- Steffen Lange, Melanie Buchmüller, Bastian Heinemann, **Mateescu Ruxandra Maria doctorand**, 4 - The *Driver for the Backsourcing Phenomenon under the Force of Globalization*, 4th BASIQ International Conference on New Trends in Sustainable Business and Consumption, **11-13 June 2018**, Heidelberg University, Heidelberg, Germany, pp. 116-123, **ISI Web of Knowledge** indexing in progress.

[7] **Mateescu Ruxandra Maria doctorand**, Lange Steffen, Bastian Heinemann, 3 - *The Role of Process Interactions Management in Ensuring Business Sustainability*, The International Conference Global Economy Under Crisis - 4th Edition, **18-20 December 2015**, Constanţa, România, published in Ovidius University Annals, Economic Sciences Series, Vol. XV, Issue 2, pp. 287-291, 2015, ISSN-L 2393-3119, ISSN 2393-3127. The

journal "Ovidius University Annals, Series: Economics" is recognized by the National Council of Scientific Research in Higher Education (CNCSIS) in B+ category, code 444. The journal is indexed in RePEc, DOAJ, EBSCO host, Cabell's Directories, Ulrichs Web, J-Gate, Erih Plus, Index Copernicus, Scientific Indexing Services, INFOBASE INDEX, ResearchBib, http://stec.univ-ovidius.ro/html/anale/ENG/wp-content/uploads/2015/03/ANALE-vol-15-issue_2_2015_site_v2.pdf, cited by:

- Steffen Lange, Melanie Buchmüller, Bastian Heinemann and Andreas Kompalla, *The Importance of a Well Defined Corporate Governance*, Proceedings of BASIQ 2017 - New Trends in Sustainable Business and Consumption, Graz, Austria, **31 May – 3 June 2017**, pp. 378, http://conference.ase.ro/wp-content/uploads/2018/01/Volum_BASIQ-2017.pdf.

[8] **Mateescu Ruxandra Maria doctorand**, Lange Steffen, Bastian Heinemann, 3 - *The Role of Process Interactions Management in Ensuring Business Sustainability*, The International Conference Global Economy Under Crisis - 4th Edition, **18-20 December 2015**, Constanţa, România, published in Ovidius University Annals, Economic Sciences Series, Vol. XV, Issue 2, pp. 287-291, 2015, ISSN-L 2393-3119, ISSN 2393-3127. The journal "Ovidius University Annals, Series: Economics" is recognized by the National Council of Scientific Research in Higher Education (CNCSIS) in B+ category, code 444. The journal is indexed in RePEc, DOAJ, EBSCO host, Cabell's Directories, Ulrichs Web, J-Gate, Erih Plus, Index Copernicus, Scientific Indexing Services, INFOBASE INDEX, ResearchBib, http://stec.univ-ovidius.ro/html/anale/ENG/wp-content/uploads/2015/03/ANALE-vol-15-issue_2 2015 _site_v2.pdf, cited by:

- **Mateescu Ruxandra Maria doctorand**, Maftei M., Verjel A., Lange S., 4 - *The Interrelation between Risk Management and the Organizational Context: Influence, Support and Barriers,* The 29th IBIMA conference on Education Excellence and Innovation Management through Vision 2020: from Regional Development Sustainability to Global Economic Growth, Vienna - Austria, **3-4 May 2017**, ISBN: 978-0-9860419-7-6, pp. 3292-3308, indexed in **ISI Web of Knowledge**, IDS Number: BI2TP, Accession number: WOS:000410252702078, http://apps.webofknowledge.com/full_record.do?product= WOS&search_mode=GeneralSearch&qid=9&SID=C3IG5LGF wucAMLbEPDa&page=1&doc=1.

[9] **Mateescu Ruxandra Maria doctorand**, Lange Steffen, Bastian Heinemann, 3 - *The Role of Process Interactions Management in Ensuring Business Sustainability*, The International Conference Global Economy Under Crisis - 4th Edition, **18-20 December 2015**, Constanţa, România, published in Ovidius University Annals, Economic Sciences

Series, Vol. XV, Issue 2, pp. 287-291, 2015, ISSN-L 2393-3119, ISSN 2393-3127. The journal "Ovidius University Annals, Series: Economics" is recognized by the National Council of Scientific Research in Higher Education (CNCSIS) in B+ category, code 444. The journal is indexed in RePEc, DOAJ, EBSCO host, Cabell's Directories, Ulrichs Web, J-Gate, Erih Plus, Index Copernicus, Scientific Indexing Services, INFOBASE INDEX, ResearchBib, http://stec.univ-ovidius.ro/html/anale/ENG/wp-content/uploads/2015/03/ANALE-vol-15-issue_2_2015_ site_v2.pdf, cited by:

- **Mateescu Ruxandra Maria doctorand**, Melanie Buchmüller, Vanessa Just, 3- *Research on Key Factors Impacting Process Sustainability in Global Organizations*, Proceedings of BASIQ 2016 - International Conference, New Trends in Sustainable Business and Consumption, Konstanz, Germany, **2-3 June 2016**, ISSN: 2457-483X, pp. 22-31, indexed in **ISI Web of Knowledge**, IDS Number: BF6YS, Accession number: WOS:000383845100002, http://apps.webofknowledge.com/full_record.do?product=WOS&search_mode=GeneralSearch&qid=12&SID=C3lG5LGFwucAMLbEPDa&page=1&doc=2.

[10] **Mateescu Ruxandra Maria doctorand**, Lange Steffen, Bastian Heinemann, 3 - *The Role of Process Interactions Management in Ensuring Business Sustainability*, The International Conference Global Economy Under Crisis - 4th Edition, **18-20 December 2015**, Constanţa, România, published in Ovidius University Annals, Economic Sciences Series, Vol. XV, Issue 2, pp. 287-291, 2015, ISSN-L 2393-3119, ISSN 2393-3127. The journal "Ovidius University Annals, Series: Economics" is recognized by the National Council of Scientific Research in Higher Education (CNCSIS) in B+ category, code 444. The journal is indexed in RePEc, DOAJ, EBSCO host, Cabell's Directories, Ulrichs Web, J-Gate, Erih Plus, Index Copernicus, Scientific Indexing Services, INFOBASE INDEX, ResearchBib, http://stec.univ-ovidius.ro/html/anale/ENG/wp-content/uploads/2015/03/ANALE-vol-15-issue_2_2015_site_v2.pdf, cited by:

- Steffen Lange, Laurenţiu Tăchiciu, Ionela Carmen Pirnea, Andreea Maier, 4 - *A Case Study on Effectiveness of Organisational Structures under the Effect of Globalization*, BASIQ International Conference, Konstanz, **2-3 June 2016**, pp. 167-174, http://conference.ase.ro/wp-content/uploads/2018/01/BASIQ_Volume2016.pdf.

[11] **Mateescu Ruxandra Maria doctorand**, Professor Marieta Olaru, Lange Steffen, Rauch Manfred, 4- *Study on Supplier Invoice Risk Management in a Global Supply Chain*, Proceedings of the International Business Information Management Conference (26th IBIMA) - Innovation Management and Sustainable Economic Competitive Advantage: From Regional Development To Global Growth, Vols I - Vi,

Madrid, Spain, **11-12 November 2015**, ISBN:978-0-9860419-5-2, pp. 2579-2590, indexed in **ISI Web of Knowledge**, IDS Number: BE0SX, Accession number: WOS:000366872700265, http://apps.webofknowledge.com/full_record.do?product =WOS&search_mode=GeneralSearch&qid=18&SID=C3lG5LGFwucAMLbEPDa&page= 1&doc=1, cited by:

- **Mateescu Ruxandra Maria doctorand**, Melanie Buchmüller, Vanessa Just, 3- *Research on Key Factors Impacting Process Sustainability in Global Organizations*, Proceedings of BASIQ 2016 - International Conference, New Trends in Sustainable Business and Consumption, Konstanz, Germany**, 2-3 June 2016**, ISSN: 2457-483X, pp. 22-31, indexed in **ISI Web of Knowledge**, IDS Number: BF6YS, Accession number: WOS:000383845100002, http://apps.webofknowledge.com/full_record.do?product= WOS&search_mode=GeneralSearch&qid=12&SID=C3lG5LGFwucAMLbEPDa&page=1 &doc=2.

[12] **Mateescu Ruxandra Maria doctorand**, Professor Marieta Olaru, Lange Steffen, Rauch Manfred, 4- *Study on Supplier Invoice Risk Management in a Global Supply Chain*, Proceedings of the International Business Information Management Conference (26th IBIMA) - Innovation Management and Sustainable Economic Competitive Advantage: From Regional Development To Global Growth, Vols I - Vi, Madrid, Spain, **11-12 November 2015**, ISBN:978-0-9860419-5-2, pp. 2579-2590, indexed in **ISI Web of Knowledge**, IDS Number: BE0SX, Accession number: WOS:000366872700265, http://apps.webofknowledge.com/full_record.do?product =WOS&search_mode=GeneralSearch&qid=18&SID=C3lG5LGFwucAMLbEPDa&page= 1&doc=1, cited by:

- **Mateescu Ruxandra Maria doctorand**, Dinu V., Maftei M., 3 - *Research on Using FMEA as a Risk Assessment Method in order to Reduce Risk Handling Costs*, Proceedings of BASIQ 2017 - New Trends in Sustainable Business and Consumption, Graz, Austria, **31 May – 3 June 2017**, ISSN: 2457-483X, pp. 419-427, indexed in ISI Web of Knowledge, IDS Number: BJ6MF, Accession number: WOS:000426833400048, http://apps.webofknowledge.com/full_record.do?product=WOS&search_mode=Gen eralSearch&qid=5&SID=C3lG5LGFwucAMLbEPDa&page=1&doc=1.

[13] **Mateescu Ruxandra Maria doctorand**, Professor Marieta Olaru, Lange Steffen, Rauch Manfred, 4- *Study on Supplier Invoice Risk Management in a Global Supply Chain*, Proceedings of the International Business Information Management Conference (26th IBIMA) - Innovation Management and Sustainable Economic Competitive Advantage: From Regional Development To Global Growth, Vols I - Vi, Madrid, Spain, **11-12 November 2015**, ISBN:978-0-9860419-5-2, pp. 2579-2590,

indexed in **ISI Web of Knowledge**, IDS Number: BE0SX, Accession number: WOS:000366872700265, http://apps.webofknowledge.com/full_record.do?product =WOS&search_mode=GeneralSearch&qid=18&SID=C3lG5LGFwucAMLbEPDa&page= 1&doc=1, cited by:

- Elisa Gotesman Bercovici, Alexandra Mateiu (Sârbu) and Adrian Bercovici, *Evaluation of Outsourcing Performances a Study of Outsourcing in the Area/Field of NGOs*, Proceedings of BASIQ 2017 - New Trends in Sustainable Business and Consumption, Graz, Austria, **31 May – 3 June 2017**, pp. 302, **ISI Web of Knowledge**, IDS Number: BJ6MF, Accession number: WOS:000426833400034, http://apps.webof knowledge.com/full_record.do?product=WOS&search_mode=GeneralSearch&qid=2 1&SID=C3lG5LGFwucAMLbEPDa&page=1&doc=1.

[14] **Mateescu Ruxandra Maria doctorand**, Professor Marieta Olaru, Lange Steffen, Rauch Manfred, 4- *Study on Supplier Invoice Risk Management in a Global Supply Chain*, Proceedings of the International Business Information Management Conference (26th IBIMA) - Innovation Management and Sustainable Economic Competitive Advantage: From Regional Development To Global Growth, Vols I - Vi, Madrid, Spain, **11-12 November 2015**, ISBN:978-0-9860419-5-2, pp. 2579-2590, indexed in **ISI Web of Knowledge**, IDS Number: BE0SX, Accession number: WOS:000366872700265, http://apps.webofknowledge.com/full_record.do?product =WOS&search_mode=GeneralSearch&qid=18&SID=C3lG5LGFwucAMLbEPDa&page= 1&doc=1, cited by:

- **Mateescu Ruxandra Maria doctorand**, Maftei M., Verjel A., Lange S., 4 - *The Interrelation between Risk Management and the Organizational Context: Influence, Support and Barriers,* The 29th IBIMA conference on Education Excellence and Innovation Management through Vision 2020: from Regional Development Sustainability to Global Economic Growth, Vienna - Austria, **3-4 May 2017**, ISBN: 978-0-9860419-7-6, pp. 3292-3308, indexed in **ISI Web of Knowledge**, IDS Number: BI2TP, Accession number: WOS:000410252702078, http://apps.webofknowledge.com/ full_record.do?product = WOS&search_mode=GeneralSearch&qid=9&SID=C3lG5LGF wucAMLbEPDa&page=1&doc=1.

[15] **Mateescu Ruxandra Maria doctorand**, Professor Marieta Olaru, Lange Steffen, Rauch Manfred, 4- *Study on Supplier Invoice Risk Management in a Global Supply Chain*, Proceedings of the International Business Information Management Conference (26th IBIMA) - Innovation Management and Sustainable Economic Competitive Advantage: From Regional Development To Global Growth, Vols I - Vi,

Madrid, Spain, **11-12 November 2015**, ISBN:978-0-9860419-5-2, pp. 2579-2590, indexed in **ISI Web of Knowledge**, IDS Number: BE0SX, Accession number: WOS:000366872700265, http://apps.webofknowledge.com/full_record.do?product =WOS&search_mode=GeneralSearch&qid=18&SID=C3lG5LGFwucAMLbEPDa&page= 1&doc=1, pp. 420, cited by:

- **Mateescu Ruxandra Maria doctorand**, Lange Steffen, Bastian Heinemann, 3 - *The Role of Process Interactions Management in Ensuring Business Sustainability*, The International Conference Global Economy Under Crisis - 4th Edition, **18-20 December 2015**, Constanţa, România, published in Ovidius University Annals, Economic Sciences Series, Vol. XV, Issue 2, pp. 287-291, 2015, ISSN-L 2393-3119, ISSN 2393-3127. The journal "Ovidius University Annals, Series: Economics" is recognized by the National Council of Scientific Research in Higher Education (CNCSIS) in B+ category, code 444. The journal is indexed in RePEc, DOAJ, EBSCO host, Cabell's Directories, Ulrichs Web, J-Gate, Erih Plus, Index Copernicus, Scientific Indexing Services, INFOBASE INDEX, ResearchBib, http://stec.univ-ovidius.ro/html/anale/ENG/wp-content/uploads/2015/ 03/ANALE-vol-15-issue_2_2015_site_v2.pdf

[16] **Mateescu Ruxandra Maria doctorand**, Professor Marieta Olaru, Lange Steffen, Rauch Manfred, 4- *Study on Supplier Invoice Risk Management in a Global Supply Chain*, Proceedings of the International Business Information Management Conference (26th IBIMA) - Innovation Management and Sustainable Economic Competitive Advantage: From Regional Development To Global Growth, Vols I - Vi, Madrid, Spain, **11-12 November 2015**, ISBN:978-0-9860419-5-2, pp. 2579-2590, indexed in **ISI Web of Knowledge**, IDS Number: BE0SX, Accession number: WOS:000366872700265, http://apps.webofknowledge.com/full_record.do?product =WOS&search_mode=GeneralSearch&qid=18&SID=C3lG5LGFwucAMLbEPDa&page= 1&doc=1, pp. 420, cited by:

- **Mateescu Ruxandra Maria doctorand**, Professor Olaru Marieta, Sârbu Alexandra, Surugiu (Farcaş) Ioana, 4 - *Research on Increasing Risk Management Efficiency as Support for Corporate Sustainable Development,* International Conference on Management, Leadership and Governance (4th ICMLG), St. Petersburg, Rusia, **14-15 April 2016**, pp. 451, ISBN: 978-1-910810-84-2, indexed in ISI Web of Knowledge, IDS Number: BH5MP, Accession number: WOS: 000401232800055, https://apps.webofknowledge.com/full_record.do?product=UA&search_mode=Gen eralSearch&qid=21&SID=1E7sTR4XNLkznRxUiPJ&page=1&doc=1.

[17] **Mateescu Ruxandra Maria doctorand**, Professor Marieta Olaru, Lange Steffen, Rauch Manfred, 4- *Study on Supplier Invoice Risk Management in a Global Supply Chain*, Proceedings of the International Business Information Management Conference (26th IBIMA) - Innovation Management and Sustainable Economic Competitive Advantage: From Regional Development To Global Growth, Volumes I - VI, Madrid, Spain, **11-12 November 2015**, ISBN:978-0-9860419-5-2, pp. 2579-2590, indexed in **ISI Web of Knowledge**, IDS Number: BE0SX, Accession number: WOS:000366872700265, http://apps.webofknowledge.com/full_record.do?product =WOS&search_mode=GeneralSearch&qid=18&SID=C3IG5LGFwucAMLbEPDa&page= 1&doc=1., cited by:

- **Mateescu Ruxandra Maria doctorand**, Vasile Dinu, Mihaela Maftei, 3 - *Improving Risk Management Methods: FMEA and its Influence on Risk Handling Costs*, **2018**, Springer Verlag.

[18] Alexandra Mateiu, **Mateescu Ruxandra Maria doctorand**, Melanie Buchmüller, Vanessa Just, 4 - *Governance as a Key Factor for Ensuring the Sustainability of Outsourcing Models*, Proceedings of the International Conference on Management, Leadership and Governance (4th ICMLG), St. Petersburg, Rusia, **14-15 April 2016**, pp. 466-474, ISBN: 978-1-910810-84-2, indexed in **ISI Web of Knowledge**, IDS Number: BH5MP, Accession number: WOS:000401232800057, https://apps.webofknow ledge.com/full_record.do?product=UA&search_mode=GeneralSearch&qid=16&SID= 1E7sTR4XNLkznRxUiPJ&page=1&doc=6, cited by:

- Elisa Gotesman Bercovici, Alexandra Mateiu (Sârbu) and Adrian Bercovici, *Evaluation of Outsourcing Performances a Study of Outsourcing in the Area/Field of NGOs*, Proceedings of BASIQ 2017 - New Trends in Sustainable Business and Consumption, Graz, Austria, **31 May – 3 June 2017**, pp. 302, **ISI Web of Knowledge**, IDS Number: BJ6MF, Accession number: WOS:000426833400034, http://apps.webof knowledge.com/full_record.do?product=WOS&search_mode=GeneralSearch&qid=2 1&SID=C3IG5LGFwucAMLbEPDa&page=1&doc=1.

[19] Alexandra Mateiu, **Mateescu Ruxandra Maria doctorand**, Melanie Buchmüller, Vanessa Just, 4 - *Governance as a Key Factor for Ensuring the Sustainability of Outsourcing Models,* Proceedings of the International Conference on Management, Leadership and Governance (4th ICMLG), St. Petersburg, Rusia, **14-15 April 2016**, pp. 466-474, ISBN: 978-1-910810-84-2, indexed in **ISI Web of Knowledge**, IDS Number: BH5MP, Accession number: WOS:000401232800057, https://apps.webofknow

ledge.com/full_record.do?product=UA&search_mode=GeneralSearch&qid=16&SID=1E7sTR4XNLkznRxUiPJ&page=1&doc=6, cited by:

- Roxana Maria Gavril, Olaru Marieta, Irmer Sven-Joachim, Verjel Ana-Maria, 4 - *Managing Contract Performance for Sustainable Business*, The 29th IBIMA conference on Education Excellence and Innovation Management through Vision 2020: from Regional Development Sustainability to Global Economic Growth, Vienna - Austria, **3-4 May 2017**, ISBN: 978-0-9860419-7-6, pp. 3624-3637, **ISI Web of Knowledge**, IDS Number: BI2TP, Accession number: WOS:000410252702110, http://apps.webofknowledge.com/full_record.do?product=WOS&search_mode=GeneralSearch&qid=24&SID=C3lG5LGFwucAMLbEPDa&page=1&doc=2.

[20] Alexandra Mateiu doctorand, **Mateescu Ruxandra Maria doctorand**, Melanie Buchmüller, Vanessa Just, 4 – *Governance as a key factor for ensuring the sustainability of outsourcing models*, Proceedings of the International Conference on Management, Leadership and Governance (ICMLG 2016), Sankt Petersburg, Russia, **14-15 April 2016**, pp. 466-474, ISBN: 978-1-910810-84-2, indexed in **ISI Web of Knowledge**, IDS Number: BH5MP, Accession number:WOS:000401232800057, https://apps.webofknowledge.com/full_record.do?product=UA&search_mode=GeneralSearch&qid=16&SID=1E7sTR4XNLkznRxUiPJ&page=1&doc=6, cited by:

- **Alexandra MATEIU doctorand**, Elisa Gotesman, Irmer Sven-Joachim, Mihaela Maftei - *Research on Current Global Market Trends in the Business Process Outsourcing Industry*, Proceedings of the 28th IBIMA conference on Vision 2020: Innovation Management, Development Sustainability and Competitive Economic Growth (IBIMA 2016), Sevilia, Spania, **9-10 November 2016**, pg.1176-1184, ISBN: 978-0-9860419-8-3, **ISI Web of Knowledge**, IDS Number: BG8XT, Accession number: WOS:000392785700116, http://apps.webofknowledge.com/full_record.do?product=WOS&search_mode=GeneralSearch&qid=30&SID=C3lG5LGFwucAMLbEPDa&page=1&doc=3.

[21] Gregor Weber, **Mateescu Ruxandra Maria doctorand**, Lange Steffen, Rauch Manfred, 4 – *Knowledge intensive Business Services (KIBS) in the context of changing energy economics in Germany*, Revista Amfiteatru Economic, "Amfiteatru Economic Journal", Vol. XVIII, Nr. 41, pp. 89-103, **February 2016**, Editura ASE, Bucharest (Romania), ISSN 2247-9104, classified in category A of CNCSIS, **ISI Thomson Reuters Services**: Social Sciences Citation Index®, Social Scisearch®, Journal Citation Reports/Social Sciences Edition. Impact factor in the year 2012: 0,953. Available http://www.amfiteatrueconomic.ase.ro. IDS Number: 710QA, Accession number:

WOS: 000286525100013, http://apps.webofknowledge.com/full_record.do? product =WOS&search_mode=GeneralSearch&qid=3&SID=R1OH4eicMMf5M8i6pPp&page=1 &doc=1, http://www.amfiteatrueconomic.ase.ro, cited by:

- **Mateescu Ruxandra Maria doctorand**, Melanie Buchmüller, Vanessa Just, 3-*Research on Key Factors Impacting Process Sustainability in Global Organizations*, Proceedings of BASIQ 2016 - International Conference, New Trends in Sustainable Business and Consumption, Konstanz, Germany, **2-3 June 2016**, ISSN: 2457-483X, pp. 22-31, indexed in **ISI Web of Knowledge**, IDS Number: BF6YS, Accession number: WOS:000383845100002, http://apps.webofknowledge.com/full_record.do?product =WOS&search_mode=GeneralSearch&qid=12&SID=C3lG5LGFwucAMLbEPDa&page= 1&doc=2.

3. Articles presented at national and international scientific conference proceedings

[1] **Mateescu Ruxandra Maria doctorand**, Melanie Buchmüller, Vanessa Just, 3-*Research on Key Factors Impacting Process Sustainability in Global Organizations*, Proceedings of BASIQ 2016 - International Conference, New Trends in Sustainable Business and Consumption, Konstanz, Germany, **2-3 June 2016**, ISSN: 2457-483X, pp. 22-31, indexed in **ISI Web of Knowledge**, IDS Number: BF6YS, Accession number: WOS:000383845100002, http://apps.webofknowledge.com/full_record.do?product= WOS&search_mode=GeneralSearch&qid=12&SID=C3lG5LGFwucAMLbEPDa&page=1 &doc=2.

4. Seminars

[1] **Mateescu Ruxandra Maria doctorand**, *Study on Systemic Risks Management in the Context of Globalization in Multinational Organizations*, Doctoral Seminar ASE Bucharest, **20 May 2016**, Friday, 10.00-15.00, Room 1407

[2] **Mateescu Ruxandra Maria doctorand**, *Research on Assessing and Optimizing Control Mechanisms related to the Risk Evaluation Process*, Doctoral Seminar ASE Bucharest, **16 June 2017**, Friday, 10.00-15.00, Room 1407

The manufacturer's authorised representative in the EU is Springer Nature Customer Service Centre GmbH, Europaplatz 3, 69115 Heidelberg, Germany. If you have any concerns regarding our products, please contact ProductSafety@springernature.com

Printed and bound by CPI Group (UK) Ltd, Croydon, CR0 4YY
30/09/2026
02225601-0005